READING *I*

Reading "Piers Plowman" is an indispensable scholarly guide to a magnificent – and notoriously difficult – medieval poem. With *Piers Plowman*, the fourteenth-century poet William Langland proved that English verse could be at once spiritually electrifying and intellectually rigorous, capable of imagining society in its totality while at the same time exploring heady ideas about language, theology, and culture. In her study of *Piers Plowman*, Emily Steiner explores how Langland's ambitious poetics emerged in dialogue with contemporary ideas; for example, about political counsel and gender, the ethics of poverty, Christian and pagan learning, lordship and servitude, and the long history of Christianity. Lucid and comprehensive, Steiner's study teaches us to stay alert to the poem's stunning effects while still making sense of its literary and historical contexts.

EMILY STEINER is Associate Professor of English Literature and an award-winning teacher at the University of Pennsylvania. She is presently co-editor of the *Yearbook of Langland Studies*. She is the author of *Documentary Culture and the Making of Medieval English Literature* (Cambridge, 2003), and co-editor with Candace Barrington of *The Letter of the Law: Legal Practice and Literary Production in Medieval England* (2002).

READING *PIERS PLOWMAN*

EMILY STEINER

University of Pennsylvania

CAMBRIDGE
UNIVERSITY PRESS

CAMBRIDGE UNIVERSITY PRESS
Cambridge, New York, Melbourne, Madrid, Cape Town,
Singapore, São Paulo, Delhi, Mexico City

Cambridge University Press
The Edinburgh Building, Cambridge CB2 8RU, UK

Published in the United States of America by Cambridge University Press, New York

www.cambridge.org
Information on this title: www.cambridge.org/9780521868204

First published 2013

Printed and bound by CPI Group (UK) Ltd, Croydon CR0 4YY

A catalogue record for this publication is available from the British Library

Library of Congress Cataloguing in Publication data
Steiner, Emily.
Reading 'Piers Plowman' / Emily Steiner.
pages   cm
Includes bibliographical references and index.
ISBN 978-0-521-86820-4 (hardback) – ISBN 978-0-521-68783-6 (paperback)
1. Langland, William, 1330?–1400? Piers Plowman.   I. Title.
PR2015.S74   2013
821'.1–dc23
2012044191

ISBN 978-0-521-86820-4 Hardback
ISBN 978-0-521-68783-6 Paperback

For Sophie and Asher

Contents

Contents

Illustrations

Acknowledgements

This book is a labor of love for my students past and present who committed themselves to reading *Piers Plowman*. To dedicate oneself to this magnificent poem is not only to face some major interpretative challenges, but also to risk losing oneself in a text that offers no easy way out. Stirring and confounding by turns, *Piers Plowman* asks its readers to forgo the safety of narrative and trust in a poetic process that is all-consuming and frequently unmanageable.

Piers Plowman promises that salvation lies in community, a promise on which I depend. I thank Candace Barrington, Maura Nolan, and Rosemary O'Neill, who read chapters in draft, and Lawrence Warner, expert in all things Langlandian, who generously commented on the entire book. Kara Gaston, Jennifer Jahner, and Sarah Arkebauer helped with various stages of research, Sierra Lomuto assisted valuably with the index, and Marie Turner edited the manuscript with her characteristic intelligence. Penn undergraduates Katie Thackray and Shoshana Akabas helped compile the bibliography. My dear colleagues Rita Copeland and David Wallace weathered this project for my own good, and it is much better for their friendship.

Piers Plowman has taught me some patience with my own shortcomings and with other people's needs. Its striking beauty comes from its ability to address the demands of a clamorous world, while holding out for a time in which people will live simply on love. My family wagered that I could be a good scholar and a good mother at the same time. I am grateful to them for taking that bet.

EMILY STEINER
University of Pennsylvania

x

CHAPTER I

Introduction
(Prologue)

"Thow myghtest bettre meete myst on Malverne Hilles . . ."
(Prol. 215)

The poem we call *Piers Plowman* is testimony to the massive literary output of late fourteenth-century England, the period that produced works as diverse as *Troilus and Criseyde*, *Sir Gawain and the Green Knight*, and the English Wycliffite Bible. The reputation of *Piers Plowman* does not ride on the life of its author, about whom we know little more than what the unique note in Trinity College, Dublin, MS 212 reports, that William of Langland was a son of Stacy de Rokayle, a gentleman dependant of the lords Despenser in Oxfordshire.[1] By contrast, Geoffrey Chaucer's activities as page, diplomat, and bureaucrat are well known, the translator John Trevisa's Oxford career can be traced from the 1360s through the 1390s, and John Gower's tomb can still be visited at his senior residence, St. Mary Overie, Southwark. The Protestant reformer, John Bale, writing the history of English reform, named Robert Langland as the author of *Piers Plowman*; in his inscription in a Huntington Library manuscript, Hm 128, Bale places the poet at Cleobury Mortimer, not far from the Malvern Hills in south-west Worcestershire, the dialectal region of the poet.[2] However, medieval readers, such as the early fifteenth-century poets who penned Langlandian poems like *Pierce the Ploughman's Crede*, were not especially invested in naming an author. They cared about the social imperative embodied by Piers the Plowman, the poem's critique of the clergy, and its program for spiritual reform.[3]

In many ways, *Piers Plowman* is a cultural phenomenon that exceeds the documentable life of its author. For one thing, the dreamer's evasive self-naming and the poet's apparent reluctance to identify himself, patron, or other writings, suspends the text between authorship and anonymity. In B.15, for example, the dreamer hints at the presence of a historical author at the very same moment in which he describes the general will to gain knowledge through a lifetime of moral choices: "'I have lyved in londe,'

quod I, 'my name is Longe Wille – /And fond I nevere ful charite, before ne
bihynde'" (15.152–53).[4] It is hard to say whether this authorial presence is
meant to be common, as Anne Middleton explains, the author's name
embodying everyman's "unsatisfied desire" or "ethical volition" ("Longe
Wille" + "in londe" = the longstanding desire to know), or whether it is
supposed to be proper, functioning like an authorial apology or signature
("Longe Wille" + "in londe" = William Langland).[5] The poem holds these
two possibilities continually in tension. For another thing, though widely
influential in the 1380s–1400, the poem was a work-in-progress even by the
standards of manuscript culture. The poem survives in a remarkable fifty-
eight+ manuscripts, perhaps as many as a dozen copied before 1400. It was
composed in at least three versions, between about 1362 and 1388, dates
wrested both from events internal to the poem (a 1362 hurricane is mentioned in A.5.13–14, for example) and external references (for example,
the C.5 "autobiographical" passage evokes the language of the 1388
Cambridge Labor Statutes[6]). The A-text, which abruptly breaks off ninety-
eight lines into passus 12,[7] is probably the earliest version, although it
seems to have had the latest circulation.[8] The B-text, on which this
present study is based, is a complete, intermediate version of the poem,
running to about 7,000 lines of twenty passūs and a prologue
(containing altogether eight dreams and two inner dreams). It is the most
formally and intellectually experimental of the three main versions, possibly
written when the poet was about 45, the dreamer's age during his mid-life
moral crisis in B.11.[9] In the B-text, the poet writes his way out of a
theological problem regarding predestination, posed at the end of A, and
he exploits the resources of a "bilingual textuality" only thinly mined in A.[10]
The C-text, an authorial revision of B, possibly released in several stages,
contains twenty-two passūs plus a prologue. A fourth version of the poem,
surviving in one manuscript, which scholars call the Z-text, may be an
authorial proto-A text or a scribal creation influenced by readings from A
and C.[11]

   To what literary tradition or genre does *Piers Plowman* belong? The
poem's early readers did not form a consensus on this question. Eighteen
Piers manuscripts have *explicits* that refer to the work variously as the
dialogue, vision, debate, or book of Piers Plowman.[12] That the poem in
any version was a must-have item at the end of the fourteenth century is
evident from the sheer number of manuscripts that survive; among medieval literary works in English, *Piers Plowman* is fifth only to the *Prick of
Conscience* (*c.*1350), the two versions of the Wycliffite Bible (*c.*1380), the
prose *Brut*, and the *Canterbury Tales* (*c.*1390). According to chroniclers of

the 1381 Peasants' Revolt, the leaders of the revolt carried English broadsides, which mention Piers the Plowman and may have been inspired by the poem.[13] *Piers Plowman* appears in a variety of manuscript contexts: it is compiled, for instance, in the deluxe Vernon manuscript (*c.*1390), a veritable archive of English religious works, as well as in the hulking Cambridge University Library, MS Dd.i.17 (s.xiv/xv), a collection of English chronicles, world histories, and travel narratives, mainly written in Latin. Of *Piers* manuscripts, only Huntington Library MS, Hm 114, which consists primarily of long narrative works, can be described as a literary anthology in the modern sense: its scribe copied *Piers, Mandeville's Travels, The Epistle of Sweet Susanne, The Legend of the Three Kings, Troilus and Criseyde,* and a fictive letter to Lucifer, the last item suggestive of *Piers Plowman,* which enrolls several fictive documents.

Medieval texts in manuscript are beholden to *ordinatio,* the divisions of a text, and they often contain abundant apparatus, such as tables of contents, running titles, book and chapter summaries, paraph marks, and commentary. *Ordinatio,* in turn, helped foster a taste for literary texts with legible schemes, such as the *Prick of Conscience,* a 10,000-line Northern poem, divided into a prologue and seven books neatly arranged by religious theme (the wretchedness of mankind, death and the afterlife, and so forth). Early readers of *Piers Plowman* were discouraged neither by its narrative incoherence nor by its confusing and overlapping textual divisions, as evidenced by the haphazard state of the rubrics. In most manuscripts the poem is divided into passūs ("steps") and into two large sections, the *Visio* (passus 1–passus 7, 8, or 9) and the *Vita,* the latter being subdivided (most consistently in the C tradition) into three lives: the lives of Dowel, Dobet, and Dobest. Some scribes also divided the poem into dream-visions (e.g., in Corpus Christi College MS 201); some envisioned the whole poem as a *Visio;* and many scribes double-numbered passūs (e.g., the title for B.16 in Cambridge, Trinity College MS B.15.17, "Passus xvjus & cetera et primus de Dobet," or the "16th Passus, etc., and the first of Dobet").[14]

From a modern critical perspective, *Piers Plowman* draws heavily from two literary traditions, alliterative long line poetry, which describes the poem's meter, formulas, and some of its diction, and French and Latin dream poetry, which describes the poem's overall structure, many of its characters, and much of its dialogue. The poet resorts to many other genres: sermons, liturgy, satire, penitential treatises and confessional handbooks, proverb collections and bestiaries, chivalric romances, and above all, the bible, in its multiple and various incarnations. *Piers Plowman,* like other

Middle English unrhymed alliterative poems, such as the *Siege of Jerusalem* or the *Wars of Alexander*, features a four-stress line with a medial caesura dividing the line into two syntactical half-lines. As with other alliterative poems, Langland's line is heteromorphic, that is, not governed by one metrical foot, such as the iambic foot (x') in iambic pentameter.[15] The first half-line (a-verse or on-verse) typically contains two and sometimes three metrically stressed syllables or staves. The second half-line (b-verse or off-verse) is normally restricted to two staves. The two half-lines are bound by alliteration, the first half-line alliterating on one or both staves, the second half-line alliterating only on the first of two staves. By far the most common of these patterns is aa/ax.[16]

In what way *Piers Plowman* relates to this corpus and in what sense it helps to define that corpus as a tradition depends on which metrical rules we take to be normative or categorical, and how we construe the relationship between alliteration and meter. Hoyt Duggan argues, for example, that Middle English alliterative poets composed with a limited number of syntactic patterns and in metrical patterns as regular, if more varied, than those used by Old English poets. He argues, too, as do many scholars, that alliteration works as a structural feature in the long line: for example, it does not confer metrical stress on an unstressed syllable. In his view, deviations from these rules were the fault not of poets but of scribes.[17] The implications of these rules for editing long line poetry are considerable, and the problems modern editors face when emending a poem like *Piers Plowman* are compounded by the number of extant manuscripts and the propensity of a text for scribal error and innovation, as well as for authorial revision. For example, *Wars of Alexander*, in many ways a paradigmatic alliterative poem, survives in just two manuscripts, in contrast to *Piers Plowman* with its convoluted history of transmission.

Piers Plowman has more syntactical variation than most alliterative poems; it has a roving medial caesura, which often disregards regular syntactic disjuncture;[18] its lines are longer than average with more syllables; and it contains many more rhythmically and semantically heavier b-verses than do other alliterative poems (e.g., B.Prol. 51, "To ech a tale that thei tolde hire tonge was tempred to lye," or Prol. 64, "For sith charite hath ben chapman, and chief to shryve lordes").[19] Correspondingly, *Piers Plowman* has a much higher rate of metrical variation and metrical irregularity, which the poet as reviser did not always see the need to fix. In short, although the poem is composed as if according to a system governed by strict metrical rules, it also presents a special case to the alliterative corpus. (In the case of

Piers Plowman, for example, Duggan concedes that, if there is a conflict between alliteration and stress in a line that seems authorial, for example, on the second stressed syllable of a b-line, alliteration can be assumed to confer stress.[20]) If metrical rules are categorical, *Piers Plowman* should be considered not an exemplar of long line poetry, but either a seriously flawed instance or a different beast entirely; if metrical rules are normative, *Piers Plowman* demonstrates a high degree of modulation within a standard metrical scheme.[21]

Taking a very different approach, Ralph Hanna has proposed that alliteration in Middle English alliterative poetry is not a central metrical feature but a "regularization of an ornamental feature."[22] By unyoking alliteration from meter, Hanna situates unrhymed long line poems like *Piers Plowman* in wider literary contexts: end-rhymed alliterative poetry, shorter-lined poetry with ornamental alliteration, and even alliterative prose. David Lawton and Ian Cornelius likewise note the affinities between alliterative long line poetry and Latin prose.[23] Along similar lines, Lawton speculates that unrhymed long line alliterative poetry in the late fourteenth century owed its vogue to *Piers Plowman*: though it likely already existed as performed entertainment – as the poet assumes to be the case – Langland reclaimed it for a sober, more penitential age.[24] In this reading, alliterative poetry does not account for the metrical form of *Piers Plowman* as much as *Piers Plowman* explains something about the pieties of fourteenth-century long line poems.

It may be, too, that *Piers Plowman* helped make alliterative poetry appealing to a wide readership, especially in London. Most fourteenth-century alliterative poems cannot confidently be assigned a date earlier than their manuscripts (usually after *c.*1390) so it is difficult to say when and if they coalesced into a tradition. Of the long narrative poems, only *William of Palerne*, a werewolf romance written before 1361 for Duke Humphrey of Bohun, surely predates *Piers Plowman*.[25] *Wynnere and Wastour* (*c.*1352–70), like *Piers Plowman* a dialogue concerned with broad social reform, may or may not predate the A-text. In either case, *Piers* and *Wynnere and Wastour*, along with *The Parliament of the Three Ages* – another alliterative poem about social abuses – shows that, by the early 1370s, alliterative poetry was considered an appropriate form for spiritual exhortation and political counsel; *Piers Plowman* may have been the text that made the difference. Chaucer's Parson, defending his choice of prose, says that, as a Southern man, he does not know how to "geeste 'rum, ram, ruf,' by lettre," nor does he prefer (end) rhymed poetry.[26] In these much-cited lines, the Parson regionalizes alliterative poetry as a Northern phenomenon, which it was in part: *The Siege of Jerusalem* was likely composed at Bolton Abbey, Yorkshire;[27] the poems collected in Cotton Nero A.x. share a north-west dialect.[28] But the Parson may also be paying homage to *Piers Plowman* as a successful – and accessible – penitential poem, which, although Northern in poetic form, circulated not only in the West Midlands, the poet's birthplace, but also in London, where scribes produced B-texts in a range of dialects, and where the poet may have first circulated his C-revision. In London a scribe of a *Troilus and Criseyde* manuscript also copied a *Piers Plowman* manuscript, British Library, MS Additional 35287, a manuscript which, in turn, was corrected by Adam Pinkhurst, the London scribe of the Ellesmere *Canterbury Tales* and the *Piers Plowman* manuscript, Trinity College, Cambridge, MS B.15.17.[29]

What most distinguishes *Piers Plowman* from other alliterative poems, and helps to explain its metrical irregularities, is its bilingual embrace.[30] Langland thinks and composes in Latin as well as in English, often translating scriptural passages from Latin to English and *vice versa*, or patching Latin quotations into English passages, sometimes ingeniously incorporating Latin tags – names, technical words, and bits of prayer – into the long line. As Tim Machan points out, the breakdown of Latin–English diglossia in England and the ascendance of English as a literary, administrative, and devotional language, was a condition of the poem's existence.[31] To be sure, the major linguistic trends that would eventually sideline Latin, would first exclude *Piers Plowman*, the dialect and meter of which made small impact on the age of print. In this view, *Piers Plowman* represents a double loss: the loss of multilingualism in the making of English poetry and the loss of a medieval alliterative tradition.

However, *Piers Plowman*'s bilingualism does not simply gesture to some future estrangement from literary culture; more importantly, it shows what was required to fashion a supple literary vernacular in the 1360s and 1370s, a vernacular both spiritually electrifying and intellectually rigorous. Latin in *Piers Plowman* appears most frequently as citation as, for example, in the Prologue, where a politically savvy mouse laments the instability that a child-king brings to a realm: "For I herde my sire seyn, is seven yeer ypassed, / 'Ther the cat is a kitoun, the court is ful elenge.' / That witnesseth Holy Writ, whoso wole it rede: *Ve terre ubi puer est rex*" [For, seven years ago, I heard my father say, / "Where the cat is a kitten, the court is completely miserable." / Holy Writ confirms this, for whomever should consult it: "Woe to the land where the king is a child."] (Prol.193–95a) (Ecclesiastes 10:16). In this scene, introduced in the B Prologue, a company of rodents has failed to bell a frightful cat, and its spokesman – a mouse – decides that quietism is the best course during a period of political uncertainty. Royal succession has skipped a generation, and the throne has passed, or is about to pass, from a long-reigning king, presumably Edward III, to his grandson, who, if Richard II, was only ten years old when crowned in 1377. As topical political allegory, the mouse may stand for Commons speaker Peter de la Mare, whose outspokenness was praised in the records of the 1376 Parliament (a session which strongly impressed contemporary writers) but was denounced by Richard's uncle, the powerful John of Gaunt, a likely candidate for the Cat.[32]

In this passage, the Latin biblical proverb endorses the mouse's warning about royal minorities. The quotation, however, has already been rendered into English two lines earlier, or perhaps the English proverb has recalled to the poet its Latin equivalent. Together, the two versions shape the topicality of the political moment. The English proverb acts as a bridge between the cat and mouse allegory and general political wisdom ("Ther the cat is a kitoun . . ."). It also personalizes proverbial wisdom, incorporating it into a recent oral history – the mouse's ("For I herde my sire seyn, is seven yeer ypassed"). The Latin quotation, by contrast, highlights the written authority behind the proverb ("That witnesseth Holy Writ, whoso wole it rede"), while at the same time insisting upon its relevance to contemporary politics. In both languages the proverb substitutes for the political action that the rodents dare not perform. And yet, some of Langland's contemporaries may have recognized the Belling of the Cat fable from a Latin sermon preached by Thomas Brinton, Bishop of Rochester, to a convocation of clergy at the 1376 Parliament. In this well-known sermon, Brinton rebukes the lords spiritual and temporal for not fighting injustice and the King for not hearing the wisdom of his many counselors.[33]

No doubt Latin's traditional authority made it attractive to a poet striving for the total reform of society and self, of clergy and laity, rich and poor alike. Indeed, its authority serves many purposes in *Piers Plowman*. As the language of medieval learning, liturgy, and law, for instance, Latin tends to divide lay from clerical audiences and restricts lay access to information, thus enabling the poet to address – and suppress – different audiences. There is perhaps no better example of the restrictiveness of Latinity in the poem as the Prologue's "Coronation" scene, in which a lunatic, an angel, a goliard, and the Commons presume to offer advice to the monarch about his obligations to his subjects, to the law, and to God. The angel, goliard, and Commons speak in untranslated and, in the case of the angel, fairly difficult blocks of Latin. As one would expect, the presentation of this scene

in manuscript preserves the hierarchies between languages and between text
and citation: though practices were variable, *Piers* scribes bolded, boxed,
enlarged, and rubricated Latin quotations as well as individual Latin words
within the English line, producing a *mise-en-page* in which Latin was
distinguished from the vernacular, and learned citation from everything
else. As Fiona Somerset points out, however, Latin in England was itself
multilingual, and the quotations in the "Coronation" scene do not portray
Latin as an undifferentiated language of power.[34] Importantly, too, the
contrast between Latin and English in this scene is tactical: it enables the
speakers to give radically different political advice. Finally, Latinity activates
the relation of speaker to language, showing how an ethical discourse might
actually be performed as counsel in the presence of a silent king. Although
the angel speaks in Latin on behalf of "lewd" men whose status or ignorance
disqualifies them from political conversation, he does not merely speak, he
"*Lowed* to speke in Latyn – for lewed men ne koude / jangle ne jugge" (Prol.
129–30, my emphasis), and the goliard, though laconic, is called a "gloton of
wordes" (Prol.139). In this scene, the gap between Latin and English, like
the marginal identities of the speakers, highlights the difficulties of obtaining a political voice.

Generally, however, Latin in *Piers Plowman* is not hard Latin. Its scope is
fairly limited – for example, it hardly ever references scholastic literature or
classical mythology. It is nearly always translated or summarized, with the
translation often preceding the quotation. In fact, at the very moments
where the poet uses Latinity as a trope of inaccessibility, he conjures up a
range of audiences, democratizing the *lingua franca* of scholars for those for
whom it is, in theory, incomprehensible. In B.15, for example, Anima
excoriates the clergy for their hypocrisy in no uncertain terms: "I shal tellen
it for truthe sake – take hede whoso liketh" (15.91). Anima's ostensible
audience of address is the clergy themselves, "Forthi wolde ye lettrede leve
the lecherie of clothyng ... Lothe were lewed men but thei youre loore
folowede" [And if you learned men would cast off worldly pomp ...
unlearned men would wish to do nothing else but follow your example]
(15.103–08), and yet his message to the clergy requires deliberate acts of
translation, as a medieval preacher might perform when adapting Latin
preaching materials to an English sermon: "For [in Latin ypocrisie] is likned
to a dongehill," etc. (15.111). A few lines later, however, Anima peculiarly
refuses to translate a block quotation from a homily by the patristic
theologian John Chrysostom, in which Chrysostom warns priests that
they are responsible for good and evil in their communities. Anima glosses
this act of non-translation:

If lewed men wiste what this Latyn meneth,
And who was myn auctour, muche wonder me thinketh
But if many preest beere, for hir baselardes and hir broches,
A peire of bedes in hir hand and a book under hir arme (15.119–22)

[If only the laity knew what this Latin means,
And who the author is, I would not be surprised
If many priests exchanged their swords and their brooches
For a rosary in their hands and a (prayer)book under their arm.]

Anima's refusal to translate does not conceal Chrysostom's thoughts on clerical responsibility; in fact, the gist of the homily has just been explained in English. Instead, Anima's refusal to translate shifts his address to a lay audience, characterized by their ignorance, their potential understanding, and their capacity for violence or their ability to "make good" on Chrysostom's exhortation to priests, thereby filling a vacuum of corrective agency ("If lewed men wiste ... But if many preest beere"). The non-translatability of the Latin quotation, in other words, calls into being a lay audience ready to disarm delinquent priests (see 15.125, 128).

As these examples suggest, the poem's bilingualism is at the core of its vernacular inventiveness. Recently, Traugott Lawler has argued that foremost on the poet's mind as he revised his poem was introducing more Latin quotations (from A to B) and perfecting his existing translations (from B to C).[35] As John A. Alford and Judson Boyce Allen have persuasively shown, Langland constructed entire scenes around quotations derived from Latin biblical commentaries.[36] In *Piers Plowman*, moreover, Latin amplifies the rhythmical quality of alliterative meter, as in the lines from the Prologue condemning ribald entertainers, in which the Latin phrase forms a perfectly metrical half-line: "That Poul precheth of hem I wol nat preve it here: / *'Qui loquitur turpiloquium* is luciferes hyne" [What Paul preaches I will not elaborate here: / "He who speaks evil" is Lucifer's servant] (Prol.38–39, alluding to 5 Ephesians 3–5). As with the Chrysostom passage, the Latin quotation ostensibly masks the object of criticism and the dreamer's critical appetites. However, as the nominal subject of the English sentence and the driving a-verse of the alliterative line, the quotation deepens the criticism of "japeres and jangleres" (Prol.35), described just a few lines above. Latin further gives the impression of depth by creating interplay between metrical and ornamental alliteration, for example, in the lines from B.1 about Lucifer's fall. "And mo thousandes myd hym than man kouthe nombre / Lopen out with Lucifer in lothliche forme / For thei leveden upon hym that lyed in this manere: / *Ponam pedem in aquilone, et similes ero Altissimo* [And with him many more thousands than one could count / Leapt out with Lucifer in hideous form, / Because they believed in him, who lied in this manner: / "I will place my foot in the North and be like the Most High"] (1.116–19). Here as elsewhere in *Piers Plowman*, linguistic difference achieves a variety of poetic effects: Latin boosts the effects of a learned vernacular poetics at the same time that alliterative meter recuperates the cultural distance between languages.

Ranulph Higden, a Latin historian writing in the second quarter of the fourteenth century, wonders why the English of his day has so many dialects but the Norman French of England only one. His translator, John Trevisa, responds by pointing out that, in France, French comes in multiple dialects, just as English does in England.[37] Langland does not comment on the state of French in England – the Norman legacy, reinforced by contact with continental French through war, trade, and cultural exchange – but he does capitalize on the several registers of French available to English speakers in order to show how language shapes moral behavior. In the Prologue, for instance, French is an integral part of London speech, as in the hypermetric line in which shiftless laborers sing snatches of French songs (or catcalls) to pass the time: "As dykeres and delveres that doon hire dedes ille / And dryveth forth the longe day with 'Dieu vous save dame Emme!'" [As dike-diggers and delvers, who do their jobs badly / And drive forth the long day with "God save you, Dame Emme"] (Prol.224–25). Although the poet quotes the line in French, he does not mark it as French in the same way that Covetousness in B.5, claiming to be a bumpkin and therefore unable to grasp the language of penance, makes French the limit to pastoral care: "And I kan no Frenssh, in feith, but of the fertheste ende of Northfolk" (5.235), he says, explaining why it is that he cannot practice "restitucioun." The Latin term "restitution" may have been absorbed into English via Anglo-Norman, or through translations of continental French, but in the 1370s it was not foreign, just technical, and that's the joke. In this line, which deftly maps status onto region and culture, French establishes a geographical limit in a way that Latin does not. Like Latin, however, French characterizes audiences: Norfolk "hicks" apparently do not know French!

The one full French quotation in *Piers Plowman*, two couplets on the virtues of sufferance at B.11.384a–b, the poet chose not to translate: "Bele vertue est suffraunce, mal dire est petite vengeance. / Bien dire et bien suffrir, fait lui suffrant a bien venir" [Suffering is a fine virtue; to speak evil is little vengeance. / To speak well and to suffer well causes a person to come through well]. The poet identifies this quotation as linguistically and culturally French – this is the kind of thing, he says approvingly, that French men and gentlefolk ("Frenche men and fre men," II.384, with a pun on franche/free[38]) teach their children. Still, the poet must have thought the quotation perfectly understandable, perhaps because the trilingual context in which it appears (following Reason's explanation of sufferance in English and preceding a Latin quotation on sufferance from Peter 2:13) clarifies the French. The poet would certainly have had many bilingual and trilingual examples to imitate: from English verses in sermons, to bilingual satire, and to trilingual collections of proverbs, which often showcased more than one verse form or alternated prose Latin quotations with French and English verse translations.[39] Higden, writing a generation before Langland, observes that children are compelled to learn Latin through French to the detriment of spoken English; Trevisa, writing a decade after the B-text, comments that grammar school children in his day (1385) now learn Latin through English, but they have lost the competence in French so crucial for traveling abroad.[40] For Langland, who keeps a noble readership continually in view, French may still have been the language of Latin instruction and of aristocratic moral education.

Although the poetics of *Piers Plowman* is essentially English, in dialogue with Latin, the three languages work together to layer meaning, as in the following two verses: "A proude prikere of Fraunce, *Princeps huius mundi*" [A proud rider from France, "The prince of the world"] (9.8) (John 16:11), and "Thanne was Feith in a fenestre, and cryde, '*A! Fili David*'" [Then Faith was in a window, and cried, "Oh! Son of David!"] (18.15). In the first line, taken from Wit's allegorical castle of the soul, the phrase "proude prikere of Fraunce" invokes genres in French: secular romances, but also courtly literatures of penance, such as Robert Grosseteste's religious allegory *Le chasteau d'amour* (*The Castle of Love*) (c.1250), the likely source for this passage, originally written in "romanz" for an audience of "seigneurs" who may have had neither "lettrure ne clergie" (Latin training).[41] The Latin scriptural quotation that triumphantly completes the line glosses the French knight, naming the devil as the would-be rapist and linking Wit's story about lady Anima in her fortified castle to a larger history of sin. In the second line, taken from B.18, Faith/Abraham ventriloquizes the cheering crowd in Matthew 21:9, when Jesus and his disciples enter Jerusalem. The Latin quotation makes Faith/Abraham an eyewitness to Christ's life, at the same time that it confirms Christ's royal lineage. The word "fenestre" further calls attention to the poet's macaronic acrobatics. "Fenestre" may be merely an f-line English synonym for window, but in this line it retains a

French, and distinctly courtly, valence, which helps the poet recontextualize the Latin quotation "*A! Fili David.*" Faith, lovelorn, watches Jesus from the window, rather than jostling with the crowd below.

Piers Plowman's multilingualism makes it an exemplary English poem in ways strikingly different from Chaucer's poetry. Chaucer became a national English poet because he so successfully adapted continental poetry to an English literary vernacular and in a variety of genres. In the process, he aggrandized London English within English court culture, and he pioneered a model for authorship imitated by fifteenth-century poets and disseminated by early English printers.[42] By contrast, Langland, writing in an insular metrics and in a West Midlands dialect, did not father a tradition of English letters in the long run. But for late fourteenth-century readers and writers including Chaucer, *Piers Plowman* exemplified a vernacular poetics of social vision and spiritual power, a poetics enriched by the poet's creative use of Latin.

Significantly, too, *Piers Plowman* advertises itself as an English poem as well as a vernacular one. Its special claim to Englishness rests on its ability to create the effect of total vision, as if it really encompassed everything: all subjects and – crucially for the poet – all persons. In the Prologue especially, Langland constructs a capacious poetic vision, which Chaucer, in his Prologue to the *Canterbury Tales*, seems to have found irresistible.[43] The dreamer falls asleep by a brook and discovers the marvels of vision, an otherworldly dreamscape with a tall tower and a dark valley and between the two a "fair feeld ful of folk" (17) populated by "alle manere of men, the meene and the riche" (18). The phrase "alle manere of men" is not so much a celebration of humanity in its diversity as it is an invitation to satire: the fair field is stocked with laborers, beggars, retailers, and clergy of every social type, many of whom fail to do their duty. "Somme putten hem to the plough, pleide ful selde" (20), but "somme putten hem to pride" (23), and some take up professions of dubious social value, such as trade or minstrelsy ("somme chosen chaffare . . . .. somme murthes to make as mystralles konne" [31, 33]). The worst offenders – professional religious – contravene their mission in order to line their pockets: friars concoct self-serving interpretations of scripture; a pardoner, canvassing the parish, pulls the wool over the eyes of credulous layfolk; and learned clerks count money in the Exchequer, draw up documents in Chancery, and manage estates, when they should be singing masses.

And yet, in *Piers Plowman*, satire does not simply uncover corruption and sin; it also fuels a vision that is all-inclusive and therefore supremely ethical, committed to the salvation of everyone. In the Prologue, moreover, the capaciousness of poetic vision is an aesthetic as well as an ethical proposition, which the poet has inherited from French dream poetry. Langland was deeply influenced by the tradition of the *Roman de la rose*, an allegorical dream-vision written by Guillaume de Lorris and Jean de Meun (*c*.1230, 1270), the first section of which Chaucer translated into English verse. In the *Rose*, a courtly Lover falls asleep, joins Love's service, and spends over 21,000 lines penetrating a tower in order to capture a "rose." Along the way, he has conversations about love, beauty, justice, manners, language, and adultery, with Love, Reason, Nature, and an Old Woman, among many other characters. In the 1330s the Cistercian monk Guillaume de Deguileville converted the *Rose* from a courtly seduction into a spiritual "pilgrimage" (the *Pèlerinage* trilogy) widely read in England. Although the goal of the lover in the *Rose* – the seduction of a virginal "rose" – is very different from the dreamer's spiritual quest in *Piers Plowman*, Langland, like Deguileville, was attracted to the *Rose*'s loveable and much-maligned dreamer and the garrulous parade of personifications who engage him. Like Deguileville, too, Langland discovered in the *Rose* the luxury of total vision, in which, theoretically, everything could be discussed over the course of many lines. In Deguileville's redemptive rewriting, the capaciousness of dream poetry conduces to spiritual reform. His monastic dreamer invites all audiences to hear his dream, inspired by the "faire romaunce of the Rose": "Now cometh neer and gadreth you togideres alle folk, and herkeneth wel; let ther be no man nor woman that drawe bakward . . . for this towcheth alle, bothe grete and smale, withouten any owtaken."[44] At the disorienting moment in the *Piers* Prologue, in which the dreamer turns his gaze from the tower and the dale to "alle manere of men," Langland invokes the *Rose*'s visionary aesthetic, translating the capaciousness of French dream poetry into an English social world. In this sense, *Piers Plowman* could be said to be the culmination of Deguileville's penitential project and a true English heir to the *Rose* tradition.

The *Piers Plowman* Prologue, a show-stopping example of medieval visionary poetics, employs a variety of techniques to conjure up the image of a society in its totality, as we have already seen, for example, with its brilliant use of the quantifier "some . . . some." Critical to achieving that effect in the Prologue is the alliterative long line. As many scholars have observed, the *Piers Plowman*-poet eschews the ornate and often archaic vocabulary of alliterative romances, the traces of which can be seen, for instance, in the poet's many words for man, such as "gome" and "freke". That vocabulary, in turn, is key to the many decorative lists found in alliterative poetry, which exploit the four semantically heavy words that make up a typical metrical line, and which raid the alliterative storehouse of near-synonyms pertaining to weaponry, textiles, bodies, music, hunting, and feasts. These lists are sources of aesthetic pleasure but also of ethical purpose insofar as they aim for completeness. For example, the *Wars of Alexander* ends with a description of Alexander's wonderfully wrought throne made of diverse materials and inscribed in various languages with the names of territories over which he has dominion (twenty-two lines total). This inscription is an ornamental geography of the known world:

> Portingale & Paiters, it paies me trouage [tribute];
> Arrabe & Artoyes and Assie þe mare [greater],
> Abbeon & Aufrike, and Acres anothire,
> Effosym & Ethiops, þire Ebrues folke
> Alle Ermony & Ewrope enterely me serues,
> Ingland, Itaile & Yndee, & Ireland costis.[45]

This list varies considerably in the Latin *Wars*, and the English poet has included many places not listed in any of the Latin versions. Yet the goal of the list remains the same: to convey the fullness of imperial power while, at the same time, satisfying readers' desire for exoticism and diversity.

Towards the end of the *Piers Plowman* Prologue, the poet, tapping the resources of alliterative metrics, lists persons of different estates and professions in order to evoke a comprehensive social world. For the poet, imagining all people all at once in their supposed diversity is a moral imperative, even those estates and crafts not explicitly targeted for critique:

> Barons and burgeis and bondemen also
> I seigh in this assemblee, as ye shul here after;
> Baksteres and brewesteres and bochiers manye,
> Wollen webbesters and weveres of lynnen,
> Taillours and tynkers and tollers in markettes,
> Masons and mynours and many othere craftes: (Prol. 216–21)

> [Barons, and burgess, and bondsmen also
> I saw in this assembly, as you shall hear next:
> Bakers, and brewers, and butchers many,
> Weavers of wool, and weavers of linen,
> Tailors, and tinkers, and toll-collectors in markets,
> Masons, and miners, and many other crafts:]

This idea, that a compendious world could be summoned with a London crowd, would also appeal to the author of the alliterative poem *St. Erkenwald* (*c.*1390). In *St. Erkenwald*, a civic-minded poem about an Anglo-Saxon saint, a British tomb is exhumed in the crypt of a newly renovated St. Paul's Cathedral. As news leaks out, "Mony hundrid hende men highhide þider sone. / Burgeys boghit therto, bedels and oþire, / And mony a mesters mon of maners diverse . . . þer common þider of alle kynnes so kenely mony / þat as alle þe worlde were þider walon wytin a honde- quile" [Many hundreds of able men rushed there immediately. / Burgess hastened there, beadles and others, / And many guildsmen of different types . . . There came there of all kinds so swiftly many / That it seemed as if the whole world was there in an instant].[46]

The desire to fashion a capacious poetics gives further insight into Langland's eclectic use of personifications. *Piers Plowman* is stuffed with the materials of allegorical dream-vision: set pieces, such as Wit's Castle of the Soul in B.9 or Piers's directions to Truth in B.5; fictive letters, such as Truth's Pardon in B.7; and philosophical dialogues between personified institutions or faculties, such as the dreamer's dialogue with Holy Church in B.1. Compositionally, however, the poem is not consistently allegory, in the sense that the narrative as a whole transparently stands in for another narrative as whole (for example, a literary pilgrimage figures an inward spiritual journey or the invasion of a fortress figures a sexual act). Nor is it an allegory in the hermeneutical sense, in which the text points to a moral or typological interpretation, although many passages certainly allude to the hermeneutical senses and even lay them side by side (as in the story of Abraham/Faith, Moses/Hope, and the Good Samaritan/ Charity in B.16–17).

The poem's use of personification is analogous to its use of allegory, insofar as it treats personification as only one of many possibilities for describing persons. We might say that the poet has drafted his eclectic literary materials into the service of the literal sense. The poet handily mixes personified virtues, vices, or faculties (Patience, Envy, or Conscience) with representatives of trades or estates (tinkers and tailors), the trade or estate itself (Knighthood, Religion), and generic persons named and unnamed, who never quite develop into characters (a reeve, a lord, Munde the Miller, Rob the Robber, even Piers the Plowman). This technique marks the poem as a distinctly English enterprise, in part because it highlights the English vernacular and an insular metrics, and it part because in grounds the universal – sin, penance, love – in the local and familiar. We see this

domestication of personification allegory at work in the estates passage in
the B Prologue, a short tale about political society. In this passage, a king
enters, led by Knighthood. The Commune (alternatively the parliamentary
Commons, the community of the realm, and the third estate) supports his
rule, and Kind Wit invents Clergy to protect the Commune and advise the
King. Together, the King, Knighthood, and Clergy arrange for the
Commune to provide food for them ("casten that the Commune shulde
hem [communes] fynde," 117), and the Commune, in collaboration with
Kind Wit, ordains plowmen to labor in the fields for "profit of al the peple"
(119). This passage describes political society very generally: it fashions an
originary narrative for the three estates, and, in doing so, it naturalizes the
relationship between economic labor and political participation (the labo-
ring classes are represented in government insofar as they provide food for
everyone). However, the curious mix of persons in this passage – a single
king, a generalized knighthood, a personified natural reasoning (Kind Wit),
a generic plowman, and a commons doubling as political abstraction and
material sustenance – together give this narrative of political origins a
distinctly English cast.

A more obvious example of the domestication of personification is Meed's
marriage charter in B.2. In this episode, the dreamer once again addresses "alle
manere of men, the meene and the riche" (2.56), whom he sees massing
together to get Meed married.[47] The assembled crowd with its countless types
attests to the universality of sin, at the same time that it models the art
required to describe everyone. The dreamer exclaims, "I kan noght rekene the
route that ran aboute Meed" [I cannot count the crowd that ran about Meed]
(2.62), and later, "I have no tome to telle the tail that hem folweth, / Of many
maner men that on this molde libbeth, / Ac Gyle was forgoer and gyed hem
alle" [I have no volume to record the number (or story) of those who followed
them, / [Made up] of all kinds of men who live on this earth, / Except that
Guile went before them and led them all] (2.186–88). At the center of this
activity is a notorious charter drawn up by Civil (law) and Simony for the
betrothed couple Meed and False. Civil and Simony read the charter aloud,
translating its Latin opening clause as if it really were addressed to everyone in
the world: "*Sciant presentes et futuri* / Witeth and witnesseth, that wonieth
upon erthe . . ." ["Let all present and future know"/Know and witness those
who live upon this earth . . .] (2.74a–75). The charter endows Meed and False
with an allegorical landscape of sins (the earldom of Envy, the country of
Covetousness, the lordship of Lechery), but it soon unfolds into a narrative
about all people, who bequeath and inherit, hear and testify, when they enter
into a contract of sin.

In witnesse of which thyng Wrong was the firste,
And Piers the Pardoner of Paulynes doctrine,
Bette the Bedel of Bokynghamshire,
Reynald the Reve of Rutland Sokene,
Munde the Millere – and many mo othere.   (2.108–12)

[In witness of this act, Wrong was the first,
And Piers the Pardoner, of the order of St. Paul,
Bette the beadle of Buckinghamshire
Reginald the reeve from the Rutland area,
Munde the Miller – and many others more.]

Though an aristocratic land-grant, the charter spews forth a welter of human figures, who are domesticated in each other's company. Wrong is the first in the line of witnesses to Meed and False's charter, but he stands in line in front of a generic beadle named Bette "of Bokynghamshire" and a reeve named Reynald "of Rutland Sokene," whose names locate them in English places. Even the descriptor "of Paulynes doctrine" (the order of the Crutched Friars), which might not seem to indicate a particular place, may refer to a neighborhood in London (Tower Hill). Everyone is willing to be taken for a ride: Meed mounts a sheriff, newly shod, while her consort False rides a juryman who softly trots (2.164–65).

The commixing of allegorical figures and social types is not uncharacteristic of medieval satire, as, for example, Nicole Bozon's poem *Le char d'Orgeil* (*c*.1320), a charming exposé of pride in courtly society. Using the device of a horse-drawn carriage, Bozon describes three chevaliers (clerics) with Anglo-Norman names, who attend Lady Pride's chariot: "Sire Herege de Heresye," "Cymon de Symonye," and "sire Torcenous en sa dymerye" (Sir Heretic of Heresy, Simon of Simony, and Sir Wicked in his territory where he is authorized to collect tithes).[48] These names invoke insular naming patterns in order to dramatize the sins they illustrate – heresy, simony, and greed. But where descriptors like "de Heresye" return the local to the universal, and the individual sinner to the sin, the plebian witnesses to Meed's charter give a heightened sense of regionalism at the expense of satire. The names of the witnesses anchor the charter in an English context in which names, local and seemingly familiar, identify persons.[49]

The dreamer of *Piers Plowman*, like the courtly dreamer of the *Rose*, brims with desire, both the desire to seek wonders ("Wente wide in this world wondres to here," Prol. 4), and the desire to attain the thing for which he longs – spiritual understanding. In the case of Langland's vaguely clerical dreamer, his desires are both enabling and misleading: he is a hermit "unholy of werkes," who strays from his proper place. Indeed, the dreamer exemplifies the poet's biggest complaint in the Prologue, that people whose duties lie in the parish or on the manor abandon those duties to seek opportunity elsewhere (Prol. 87–91).

From the very beginning, however, the poem is defined by travel. To be sure, some parts of *Piers Plowman* are leisurely and discursive, played out on a courtly landscape detached from time and place, but the poem as a whole is trafficked by beggars, pilgrims, merchants, messengers, and missionaries, all of them constantly in motion. In general, the poem gains a lot of momentum from the very things it seeks to reform, whether secular entertainment in B.9–10, or the institutional church in B.20. Travel is no exception. But the poem's abiding concern with people in motion also forms part of its self-identification as an English work. One itinerary that informs the poem's geographical imaginary is the trip from the hinterland to the urban center, and, specifically, from the Malvern Hills to London. In the defense of his life in C.5, the dreamer identifies himself as someone from "London and opelond bothe" (44). At the beginning of the Prologue, the dreamer falls asleep in the Malvern Hills, and wakes up in a version of London, the place of greatest temptation and, therefore, of ripest imagination. There sleazy retailers rub shoulders with foreigners in the bar (like the tavern-goers in Gluttony's confession B.5.306–25, who include Tymme the Tynkere, Clarice of Cokkeslane and Pernele of Flaundres [these last two likely prostitutes], Godefray of Garlekhithe, and Griffyth the Walshe), and there the proximity of Westminster means plenty of clerks angling for positions in the royal bureaucracy or in noble entourages.

A second set of itineraries radiating from London leads to major English pilgrimage sites: to the north-east of London, to Our Lady of Walsingham, Norfolk, a shrine reviled by medieval and early modern English reformers ("Heremytes on an heep with hoked staves / Wented to Walsyngham," Prol.53–54), and to the Rood of Bromhold, also in Norfolk; to the south-east, to St. Thomas's shrine at Canterbury; and north-west on Watling Street to Chester, where pilgrims flocked to see the nail of the Holy Cross at St. John's Church. The poet gestures to pilgrimages abroad, and disapproves of those folk who, consumed by wanderlust, cross the channel "To seken Seint Jame and seintes in Rome" (Prol.47). Yet for Langland the significance of continental travel always refers back to English places. In an ironic exchange of Rome and Chester, a repentant Sloth swears by the "Rode of Chestre" that he will settle his debts and use what's left of his money to "seken truthe erst er I see Rome" (5.461).

Piers Plowman's great achievement as an English poem is to portray a very dense and heterogeneous social world within an England narrowly defined. The poet has scant interest in Wales, the North of England, Scotland, or the borderlands. His gaze is trained on London and its vicinity: Westminster, Stratford, Cornhill, Essex, Hertfordshire, Buckinghamshire, and Abingdon. He is aware that wine is imported to London from Alsace, Gascony, the Rhineland, and La Rochelle, and he is cognizant of recent wartime negotiations in France and papal politics in Avignon. Far off in the distance and in the remote past of his poetic imagination lies Jerusalem. Most Middle English alliterative poems, by contrast, tend to cover a broad territorial swathe, either because they are set in foreign countries or because they are preoccupied with warfare and conquest, like the *Siege of Jerusalem*, *Wars of Alexander*, *William of Palerne*, and *Gawain*. At the beginning of the *Alliterative Morte Arthure*, for example, the narrator tracks Arthur's conquests from the Orkneys, Hebrides, Ireland, Scotland, and Wales, to Flanders and France, Holland, Hainault, Navarre, Norway, Normandy, and beyond.[50] Langland is not directly interested in conquest – the only comparable list of foreign places in his poem occurs in B.15.520, where the poet imagines the conversion of the infidel in India, Alexandria, Armenia, and Spain. In *Piers Plowman*, however, travel, and especially English travel, is vital to a poetics capable of describing all persons and a range of social and spiritual conditions.

I conclude with one of the poem's loveliest passages, Recklessness's parable in C.13 about Winchester Fair, one of the most famous fairs in England, attracting foreign merchants as well as English ones. The poet is deeply ambivalent about mercantilism: after all, merchants often profit at the expense of needy consumers. In the Confession of the Sins in B.5, for example, Covetousness confesses that he sells merchandise for his master at Winchester Fair and at Wye in Kent, a regional market popular with London merchants (B.5.201–02). However, the poet acknowledges that merchants take huge personal and financial risks in order to turn a profit; as a result, they have a special purchase on the spiritual risks assumed by all earthly "travelers," both prosperous and mendicant (compare C.5.92–101).

In C.13 Recklessness argues rather tendentiously that patient poverty is the only sure route to heaven ("Ac the pore pacient purgatorye passeth / Rather then the ryche thogh they renne at ones" [And the patient poor pass through Purgatory quicker than the rich, though [the rich] run headlong] C.13.30–31), and of course his name, Recklessness, implies a calculated indifference to moderation. For this reason, he is the ideal spokesperson for the spiritual value of itinerancy because he is willing to take big rhetorical risks. For Recklessness, moreover, the spiritual value of travel is profoundly English in orientation. If, he says, a merchant and a messenger were traveling on the same road and stopped at a toll booth, the merchant, laden with goods, would surely be delayed, while the messenger, who need only "with his mouth telleth his erende" and "his letter sheweth" (39–40) would pass straight on through. If, then, the two men were to travel through a manor, "amydde the fayre whete" (42), the messenger would not likely be stopped by the hayward. But if a merchant should make his way "ouer menne corne" (45) and should run into the hayward, the hayward would surely force him to pay a fine or to pledge something to guarantee his conduct, even his purse. If the merchant and the messenger should "wende o way" to Winchester fair (51), the merchant, weighed down with merchandise, would travel more slowly than the messenger, who carries only his letterbox with the brevet inside. The merchant, too, has cause to fear robbers, whereas the messenger's mouth is "ful of songes" (58) because he knows no one would jump him for a letter.

And yet, says Recklessness, both men, in the end, will arrive safely at the inn, if the merchant is willing to hire a bodyguard! He explains that the merchant represents the rich man, whom God holds accountable for his worldly goods, and who must give alms to those who have fallen on hard times, represented by toll booth attendants, haywards, robbers, and bodyguards (70). The messenger represents beggars ("mendenantz"), who, if true believers, have only to show the letter and seal – their contract with Christ – to be admitted to the heavenly kingdom. This parable, which charts the perilous journey of the merchant, in contrast to the carefree route of the messenger, turns England into a complex moral landscape. This landscape, which encompasses all social worlds but which is mapped on a particular idea of England, is *Piers Plowman*'s poetic subject.

CHAPTER 2

Value
(B.1–4)

"Teche me to no tresor" (1.83)

Introduction

At the beginning of passus 1, the dreamer promises to interpret the land-scape he beheld in the Prologue: "What this mountaigne bymeneth and the merke dale /And the feld ful of folk, I shal yow faire shewe" [What this mountain signifies, and the dark valley, /And the field full of folk, I will show you well] (1–2). Unsurprisingly, the tower on the mountain represents Truth (God), the dungeon in the dale the Devil, and the field the World. For the poem's inquisitive dreamer, the allegorical landscape is also a place of departure for the pursuit of moral and spiritual knowledge, and passus 1 introduces us to the first of many interlocutors who will aid him in that pursuit: Holy Church. The dreamer's dialogue with Holy Church, which I argue is indebted to Boethius's *Consolation of Philosophy*, transforms Piers *Plowman* into a philosophical work about the relationship between know-ledge, virtue, and salvation.

The subject of the dialogue between the dreamer and Holy Church is value: what is valuable in this life, and what constitutes the highest good? In this dialogue, the dreamer tries to figure out what is most valuable to the soul, what lacks real value, and, how value can be talked about in the first place. Passus 1, which initially takes the form of a dialogue, develops into a sermon on moderation and charity, two of the virtues most praised by the poet. And yet this passus, with its abiding interest in value, also provides an occasion for the poet to flex the philosophical muscle of English poetry. The subject of value – or, what material goods have to do with spiritual goods – turns Holy Church's sermon into a philosophical dialogue, anticipating the poet's turn to political philosophy and counsel in B.2–4. Passus 1 asks, what is the true relationship between virtuous behavior and worldly things?

Which literary forms give substance to those abstract values – integrity, love, grace – that people are supposed to cherish? How does gender, like the gender of Holy Church, convey something about value? Finally, it asks more indirectly, how do literary effects contribute to a philosophical discussion about value?

Similar questions about the relationship between language and value and between spiritual and material goods emerge in passūs 2–4 with the introduction of Holy Church's rival, Lady Meed. As the personification of reward, Meed returns the dreamer to the hectic world pictured in the Prologue and to contemporary problems having to do with service, warfare, counsel, and above all, justice. In these passūs, the poet inveighs against a society corrupted by money, so evident in marriage, bureaucracy, law, war policy, and the court. The poet's critique is primarily directed at the way that money affects human behavior: some people will do anything for preferment or gold, because they value the things of this world over moral principles such as honesty, pity, and love.

In this sense, B.2–4 deal much more straightforwardly with the subject of value than does passus 1, where the discussion of value is less engaged with contemporary life. Yet, by placing Lady Meed at the center of this critique, the poet broadens his investigation of value in ways already anticipated by passus 1; in doing so, he continues to channel Boethius's attempt in the *Consolation* to cultivate a philosophical attitude through his discontents with contemporary politics. Langland asks in B.2–4, for example, how does one choose between competing systems of value? Must the dynamics of service and reward, so essential to medieval rule, depend on vices like wantonness and greed? Which literary fictions are necessary for talking about money in the first place? How might gender – in Meed's case, the gender of money – subvert Christian morality and threaten the health of the realm? Finally, how might English poetry convey philosophical values, offering a counsel worthy of a king?

Boethian gender

In passus 1, the satirical energies of the Prologue are suspended by a leisurely interlude inspired by one of the most influential works in the medieval West, Boethius's *De consolatione philosophiae* (*The Consolation of Philosophy*). The *Consolation*, a sixth-century treatise written in prison by a Roman senator condemned to death by Emperor Theodoric, made a huge impression on medieval thought and letters. It generated a number of translations, including Jean de Meun's *Li livres de confort* (*c.*1300) and

Geoffrey Chaucer's *Boece* (*c*.1380), several commentaries, such as those of William of Conches (before 1150) and Nicholas Trevet (1307), and many Boethian dialogues, including Alain de Lille's *Anticlaudianus* and Jean de Meun's *Le roman de la rose*. In the 1370s and 1380s, Chaucer and his unfortunate contemporary, Thomas Usk, successfully converted the *Consolation*'s ideas about fortune and suffering into English literature, for example, with Chaucer's *Book of the Duchess* (*c*.1369–72), which may have been written for the bereaved duke John of Gaunt, and with the *Testament of Love* (*c*.1387), which Usk wrote while in prison awaiting execution. For Chaucer and Usk, Boethian dialogue gave the literary subject a language with which to lament the vicissitudes of fortune and the reversals of love, money, and power. At the same time the *Consolation* taught readers to get a better perspective by transcending worldly things and aiming for higher ones, such as salvation, eternal love, and the elevation of literary letters.

Like his contemporaries, Langland capitalizes on the *Consolation*'s prestige in order to create a philosophical English poem. Like them, too, he contends with the two questions that drive the *Consolation*: what attitude should a person cultivate toward worldly things, and what is the highest good? Langland, like Boethius, identifies the highest good as a providential God (Truth), but his goal with respect to that good, salvation, is a goal to which Boethius's Stoic narrator does not aspire, concluding that a virtuous mind directed toward higher things is its own reward. Medieval glossators on the *Consolation* tried to close the gap between divine providence and Christian salvation,[1] and passus 1, like many a medieval gloss, Christianizes Boethian dialogue (unlike Boethius's narrator, for example, Langland's dreamer wants to be good, not happy, so he will earn his reward in the afterlife). As we will see below, the poet further Christianizes Boethian dialogue by intercalating two biblical lyrics about the fall of Lucifer and the incarnation of Christ.

In passus 1, however, the poet explores other questions central to Boethian dialogue: how exactly does language raise us from ignorance to understanding, and how does it teach us what we should value? For Langland, as for Boethius, personification, and especially the gender of personification, is critical to understanding the relationship between language, knowledge, and value. In *Piers Plowman*, this relationship is first grounded in the figure of Holy Church, a lady elegantly arrayed ("A louely lady of leere in lynnen yclothed," 1.3), who introduces herself as the institutional Church, font of baptism and instruction. Medieval writers personified the Church as female (following the Latin feminine noun), calling her

the *mater ecclesia* (mother church) or the *sponsa Christi* (bride of Christ), and
sculptors carved her on the portals of Gothic cathedrals as an antitype to
another female personification, the lovely but blindfolded *synagoga*, who,
like Lady Meed, suffers a loss of prestige in a Christian world. Although the
dreamer needs to ask Holy Church's name ("Thanne hadde I wonder in my
wit what womman she weere ... And halsede hire on the heighe name, er
she thennes yede, / What she were witterly that wised me so faire" [Then
I wondered what woman she was ... And entreated her, in God's name,
before she went away, /(To tell me) who she really was who taught me so
well], 1.71, 73–74), he immediately recognizes her superior authority, and
her formidable appearance stuns him into an appreciative silence: "I was
afered of hire face, theigh she faire weere" [I was afraid of her countenance,
though she was beautiful] (1.10). In this exchange, female personification is
crucial to spiritual understanding because it embodies a way of learning
about value.

   Later, Holy Church will explain that she is the daughter of God, as
opposed to Lady Meed with her dubious lineage (2.24–35). In this first
encounter, however, Holy Church descends from a literary line of female
personifications, beginning with Boethius's Lady Philosophy, for whom
grandeur and condescension comprise the twin pillars of pedagogy. In the
first book of the *Consolation*, Boethius's narrator, wallowing in self-pity,
beholds a woman

> Most awe-inspiring to look at, for her glowing eyes penetrated more power-
> fully than those of ordinary folk, and a tireless energy was reflected in her
> heightened colour. At the same time she was so advanced in years that she
> could not possibly be regarded as a contemporary. Her height was hard to
> determine, for it varied; at one moment she confined herself to normal
> human dimensions, but at another the crown of her head seemed to strike
> the heavens. When she raised it still higher, it even broke through the sky,
> frustrating the gaze of those who observed her. Her robe was made from
> imperishable material and was sewn with delicate workmanship from the
> finest thread ... At the lower edge of the robe was visible in embroidery the
> letter Pi, and the neck of the garment bore the letter Theta; between them
> could be seen the depiction of a ladder, whose rungs allowed ascent from the
> lower letter to the higher. But the robe had been ripped by the violent hands
> of certain individuals, who had torn off such parts as each could seize. In her
> right hand she carried some books, and in her left hand a scepter.[2]

Lady Philosophy invites Boethius to read her as a "set piece": he learns
something about her by reading her costume allegorically, which in turn
prepares him to be her student. Her status is expressed as stature – philosophy

is a lofty if human science – and as material richness – though an enlightening pursuit, philosophy is ransacked and abused by unprincipled persons. In short, Philosophy's appearance is Boethius's initiation into profitable reading, and it is in reading female nobility that he accepts her as an instructor. In this way, the material signs of female status, ripe for interpretation, offer a fictional alternative to the traditionally male pedagogy of the Middle Ages. Medieval writers tended not to regard women as proper instructors, either in the classroom or in the pulpit, but so long as institutions, faculties, and texts could be personified and so long as pedagogy depended on the imbalance of power between teacher and student, a lady theoretically could instruct a male clerk.

Langland likely knew the *Consolation* from the schools, where it was part of the curriculum in dialectic; Boethius's treatise was one of the most widely circulated of medieval academic texts.[3] The poet, however, probably owed his version of Lady Philosophy to a proximate literary source, *Le pélerinage de la vie humaine* (*The Pilgrimage of the Life of Man*, c.1330–55; hitherto *Vie*), the first of three allegorical dream-visions written by the French Cistercian monk, Guillaume de Deguileville.[4] Deguileville's trilogy was well known to late medieval English writers – the *Vie* was the source for Chaucer's "ABC" hymn to the Virgin, and was later translated into English by John Lydgate and William Caxton – and its success in England was largely due to the author's adaptation of the popular thirteenth-century secular allegory, *Le roman de la rose*. In the *Vie*, the pilgrim-narrator first meets Grace Dieu (God's grace), who appears in an outfit studded with precious stones, as befitting the daughter of a great lord.[5] Her dress calls attention to her status but, more significantly, it produces the dreamer as a student, who learns from the lady's condescension a lesson about spiritual attitude:

> Curteis she was as me þohte, for she saluede me first, and askede me goodliche what I wente so seeching. And þanne I was al abashed, for I hadde not lerned þat a ladi of so gret array shulde deyngne to caste hire chere to meward. But anoon I avisede me þat as I hadde lerned and woot wel, þat who þat hath in him most bountee hath in him most humblesse, and þe mo appelen þe tre bereth þe more she boweth to þe folk.[6]

> [She seemed very courteous to me: she greeted me first, and asked me politely what I was looking for. And then I was all abashed, because I would never have assumed that a lady of such noble appearance would acknowledge my presence. But, presently, I assured myself that, as I had formerly experienced, the best people are the most humble, and the more apples a tree bears the more she bows down to the common people.]

The pilgrim, flattered by her notice, remembers that those who truly have something to offer do not scruple to address those beneath them. Here, as in the *Consolation*, female nobility serves as a figure for both pedagogical relations and allegorical interpretation. The splendor of Grace Dieu's costume discloses information about her value. Her dignity, advertised by her jewels, proves her authority, which is vital both to learning and to salvation; and her condescension to the pilgrim, like Holy Church's condescension to the dreamer, recommends her as a teacher, just as the pilgrim's admiration shows his readiness to learn.

In Deguileville's reading of Boethius, value is intimately related to form: personification gives a body to an abstract concept, thereby investing it with value; and personification reveals the hermeneutic or spiritual worth of something by representing it materially (Philosophy's robes; Grace Dieu's jewels). In this respect, a personification's gender and status (whether, for example, she is a nursemaid, lady, daughter or queen) matter. Holy Church's costume is not as detailed as Grace Dieu's or Lady Philosophy's, yet her appearance induces in the dreamer the awe necessary to enter into a learned dialogue in which he will play a subordinate role. Significantly, Langland has distributed the details of dress – fur-trimmed gown, jeweled bracelets, scarlet robe – to Lady Meed, whose lack of moral authority makes her ill equipped to instruct anyone. Meed has absorbed the material trappings of the authoritative female personification, and indeed, within the context of Langland's satire, a sumptuous Holy Church might have been vulnerable to the kind of critique that Protestant readers would later find irresistible.

But the question of material value and its relation to knowledge remains a critical part of Holy Church's vocabulary: what is the dearest "treasure," and how can it be known? Moreover, it is Holy Church who allows the poet to explore the relation of value both to learning and to literary form. Holy Church's appearance attracts the dreamer's attention and, like Grace Dieu, she serves as a means to the end; just as God's grace is a helping gift, so the sacraments administered by the Church help to bring about salvation. Additionally, like her predecessors, Holy Church's gender makes her an integral part of the dreamer's remembered education. Lady Philosophy accuses the *Consolation*'s narrator of having forgotten her, "Are you the man whom once I nurtured with my milk and reared on my solid food until your mind attained full maturity? . . . Do you recognize me?"[7] In a Boethian universe, one needs to remember having learned in order to learn again for it is by forgetting that one has learned that one loses one's innate capacity to know. Like a nursemaid or godmother, Holy Church chastises the dreamer for forgetting the circumstances in which he was "brought up," i.e., the pledges made on his behalf at the baptismal font to serve and love Holy Church: "thow oughtest me to knowe. / I underfeng thee first and the feith taughte. / Thow broughtest me borwes my biddyng to fulfille, / And to loven me leelly the while thi lif dureth" [You ought to know me: / I received you first and taught you the faith. / You brought me pledges that you would follow my precepts, / And love me faithfully as long as you live] (1.76–79). Holy Church represents in maternal guise the dreamer's institutional origins, as well as the feeling of shame that often accompanied a medieval student's initiation into learning.[8] For the dreamer, it is the experience of being a student – of having had an incomplete or imperfectly remembered education – that produces him as a Christian subject.

True worth

Holy Church begins by reading the poem's allegorical landscape through a critique of greed, and the passus quickly becomes a sermon on measure and excess: how one can earn heaven by restricting consumption, striving for integrity, and acting charitably. She explains that most people care only about earthly reward, oblivious to the demands of Truth, the supreme authority residing in the Tower. Truth ordained the world according to "mesurable manere" (1.19), providing for human beings' basic needs. As Holy Church explains, moderation is both an act of obedience and a check to sin: by living moderately, one avoids the sins that arise from bodily desires, like gluttony and lechery, for "It is nought al good to the goost that the gut asketh, / Ne liflode to the likame that leef is to the soule" (1.36–37). These lines articulate one of the poet's strongest convictions, that intemperance is the major cause of social and spiritual ills. They also illustrate Langland's habit of restating an important idea in a way that changes the meaning of the original formulation. This tendency is characteristic of alliterative poets, but it is worth pausing at these lines, which analyze the relationship between form and value. In the first line, "not everything is beneficial to the spirit that the body demands," Holy Church recommends moderation; in the second line, "nor is it nourishment to the body that is precious to the soul," she pits body against soul.[9] Notably, if the two lines take different positions toward consumption, they share metrical values. Each line follows a slightly different pattern of lifts and dips within the general scheme aa/ax, but they interpret stress very similarly, marking the same semantic range, and emphasizing in parallel ways the relationship between metrical value and physical consumption. Compare "good/goost/gut/asketh" (good, spirit, belly, ask) in line 36 to "liflode/ likame/leef/soule" (nourishment/body/precious/soul) in line 37. Together, they show how theories of value, moderation or asceticism, depend upon the formal values of poetic language.

Holy Church's denunciation of greed is typical sermon fare, but her tone soon becomes more philosophical than homiletic. The dreamer asks her opinion on "moneie" or "tresour," by which he hopes to figure out the difference between necessary things which keep you alive, and worldly things which can be amassed and dispended ("render unto Caesar," etc., 1.51–54) and get in the way of salvation: "Ac the moneie of this molde that men so faste holdeth / Telleth me to whom that tresour appendeth" [And the money of this earth, to which people cling / Tell me to whom that treasure belongs] (1.44–45). Holy Church, rather than answering his question directly, seizes upon the word "tresour" to talk about value in the most expansive way possible, both as a material good and as an abstract idea. As the passus progresses, "tresour" accumulates a bewildering range of meanings. At one point, Holy Church uses it very concretely in the context of wealth management, urging rich people to appoint kind wit (here, common sense) as warden of their wealth and tutor of their treasure (1.55–56). Just a few lines later, however, she uses "tresour" more abstractly to mean something like "creed" or "capital," that which one holds with or stands for. Wrong causes people to sin – he is the "lettere of love" [the hinderer of love] – and those who "trusten on his tresour bitrayed arn sonnest" [trust in his treasure are soonest betrayed] (1.70). The dreamer tries to force the issue by rejecting "tresour" altogether, insisting upon its literal meaning and opposing it to salvation: "Teche me to no tresor, but tel me this ilke – / How I may save my soule, that seint art yholden" [You, who are considered a saint, do not talk to me about treasure; / Tell me this instead: how may I save my soul?] (1.83–84). For the dreamer, the problem with "tresor" is that it refers *both* to a storehouse of material riches *and* to those things that one values in the way that one values a storehouse of material riches. If only necessary things are worth valuing, how can they be compared to the amassing of goods (treasure)? How can true value be signified by something in excess of need? Holy Church, to the dreamer's frustration, persists in collapsing the signifier and the signified, insisting on the positive value of "tresour"': "'Whan alle tresors arn tried,' quod she, 'treuthe is the beste'" (1.85, repeated at 135, 137, and 207). For Holy Church, treasure posits a fundamental connection between material goods and moral concepts such as moderation or obedience, which one should truly value.

From the moment that Holy Church equates "treasure" with "truth," the meaning of "truth" also begins to proliferate. Within the allegorical landscape, Truth, in his tower, stands for God the Father, the dispenser of goods and progenitor of humankind. Truth's foe, naturally, is the devil or Wrong, who is at once the denizen of the dale and the supernatural agent who spawned generations of evildoers: "Fader of falshede, founded it hymselve. / Adam and Eve he egged to ille, / Counseilled Kaym to killen his brother, / Judas he japed with Jewen silver" [Father of falsehood, which he himself established. / He incited Adam and Eve to sin, / Counseled Cain to kill his brother, / deceived Judas with the Jews' silver] (1.64–67). At line 84, the meaning of Truth abruptly shifts from divine agency to human, and specifically aristocratic behavior. Holy Church first identifies Truth with the set of values that rationalizes the existence of the armigerous classes. The job of the gentry, she says, is to bring transgressors of the law to justice ("And taken *transgressores* and tyen hem faste / Til treuthe hadde ytermyned hire trespas to the ende" [And take "transgressors" and bind them fast / Until Truth has determined the extent of their punishment], 1.96–97). A few lines later Holy Church links Truth to another kind of noble duty, the fealty that vassals owe to their sovereign lord. She gives the negative example of Lucifer: true knights are supposed to "sweren on hir swerd to serven truthe ever" and to "holden with hym and with here that wolden alle truthe" (1.99, 102), but Lucifer broke his bonds of obedience to his lord, and was punished accordingly (1.114). In these two examples "truth" refers both to feudal service and to the lord God himself, who first established "truth" as a moral code.

By this point, the landscape of the tower and the dale, once a diagram of good and evil, has become a constellation of philosophical abstractions. The dreamer quite understandably wants a prescriptive *bonum*, a proper sermon not a philosophical treatise, but Holy Church just repeats the same precept, that truth is the best treasure. Holy Church is trying to say that the sovereign good is like a treasure because we value it so highly, and the false value of excess goods reveals the true value of a Christian moral code. As she suggests, too, if material goods are required to talk about moderation and salvation then perhaps no sure distinction exists between material and spiritual value. In the *Consolation*, Lady Philosophy urges Boethius to abjure his faith in Fortune, who only appears to control the material goods he wrongly believes constitute his happiness. But once a writer introduces a personification like Fortune, Lady Philosophy, or Holy Church into moral philosophy, he makes it clear that philosophical discourse depends upon literary forms that give substance to moral concepts, even those concepts which are supposed to lead us away from worldly things. Likewise, a philosophical discourse that personifies reason, or evil, or fortune begs questions regarding moral agency. Just as Fortune is a kind of false consciousness, so all personification obscures the nature of choice.[10] Similarly, when abstract concepts such as Truth and Wrong intrude upon a biblical narrative starring Adam and Eve, Cain, Lot, Judas, Lucifer, and Christ, they enter the material world of history. As passus 1 shows, the way in which language assigns value helps us determine what is valuable, what has intrinsic worth, and how good and evil should be understood in a world in which God is the protagonist, dealing out punishment and reward. In this respect, passus 1 serves as Langland's response to Boethian philosophy and its literary traditions. It also can be understood as an attempt to frame a religious vernacular poem in philosophical terms.

Embodiment

This tension between a philosophy that rejects worldly things and a language that stresses agency, embodiment, and weight is one that Boethius brilliantly explores in the *Consolation* through the prosimetrum. At the beginning of the dialogue, Lady Philosophy condemns the muses whose mournful songs have reduced Boethius to tears, and her timely intervention prevents him from recording their songs as his consolation. But the *Consolation* immediately unfolds into a prosimetrum, a prose work interspersed with verse in various metrical patterns. The poems do not plunge Boethius into self-pity, as the songs of the muses did; instead, they encourage him to embrace the attitude prescribed by Philosophy in the prose sections, to disinvest in mutable things. The purpose of the *metra* is to transmit images that support Philosophy's argument that to be truly happy one must mentally transcend the boundaries of the world, leaving fame and riches behind. As Book 1, poem 7 explains, Boethius once explored the mysteries of Nature, but now he is shackled by his passions, which keep him from attaining the clarity he seeks: "If the stormy south wind, / Assaulting the sea / Stirs up the salt-surge, / The waves that lay free / And were glassy, encalmed / As unclouded days, / Are fouled with dredged mud / And opaque to our gaze."[11]

And still these poems, which urge Boethius to rise above the confines of the earth, depend upon likenesses drawn from the material world. This philosophical dependence on earthly things, and on the literary forms capable of drawing likenesses between earthly things and mental states, becomes even more apparent in later *metra*, which moralize tales of classical heroes who rose high or fell into confusion. In Book 4, poem 3, Boethius describes Odysseus's great escape from Circe, who plied his men with drink and turned them into pigs, or, in other words, says Boethius, a true philosopher is liberated from the excessive desires of the body, since real strength lies in the mind, not in monstrous and changeable forms. In Book 3, poem 12, Orpheus breaks the bonds of earth when he penetrates the underworld, but he casts his eyes back to hell when he turns to gaze at his trailing wife, Eurydice. In Book 4, poem 7, Hercules's twelve labors are a model for all determined men. In this mythography, philosophical heroes inhabit tales of embodiment and transcendence, triumph and defeat.

According to Boethius's *metra*, to know what is truly valuable, and to translate this knowledge into moral action, one needs to grasp the main concepts with respect to something substantial, material, even incarnate. In passus 1, Langland zeroes in on this central idea of Boethian dialogue. In the *Consolation*, this idea is structurally prosimetrical, that is, it emerges through the juxtaposition of poetry and prose. *Piers Plowman* is not prosimetric in this sense: although it alternates between Latin and English, it does not do so consistently, and it certainly does not alternate prose and verse in that way that many Boethian dialogues tend to do, such as Bernardus Silvestris's *Cosmographia* (1147) or Alain of Lille's *De planctu Naturae* (c.1160–70). Yet the poet does work with some prosimetric principles, namely, that the versatility of literary language makes it a perfect vehicle for philosophical reflection, and that certain literary forms trouble distinctions between material and spiritual values. In passus 1, Langland highlights the protean quality of alliterative verse in order to make the case for vernacular poetry as a vehicle for thought. And he does so, as Boethius does in the *metra*, by showing how poetry teaches us how to transcend worldly values by embracing material things.[12]

As a medieval poet talking about value, Langland is committed to representing the God–man relationship as the source of happiness and of eternal life, as well as of suffering and death. As discussed above, he departs from Boethius by identifying heaven as the reward for a virtuous life, and charity as the virtue that leads to heaven. Of course, this is a critical difference. A Christian writer concerned about salvation has committed himself to reward after death, as well as to the belief that God has doubly invested himself in the material world, both through creation and through the Incarnation of Christ. In the second half of passus 1, Holy Church dramatizes the God–man relationship with the main events of Christian narrative: the fall of Lucifer and the Incarnation of Christ, the counterparts to the exploits of Odysseus, Hercules, and Orpheus. Langland's description of these events – two

intercalated lyrics – serves as his Boethian prosimetra. With these, he shows
how spiritual values and divine love are grounded in the material world.

From line 138, the keywords of passus 1 switch from "treasure" and
"truth," to "kind wit" and "charity." These new terms adjust the passus's
focus from an abstract Truth to God in history, and from sin to love. In
Piers Plowman "kind wit" means something like natural wisdom or innate
understanding, knowledge gained through experience or the knowledge
that one should have realized one had all along. In passus 1, kind wit refers
more specifically to the inborn understanding of the God–man relationship. Holy Church first associates kind wit with formal learning: when the
dreamer complains he lacks kind wit, she rebukes him for neglecting his
education: "'Thow doted daffe'! Quod she, 'dulle are thi wittes. / To litel
latyn thow lernedest, leode, in thi youthe'" ["You ignorant fool!," she said,
"Your wits are dull. / Man, you learned too little Latin in your youth"]
(1.140–41). With this reproof, Holy Church ushers in a pageant of imperi-
ous characters who will humiliate and educate him (1.145–46).

Holy Church is not arguing, however, that higher education is required for
innate understanding, even if she would agree that the study of (Latin)
grammar is the first step toward grasping big ideas about God and the universe.
Rather, she means that if the dreamer regards himself as teachable he will
understand that knowing what is truly valuable is something heart-felt or
childlike, a return to institutional origins. In this sense, Holy Church explains,
kind wit is less a mode of cognition than it is a spiritual attitude toward God
and one's neighbor, which induces charity or love in the subject. In sum, kind
wit signifies two kinds of natural-born understanding: the recognition of the
relationship between God and man, and the fulfillment of the ethical demands
of that relationship (charity, or love of God and neighbor).

We saw that Boethius, in the later *metra*, uses mythological heroes to
show what it means either to go higher and to extricate oneself from earthly
constraints, or to succumb to materiality – to bodies, desire, and death. At
the same time these heroes show how poetry aids philosophy through its
particular investments in the material world. In the second half of passus 1,
Langland depicts the main events of Christian mythology – the fall of
Lucifer and the incarnation and resurrection of Christ – in order to portray
the ethical requirements of love. These two gorgeous passages, which show
charity in action, take their cue from Boethian *metra*. In the first passage,
the poet describes the fall of Lucifer, with awesome concision, distilling all
the drama and pathos of that story into just a few lines. Beginning at line 111,
Lucifer breaks his obedience and falls with his legions out of God's fellowship and heaven's sphere:

And fel fro that felawshipe in a fendes liknesse
Into a deep derk helle to dwelle there for evere.
And mo thousandes myd hym than man kouthe nombre
Lopen out with Lucifer in lothliche forme
For thei leveden upon hym that lyed in this manere:
Ponam pedem in aquilone, et similis ero altissimo
And alle that hoped it myghte be so, noon hevene myghte hem holde
But fellen out in a fendes liknesse [for] nyne dayes togideres,
Til God of his goodnesse gan stable and stynte
And garte [to stekie the hevene], and stonden in quiete.   (1.114–23)

[And fell from that fellowship, in a devil's guise
Into a deep, dark, hell, to dwell there for ever.
And with him many more thousands than one could ever count
Leapt out with Lucifer in hideous form,
Because they believed in him, who lied in this way:
"I will place my foot in the North and be like the Most High."
And no heaven could hold those who believed it to be so,
But they fell out, like devils, for nine straight days.]

Lucifer's wicked followers fall everywhere in the world, but Lucifer hits rock bottom:

Whan thise wikkede wenten out, wonderwise thei fellen –
Somme in eyr, somme in erthe, somme in helle depe,
Ac Lucifer lowest lith of hem alle:
For pride that hym pulte out: his peyne hath noon ende.   (1.124–27)

[When these wicked left, they fell every which way:
Some in air, some in earth, some into deep hell.
But Lucifer lies lowest of all;
Because of the pride that pulled him down, his pain has no end.]

In this passage, alliterative verse becomes the consummate verse form for heroic narrative, supremely capable of describing archetypal events: ascent and descent, triumph and defeat, darkness and light, buoyancy and weight. These virtuosic lines, which look forward to Milton, portray the swiftness of Lucifer's punishment and his sudden and improbable transformation from angel to devil ("in a fendes liknesse"). They also proclaim the terror of falling and the rupture of the heavens: God shows his goodness both by meting out justice – heaven could not hold those who hoped to remain there, because the "weight" of their sin literally dragged them down – and by quieting the heavens once more. Like many of Boethius's *metra*, Langland's Lucifer passage celebrates God's ability to establish order and, like many of the *metra*, which employ a variety of meters, it extravagantly displays the materiality of poetic form. For example, the hypermetric line at 120 expresses the breathless anticipation of the supernatural cohort teetering on the brink. Conversely, line 126, "Ac Lucifer lowest lith of hem alle," the shortest of metrically regular lines, describes with laconic pathos the lowest place where Lucifer dwells.

The poet saw all kinds of potential in the Lucifer passage. Between the A-text and B-text he tested its epic proportions. The A-text alludes only briefly to Lucifer's fall, whereas the B-text expands the Lucifer passage into a dramatically charged episode, exploiting to the hilt the Latin quotation he has introduced to the scene – "Ponam pedem in aquilone, et similis ero Altissimo" (119a) ("I will set my foot in the North and be like the Most High," from Augustine's *Ennarratio in Psalmos*, following Isiah 14:14) – and adding the details about Lucifer's legions of followers and about the heavens collapsing and stabilizing. In the C-text revision, the poet rewrites B's cosmic drama into a crowd-pleasing sermon developed from the same Latin quotation. In this revision, which spoofs the lofty didacticism of Boethian dialogue while undercutting the epic majesty of Lucifer's fall, Holy Church does an impression of a local preacher who does not mind knocking Northerners to get a point across. Why, she asks, did that wicked Lucifer not stay to the south, on God's sunny side? She demurs, "'Nere hit for northerne men, anon Y wolde yow telle / Ac Y wol lacky no lif,' quod that lady sothly ... 'Ac of This matere no more nemnen Y nelle'"] ["If it weren't for Northern men, I would tell you straight away, / But I never insult anyone," said that lady truly ... "And I'm not going to speak any more about this!"] (C.1.115–16, 123).

In the second lyric, on Christ's heroic dive into human form, Langland again invokes Boethian *metra* and specifically the way in which they celebrate aristocratic values. Boethius is an aristocrat's philosopher. As a high-ranking public servant from an ancient Roman family, he once had it all – power, riches, fame – and he must now reckon with his losses. Langland, by contrast, is a reformer, who pursues the *summum bonum* through a landscape of poverty and greed. But in passus 1 Langland shares with Boethius both an interest in value – by its nature, a subject for the rich, who can afford to be moderate, and who enjoy the favor of Fortune – and a confidence in poetry to convey the material values of philosophical thought (e.g., truth is the best treasure). Like Boethius, too, he situates Christian morality within an aristocratic framework, as he will elsewhere in the poem. As we have seen, Holy Church's status, like Lady Philosophy's, foregrounds the nobility of philosophical discourse; it also frames passus 1 in decidedly aristocratic terms. For instance, she continually addresses topics of interest to the nobility, such as stewardship, husbandry, chivalry, and lineage, and she cites Lot, Abraham's notorious nephew, as an example not only of the price of gluttony (Lot's daughters seduced him with drink) but also of the tragic failure of a noble line: he "gat in glotonie gerles that were cherles" [he begat in his gluttony children who were churls] (1.34). This attention to aristocratic subjects is important because it enables the poet to valorize material goods (truth is the best treasure), even while presenting moderation, charity, and obedience as the keys to Christian salvation. This sustained attention to aristocratic subjects also allows him to explore the relationship between value and love (*caritas*). According to Holy Church, for example, love means giving away material goods in order to attain the sovereign good; in this view, love is a magnanimous act performed by those of higher birth. Holy Church exhorts the rich to humble themselves by showing pity for the poor: "Forthi I rede yow riche, haveth ruth on the povere, / Though ye be mighty to mote, beeth meke in youre werkes" [Therefore, I counsel you rich, have pity on the poor, / Though you be mighty in your summons, be meek in your works] (1.175–76).

Most significantly for the poet, the aristocratic virtues of magnanimity and pity, or what might be called the noble condescension to lower forms, are the same virtues exemplified by God when he sent his Son to earth to redeem humanity and restore the balance upset by the Fall. In the *Consolation*, Book 4, poem 7, Lady Philosophy explains that the earth's caves contain treasures, which bring no happiness to avaricious men. The goal is to soar beyond the treasure-hoard. Langland, too, condemns greed and urges his dreamer to go higher. But because he is finally interested in charity, he needs to find a discourse capable of describing the earthly instantiation of love, the virtuous descent into form, i.e., Christ's incarnation and resurrection, the ultimate sacrifice for love. Beginning at line 148 ff., Holy Church describes divine love in a sequence of images as compressed as a John Donne sonnet:

> For Truthe telleth that love is a triacle of hevene:
> May no synne be on hym seene that that spice useth.
> And alle his werkes he wrought with love as hym liste,
> And lered it Moyses for the leveste thyng and moost lik to hevene,
> And also the plante of pees, moost precious of vertues:
> For hevene myghte nat holden it, so was it hevy of hymselve,
> Til it hadde of the erthe eten his fille.
> And whan it hadde of this fold flesh and blood taken,

Was never leef upon lynde lighter therafter,
And portatif and persaunt as the point of a nedle,
That myghte noon armure it lette ne none heighe walles.   (1.148–58)

[For Truth says that love is heaven's remedy.
No sin will be seen in him who uses that spice!
And all his works he wrought with love, as it pleased him,
And taught it to Moses as the dearest thing and most like to heaven;
And also the plant of peace, most precious of virtues:
For heaven couldn't hold it, it was so heavy of itself,
Until it had eaten its fill of earth.
And when it had taken from this earth flesh and blood,
[There] was never a linden leaf lighter after that,
Or as portable and sharp as the point of a needle,
So that no armor could stop it, and no high walls.]

These lovely lines blend a number of images from chivalric romance:
superlative love, magical herbs, and armor.[13] Love is a remedy and therefore a curative spice, and therefore a medicinal plant, but a metaphorical
plant of peace so weighty that, as Christ incarnate, heaven could not hold
it until it had "eaten of the earth" and taken flesh and blood, with the
result that it became, paradoxically, lighter than any linden tree leaf, and
as slender as the point of a needle, which can pierce anything, whether the
walls of the heavenly city or the defenses of the human heart. This string
of images recalls the cosmic language of Lucifer's fall: just as Lucifer
crashed through the heavens, so divine love was too heavy for the heavens
to hold. Whereas the fall of the angels passage relies on puns (Lucifer
"broke" his buxomness and literally "fell" out of fellowship), however, this
passage relies on paradox: weight is levity and humility is strength. This
kind of paradox is a familiar trope of a medieval religious poetry which
seeks to explain the mystery in which God assumes human form out of
strength rather than out of weakness, as in a lyric from MS Ashmole 189,
whose speaker exclaims, "The to redeme / He founde sone remedye, /
Vsynge humylite to thi pride clene contrary" [In order to redeem you, /
He immediately found a remedy, / Using his humility entirely against
your pride].[14] In this lyric, as in Langland's "plant of peace" passage,
paradox also signals an aristocratic ethics: the voluntary condescension to
embodiment. This condescension is at the heart of the Redemption, and
embodies for many medieval writers the noblest form of love.

In his loving descent, Langland's Christ begins to resemble medieval
moralizations of Orpheus, whose noble love for Euridice drives him down

to the underworld. Medieval commentaries on Boethius tend to allegorize Orpheus as a moral faculty, for instance, the rational mind overcome by desire for those earthly things represented by Euridice, but more than one author saw a likeness between Orpheus and Christ, two noble lovers bound by love, an analogy first disseminated by commentators on Boethius and later by Ovidian mythographers.[15] In this analogy the descent into hell, or the condescension to form, testifies to a divine love so compelling that it postpones indefinitely the moment of Orpheus's backward glance. According to one early fourteenth-century French version of Boethius's Orpheus, up until the moment he looks back to the trailing Euridice, Orpheus represents the power of love overcoming lust, a love internalized in man and externalized in Christ as redeemer.[16] As the influential Ovidian moralist Pierre Bersuire (d.1362) explains, Orpheus is the Christ who draws to himself, his lover, the human soul: "Allegorically speaking, Orpheus, son of the sun, is Christ, son of the Father, who from the beginning, led Euridice, that is, the human soul, through charity and love, and joined himself to her, through special prerogative." In another place, Bersuire describes Orpheus's attempt to recover Euridice as Christ's successful harrowing of hell and his redemption of human nature. His Christ-Orpheus leads the Soul-Euridice to the upper world while singing a verse from the Song of Songs: "In this way resembling Christ, Orpheus wished to descend into hell personally, and, in this way, he recovered his wife, that is, human nature, snatching her away from the realm of darkness, and led her with him to the upper world, saying this from Canticles 2: 'Rise up my love.'"[17]

Although the reception of the *Consolation* underwrites much of medieval personification allegory, Langland's Christ is not Orpheus, and Langland does not appear to be following a particular commentary. But the "fall of Lucifer" and "plant of peace" passages, like Boethius's *metra*, show how the material values of form both offset and ratify a philosophy of moderation and restraint. In this way, passus 1 does not merely borrow the form of Boethian dialogue; it also serves as Langland's defense of poetry, showing how vernacular poetry can transmit cultural ideas about value.

At the end of passus 1, Holy Church declares that she has educated the dreamer in matters of the faith: "Now have I told thee what truthe is – that no tresor is bettre - / I may no lenger lenge thee with; now loke thee Oure Lord!" [Now I have told you what truth is – that no treasure is better – / I may no longer stay with you; may God watch over you!] (1.208–9). But the dreamer has learned from Holy Church a language for *thinking* about value, not advice he can put to immediate use. In the course of the passus, the dreamer has managed to ask the major question that drives the poem as a whole – how do I save my soul? – and he has taken the habit of a student, which will serve him well later on. But if Holy Church has established that the best truth is love – the bond between human beings and God, wherein true value lies – she still has not given the dreamer the answer he seeks. He has nineteen more passūs to figure it out.

The gender of money

Passus 1 interrupts the poem with a dialogue that raises the intellectual stakes of the poem, setting to one side the bustle and sprawl of the Prologue. Just as the Prologue shows the spectacular range of a socially oriented dream-vision, passus 1 shows how penitential poetry can approximate Boethian philosophy. It is something of a relief, however, to return to the everyday business of marriage, law, and governance critiqued in passūs 2–4. In the *Consolation*, Boethius teaches his readers how to deal with adversity and how to adjust their attitude toward mutable things, like public honor and material goods. He does not teach them, however, how to be good in a Christian world, a world which Langland pictures teeming with bureaucrats, confessors, and crooks, whose activities revolve around a king eager to put things right. Through the adventures of Lady Meed, the poet reminds us that political counsel is the counterpart to moral philosophy; after all, it might be better to leap into the saddle and go counsel the King at Westminster than to be like Boethius in exile, philosophizing on death row. With Meed, his second female interlocutor, the poet reconsiders the question of value within real-life nexuses of counsel, service, and reward.

Passūs 2–4, which contains the poem's first "dream within a dream" (beginning 2.52), is one of the most dynamic episodes in the poem. It tells the allegorical tale of a lady named Meed, who contracts marriage with False through a wonderfully wicked charter. The King gets wind of the plot and summons the whole gang to his court at Westminster, where, in passus 3, Meed agrees to marry Conscience, the King's choice, instead. She is refused by Conscience on the grounds of moral character and she attempts, unsuccessfully, to defend herself. In passus 4, the King banishes Meed from court after Conscience and Reason, royal advisors, convince him to wash his hands of her. Meed's story culminates in two debates about the relationship between governance and reward. The first debate has to do with the nature of compensation: is it ethical and in what form, and to what degree is it instrumental in its own corruption (can money be said to be the root of all evil?). The second debate concerns the nature of justice: can justice be preserved through personal and local interests (feuding, for example, or

Figure 1. "Lady Meed riding a sheriff." William Langland, *Piers Plowman* (C-Text). Oxford, Bodleian Library, MS Douce 104. f.10r. (Anglo-Irish, 1427).

maintenance, or settling out of court), or only through the long arm of a centralized royal government? Both debates portray abstract ethical topics, such as reward and justice, as the matter of political counsel. Both show, moreover, that a society's moral health depends on its interpretation of value.

In the fourteenth century, meed was most commonly used to mean "just deserts," a fitting reward for services rendered, or a punishment for crime. Originally derived from the Old English feminine noun, meed became a useful term to talk about spiritual reward – a person gets what she deserves after death, whether the consolation of heaven or the pains of hell. Insofar as it refers to actions and outcomes, meed obviates the need to evaluate the workings of justice; it assumes that the process is fair, that a decision has already been made, and that compensation is being distributed accordingly. We see this unexamined quality of meed in a famous line from the Prologue to the *Canterbury Tales*, in which the Host hopes that St. Thomas of Canterbury will "quite" the pilgrims' meed, or grant whatever they request.[18] The bestowal of the reward is at issue, not the saint's motivations or the pilgrim's deserts. It is, moreover, the unexamined nature of meed that makes it indispensable to princely rule. It is a commonplace in medieval romances, for example, that a ruler earns his heavenly reward by allocating his treasure wisely. In an early Middle English metrical romance about the legendary King Horn, "Horn Childe – Maiden Rimnild," compiled in the Auchinleck manuscript (c.1330s), Horn's father, having defeated a company of Danish raiders on the Yorkshire coast dubs sixty knights on the spot. The narrator approves of this decision:

> [He] ȝaf hem riche mede,
> Sum baylis he made,
> &sum he ȝaf londes brade;
> His ȝiftes were nouȝt gnede.
> & seþþen he dede chirches make,
> To sing for þe dedes sake –
> God quite him his mede![19]

> [(He) gave them rich reward:
> Some he gave strongholds,
> And some he gave extensive lands.
> His gifts were not paltry.
> And then he endowed foundations
> To sing for the sake of the dead.
> May God reward him!]

In this passage, munificence is a function of monarchical power and its reflex. Royal sovereignty is based on a *quid pro quo* with God – a worthy king justifies his actions only to God, and God rewards a king who supports his men, regardless of his intentions or their individual deserts.

Distributing wealth is a royal duty, whether as charity to priests, who pray on the King's behalf, or as reward to the men who fight Vikings by his side.

Langland, by personifying Meed, has re-created a vernacular ethical concept and invested it with ideological complexity. Meed, in *Piers Plowman*, means not simply "what one deserves" but also "how one desires," whether that desire is directed to reward for its own sake, or to what can be won with gold, such as victory, or honor, or a path through the thickets of bureaucracy. As unexamined compensation, meed sidesteps questions of corruption or injustice, instead directing attention to actions and outcomes. But, as a complex of desires, Meed tells a different story: she uncovers the sinful motivations (pride, greed, lechery) which jeopardize the soul of the sinner and the promise of a just society.[20] Lady Meed, in other words, turns reward into a subject of moral investigation and the locus of injustice. In the end, the poet's re-creation of meed as an ethical problem and as a female personification enables him to offer up the matter of good governance with which to advise the King.

Lady Meed is the protagonist of a riveting narrative about the way that reward operates in society. As a person, Meed exposes the universal desire for gain – everybody wants her – as well as the crimes and deceptions prompted by that desire. As a woman, Meed refracts this desire through assumptions about female sexuality for instance, that it is conductive and insidious, directed toward bad ends and difficult to control. As the analogy goes, like female sexuality, (and like other forms of sexuality outside of approved heterosexual marriages), money forges unholy unions, undermines right relations, and sexualizes all relationships: False and Meed will "ligge togideres" (2.136) through an improper marriage; Meed "coupleth togiders" clergy and covetousness (3.165); both "lewed men and lered men" (3.38) will lie with Meed. Consequently, money compromises intimacy and, in the process, reveals even courtesy to be a network of sordid exchanges. At the King's court at Westminster, for example, Meed is received with a courtesy befitting her station, but the wrong people welcome her for the wrong reasons. A clerk, hoping for favor, "took Mede bi the myddel and broghte hire into chambre" [wrapped his arm around Meed's waist and escorted her into the room] (3.10), and some justices "gentillische with joye … busked hem to the bour ther the burde dwellede" [nobly with joy … hurried to the apartments where the lady was staying] (3.13–14). Money, like female sexuality, further disguises vice under the cover of beauty, piety, or art. Lady Meed,

sometime romance heroine, is dressed in furs and precious stones with
no allegorical fleas or patches to give the besotted dreamer pause for
thought: "Hire array me ravysshed; swich richesse saugh I neuere"
[Her costume ravished me; I never saw such finery] (2.17), he says.
The dreamer likewise admires False's "riche retenaunce" (2.54), his
powerful and well-dressed entourage, and in a different context, this
might be honest praise. One of the claims of courtly literature is that
status and virtue are intertwined: valiant knights wear dazzling armor
and noble ladies rarely appear in smocks. With Meed, however, the
poet demystifies the riches of romance, suggesting that the material
goods that underwrite courtly values mask all sorts of depravity, such
as insincere penance and adulterous sex. Meed, too grateful for her
reception at court, promises to advance clerks in their profession, no
matter how ignorant. She even agrees to sponsor stained glass windows
in the friars' church, so long as the friars forgive lechery. As she tells
her friar confessor, he is justified in absolving adulterers because love is
a natural act, if a weakness of the flesh:

> While ye love lordes that lecherie haunten
> And lakketh noght ladies that loven wel the same.
> It is a freletee of flesh – ye fynden it in bokes –
> And a cours of Kynde, wherof we comen alle. . .   (3.53–56)

> [As long as you love lords who pursue lechery,
> And don't disparage ladies who love the same way.
> It is a fraility of the flesh – you find it in books –
> And the way of Nature, from which we all come.]

Meed continues with a sentiment from romance: "Who may scape the
sclaundre, the scathe is soone amended" (3.57), or, in other words, if no one
knows, no harm done. In *Sir Gawain and the Green Knight*, Bertilak's wife,
another dealer in moral fictions, begs Gawain to sleep with her, reminding
him that, as an icon of courtesy, he is supposed to instruct her in the arts and
letters of courtly love.[21] Gawain is puzzled to have his reputation for
courtesy reflected back to him as adultery. Lady Meed's speech to the friars
similarly parodies the "textbook" ethics of romance, which naturalizes
adultery as a species of courtliness, and hides vice under art.

In passus I, the gender of Holy Church, pedagogue and nursemaid, is the
starting point of an investigation into the relationship between value and
language: how does one's attitude toward material goods determine the way
that one understands the sovereign good, and in what way might literary
language explain the relationship between materiality and spirituality? As

Holy Church's alter ego, Lady Meed transposes these questions into the realm of social life and politics, and in doing so incorporates certain assumptions about the relationship between women, value, and language which implicate Holy Church as well. Although Holy Church would have the dreamer believe that she and Meed are opposites – she orders him to choose between them, just as Boethius's Philosophy opposes herself first to the Muses and later to Fortune – the two personifications function within the same discourse of desire and reward (though only Holy Church has managed to escape the slander). At the beginning of passus 2, she complains that Meed has disparaged her lover, Leaute (integrity, equity, justice), and that she and Meed have become rivals in the Pope's palace, where they are equally intimate ("pryvee," 2.23). Holy Church assures the dreamer that any man who loves what she stands for will be properly rewarded in heaven by claiming her as his wife (he "Shal be my lord and I his leef in the heighe hevene," 2.33), but any man who loves Meed will "lese for hire love a lappe of *Caritatis*" [lose a chunk of *Charity* on account of her love] (2.35).

One medieval reader saw the relationship between Holy Church and Meed similarly. In Lincoln's Inn manuscript 150, a *Piers Plowman* A-text, the scribe made the following revisions: he replaced the b-verse of A.1.82, "that saint are yholde," referring to Holy Church, with "fro synnes in þis eorþe," and then he inserted a second line about Holy Church, "Than þat louely lady with laghyng chere," which he lifted from C.3.55, where Meed is described as a lovely lady with a laughing expression.[22] The scribe, who was familiar with multiple versions of the poem, seems to have been a poor judge of literary character: Holy Church is, after all, rather stern. But the transposition of that second line from Meed to Holy Church suggests that built into personification is a basic interchangeability, even and precisely at those moments where personifications are used to compare values. The antagonism between Holy Church and Meed, for example, is supposed to show that salvation obtained through the church, which promotes moderation and alms, is better than any earthly reward. Female personification, always sexualized, underlines the interchangeability and the relationality of personification allegory. According to Holy Church, Meed, a bastard, comes from impure stock, whereas Holy Church is the daughter of God. Later, however, Theology gives a different account of Meed's lineage, protesting that Meed comes from good stock, because Amends (compensation) is her father (or mother) and God has intended her as Truth's wife (2.119–21). This relationality is didactic: it explains difficult concepts, such as the ethics of reward or the operations of divine grace. In the Meed episode, however, it also shows that value itself, what a culture deems most important, is subject to exchange.

As discussed above, once desire is factored in, the ethics of reward – gifts, wages, even almsgiving – become very complicated. Langland reminds us that it is easy to pretend that money acts through its own volition and that, like fortune, it favors one person over another, or can be appeased or coerced. The men at court swear to Meed, "For we beth thyne owene / For to werche thi wille the while thow myght laste" [For we are yours / To work your will, as long as you last] (3.27–28). The men who swarm around Meed invest her with will, a will they also attempt to master so that she may act on their behalf. False's clerks promise that they will persuade Meed to accompany them to London to defend her marriage to False: "Certes, sire, cessen shul we nevere / Til Mede be thi wedded wif thorugh wittes of us alle; / For we have Mede amaistried thorugh oure murie speche, / That she graunteth to goon with a good wille" [Truly, sir, we will never cease / Until Mede becomes your wedded wife through our clever stratagems] (2.152–55). This fiction of will and agency goes both ways: whether Meed is said to be mastered or whether she is declared sovereign, she exposes the desire for possession and dominance.[23]

The poet takes pains to show that Meed, like Boethius's Fortune, is universal. Insofar as reward is figured through human (and in *Piers Plowman*, nearly exclusively male) desire, it is theoretically available to everyone, of every class and gender, and to suggest otherwise would be to deny human moral agency altogether. This is the conceit, for example, of Meed's marriage charter, the diabolical land-grant witnessed by common folk such as Piers the Pardoner and Reynald the Reeve: everyone wants reward, and everyone has the chance of getting it in some form.

At the same time, Langland's analogy between women and money, and between sexual desire and greed, calls attention to the constructedness of will and agency, both female and male. Gender, in other words, links universalized sinfulness to the human construction of desire. As Elizabeth Fowler has influentially argued, for example, the character of Meed participates in the medieval legal concept of civil death, a "specially structured" agency in law, in which women who marry consent to the loss of power to intend or act in law. Their consent means that henceforth their actions, such as alienating land or committing a crime, will always make reference to the actions of their husbands, or in other words, a wife's actions are always "covered" by her husband's will. In this view, the feminine is something amoral or immoral, continually rationalizing the need for male sovereignty.[24] Like women in medieval law, Meed's character emerges from a cultural fantasy about female will and agency, which is really a cover for (male) desire. Even the King, determined to stay above the fray, believes that mastering Meed is a moral imperative, requiring the exercise of royal authority and pity. As he says, "I shal assayen hire myself and soothliche appose / What man of this world that hire were levest. / And if she worche bi my wit and my wit folwe / I wol forgyven hire this[e] giltes, so me God helpe!" [I will interview her myself, and ask her directly / Which man of this world is most pleasing to her. / And if she works by my wit and follows my advice, / So God help me, I will forgive her these offenses] (B.3.5–8).

From a satirist's point of view, Meed is a potent allegory, morally fraught and infinitely generative. Her character also highlights the historicity of personification allegory, and especially of female personifications. One of the most memorable scenes in passūs 2–4 is the marriage charter drawn up between Meed and False, which grants the couple territories of sin. This charter is a cleverly compressed allegorical fiction, which traces the spiritual life of an everyman who falls into despair,[25] at the same time that it charts a topography of sin on a generic aristocratic landscape, "with the chastilet of cheste ... The countee of Coveitise and alle the costes aboute" (2.85–86).[26] But as a record of a transaction, and specifically of the transfer of property, it grounds Meed in a pseudo-history, pointing to another identity for Meed besides the female personification of reward. In medieval historical writing, women who make too great a mark on political life tend to be accused of improvidence or licentiousness; conversely, these accusations have huge explanatory power, explaining how women can be historical actors in the first place, worthy of record. It is little wonder, then, that modern scholars have often compared Meed to her "contemporary" Alice Perrers, the formidable landholder and mistress to Edward III, who wielded influence at court during the King's declining years, making enemies of generations of chroniclers who derided her as a low-born whore.[27] In 1377 Perrers was banished from court, although for years she continued to exercise power as a major landholder. The resemblance between Alice Perrers and Meed is remarkable: like Perrers, Meed establishes her presence in the King's court, presumably the court of Edward III, but she is eventually thrown out amid accusations of whoredom and obstruction of justice.

Like Perrers, too, Meed discloses the difficulty – and the attraction – of recording women for posterity. In this respect, Meed resembles yet another powerful woman from three centuries earlier, Queen Maud (or Matilda) (b.1080). Medieval chroniclers praise Maud for her piety and chastity but, at the same time, following William of Malmesbury's account, they suspect her influence at court, and particularly her liberal patronage, which belies her other virtues. According to William, Maud, plucked from Wilton Abbey by Henry I, continued her pious habits after marriage, for example, routinely washing the feet of lepers and remaining faithful to Henry during his long absences. Some of that piety, however, says William, was misguided. For example, the Queen would reward any cleric who could sing the liturgy, which was dear to her heart, consequently attracting a bevy of international scholars and performers to the English court. According to William, who was jealous of her favors, she "would give them rich gifts, and promise richer" [*multa largiri plura polliceri*].[28] But her openhandedness apparently made her susceptible to flattery and profligate in the name of piety. Though a chronicler ought to portray a former benefactress in the best possible light, William of Malmesbury struggles with Maud and bequeaths his struggle to later chroniclers. In the *Gesta* he is troubled by her sexuality (he is uncertain whether she took solemn vows at Wilton before her marriage), as well as by her liberality, from which Malmesbury Abbey sometimes profited. The Queen, he says bitterly, was beguiled into promising presents to the throngs of foreigners at court while at the same time, misusing her own tenants; or perhaps, says William, it would be safer to blame her greedy servants for misleading her.

Maud's resemblance to Meed as patroness is striking: Meed lavishes gifts on her followers and procures justice for all comers (see B.3.20–24); she is easily seduced by courtiers and clerks; her sexuality and liberality are linked in the act of patronage; it is hard to know whom to blame for her excess (indeed, Meed and Maud, with their abundance of gifts, represent the flip side of medieval justice exemplified by those fourteenth-century queens, so valuable in the pursuit of royal justice, such as Queen Philippa, who interceded with Edward III for the lives of the burghers of Calais in 1347, or Queen Anne, who interceded with Richard II for the citizens of London in 1392). This is not to say that Meed represents an early twelfth-century queen any more than she represents Alice Perrers; the point is rather that the poet has fashioned Meed from stereotypes about prominent women, stereotypes which in turn, allow him to present Meed as a moral and historical actor. It is by virtue of this pseudo-historicity, her claim to be present at a significant moment in English history, that Meed occupies the position of counselor to the King.

Valuable advice

When False and his minions get wind of the King's plans to stop the marriage, they flee the scene, forsaking Meed, who piteously weeps and wrings her hands (2.234–37). The King, having already secured Meed's consent, attempts to arrange a marriage between Meed, his ward, and his tried-and-true counselor Conscience.[29] Conscience refuses, explaining that Meed has ruined everything: she is a prostitute, a "baude" (3.129), as "commune as the cartwey" (3.132); she corrupts justice and competes with royal authority. "She may neigh as muche do in a monthe ones /As youre secret seel in sixe score dayes!" [She can do nearly as much in a month /As your secret seal (can do) in four months] (3.145–46). She is intimate with the Pope, she greases the wheels of his machine, and she confounds lowborn men who cannot pay for justice. This, says Conscience, "is the lif of that lady" (3.166), and indeed, Meed's "life" for an instant looks absurdly like the *vita* of a female saint. Like a St. Cecilia or St. Catherine, Meed's background is noble, and her story plays out accordingly: she is misunderstood, she is compelled to marry, she is accused of being a hypocrite and a whore, she must defend herself publicly, and suffer questioning by a ruler who finds her captivating, not just because she is lovely – as young female saints were reputed to be – but also because her influence nearly rivals his.

Like many a female saint, too, Meed is a rhetorical force to be reckoned with and her answer to Conscience is one of the very best speeches in the poem. Meed argues that Conscience, who is supposed to help the King distinguish good from bad, is a bad counselor masquerading as a moral guide. By Meed's account, Conscience is not high-minded but dithering and cowardly, a poor strategist who dishonors his king and nation. Most damningly, Conscience let the King debase himself in the war with France: in 1360, spooked by a hailstorm outside of Chartres, the King agreed to a peace. Says Meed to Conscience,

> In Normandie was he noght noyed for my sake –
> Ac throw thiself, soothly, shamedest hym ofte:
> Crope into a cabane for cold of thi nayles,
> Wendest that winter wolde han ylasted evere,
> And dreddest to be ded for a dym cloude,
> And hyedest homward for hunger of thi wombe. (3.189–94)

[In Normandy, [the King] was not the least bit vexed for my sake,
But rather for yours; truly, you shamed him often:
You crept into a hut because your fingernails were cold,
You expected winter to last for ever,
And because of a dark cloud, you were afraid to die,
And set off for home because of the hunger in your belly.]

Though the king was destined to fell his foes, Conscience persuaded him to exchange his claim to the "richeste reaume" of France for a "litel silver" (3.207) referring to the staggering 3,000,000 ecues paid by the French Crown at the Treatise of Bretigny (1360). In the C-text, Meed severely rebukes Conscience on this score: "Caytifliche thow, Conscience, consei-ledest the kyng to leten / In his enemyes handes his heritage of Fraunce" [Cowardly, you, Conscience, counseled the King to let / his French inher-itance fall into enemies' hands] (C.3.242–43). If the King had only listened to Meed, his concession would have been unnecessary: somehow, she would have raised the money and paid the soldiers so well from the start that they would have conquered France and enjoyed all the benefits of conquest. Nor would they have had to stoop to practices like *chevauchée*, the Black Prince's specialty, which the English army practiced again in the 1370s campaigns, pillaging the French countryside to pay and feed the soldiers (B.3.195–96) who, with no passage home, became roving men-aces.[30] Meed says she would have laid down her life as surety that the King would be lord of France and his every last relative promoted: "The leeste brol of his blood a barones piere!" (B.3.204–5) – just as Meed herself doles out cups and rings to her followers and to "The leeste man of hire meynee a moton of golde" [a gold coin even to the lowest man in her entourage] (B.3.24).

In Meed's view, monarchical rule is an expression of the ethics of the noble household, demonstrated in grand feasts and well-planned campaigns, both of which depend on the lord's willingness to expend his personal wealth. Meed defines royal virtue as lordly valor and magnifi-cence displayed both at home and abroad. A good king subdues realms, gratifies his nobles, leads soldiers, commands servants; in short, he proves himself a man:

> It bicometh to a kyng that kepeth a reaume
> To yeue [men Meed] that meekly hym serveth –
> To aliens and to alle men, to honouren hem with yiftes;
> Meed maketh hym biloved and for a man holden.
> Emperours and erles and alle manere lordes
> Thorugh yiftes han yomen to yerne and to ryde.   (3.209–14)

> [It is fitting for a king who maintains a realm
> To give reward to men who humbly serve him,
> To foreigners and to all men, to honor them with gifts;
> Meed makes him beloved and held to be a man.
> Emperors, and earls and all kinds of lords
> Through gifts have the desire to go forth and ride.]

If a king wants to maintain his honor, he must be prepared to give generously to those who serve him. According to Meed, even the ability of the King to act conscientiously in ways that support Christian morality is upheld by the wealth on which male noble virtue rests. As Meed warns Conscience, I "menske thee with yiftes / And mayntene thi manhode moore than thow knowest" [I reward you with gifts / And maintain your manhood more than you know] (3.184–5). Moreover, says Meed, this ability to reward one's followers, which makes the King a mensch, is a model for society in general: just as royal munificence wins the loyalty of the great lords who ride with him in battle, so compensation is due to every person of every station and walk of life. Beggars get alms in return for prayers, minstrels for their mirth. Even the Pope and prelates receive gifts, and in turn they "medeth men" (3.216) who administer canon law. Or, in other words, just as the nation can be defined by the figure of the conquering King, who rewards his kinsman and servants in his wars, so all of western Christian society operates through networks of service and reward.

Although Meed's model of the English nation is colored by relatively recent events, her theoretical apparatus is derived from medieval mirrors-for-princes literature, such as *De regimine principum* (*On the Governance of Princes*, henceforth, *DRP*) (*c.*1280), written for the future French king Philip the Fair by his tutor, Giles of Rome. The *DRP*, which survives in over 350 Latin manuscripts and in several translations, is a compendium of Aristotelian material divided into three books: ethics (rule of the self), economics (rule of the household), and politics (rule of the realm).[31] Book 3, part 3, is a close adaptation of Vegetius's *De re militari*, a late antique guide to warfare popular among the medieval aristocracy. According to the *DRP*, a prince needs a good education and he should chiefly study political philosophy in the vernacular so that he can learn how to be a good ruler and foster virtue in his subjects.[32] A ruler ought to have this matter explained to him in the common idiom and read to him at the table, ideally from a copy of the *DPR*, which offers virtual counsel in the presence of the prince.[33]

In *Piers Plowman*, it is Meed who brings this material to the King's court in the common idiom. Specifically, she transmits that advice most flattering to the monarchy: a good ruler is one who exemplifies aristocratic virtues, someone who knows how to walk the fine line between moral extremes, such as profligacy and liberality, waste and magnificence, tyranny and rule. A prince can walk that line because he is financially sufficient: the monarchy is an extension of lordship because a king ideally performs great deeds at his own expense without abusing his tenants or ravaging the countryside; as Giles explains, the sixth quality of magnanimity, as it pertains to a ruler, is sufficiency in goods.[34] An anonymous French mirror-for-princes, "L'estat et le gouvernement," written in 1347 on Giles's model and translated into English in the fifteenth century, explains that a good king needs to consider three things: the state of himself, the management of his household, and his fear of God. Concerning the second, a good ruler is by definition rich. His treasure attests to his ability to defend himself, his lands, and the realm,[35] and he can maintain his troops without encroaching upon the good will and possessions of his subjects.

Of course, the proposition of a king paying for his own wars was untenable by the mid fourteenth century, and by defining good rule as the ability to do great deeds, to pay and conquer, Meed ignores the elephant in the room: taxation. Edward III had to raise money to fund the wars in France from the subsidies that were both a bone of contention in Parliament and seemingly its raison d'être in the fourteenth century (parliamentary sessions from mid century were characterized by wrangling over taxes and subsidies). Taxation effectively disrupts the link between monarchical and aristocratic virtue. How can a king be said to reward those who defend the nation when that reward comes from subsidies levied on wool and the taxes collected from the population as a whole?

According to Meed, it is Conscience's failure to support her model of kingship that disqualifies him as a counselor. Conscience does not count as a royal virtue because he can't manage the ethical distinctions that confer honor on the King and profit to the realm: "'Forthy y consayl no kynge eny conseyl aske / At Concience, þat coueiteth to conquere a reume. / For sholde neuere Conscience be my constable were y a kyng,' quod Mede, / 'Ne be marschal ouer my men there y moste fyhte'" ["Therefore I advise no king, / to ask Conscience's counsel, who wishes to conquer a realm. / I would never have Conscience as my constable, if I were king," said Meed, / "Nor have command over my men wherever I might fight"] (C.3.253–56). By contrast, Meed's description of an English nation led by an openhanded warrior-king would seem to make her the ideal counselor, precisely because she is channeling, however selectively, the moral matter of medieval political philosophy. No wonder the King is ready to award Meed the "maistrie" in the debate. If he did, he would endorse an ethical system in which reward is defined as munificence, and in which action and outcome trump intention and desire. Meed argues this point most strenuously in C: "And þat is þe kynde of a kyng þat conquereth on his enemys, / To helpe heyliche alle his oste or elles graunte / Al þat his men may wynne, do therwith here beste" [And that is the nature of a king who defeats his enemies. / [Who] generously supports his troops or else ordains / That everything his men win, they can do with as they wish] (C.3.250–52).

If the King were to declare Meed the champion, moreoever, he would endorse a national policy defined by female eloquence. Meed's self-defense turns out to be a species of female counsel; the King's female ward presumes to tell him how he should rule and what he should value. Though Meed eventually loses her bid to shape national policy, she has effectively advised the King. Through Meed, moreover, the poet has tried out a form of vernacular counsel which, in medieval letters, was the route to talking about good governance. In the Prologue, the poet attempts several times to imagine a new discourse of political counsel: the story of political origins in the three estates passage, the "outsider" advice offered by a goliard, angel, and lunatic, and the allegory of contemporary politics in the "Belling of the Cat" episode. Meed, a woman and the quintessential insider, gives the most convincing impression of political counsel and models a new political literature in a post-treaty world.

Conscience takes the stand against Meed and forestalls her victory, and, in doing so, he reimagines the role of counsel and sets the agenda for a peacetime nation. His first task is to redefine meed, just as Meed has redefined conscience. According to Conscience, there are two kinds of meed, temporal and spiritual: the first is characterized by the greed that obstructs justice and knows no bounds, fueled by the desire for that which has not been earned or deserved (including kickbacks, price inflation, and usury, or in other words, transactions motivated by personal gain); the second is the spiritual reward that one receives in heaven if one has lived a life of charity and restraint. With this second definition, Conscience dismantles the analogy inherent in meed between temporal and spiritual reward: whereas temporal meed is always in excess of what it should be – always about avarice rather than liberality – spiritual meed signifies God's perfect justice. Conscience concedes that there is a third kind of meed, just payment for services rendered, given and received within the constraints of proper desire. But, he says, this kind of reward is not rightly called meed at all; rather, it falls under a third category, what Conscience calls "measurable hire" (B.3.256). This is very like Holy Church's "moderation in all things," but it anticipates the poet's increasingly stern view of that ethic in which poor laborers receive just enough money to sustain their basic needs, retailers earn little profit, beggars beg only as a last resort, clergy neglect their own well-being, and the rich win heaven only by the skin of their teeth.

Conscience's definition of meed undermines Meed's feudal economy in all sorts of ways, most conspicuously by erasing the category of magnificence. It also reimagines the English nation as one constituted not by royal derring-do, but by just governance and sober, religious-minded advice. Conscience's proposal of a political ethics severed from the war with France notably fails to address the pragmatics of rule, such as rewarding one's servants and recruiting soldiers, which Meed regards as political virtues. But it also recuperates counsel for a new age, an age supervised by an educated male clergy. Conscience tells the tale of King Saul's battle against the Amalekites, in which Samuel, Saul's high priest and counselor, advises the King to kill every person and animal, including the Amalekite King. Saul, however, allows greed to get the better of him: he disobeys Samuel, holds the King for ransom, and lets the best livestock live. God punishes Saul for his disobedience in the worst possible way – by discontinuing his bloodline and replacing it with David's. Conscience audaciously frames this story as a prophecy about future kings in England and predicts a new era of reform.

At first glance, the story of Saul and the Amalekites seems a very odd tale for Conscience to tell in this context. After all, it advocates war and genocide and predicts the failure of the royal line. One can only guess what this dire prediction meant to readers of *Piers Plowman* at the end of Edward III's reign, when the king was fading, and his heir, the Black Prince, dying of a progressive disease, leaving the kingdom in the hands of the Black Prince's underage son. It shows, however, that Conscience is capable of talking about kingship and war on his own terms, with Conscience standing in for the prophet Samuel, more hawk than dove, who understands better than anyone the price paid by the nation for the disobedience of its king. Telling of Conscience's "peacetime" counsel is his interpretation of Isaiah, "and they shall turn their swords into ploughshares":

Alle that beren baselard, brood swerd or launce,
Ax outher hachet or any wepen ellis,
Shal be deemed to the deeth, but if he do it smythye
Into sikel or to sithe, to shaar or to kultour –
Conflabunt gladios suos in vomeres
Ech man to pleye with a plow, pykoise, or spade,
Spynne, or sprede donge, or spille hymself with sleuthe.   (B.305–10)

[All those who bear dagger, broad sword, or lance,
Axe or hatchet, or any other weapon,
Shall be sentenced to death, unless he beat it
Into sickle, or scythe, plowshare or blade –
"And they will turn their swords into plowshares (and their spears into pruning
   hooks)" –
Each man to play with a plow, pickaxe, or spade,
Spin, or spread dung, or waste himself with sloth.]

In this passage, an arsenal of weapons is converted to tools of peace – the poet can never resist a catalog – but Conscience does not favor peace *per se*. He is interested, instead, in developing a discourse of nation and governance unmoored from aristocratic values. In the plowshares passage this discourse is defined, not by the noble arts of war, but by the wholesale commutation of war into agricultural labor. The result is a nation defined by the commons rather than the baronage. This commons is not identical to the Commons, the merchants and knights of the shire, the upper echelons of the third estate, who had a stake in government, and whose consent to taxation was crucial for filling the war-chest. Conscience's commons is the lowest common denominator of that estate, agricultural laborers who, because they are not represented in government, can be used to symbolize the nation, as in the estates model in the Prologue, in which plowmen stand for the whole edifice supporting the King's rule.[36]

We saw that Meed's flattering subject is the King as lord for whom value is linked to masculine codes of honor, and whose identification with the nation is bound up in national defense and its material rewards. Though Conscience does not confront Meed's model directly, he is as keen as she is to present a masculinist nation, in his case, one that privileges high-minded governance over war. Notably, Conscience's model of a masculinist nation is categorically insular. Meed's ideal nation hearkens back to the glory days of the campaign in France, in which the English kingdom, through the ambitions of its king, straddled the Channel. By contrast, her two opponents, Conscience, and Conscience's collaborator, Reason, want to constrict the nation's geographical imaginary. In a fascinating passage, Reason addresses the passage across the Channel, and the relationship between travel and value: pilgrims, he says, shouldn't be carrying money– they are not tourists (or merchants or legates) after all – and although the English coinage is stamped with a picture of the king, the king's image is not a form of currency to be recklessly spent by English "Rome renneres" [runners to Rome] and misused by "robberes of biyonde" [robbers from across the sea] (B.4.128; in C, more explicitly, "ruyflares in Fraunce" C.4.125). The poet may have been thinking about the fourteenth-century English noble, stamped with an image of Edward III as warrior king standing in the middle of a ship while brandishing a sword and shield. Though the image stayed the same, the legend changed in the treaty period (1361–69) from "Edward by the grace of God King of England and France, Lord of Ireland," to the less ambitious "Edward by the grace of God King of England, Lord of Ireland and Aquitaine," and eventually reverting back to a combination of the two in the post-treaty period (1369–77), "Edward, by the grace of God King of England and France, Lord of Ireland and Aquitaine." In the Channel passage

Reason is talking about pilgrimage reform, which he sees as emblematic of the reform of society as a whole; he is also, however, talking about fluctuations in the nation's symbolic economy and the restrictions that should be imposed upon it. Any pilgrim who tries to carry English currency across the Channel should have his money seized at Dover (B.4.131), which, for Reason, marks the limits of the nation.

As suggested above, the debate staged between Meed and Conscience and continued by Reason looks like a new kind of mirror-for-princes literature, created to address national politics between the Treaty of Brétigny in 1360 and the coronation of Richard II in 1377, the period in which the A and B texts were probably composed. In this sense, it closely resembles another alliterative dream-vision, *Wynnere and Wastour* (c.1351–70), which also reckons with the Treatise of Brétigny and its aftermath, and concomitant shifts in national policy.[37] *Wynnere and Wastour* opens with the King's pavilion, from which the King and his knights behold the troops of European society converging on a battlefield, each company representing a major social order: ecclesiastics, merchants, lawyers, and the four orders of friars. The King commands the leaders of the two armies, Winner and Waster, to cease hostilities and let him adjudicate their quarrel. A debate ensues between Winner and Waster conducted in front of the royal audience. Winner defines himself as desirable gain (good husbandry) and accuses Waster of prodigality; Waster defines himself as efficacious expenditure (maintaining the honor of lords, who hold lavish feasts and distribute alms) and accuses Winner of avarice. At the conclusion of the debate, the amiable King pokes fun at them both, and promises to make them work for him.[38] *Wynnere and Wastour* makes a fitting prequel to the Meed episode, and indeed, it may have been written shortly before *Piers Plowman*: both texts aim for a vernacular discourse about princely virtue on a national scale, and both texts present the noble household as a repository of competing theories of value, with implications for good governance. Like the debate between Meed and Conscience, the debate about value in *Wynnere and Wastour* is staged against a backdrop of war and presents royal justice as a substitute for war, with the King as sole arbiter of value.

Significantly, *Wynnere and Wastour* is more successful than *Piers Plowman* at presenting a powerful king at the center of a national imaginary, who rules as if from the battlefield, who surveys the economic landscape, and who renders absolute judgement. Langland has placed his King in a trickier position. Whereas *Wynnere and Wastour* negotiates aristocratic values in the name of good governance, the debate in *Piers Plowman* opposes these values to royal rule. Bubbling over with good intentions, Langland's King loses control over his court: he is indecisive, he flounders, and though he exclaims to Meed and Conscience, "Ye shul saughtne [be reconciled], forsothe, and serve me bothe" (4.2), his attempt to reconcile them comes to nothing.

Meed's defeat entails other losses as well. For one thing, it excludes Meed from governance, when Conscience rejects her as a counselor as well as a marriage partner. Conscience's victory, we might say, is won at the price of female counsel. The poet has assigned Meed the task of advocating an ethics of reward and a national war policy not because these arguments are weak, but on the contrary, because they are extremely persuasive, and can be discounted only when associated with female reasoning.

Conscience's dismissal of women's counsel and its values requires not only that Conscience radically define meed but also that he deconstruct female learning in the process. Conscience insists that the King's most reliable counselors are his best-educated men, counselor-scholars who can expound Latin texts in the vernacular but understand them in the original, and his discourse on meed is aggressively clerical, chockfull of Latin proverbs and prophecies drawn from scripture. Meed protests that she, too, can read Latin and cites Proverbs on the usefulness of giving presents: generosity assures victory or "Honoram adquiret, qui dat munera" [he who gives gifts, acquires honor, 3.336] – but she only succeeds in citing the first half of the verse. Conscience scoffs that, while Meed was sitting in her study reading "Sapience" (Proverbs) (3.345), she might have hired a "konnynge clerk" (3.347) to help her turn the page. Relying on her own powers of study instead, she contented herself with the first half of the line, because it happened to support her aristocratic world-view: "This text that ye han told were [tidy] for lordes" [The text which you have cited is fitting for lords] (3.346). Had she bothered to turn the leaf, says Conscience, (or learn her lesson twice), she would have discovered the crucial second half of the line "Animam autem aufert accipientium" [but he carries away the soul of the receivers] (B.3.350), which makes Conscience's point, that those who give gifts lose heaven both for themselves and others.

What might be called the ethics of female instruction, how learning with women can make you good or bad, has suffered a loss of prestige from Holy Church to Meed. The poet is clearly both attracted to and repelled by the idea of a female counselor. As Deanne Williams has argued with respect to Chaucer, Langland may have been uncomfortable with the eroticization of the *Consolation* in vernacular literature with all of its ties to philosophical love poetry; it is perhaps for this reason that he chose to divvy up the character of Lady Philosophy into Holy Church and Meed, both female advisors, both skillful rhetoricians, and both capable of holding the dreamer's attention.[39] But Meed, as a counselor, is not easily disposed of, in part because, following the allegory, the corrupting effects of money are so deeply entrenched.

Passus 4 begins in a moot-hall, the King's law court, where the King, still gung-ho for justice, begins to hear cases, guided by his advisors Conscience and Reason.[40] The main event at court is Peace's petition against Wrong, a local thug, whom Peace accuses of a number of crimes. Wrong has abducted "Rose, Reignaldes loove" (4.49) and ravished "Margrete of hir maydenhede" (4.50). Like a mob boss, he has sicced his "gadelynges" [hangers-on], (4.51) on Peace, intimidating him, stealing his livestock, "borrowing" his horse, murdering his servants, and breaking up the market fairs over which Peace presides. The King orders Wrong to be cast in irons. At once, Wisdom and Wit, Wrong's smarmy associates, conspire with Meed to obstruct royal justice and save Wrong by paying off Peace. Their arguments on Wrong's behalf twist the language of compensation ("amendes" and "boote") to their own advantage. Wisdom exclaims,

> That were noght the beste!
> And he amendes mowe make, lat Maynprise hym have
> And be borgh for his bale, and buggen hym boote
> And amenden that is mysdo, and everemoore the better.   (4.86–90)

> [That were not for the best!
> And he, who must make reparations, let Mainprise help him out,
> And stand bail for his suffering (or the evil he has inflicted on others), and buy him
>   a remedy
> And fix what is broken, and no more problems.]

And Wit chimes in,

> Bettre is that boote bale adoun brynge
> Than bale be ybet and boote nevere the better.   (4.92–93)

> [Better is that remedy brings down evil
> Than evil be beaten and remedy never the better.]

These might sound like fine adages, but they are really just a jumble of juridical nonsense. The lines about mainprise, the legal procedure through which one person stands surety for another person accused of a crime (in this case associated with maintenance, the unlawful aid of a party in a legal action), have appropriated a theological vocabulary which explains the operations of divine justice and mercy and have used it to justify the abuse of human law. Wisdom's lines recall passus 11, for example, in which Reason explains the mysterious ways of a God, who could right every wrong ("amende") if he chose, but instead lets people earn heaven through their own free will. As Reason says to the dreamer, "He myghte amende in a minute while al that mysstandeth, / Ac he suffreth for som mannes goode, and so is oure bettre" [He might fix instantly everything that's amiss / But he endures it for man's good, and that is to our benefit] (11.380–81). Wit's speech recalls the arguments for the Redemption in B.18, in which God makes good by "standing bail" for his people, who have been imprisoned by the devil (e.g., 18.183–84). In the long run, of course, human beings need to learn how to choose for the good, but God was willing to level the playing field by acting like a good lord, delivering his servants from danger and compensating for their moral lack. In the King's court of justice, however, the language of surety and reparation has been severely undermined. Personal interest now passes for mercy, and "amends" has become a cover-up for injustice. Reason recognizes Wisdom's and Wit's speeches for the travesties they are: "Reed [advise] me noght," he says harshly, "no ruthe [pity] to have" (4.113). Mercy may be needed when talking about man's shortcomings with respect to God, but justice is needed when talking about a society enthralled to its own legal processes. He advises the King to kick Meed out of "moothalle"; Love and Leute spread the news, and "mooste peple in the halle and manye of the grete" are happy to repeat the tabloid news that Meed is a shrew and a whore (4.159).

In B.2–4, the poet wonders how justice can be guaranteed in a fallen world in which the administrators of justice are susceptible to corruption and the King is forced to compete with the gentry's local "solutions." In an ideal world, the answer would lie not in a representative or deliberating body, such as Parliament, but in the ruler himself, in the political virtues which he cultivates, and which radiate, metonymically, to his best advisors. At the end of the episode, the poet tries to restore the autonomy of royal virtue through a reaffirmation of political counsel. Medieval rulers, however autocratic, were obliged to seek counsel, and mirror-for-princes treatises advise rulers to be very careful about how they choose their counselors. As Giles of Rome explains, a wise prince considering matters of the realm will surround himself with people who have good track records, who make logical arguments, and who refrain from flattery. Within the household of a prince, the prince makes careful decisions about whom he will admit to his privy counsel, with whom he will share private information, and from whom he will seek advice. These are decidedly not women, who are less reasonable, or children, who are underdeveloped.[41] Those who deserve to be taken into a prince's confidence are adult men who can claim the right status, who are neither "natural servants," lowborn and therefore unwise, nor "servants by law," who serve for dread, nor "servants by hire" (in Latin, "pro mercede"), who serve for reward; rather, these are men who can afford to serve for love ("amor et dilectio principis magis"). Those who serve out of love and who, therefore, can be proved kind, loyal, and prudent, are those who should be received into the King's counsels ("secreta magnis"). What a king needs is advice money cannot buy, and advice that, in the best possible way, holds up a mirror to his own desires.[42]

With the exclusion of Meed, the poet portrays this best of all counsels as a kind of homosocial love, a counsel wrung from male friendship. When the King sees he cannot reconcile Meed and Conscience, he orders Conscience to fetch Reason and bring him to his counsel. Conscience rides off to confer with Reason and whispers something in his ear ("and rouneth in his ere," 4.14). Conscience and Reason, whispering together ("rownynge togideres," 4.25), mount their horses and ride back to Westminster, where the King takes Reason into his confidence and sets him between himself and his son on the bench (4.44–46). This scene, with its overwrought intimacies, owes much to earlier descriptions of False and Meed's entourage, their journey to Westminster, and Meed's confabulations with courtiers and clerks at court. In fact, it reminds us that the very thing that comes under scrutiny in the Meed episode – unregulated exchange – is the foundation of justice in the context of the King and his trusted male counselors. Reason and Conscience, of course, are personifications of the King's powers to discriminate and judge, and in this sense, male personification is the ultimate form of loving counsel, an expression of royal self-love and of the monarch's pleasure of having his own virtues reflected back to him while at the same time meeting his obligations as a ruler. The poet acknowledges that a king must seek unity and concord among his subjects, if he wants to enforce his policies. Conscience reminds the King, for example, that an act as far-reaching as the condemnation of Wrong may be carried out only with assent of the "commune" and the cooperation of the King's "lige leodes" (his loyal subjects) (4.184). But the poet allows no real constraints to royal authority beyond the King's own desire for reform: monarchical power is imagined to be composite only insofar as the King's counselors are personifications of his own mental faculties, a flattering portrait indeed.

In the last few lines of passus 4, the King, Conscience and Reason swear oaths between them: Reason promises to rule the King's realm, so long as the King makes everyone obey him; the King agrees to this proposition, swearing to seek counsel among lords and clerks, if Reason stays by his side; Reason agrees to stay with the King, so long as Conscience remains part of his counsel. The King grants this last request, promising that the three of them will stay together for ever: "Als longe as oure lyf lasteth, lyve we togideres" (4.195) .[43]

CHAPTER 3

Community
(B.5–7)

"[And] it are my blody bretheren, for God boughte us alle"

(B.6.207).

Introduction

In the first vision (B.Prol.–4), the poet explores a series of questions about
political society, such as how can a diverse society be imagined? What are
the origins and limits to governance, and what is the common denominator
of political rule? How might a reform-minded English poetry represent
society's underlying values and expose its greatest faults? Lastly, in which
contexts can a satire of contemporary life constitute a moral philosophy and
political counsel worthy of a king?

Entering the second vision (B.5–7), the poem's emphasis shifts from society
to community, or from the structures to the ethics of association. In these
passūs, the poem reveals the fair field of folk to be neighbors, whose collective
well-being haunts the dreamer. In *Piers Plowman*, as in medieval literature
generally, society is inseparable from morality: a person's station and occupation determine his ability to be righteous, and the sum of labors performed
impacts everyone's spiritual future. The Prologue, indebted to estates satire,
argues that corrupt and lazy people compromise the integrity of the system,
triggering famine and plague, and hastening the apocalypse. Waxing prophetic,
the poet warns that "The mooste meschief on molde is mountynge up faste!"
[The greatest calamity on earth is building momentum!] (Prol.67). In the
second vision, the poet continues to be concerned with the make-up and break-
up of society, but he is newly interested in ethical bonds, such as empathy,
reciprocity, and mastery. Whereas in passus 1 the dreamer asks Holy Church to
"tel me this ilke – / How I may save my soule" [tell me this thing in particular:
how I may save my soul] (1.83–84), in passūs 5–7, community is at the very
heart of this desire to be saved, and the ethics of association articulates the link
between being saved and doing well.

The second vision contains three discreet episodes: the Confession of the Seven Deadly Sins (passus 5), the Plowing of the Half-Acre (passus 6), and Truth's Pardon (passus 7). Each episode proposes a different model of thinking about community: penance, labor, and legal performance. These models serve as literary experiments in *community* – what if the Seven Deadly Sins confessed? What if God sent a Pardon that absolved everyone? – while at the same time staging the lived experience of the group. The figure of Piers, sometime plowman, pilgrim, and reeve, emerges in these three passūs as the leader of the community of the poem and its elusive spiritual object. In each episode, Piers represents the desire to attain salvation through the efforts of the group, and he initiates projects through which the communities of the present might approach the heavenly community of the saved. Throughout the poem, he embodies the best intentions of the earthly community – in B.19, for example, a vicar demands that Piers be crowned "emperor of the world" (431), because he provides and suffers for all people – and, in B.15 and B.18, he comes to represent the "whole Christ" or the part of human nature that unites human beings with God.[1]

In B. 5–7, the poet places his hope in community, but he shows that the difficulty of doing the right thing is compounded by the problems of working as a group. At the end of passus 5, Piers leads his motley crew on a pilgrimage to Truth, but several of them immediately lose their way and can no longer be accounted for; at the end of passus 6, idle beggars rise up against Piers, refusing to work and demanding better food, and Piers cries out for a truce; at the end of passus 7, Piers rips up Truth's Pardon and embarks upon a solitary spiritual path. As several scholars have observed, these frustrating ruptures and discontinuities, so pronounced in B.5–7, are key to the poem's experimental mode: the poet uses episodic form to try out different genres or discourses, or to highlight the subjective experience of his dreamer, who is pitched from one scene to the next.[2]

Community offers another perspective on the episodic form of the second vision; in passūs 5–7, it even begins to resemble a literary category. In many *Piers* manuscripts, the first eight numbered passūs (with the addition, in some manuscripts, of the Prologue and passus 9) are titled "de visione petri le ploughman."[3] The experiments in community in B.5–7 encapsulate the poem's notion of *visio* or what it means to have a view of a whole: of everyone who is implicated by sin, as set forth in the confessional, of all the people attached to a manor, and of all those covered by an indulgence or mentioned in a royal pardon. They show further how literary fictions can double as ethical projects, insofar as they refer to the experience of the group. Finally, if *Piers Plowman* is driven by the desire for salvation, the

Confession of the Sins, the Plowing of the Half-Acre, and Truth's Pardon show why the group effort to be saved is so fraught, provisional, and always on the verge of collapse. The problem is not only that some people are corrupt, or that the earthly city, by definition, falls short of its heavenly counterpart. The problem is also that the possibility of anyone doing well can be meaningfully imagined only through people's relationships to each other.

It is telling, in this respect, that the poem's most credic assertions are bound up with the posture that one assumes toward other people and the acts performed on their behalf. The Athanasian Creed (a prayer recited in the Divine Office, and often compiled in books of Psalms), the penultimate line of which forms the text of Truth's Pardon, requires an individual statement of belief (*Quicumque vult*): "Whosoever will be saved, before all things it is necessary that he hold the catholic faith." Yet central to that belief is the salvation and damnation of groups, the final division of the good and the bad, the sheep and goats; i.e. "those who have done well will go to eternal life; those who have done evil will go to eternal fire."[4] The collective experience, in other words, reveals the difficulty of doing well in the first place, and thus of joining the heavenly community of the saved. Giving to the poor is never a morally straightforward act (B.6 and 7, C.9) and agricultural labor, a group effort, is uneasily analogized to spiritual labor (B.6). As Repentance's prayer explains (B.5), only God's radical identification with humankind can make up the difference between what is required and what is performed, and between experiment and resolution.

Personal bonds

From the beginning, the poet's challenge is to develop a vision of community that emphasizes the ethical bonds between persons. In passūs 5–7, he develops this vision through legal contract, because it is through contract that people formalize their relationships in time; it is through contract, too, that people make ethical demands of each other that challenge social hierarchies. Medieval critics tended to lean heavily on traditional models, such as the three estates (those who fight, those who pray, and those who work) or the body politic (the ruler is the head, the laborers the feet, and so forth). What was appealing about these models was their timelessness and fixity: although they could be adapted to different uses – to castigate tyrants, for example, or denounce usurers – the problem for medieval writers was rarely the models themselves but rather people who failed to conform to them. Like many a medieval preacher and satirist before him, Langland

idealizes the estates and hates social mobility. In C.5, the dreamer, defending his life, contends that no cleric should have to perform manual labor,
and conversely that no bondman should be ordained (5.66–67). In C.9 the
poet urges everyone to show obedience to divine law by fulfilling the duties
that pertain to their estate: professional religious must obey their rules,
lowborn men ought to labor, and lords should shoot wild animals as a
public service (9.219 ff.).

At the same time, the poet sees the potential in traditional models for
innovative social and ethical thought. He develops it by writing contractual
narratives for the three estates. In *Piers Plowman*, contract proves not
whether traditional social models are practicable, but how they are ethical,
that is, what they tell us about the way that people enter into relationships
with each other. Most importantly, the poet uses contract in order to
imagine moments of origin for the three estates. Medieval writers understood hierarchy to be a consequence of human sin, but they failed to
establish a coherent originary narrative for it. Labor and servitude, for
example, were not thought to have been established at the same time:
Noah's son, Ham, punished by God for uncovering his father's nakedness,
was the progenitor of a servile class, but when Adam and Eve toiled outside
of Eden, everyone was a laborer. Hence the force of the insurrectionary
verses attributed to the preacher John Ball during the 1381 Peasants' Revolt:
"When Adam dalf, and Eve span, / Who was thane a gentilman?"[5] The
peculiar temporality of the estates left a gap in medieval social theory
between morality and ethics: if the estates lack a specific moment of origin,
can they really predetermine social roles and serve as moral guides? For
example, can a plowman do well and earn heaven simply by fulfilling the
duties that pertain to his estate, or is there a moment in which he consents
to be a plowman, willing to produce food for others, just as there is a
moment at which he chooses good over evil?

In the Prologue, lines 112–22, Langland first explores the ethics of the
estates by writing the three estates into an originary narrative about human
agency and consent. This narrative of origins in the Prologue boosts the
ethical import of the estates, asking not simply whether people act morally
when they fulfill predetermined social roles but also under what circumstances those roles came into being, through whose initiative, and for whose
benefit. In this scene, the King enters with Knighthood in the vanguard,
and propels the three estates into existence through various collaborations:
Kind Wit (natural reasoning) invents Clergy to counsel the King and
protect the Commons; the King, Knighthood, and Clergy together "casten"
that the Commons provide the necessities of life (communes); the

commons "contrived" through Kind Wit that plowmen provide food; and finally, together the King, Kynde Wit, and the Commons create ("shopen") positive law.

Thanne kam ther a Kyng: Knyghthod hym ladde;
Might of the communes made hym to regne.
And thanne cam Kynde Wit and clerkes he made,
For to counseillen the Kyng and the Commune save.
The Kyng and Knyghthod and Clergie bothe
Casten that the Commune sholde hem [communes] fynde.
The Commune contreved of Kynde Wit craftes,
And for profit of al the peple plowmen ordeyned
To tilie and to travaille as trewe lif asketh.
The Kyng and the Commune and Kynde Wit the thridde
Shopen lawe and leaute – eche lif to knowe his owene.   (B. Prol.112–22)

[Then a King came there; Knighthood led him;
Might of the Commons made it possible for him to reign.
And then came Kind Wit, and he fashioned clerics
To counsel the King and save the Commons.
Together the King, Knighthood, and Clergy
Determined that the Commons should provide sustenance for everyone.
The Commons made use of Kind Wit's crafts
And, for the profit of all the people, ordained plowmen
To till and labor, as true life demands.
The three of them, King, Commons, and Kind Wit
Created law and justice – each life to know its own (i.e., his or her rights, esp. over property, according to the law).]

This passage is generally concerned with royal accountability, a subject explored further in the "Coronation" scene that follows, that is, whether kings make the law or are made by it, and whether they are answerable only to God or also to their counselors, magnates, and commons. Under the rubric of kingship, the poet further explores the relationship between traditional estates models and ethical association or the way that people interact in ways that promote individual and collective good. By personifying the estates, and by incorporating them into an originary narrative, the poet adjusts his lens from hierarchy and duty to the shared interests and collaborative acts of people in time. Further, by portraying society as a series of dynamic collaborations between figures of the estates, the poet stresses the ethical nature of such a project: the three estates exist not only so that the needs of society may be met (i.e. the first estate provides order, the second, counsel, and the third, food), but also so that each person may know what pertains to him, and what his privileges and restrictions are under the law ("ech lif to knowe his owene," Prol.122).

In the Plowing of the Half-Acre in B.6, the poet dramatizes the heady proposition of the allegory of the estates, that the ethical meaning of traditional models resides in the contractual relationships formed between persons in time. In this scene, the poet imagines society coming into being at a particular moment in time and through the consent of individuals. In the allegory of the estates, the Commons arranged to be provisioned – and thereby represented – by plowmen ("And for profit of al the peple plowmen ordeyned," Prol.119). In the Plowing of the Half-Acre, the plowmen are represented as a single plowman – a character named Piers, who possesses legal agency and individual will. Piers invites everyone to join him on his pilgrimage to Truth but explains he must first stop to cultivate his half-acre at home, as he has sworn to do. The Knight courteously offers to labor in the fields, and Piers elects to work for both of them (6.24–25), so long as the Knight swears to protect his workers. The Knight plights his troth to fulfill these customary duties, but Piers insists upon a second contract in which the Knight promises not to abuse his tenants (6.37–42), to which the Knight declares his good faith, "I assente, by Seint Jame . . . For to werche by thi wordes the while my lif dureth" [I assent, by Saint James . . . To abide by this treaty as long as I live] (6.55–56).

The first contract, peasant labor in exchange for aristocratic protection, may seem to justify an unequal labor system through the so-called consent of representatives of the estates, Piers and the Knight. To be sure, by personifying the estates, the poet is able to construct a fiction of consent not available to most medieval peasants. The exchange between the Knight and Piers further idealizes the role of the gentry, from whose depredations peasants often needed as much protection as they did from enemy ships or from foxes in the henhouse. Importantly, though, Piers uses the legal intention that underwrites the first contract to draw up a second, which complicates the hierarchies of the first. According to this contract, the Knight should refrain from injuring his bondsmen lest at the end of the year he pays the price in Purgatory and finds himself exchanging places with his tenants in heaven (6.43–44). As Piers observes, at the charnel house it is not easy to tell a knight's corpse from a churl's. In this scene, the overlap between social and spiritual contracts highlights the true stakes of human association. The poet romanticizes feudal relations, yet with the Faustian clause, "at one yeres ende," he reminds us that the willingness to fulfill one's social obligations is always coupled with a responsibility not to hurt others. In the final hour, the ethics of association of this world is determined by the inclusions and exclusions, the rewards and punishments, of the afterlife.

This relationship between contract and community achieves its fullest expression in the Pardon episode in B.7. In a reprise of the Prologue's fair field of folk, the Pardon promises to cover every sector of society. In this passus, however, the poet is concerned less with whether people fulfill their respective social roles than with how those roles allow people to treat their fellow human beings. The Pardon first addresses all those who help Piers labor: "Treuthe herde telle herof, and to Piers sente / To taken his teme and tilien the erthe / And purchaced hym a pardoun *a pena et a culpa* / For hym and for hise heires for eueremoore after" [Truth heard all about it, and ordered Piers to take his team and till the earth, / And obtained for him a pardon "from punishment and guilt"/ For him and his heirs for posterity] (7.1–4). Next it turns to traditional representatives of the first and second estates, kings and bishops, only to abandon the estates model for an extended discussion of occupations outside the three estates: merchants, lawyers, and beggars – occupations which, for many medieval moralists, lacked any social value.

This Pardon surely captures the changing composition of society in the later Middle Ages: traditional models tended to break down when faced with the occupations generated by a profit economy.[6] At the same time, the Pardon is a stunning poetic investigation into the ethics of association. Here, for example, the poet showcases his trademark exceptionalist poetics: classifying a group of people in order to critique certain people within that classification, or *vice versa*, excluding some people in order to invent a new classification. One way in which he uses this technique is to argue for the relationship between morality and social function, as when the dreamer observes at the end of the Prologue that certain laborers stand apart ("lopen forth") from the rest, namely, those who sin by doing shoddy work:

> Baksteres and brewesteres and bochiers manye,
> Wollen webbesters and weveres of lynnen
>
> . . .
>
> Of alle lybbynge laborers lopen forth somme –
> As dykeres and delveres that doon hire dedes ille.
>
> (Prol. 219–220, 223–24)
>
> [Bakers, and brewers, and butchers many,
> Weavers of wool and weavers of linen
>
> . . .
>
> From all these living laborers some leapt forth,
> Such as dike-diggers and delvers that do their jobs badly.]

In the Pardon episode, the poet uses this technique not just to relate morality and social function, but also to explore the ethics of exceptionalism. Thus merchants, inscribed on the margins of the document, are excluded from the general pardon, but Truth sends them a separate letter under his personal ("secret") seal offering them pardon in return for charity. Ecclesiastical pardons often specified local programs to which people could contribute in return for days off punishment in Purgatory.[7] Truth's Pardon similarly alerts merchants to opportunities for charitable giving in their communities, such as to support hospitals, prisoners (who had to provide their own food), widows, and dowerless girls, and to repair broken bridges (7.23–26). Lawyers, too, are included in the Pardon, if they plead for the poor *pro bono*, and beggars are included but only if they are really incapacitated, not siphoning alms off widows, orphans, and the handicapped. As the B-text of the Pardon goes on to explain, almsgivers encounter a moral quandary every time they give: if they give to the undeserving they deprive the deserving; if they discriminate between the two, they run the danger not only of making the wrong decision, but worse, of adopting an uncharitable attitude toward the needy. In this way, exceptional occupations – those people uneasily assimilated to traditional models – throw the ethics of association into relief.

As I have suggested above, in B.5–7 contract is the form that discloses the ethical meaning of traditional models; as such, it serves as the basic unit of the poem's community-oriented vision. Significantly, in the Pardon episode, contract takes an insistently material form.[8] The poet constantly makes us aware of the Pardon's various modes of transmission, modes which change from one version of the poem to another, which draw readers and listeners into a textual community defined by anxiety and joy. Truth sends the Pardon to Piers in response to the crisis on the half-acre (7.1–4, in the C-text, the Pope sends it); Piers proffers it to the merchants, who weep for joy (7.37–38, in the A-text the dreamer writes it for the merchants); in all three versions, the dreamer stands behind Piers as he and the priest scrutinize the text: "And Piers at his preiere the pardon unfoldeth – / And I bihynde hem bothe beheld al the bulle" (B. 7.107–8). At the end of A.8 and B.7, Piers, hearing the contents of the Pardon, as explained by the priest, mysteriously rips it in two, an act that recalls Moses's breaking of the Tablets, or the ceremonial fracture of the Host in the Mass. In C.9 the tearing is just as mysteriously excised, perhaps because it appeared to Langland's readers to condone the destruction of written instruments.[9] In a Judeo-Christian scheme, a document is where human witnessing and divine revelation critically converge; it is also where law makes its most legible and therefore most contestable claims to power. Scholars often note that Piers's tearing of the Pardon conjures up the rebels' burning of legal documents during the Revolt of 1381, which was partly motivated by frustration with the administration of royal and local justice. At the same time, the Pardon reminds us that tearing a written document, even more than unfolding or writing it, underscores the power of a decree to affect the lives of readers and listeners past and present.

The contractual form of the Pardon likewise gives community a sense of imminence, reminding Piers and his fellows that every one of them is implicated by a contract drawn up between humanity and its God. By reimagining society as a written contract, with the additions and limitations that define the bonds between persons, the poet invites his audience to think about another contract – God's contract with humanity, which was drawn up at the Atonement, and which will be fulfilled at the Last Judgement.[10] This divine contract helps shape human association on earth at the same time that it threatens to exclude from heavenly communion those who do not adhere to its terms. In this way, Truth's Pardon defines the essence of earthly community by laying out the spiritual conditions of divine pardon: according to the long version of the Pardon, forgiveness for original sin through the Atonement, and the chance to earn salvation through faith and works; according to the short version, the final division at Judgement Day between those who have done well and those who have done evil (the penultimate line of the Athanasian Creed: *Et qui bona egerunt ibunt in vitam eternam; Qui vero mala in ignem eternum*). Community, insofar as it refers to association, would seem to be an inherently inclusive term. Indeed, as discussed above, the very people excepted from the general Pardon are the ones who best describe the human capacity to make ethical decisions and perform acts of charity. Yet the Pardon scene finally proves that a radical misunderstanding of community – one's attitude toward one's neighbor, what one owes and is owed by God – can exclude people from membership altogether.

Do penance!

At the beginning of passus 5, the advent of the second vision, the King and his knights go to church, and Reason preaches a public sermon, an event occasioned by the King's arrival but attended by the entire "feld ful of folk" (5.10–12). In classic medieval political theory, the king possesses two bodies: a natural body, which lives and dies, and a transcendent body, coextensive with the community of the realm, past, present, and future.[11] In passus 5, the King's body metonymically extends to the community of the realm, which the poet describes as a crowd of bodies ripe for penitential discipline. In this scene, penance transforms the political realm into a ritual community. In his sermon, Reason takes a hard line, focusing on the physical and material consequences of sin and prescribing severe remedies: he endorses corporal punishment for wives and children; he threatens monks with disendowment (deprivation of property); he urges the King to love his people, who are his sustenance, his "tresor" (treasure) and "tryacle" (remedy) in times of need (5.49); and he warns everyone, including the Pope, that those unprepared to meet their maker may be denied heaven. He quotes the Bridegroom's words to the five foolish virgins who forgot the oil for their lamps and miss the marriage feast: "Amen, I say to you, I know you not" (5.55) (Matthew 25.11). The sermon is universally affecting. Repentance repeats it, Will weeps, and the Seven Deadly Sins step forward to confess.

Modern histories of penance tend to stress the secrecy of the confessional, portraying the sacrament as a private conversation between penitent and priest. In passus 5, by contrast, Langland displays the public face of penance, portraying a confessional dynamic somewhere between modern group therapy and the revival tent. In the Middle Ages, the sacrament of penance meant continual re-admittance to the community of the faithful and the ongoing collaboration of its members, both living and dead. Public confession and reconciliation was modeled, then as now, by the liturgies of the Mass such as the *Confiteor*, during which the priest ritually confesses to his "fratres" (the congregation), taking responsibility for his own sins. A literary version of the public confession circulated with the popular tales of Théophile (mid thirteenth through fifteenth centuries). In these tales, a cleric, having been passed over for promotion, signs his soul over to the devil in exchange for worldly honors. Initially unrepentant but increasingly isolated, Théophile appeals to the Virgin, who retrieves the diabolical charter, and he subsequently reintegrates himself into the community by reading the charter aloud to an assembly of clergy and laity.[12]

This penitential group effort reached well beyond the grave: many monasteries were founded for the purposes of commemorating saints and praying for the sins of the monks and their patrons. In the later Middle Ages, wealthy donors endowed chantries (chapels), whose priests offered continual rounds of prayers for the departed in Purgatory. In England, parish fraternities organized charitable giving for the poor members of their organization, as well as prayers for departed members, and cathedral churches offered obits (annual masses) for a wide range of patrons.[13]

As in the case of Reason's sermon, moreover, the point of many medieval sermons was to make people weep publicly for their sins. Wrath reminds us in his confession that this connection between preaching and penance could be a lucrative one for preachers. Parish priests and friars, for example, would denounce each other publicly in sermons, because they were competing for the privilege of hearing confession (7.145–57). At the same time, public sermons, devoutly preached, might provide a penitential theatre spiritually beneficial to both preacher and audience. Margery Kempe, the fifteenth-century mystic and author, was a notorious weeper at home and abroad. According to Margery, in her hometown of King's Lynn she was especially well known for wailing during sermons. In the following passage, a doctor of divinity (i.e. a friar), preaching on the Assumption of the Virgin, patiently tolerates Margery's pious sobs:

> Whan the worschepful doctowr schulde prechyn and worthily was browt to the pulpit, as he began to prechyn ful holily and devowtly of owr Ladiis Assumpsyon, the sayd creatur, lyftyd up in hir mende be hy swetnesse and devocyon, brast owt wyth a lowde voys and cryid ful lowde and wept ful sor. The worschepful doctowr stod stille and suffyrd wol mekely tyl it was cesyd and sithyn seyd forth hys sermowne to an ende.[14]

> [when the illustrious doctor was ready to preach and was honorably brought to the pulpit, just at the moment that he began to preach very reverently and devoutly about our Lady's Assumption, the aforementioned creature [Margery], elevated in her mind by great sweetness and devotion, burst out in a loud voice and cried very loudly and wept very passionately. The illustrious doctor stood still and humbly waited it out, and he concluded his sermon.]

The wonderful contrast between Margery's tears and the preacher's restraint suggests that, like the "fratres" in the mass, any person, any audience, might facilitate the public penance of another. As this scene suggests, too, the sacrament of penance, whether it took place in a private chapel or town square, was basically theatrical. It was a ritual that required an audience of one or many, and it consisted of both verbal and non-verbal scripts, such as crying, kneeling, and beating one's breast, the performance of which was meant to be witnessed and judged. Like Margery Kempe, who often chastised herself for her pride, Pernele Proud-heart (Pride), the first character to react to Reason's sermon, flings herself to the ground and dons a hair shirt, causing a chain reaction among the Sins (5.62–66).

Penance in B.5 may be theatrical but it is also performative: it constitutes a sacred mystery and, through the instrument of the priest, confers grace upon the penitent. If the penitent is properly "shriven," if she gives a complete confession, demonstrates true contrition, and makes satisfaction for her sins, then she may be absolved by the priest and rejoin the community of the faithful. In *Piers Plowman*, the context for performativity is ritual community. As will become clearer below, this is not because the success of penitential performance is at issue, as, for example, when the subject offers a patently insincere confession or grudgingly accepts the penalty meted out by the priest. Rather, the context for performativity is ritual community because the sacrament of penance enables people to enter into ethical association with each other. By structuring the Seven Deadly Sins around a series of public confessions, the poet reminds us that penance is always about our relation to other people, how we behave toward others, how we acquire membership, and how we perform for the group. Confession could be a highly entertaining form of penitential storytelling, full of anecdotes about bad behavior; as such it informed a number of medieval literary genres, such as the *fabliau*. But, just as importantly, confession was and is a form of ritual communication; following anthropologist Roy Rappaport, it communicates to others not only what a person has done in the past, her good deeds and bad, but also her present state as a ritual participant.[15] And it is precisely as a communicative act that penance becomes a ritual of community. It identifies a group bonded by the effort to be saved, and it produces in its participants the compassion that allows a group effort to take place.

The personification of the sins in passus 5 is critical to Langland's exploration of penance as a ritual of community. At first glance, the Sins' confessions appear to be nothing more than a travesty of penance for the sake of satire, and personification would seem to mark this failure of penitential performance. Wrath's confession, for instance, though it demonstrates strong feeling (he is, after all, angry) never moves beyond social satire, hilariously depicting strife within different religious communities: friars, parish priests, nuns, and monks. Likewise Covetousness's "confession" pokes fun at mercantile life, specifically retailers, whose activities medieval writers loved to satirize. Covetousness recounts, for example, how he and his wife adulterated the ale, pouring penny ale and pudding ale together, and keeping the best ale in the bedchamber for unsuspecting customers to sample (5.215–21).

In the Confession of the Sins, moreover, confession is not always part of the remedy of the confessant, and indeed, the successful penance of a Sin ought to be a contradiction in terms. After all, total conversion to a life free of sin would be tantamount to a Sin's self-negation, an embodied act of will that would obliterate not only one individual's sins but also the entire human disposition to sin. Crucially, moreover, it is in the failure of a Sin to perform penance that readers receive their penitential education: they can learn about sin because it never goes away. In Gluttony's confession, for example, the first-person confession is famously hijacked by a third-person narrative about Gluttony, a drunk's tale about drunkenness. Gluttony rises to confess, is distracted by lowlife tavern friends, drinks to excess, pisses as long as it takes to recite the Paternoster, farts like a bugle at Judgement Day, passes out, is berated by his Conscience and his wife, and gets up once again to do "shrift." Gluttony's initial failure to do penance generates a ribald tavern tale, which invites the poem's readers and listeners to learn something about gluttony while simultaneously making them vicarious participants in his pleasure.

More seriously, in several instances the personification of the Sins appears to challenge the efficacy of the sacrament. Technically, the performativity of penance depends upon the link between contrition and confession: a true confession should lead to sincere contrition; conversely, sincere contrition marks a true confession. But the personification of the Sins highlights a troubling gap between feeling and narrative. In Envy's confession, for example, the feeling of sorrow – the condition of the truly contrite – turns out to be a dangerously capacious emotion, the expression of which revolves around the imprecision of the Middle English word "sorwe." Langland's Envy distorts the language of contrition by expressing sorrow entirely the wrong way. The dreamer reports that "Envye with hevy herte asked after shrifte / And carefully *mea culpa* he comsed to shewe" [Envy, with heavy heart, sought to confess / And dutifully he began to confess "through my own fault"] (5.75–76). It soon becomes obvious, though, that his "heavy-heartedness" is misdirected. His sorrow is not compunction but *tristitia*, or worldly sorrow, and however much he may pray, grieve, or cry, his regret is reserved not for his sins but for the good fortune of others. Indeed, sorrow is what defines Envy, not as a sinner but as a Sin: "I am evere sory," he says, "I am but selde oother" (5.126). It is no wonder that, in his influential *Instructions for Parish Priests* (*c.*1400), John Myrc studiously avoids translating (or even defining) envy, retaining the French word "envie" and admitting no English synonym.[16] In short, Envy's confession points to the vulnerability of an emotional language at the heart of the sacrament of penance.

Another example of such linguistic vulnerability, or the distortion of the language of feeling, has to do with the circumstances of narrative. Medieval penitential manuals like Myrc's urge priests to discover the exact circumstances of sin, asking the confessant, "quis, quid, ubi, per quos, quociens, quo modo, quando" [who, what, where, through whom, why, how, when]. The number of times a penitent has committed a sin is crucial information, because it helps the penitent shape a true (i.e., full and complete) confession while helping the priest determine the severity of the penance.[17] But, for a personified Sin, the time of sin is identical to the nature of the sin: it is not what a Sin has done but what he always does. So when Envy confesses, he describes a lifelong condition rather than a number of sinful acts. He is envious not in the past but in the continuous present, such as in his complaint to his neighbor: "His grace and his goode happes greven me ful soore, / Bitwene mayné and mayné I make debate ofte, / That bothe lif and lyme is lost thorugh my speche" [His good luck grieves me so much, / That I stir up trouble between our households, / So that both life and limb is lost on account of my speech] (5.96–98).

As the Confessions of the Sins show, no one can guarantee a meaningful link between feeling and narrative, language and performance. The real concern in this episode, however, is not how to evaluate the sincerity of another, or how to judge the efficacy of sacramental performance. Peculiarly, several of the Sins use the language of contrition and express hope in their own redemption. At the beginning of the Confessions, Repentance rehearses Reason's sermon, Will weeps (5.61), and Pernele Proud-heart (Pride) lies prostrate on the ground, promising to wear a hair shirt next to her flesh and uttering a lyrical confession: "Shal nevere heigh herte me hente, but holde me lowe" [Never shall a high heart claim me, but I shall hold myself ever low] (5.67). Lechery at once takes up the cry, begging the Virgin to pity him for his misdeeds, and swearing to fast on Saturdays for the next seven years. The assumption is that a heart-felt confession is knowable and possible, even for a Sin.

In B.5, then, the real concern is how ritual performance can create a model of community that includes and benefits all persons, even Sins. Although theoretically the Sins must resist the sacrament, confession signals the entrance of the participant into a ritual community that works on behalf of all sinners. It is a performance that communicates the state of the performers to others, as if to say, "here I am, a person with a body, participating in the sacrament, along with other people who have bodies, voices, and tears." Following Rappaport again, a confessant like Pernele Proud-heart is not simply affirming her belief; she is indicating to herself and to others that, like the priest confessing in the mass, she accepts "whatever is encoded in the canons of the liturgical order in which [she] is participating."[18] And by indicating her acceptance through ritual performance, Pernele becomes part of a community effort inseparable from that liturgical order.

The personification of the Sins further highlights the role of the body in performance, linking speaking subject to ritual performer. Conventionally, personification calls attention to the relationship between appearance and character. We "recognize" sin when we see it, because it is visually so striking: Envy looks like a leek that was laid out too long in the sun; Wrath has a runny nose and hanging neck; Covetousness is "bitelbrowed and baberlipped" (5.188), as well as old, leathery, greasy, and lousy. The fourteenth-century sermon handbook *Fasciculus Morum* describes the glutton as having the head of a pig, the body of a leech, and the hindquarters of an ass.[19] But personification also calls attention to that which the body is capable of communicating through gesture, voice, or narrative and, most importantly, the response that one body elicits from others through ritual participation. It is what the body communicates and the responses that it provokes that constitute the penitential community. In this way, a confessional narrative, even where it does not express a sincere desire to reform, nevertheless has the power to be redemptive.

In the *Canterbury Tales*, Chaucer's Parson claims that envy is an exceptional sin. It differs from every other sin in the sense that it contains nothing pleasurable; it is the very embodiment of "angwissh and sorwe": "In this manere it is divers from alle othere synnes. For wel unnethe is ther any synne that it ne hath som delit in itself, save oonly envye, that evere hath in itself angwissh and sorwe"[20] [In this way it diverges from all other sins. For there is hardly any other (i.e., no) sin that does not contain within itself some delight, with the exception of envy, which always contains within itself anguish and sorrow]. If, according to the Parson, what distinguishes envy from other sins is its double-sorrow, its anguish and resentment (unlike Langland's Envy, it has no Schadenfreude), this double-sorrow also makes envy sympathetic as a sinner. In *Piers Plowman*, even Envy's sorrow, so woefully misdirected, communicates the emotional state of the sinner in a ritual context. His insincerity is reprehensible, but it is nevertheless a form of ritual feeling that has the power to induct him into a community of penance.

In short, personification, by giving bodies to Sins, enables them to participate in ritual community despite themselves. Gluttony chooses the tavern over the confessional and ends up in bed with a hangover. But as a person, and a loveable one to boot, the very act of confessing inducts him into a supportive community of ritual participants whose members make no distinction between persons, sins, and faculties. His wife and his Conscience stage an intervention, and Repentance preaches to Gluttony, drawing an analogy between the performance of sin and the performance of penance (if you can do the one, you can do the other, because both are ritual acts): "As thou with wordes and werkes hast wroght yvele in thi lyve, / Shryve thee and be shamed therof, and shewe it with thi mouthe" [Just as you have committed evil in your life with words and words, / Confess yourself, and be shamed by what you confess, and show it with your mouth] (5.366–67). Gluttony rises guilt-stricken and admits to his dissolute ways. Repentance assures him that his confession will have merit: "'This shewyng shrift,' quod Repentaunce, 'shall be meryt to the'" ["This revealing confession," said Repentance, "will be to your merit"] (5.379). Gluttony, making "grete dole" [great sorrow], promises to perform penance by embracing that which is intrinsically opposed to his nature, abstinence.

Likewise Covetousness, as a Sin, is an "unkynde creature" [an unnatural fellow] (5.269) whom Repentance cannot absolve until he makes restitution, a practice opposed to his very nature as a Sin. Covetousness refuses at first to understand what restitution is, but when Repentance asks him whether he has restored the goods he stole, he makes an English pun on the word "restitution," pretending that it means the opposite (to steal rather than return): "I roos when thei were a-reste and riflede hire males" [I got up when they were resting and rifled through their bags] (5.230). Repentance patiently defines the concept for him, but Covetousness claims not to understand the word because it is derived from French (5.234–5). But when Repentance begins to lecture on the difficulty of making amends, Covetousness seizes the chance to act against his own "unkynde" nature. Rather than dismissing Repentance's warning, as might be expected, he falls into deep despair: "Thanne weex the sherewe in wanhope and wolde han hanged hymselve / Ne hadde Repentaunce the rather reconforted hym in this manere, / 'Have mercy in thi mynde ...'" [Then the wretch fell into despair and would have hanged himself / If Repentance hadn't comforted him in this way: "Think of God's mercy ..."] (5.279–281).

Despair should lead the sinner away from repentance: to repent is to hope for the possibility of gaining salvation through the rituals of the institutional church, whereas the Middle English word for despair, "wanhope," means literally the darkening of such a hope. But despair also elicits from the sinner bodily gestures that arouse sympathy in others and in the sinner for himself. Thus the desperate Covetousness attempts to hang himself and would have done so if Repentance had not comforted him. Here the inward feeling of repentance, one's remorse for one's own behavior, is externalized as the response of others, pity for the plight of the sinner.

Similarly, at the end of his confession, Sloth swoons. Slothfulness keeps the sinner from making the effort to learn and repent (it marks a "sterile life," see below) and it is fitting, therefore, that Sloth is the last Sin to confess in passus 5. If Sloth is critical to a penitential education, he is inimical to penance, slothfulness being a black hole for all penitents – or, as the theologian Thomas Aquinas explains, a misdirected aversion toward one's own spiritual good and a forsaking of the divine good.[21] Sloth's swoon dramatizes the torpor associated with the deadly sin of sloth, but it also indicates a heightened emotion, the grief to the point of despair that belongs first and foremost to the lover. In Chaucer's *Troilus and Criseyde*, Troilus swoons, so overcome is he with grief at the thought that he might have offended Criseyde.[22] Pandarus, the intrepid go-between, capitalizes on the timely swoon, promptly laying Troilus in Criseyde's bed. Not unlike Troilus's famous swoon, Sloth's swoon triggers a response which helps him get the very thing he despairs of ever having, forgiveness.[23] Vigilance splashes water on his face and exhorts him to beware of despair, beat himself on the breast, and pray God for grace:

> "I [yarn] aboute in youthe, and yaf me naught to lerne
> And evere sitthe [beggere be be] my foule sleuthe:
> *Heu michi quod sterilem vitam duxi iuvenilem!*"
> "Repentest the noght?" quod Repentaunce – and right with that he swowned,
> Til *Vigilate* the veille fette water at hise eighen
> And flatte it on his face and faste on hym cryde
> And seide, "Ware thee fro Wanhope, wolde thee bitraye.
> 'I am sory for my synnes,' seye to thiselve,
> And beet thiself on the brest, and bidde hym of grace,
> For is no gilt here so gret that His goodnesse is moore"...   (5.440–48)

> ["I ran around in youth, and did not apply myself to my studies,
> And ever since I have been a beggar on account of my foul sloth:
> 'What a useless life I led in my youth!'"
> "Are you not repenting?" said Repentance – and right then [Sloth] swooned,
> Until Vigilance dashed water in his eyes
> And slopped it on his face and entreated him,
> And said, "Beware of despair, which will betray you.
> Say to yourself, 'I am sorry for my sins,'
> And beat yourself on the breast, and pray to Him for grace,
> For His goodness is greater than any sin here."]

Sloth recovers, rises, and crosses himself. He vows to attend church each Sunday all day for the next seven years and swears to make full restitution, after which he will make a pilgrimage to Truth.

Although the language of penance is easily exploited and its emotions difficult to identify and feel, what bonds the penitential community are ritual acts, the performance of strong feeling and the responses of others. The Sins have the capacity to be saved because, like all persons, they are able to perform their acceptance of an order to which everyone around them subscribes. In this sense, confession even makes it possible for the confessant "to transcend his own doubt by accepting in defiance of it."[24] In other words, if ritual performance entails the acceptance of an order, thereby making truthfulness and doubt slightly beside the point, it also creates the conditions through which a divine mystery can take place.

Finally, as Sloth's swoon shows, all ritual acts are charged with feeling because they arouse feelings in others. In Langland's version of penance, there is always an onlooker, deeply affected by what he observes. Robert the Robber, overhearing the exchange between Repentance and Sloth and noting that he has nothing left with which to make restitution, weeps profusely for his own sins, hoping that, as in the case of the thief on the Cross, Christ's mercy will compensate for his lack of goods. The narrator testifies to Robert's show of feeling: "And for ther was noght wher[with], he wepte swithe soore . . . Wel I woot he wepte faste water with hise eighen" [And because there was nothing left, he wept very hard . . . I know for sure that he cried many tears with his eyes] (5.463, 473). Repentance, touched by the general drive to penance, has "ruthe" [compassion] upon all people, urging them to kneel and reciting one of the most heartfelt prayers ever written about the connection between human and divine. Heavenly and earthly communities join together, echoing Repentance's prayer:

Thanne hente Hope an horn of *Deus tu conversus vivificabis nos* (Psalm 84:7)
And blew it with *Beati quorum remisse sunt iniquitates,* (Psalm 31:1)
That alle Seintes in hevene songen at ones
"*Homines et iumenta salvabis, quemadmodum multiplicasti misericordiam tuam,*
    Deus!"(Psalm 35:7)
A thousand of men tho thrungen togideres,
Cride upward to Crist and to his clene moder
To have grace to go [to] Truthe – [God leve that they moten!]   (5.507–12)

[Then Hope reached for a horn of "God, you will turn and bring us back to life"
And blew it with "Blessed are those whose iniquities are forgiven,"
With the result that all the saints in heaven sang at once
"You will preserve men and beast, O God: how you have multiplied your mercy!"
A thousand men then assembled together,
Prayed upwards to Christ and to his Virgin Mother
For grace to reach Truth – God grant that they might!]

Blood brothers

One of the main ideas in Langland's understanding of community is "bloody brethren" (blood brothers), a complex and loaded term, which describes feelings of intimacy with and responsibility towards other people. In *Piers Plowman*, this idea turns on questions of relatedness and specifically the way that Christ's sacrifice created a shared sense of identity among those for whom he sacrificed himself. The poet asks, how does identification in Christ affect the way that rich people relate to poor people, good people to sinners, Christians to heathens?

If, in *Piers Plowman*, "bloody brethren" designates an ethical identification with all people through Christ, it is a form of identification firmly rooted in aristocratic notions of community, specifically noble kinship or affinity, the intimate relations among members of the nobility. It is true that medieval romances often oppose familial relations to the "blood brothers" of chivalric fellowship, substituting the near-sacramental bonds of comrades-in-arms for familial ties. In Thomas Malory's *Le Morte D'Arthur*, for example, Sir Gareth's loyalty to Sir Lancelot surpasses his loyalty to his own brothers, and Gareth's accidental death at the hands of Lancelot precipitates the destruction of the Round Table.[25] Yet the one could be substituted for the other because chivalric fellowship was considered a near-blood relationship and the noble estate kinship writ large. Moreover, the sheer ability to identify with the condition of another, and therefore to enter into an ethical relationship with that person, was understood to be a noble quality. In medieval literature, for example, members of the nobility tend to sympathize more with foreign nobility than with their lowborn countrymen. In Jean Froissart's account of the Battle of Caen, two French noblemen, the Constable and the Count of Tancarville, fear that they will "fall into the hands of archers" (i.e. English peasants), "who would not recognize them."[26] The noblemen appeal to an English knight named Sir Thomas Holland, with whom they have previously crusaded against the infidel in Granada and Prussia. Once acquaintance is established, Sir Thomas is more than happy to save their lives, winning marks for gallantry in addition to the hundreds of thousands of gold moutons paid through their ransom.

It is not surprising that *Piers Plowman*, a religious allegory partly indebted to chivalric romance, would propose bloody brotherhood as a model for community. For one thing, noble fellow feeling afforded medieval writers a conceptual language with which to explain tricky theological concepts, such as Christ's status as both God and man, king and pauper, victor and victim.

The paradox in which the Lord is born in a manger and crucified on a cross is supportable if Christ's radical identification with human nature, with the poor and downtrodden, stems from his inherent nobility. In B.18 the crucified Christ jousts in Piers's "armes," a gorgeous pun that incorporates (1) Christ's humanity as figured through the body of a plowman, (2) the weapons or insignia of a warrior, and (3) the loving embrace of noble friendship. In the same vein, only the blind Longinus may "joust" with the crucified Christ, not just because he alone has sufficient courage, but also because he shares with Christ an aristocratic identity which guarantees privileged physical intimacy:

> For alle thei were unhardy, that hoved on horse or stode,
> To touchen hym or tasten hym or taken hym doun of roode,
> But this blynde bacheler, that baar hym thorugh the herte.
> The blood sprong doun by the spere and unspered the knyghtes eighen.
>
> (18. 83–86)

> [Everyone present, standing or on horse, lacked the courage
> To touch him or grope him or take him down from the cross,
> Except for this blind knight who stabbed him in the heart.
> The blood sprang down his spear and opened the knight's eyes.]

In these lines, Langland's Christ is a dead-ringer for Malory's Lancelot, whose worthiness is displayed by his wondrous healing powers as well as by his martial prowess. In one spectacular scene in the *Morte*, Lancelot cures the knight Sir Urry, after every other knight has failed, by laying his hands literally upon him:

> And than, devoutly knelyng, he ransaked the three woundis, that they bled a lytyll; and forthwithall the woundis fayre heled and semed as they had bene hole a seven yere ... Than kynge Arthur and all the kynge and knyghtes kneled downe and gave thankynges and lovynge unto God and unto Hys Blyssed Modir. And ever sir Launcelote wepte, as he had bene a chylde that had bene beatyn![27]

> [And then, kneeling devoutly, he examined the three wounds, so that they bled a little; and subsequently the wounds healed nicely and seemed as if they had been whole for seven years ... Then King Arthur and all the kings and knights kneeled down and gave thanks and praise to God and to His Blessed Mother. And Sir Lancelot constantly wept, as if he were a child who had been beaten.]

In this scene, as in Langland's description of Longinus, noble identification fosters a powerful intimacy between two persons formerly unknown to each other, an intimacy that can prove redemptive.

In *Piers Plowman*, however, "bloody brotherhood" is supposed to describe a fellowship that transcends kinship ties and class identity as among brothers, bringing people of different lineages and status into ethical and spiritual understanding through Christ. The understanding between blood brothers is nothing less than a radical identification with all human beings, and as such, it lays the groundwork for Christian charity. According to the Emperor Trajan ("a knight"), for example, Christ's sacrifice made all Christians "blody bretheren":

> Almighty God [myghte have maad riche alle] men, if he wolde,
> Ac for the beste ben som riche and some beggeres and povere.
> For alle are we Cristes creatures, and of his cofres riche,
> And bretheren as of oo blood, as wel beggeres as erles.
> For at Calvarie of Cristes blood Cristendom gan sprynge,
> And blody bretheren we bicome there, of o body ywonne.
> As *quasi modo geniti* gentil men echon –   (11.196–202)[28]

> [Almighty God could have made all men rich, if he wanted to,
> But it is for the best that some men are rich while others are poor beggars.
> For all of us are Christ's creatures and rich from his coffers,
> And brothers, as if from one bloodline, beggars as well as earls.
> For Christendom sprang from Christ's blood at Calvary,
> And we became blood brothers there, redeemed from one body
> "As newborn babes", each one of us noble men.]

Trajan explains that noble feeling unites all people in Christ, conferring spiritual gentility on rich and poor alike. Importantly, as the passage shows, "blood brothers" also rationalizes material differences in wealth and status ("Ac for the beste ben som riche," 11.197 and ff.). In fact, as Trajan implies, the discrepancy between rich and poor – and, by analogy, between Christian and heathen – both elides difference, enabling the expression of Christian brotherhood, and affirms it, thereby encouraging people to give charity.

As these and other passages suggest, from an ethical standpoint, chivalric affinity might turn out to be a problematic model after all because it is nearly impossible to separate Christian fellowship from aristocratic identity. Additionally, by insisting upon chivalric affinity as a metaphor, the poet seems to suggest that ethical identification, a prerequisite for Christian community, is available only to those who naturally possess noble fellow feeling. The Emperor Trajan's capacity for fellow feeling, witnessed by the ardent speech attributed to him above, has everything to do with his social status: it was the pagan emperor's noble compassion for a lowly widow that persuaded Pope Gregory the Great to pray on Trajan's behalf and persuaded

God to include Trajan among the saved. What happens to Christian community when non-noble people cannot feel?

Toward the end of B.5, for example, the members of Reason's congregation band together in the search for Truth. Almost immediately, they fall into confusion. A pilgrim named Piers offers to guide them to Truth, but his directions are allegorical and his notion of travel steeped in the language of chivalric affinity: those who *know* how to reach Truth are those who can conceive of spiritual progress as a set of intimate social relations.

> Thenne shaltow come to a court as cler as the sonne.
> The moot is of Mercy the manoir aboute,
> And alle the walles ben of Wit to holden Wil oute,
> [The kerneles ben] of Cristendom that kynde to save,
> Botrased with "Bileef-so-or-thow-beest-noght-saved."
> And alle the houses ben hiled, halles and chambres,
> With no leed but with love and lowe speche, as bretheren [of o wombe].
>
> (5.585–91)

> [Then you shall come to a court as clear as the sun.
> The moat about the manor is made of Mercy,
> And all the walls are made of Wit to keep Will out,
> And decorated with Christendom to save that race,
> Buttressed with "Believe so or you will not be saved."
> And all the houses are covered, both halls and chambers
> With no lead but with love and humble speech, as brothers of one womb.]

> Grace hatte the gateward, a good man for sothe;
> His man hatte "Amende-yow" – many man hym knoweth.
> Telleth hym this tokene: "Truthe w[oot] the soothe"... (5.595–97)

> [Grace guards the entryway, truly a good man;
> His servant is named "Amend yourself" – many a man knows him.
> Tell him this token: "Truth knows the sooth".]

The reaction of the folk is to literalize Piers's allegorical directions by reducing chivalric affinity to relations of blood:

> "Now, by Crist!" quod a kuttepurs, "I have no kyn there."
> "Ne I," quod an apeward, "by aught that I knowe."
> "Wite God," quod a wafrestere, "wiste I this for sothe,
> Sholde I never ferther a foot for no freres prechyng."
> "Yis," quod Piers the Plowman, and poked hem alle to goode,
> "Mercy is a maiden there, hath might over hem alle;
> And she is sib to alle synfulle, and hire sone also,
> And thorough the help of hem two – hope thow noon oother –

Thow might gete grace there – so thow go bityme."
"Bi Seint Poul" quod a pardoner, "paraventure I be noght knowe there;
I wol go fecche my box with my brevettes and a bulle with bisshopes lettres."
"By Crist!" quod a commune womman, "thi compaignie wol I folwe.
Thow shalt seye I am thi suster." I ne woot where thei bicome.   (5.630–42)

["Now, by Christ!" said a cutpurse, "I have no kin there."
"Nor I," said an ape-keeper, "as far as I know."
"God knows," said a waferer [seller of cakes], "I am sure about one thing:
I won't take a step further, for no friar's preaching."
"Come on," said Piers the Plowman, and nudged them along,
"Mercy is a maiden there who has authority over everyone;
And she is related to all sinful people, and her son is as well;
And through the help of those two – and expect nothing else –
You might get grace there, if you hurry up now."
"By Saint Paul," said a pardoner, "it is possible no one will know me there;
I will go fetch my box with my papers and a papal bull with bishop's letters."
"By Christ," said a prostitute, "I will come along with you.
You shall say I am your sister." I do not know what became of them.]

For these lowborn pilgrims the intimacies of aristocratic community –
knowing the right password, for example ("telleth hym this tokene"), or
speaking in affectionate tones as with one's family ("as bretheren of o
wombe") – are obstacles to Christian identification and thus to spiritual
progress. For them, Christian fellowship, experienced through the language
of aristocratic sensibility, is unattainable without ties of blood. The cutpurse, apeward, and waferer refuse to take a step further, complaining that
they have no kin in Piers's country. Piers, reading kinship allegorically,
lightly assures them that Mercy and her son live there and, as "sib to alle
synfulle," they have special powers of intercession. A pardoner and prostitute decide the best strategy is to falsify the "blood" relations of Christian
association: the pardoner goes off to find his box of indulgences (presumably false papers) lest he "be noght knowe there," and the prostitute
pretends to be his sister.

Their failure to understand Piers's directions has serious implications for the
relationship between hermeneutics and community. Ethical identification is an
interpretative act and literal readers, always obdurate, show a churlish disregard
for true association. This comic interlude reminds us, too, that religious allegories can be awfully plodding, since no one really goes anywhere except within
themselves, a quality redeemed by Langland as interiority: "And if Grace graunte
thee to go in this wise / Thow shalt see in thiselve truthe sitte in thyn herte / In a
cheyne of charite, as thow a child were" [And if Grace allows you to travel in this

way / You will see inside yourself Truth sitting in your heart / In a chain of charity, as if you were a child] (5.605–07). But the inability of these folk to cultivate noble fellow feeling, and their concomitant failure to master Piers's lesson, highlights the stakes of true association. The dispersal of the pilgrims strikes us as both comic and poignant. As the dreamer admits, "I ne woot where thei bicome" (5.642)

Hungry for love

Key to Langland's understanding of community is the idea of fellow feeling: a person's conduct toward other people, such as praying for them and giving them alms, depends on a prior feeling of connectedness. "Blood brothers" assumes that gentility is the foundation of fellow feeling: identification with another confirms the capacity for noble feeling; at the same time, it confers gentility upon the object of identification, making all people noble kin in Christ. As we have seen, this link between gentility and fellow feeling raises difficult questions for the poet, for example, how non-noble people can grasp fellow feeling, and who exemplifies that common humanity with which all Christians are supposed to identify through Christ. If by "common" we mean the lowest folk, the poor and downtrodden, should those folk be defined by need or by estate? Are they the people to whom other people give alms, or through whose labor they live? Finally, what happens to one's relationship to others when ethical identification is determined not just by the subject's capacity to feel, but also by the object of feeling: the laborer or beggar, the vagrant or neighbor?

These are some of the questions explored in the Plowing of the Half-Acre in B.6. At the beginning of the passus, Piers declares that true pilgrimage is plowing Truth's land, and he encourages all pilgrims to embark on a spiritual journey: a stay-at-home pilgrimage on the medieval manor, counter to the itinerancy of romance. Initially satisfying, this analogy between true penitence and obedient work comes to hinge on the integrity of the laborer. Some people cheerfully toil in return for very basic food and drink, but others hold out for higher pay and fancier food (unjustly, in Piers's opinion), and still others refuse to work at all, faking injury and begging for alms. Another question arises: if agricultural labor is supposed to be equivalent to spiritual labor, what happens to Christian community when the laborer will not work?

The historical context that informs this episode, one richly documented by *Piers* scholars, is the Ordinance of Laborers of 1349, the parliamentary legislation that sought to regulate the post-plague labor market. In the aftermath of the Black Death, the English agricultural workforce was cut in half and bondsmen and free laborers found themselves able to negotiate wages and customary duties. The Ordinance of Laborers and subsequent legislation in 1351 and 1376 were designed to prop up landowners by freezing wages at pre-plague rates, forcing those who were born into servitude to stay in the service of their original masters and penalizing those who gave money to able-bodied beggars. Between the Ordinance of Laborers of 1349 and the Vagrancy Statutes of 1388, moreover, there were some further developments in the legislation of labor. These included attempts to restrict physical mobility (requiring those traveling out of their district to carry "passports"); thwart social mobility, especially among agricultural laborers; and criminalize beggars as vagrants, labeling them as menaces not only to landowners hoping to bring in the harvest as cheaply as possible, but even to the very welfare of the State.[29]

The creation of a labor market meant that the traditional estates model, as it pertained to rural laborers, was no longer tenable: plowmen could no longer be depicted as humble Christians contentedly working in their divinely appointed estate.[30] It also meant that to represent a community of laborers was to put mastery – coercion, discrimination, and punishment – front and center.[31] In the Plowing of the Half Acre, Piers the Plowman, the default protagonist of the *Visio*'s spiritual community, finds himself in an awkward position as both the representative of a common humanity and its charismatic leader, as well as Truth's reeve, with the frustrating job of making people work for their own material and spiritual good. In Piers's world, normal channels of coercion have failed: the Knight, who in regular circumstances would play the role of landowner, swears to defend his laborers from roving animals, a promise that sounds quaint once it becomes clear that the only threat to productivity is the workforce itself. Likewise in the Plowing of the Half-Acre, the labor statutes, intended to protect the rights of landowners, have been replaced by a personification named Hunger, summoned by Piers, who compels "wasters" to work:

And thanne corseth the Kyng and al his Counseil after
Swiche lawes to loke, laborers to greve.
Ac whiles Hunger was hir maister, ther wolde noon of hem chide,
Ne stryven ayeins his statut, so sterneliche he loked!   (6.315–18)

[And then (the workman) curses the King and his whole Council after
Who created such laws, which distress laborers.
But as long as Hunger was their master, none of them there would complain,
Nor strive against his statute, so stern he seemed!]

Hunger sustains the fiction that there is a natural relationship between work and food. He personifies an internal compulsion ("I work because I need to eat"), the very externalization of which disguises the fact that some people refuse to labor, not because they are lazy but because they are holding out for better working conditions ("I work because I am paid enough"). In Langland's ingenious presentation, Hunger is also the personification of an external compulsion, famine, which the poet claims to be a function of labor: if laborers demanded less compensation and tilled the fields for the common good, then hunger would be prevented; conversely, the threat of famine should force idle laborers to work. As both internal and external compulsion, Hunger fills a vacuum of coercive agency left by lordship and law.

This imagined vacuum of agency stems from the poet's very traditional view of labor relations, yet it nonetheless gives him the chance to dramatize in innovative ways the ethics of a community defined by labor. Although Piers is grateful to Hunger for forcing people to work, he is aware that the existence of Hunger presents some ethical quandaries. For one thing, to coerce people is to restrict food or money, thereby contradicting the scriptural injunction that people bear each other's burdens. For another thing, to master a labor force, as Piers does here with Hunger's help, is necessarily to discriminate between those who deserve charity (the truly needy) and those who do not (false beggars); that is, to identify with some people and not others. Piers asks Hunger how he might force the people to work in Hunger's absence, and whether mastery is, in fact, reconcilable with the imperative to love one's fellow human being:

> "Ac I preie thee, er thow passe," quod Piers tho to Hunger,
> "Of beggeris and of bidderis what best be to doone?
> For I woot wel, be thow went, thei wol werche ful ille;
> Meschief it maketh thei be so meke nouthe,
> And for defaute of hire foode this folk is at my wille.
> [And] it are my blody bretheren, for God boughte us alle.
> Truthe taughte me ones to loven hem ech one
> And to helpen hem of alle thyng, ay as hem nedeth.
> Now wolde I wite of thee, what were the beste,
> And how I myghte amaistren hem and make hem to werche."
>
> (6.202–11)

> ["But let me ask you, before you go," said Piers to Hunger,
> "What is best to be done with beggars and bidders?
> For I know well that, before you came, they seriously slacked off;
> Hard times are what cause them to be so meek,

And they do what I wish because they have no food.
And these are my blood brothers, because God bought us all.
Truth once taught me to love each one of them
And help them by giving them everything that they need.
Now I would like you to tell me the best solution,
And how I might master them and force them to work."]

In this passage, Piers uses "blody bretheren" to invoke a common humanity that brings people into ethical understanding. This common humanity is brought into focus through Christ's sacrifice on the Cross and defined by need (6.207–09). In this way, Piers can justify giving alms to beggars by invoking a sense of relatedness, a shared Christian identity with all human beings. But when the laborer is defined as a legal–political entity, which subsumes all beggars as willful non-workers, Christian kinship no longer serves. Piers must now discriminate between those who do and do not deserve his charity.

In his answer to Piers, Hunger recommends two courses of action: discriminate between false beggars and the truly needy; and provide in some way for everyone, letting the final decision rest with God:

"Ac if thow fynde any freke that Fortune hath apeired
[Other] any manere false men, fonde thow swiche to knowe:
Conforte hem with thi catel for Cristes love of hevene;
Love hem and lene hem, for so lawe of [kynde wolde]:
Alter alterius onera portate.
And alle manere of men that thow myght aspie
That nedy ben and noughty, [norisse] hem with thi goodes.
Love hem and lakke hem noght – lat God take the vengeaunce;
Theigh thei doon yvele, lat thow God yworthe:
Michi vindictam et ego retribuam."   [Romans 12.19] (6.218–26)

["But if you come across any man whom fortune has abused
Or any kind of false men, as far as you can tell:
Comfort them with your goods for the love of the heavenly Christ;
Love them and support them, as natural law requires:
'You should bear one another's burdens'."
And all manner of people whom you meet
Who are needy or destitute, nourish them with your goods,
Love them, don't judge them – let God take revenge;
Even if they do evil, let God deal with it:
'Revenge is mine, and I shall pay them back'."]

Hunger's compromise, to discriminate between false and true beggars while at the same time refraining from final Judgement, seems reasonable on the face of it. In fact, Piers has already acted on this suggestion just a few lines earlier, when he feeds false beggars bean bread – horse food – but does not deny them sustenance altogether. The problem with Hunger's compromise is that it equates divine and human mastery, making discrimination and exclusion the central terms of human association, and putting human beings in the uncomfortable position of playing God. Earlier in B.6, Piers draws up a last will and testament, discharging his debts and placing his body in the hands of his parish priest. Before he makes his will he swears, as a plowman, to provide food for everyone, with the exception of those marginal types, whose behavior he condemns. He compares his refusal to feed them with God's deletion of their names from the Book of Life:

> And alle kynne crafty men that konne lyven in truthe,
> I shal fynden hem fode that feithfulliche libbeth –
> Save Jakke the Jogelour and Jonette of the Stuwes,
> And Danyel the Dees-pleyere and Denote the Baude,
> And Frere the Faitour, and folk of his ordre,
> And Robin the Ribaudour, for hise rusty wordes.
> Truthe tolde me ones and bad me telle it forth:
> *Deleantur de libro vivencium* – I sholde noght dele with hem,
> For Holy Chirche is hote, of hem no tithe to aske,
> *Quia cum iustis non scribantur* (Psalm 68:29)
> Thei ben ascaped good aventure – now God hem amende! (6.68–77)

> [And all kinds of skilled men who are able to live in truthe,
> For them, I will provide food, those who live faithfully –
> Except for Jack the Juggler, and Jonette of the brothels,
> And Daniel the dice-player and Denote the pimp.
> And Faker Friar and the members of his order,
> And Robin the smut-seller, for his crude words.
> Truth told me once and asked me to spread the news:
> "Let them be blotted out from the book of the living" – I should not deal with them,
> For Holy Church is commanded to ask no tithes from them,
> "And with the just let them not be written."
> They have gotten away with it so far – may God make them better!

Piers's testament and his "blood brothers" represent opposing sides of human association: radical discrimination on the model of God the Father and radical identification on the model of God the Son.

The distance between the two models of association precipitates a crisis in the Plowing of the Half-Acre, where Piers continues to discriminate, defining common humanity in Christ as a motley crew of good and bad laborers, idlers and beggars. Truth's Pardon, issued from on high, proposes a remedy to the crisis: not by getting people to work, as Piers would have it, but rather by reconciling the two ethical postures, identification and discrimination. Like Piers's testament, the long version of the Pardon argues for the prerogative of a Supreme Ruler – Truth – to exclude and punish those who break the law, but then, through special dispensation, include them through the liberal use of the personal seal. As discussed above, the poet uses this passage to showcase his exceptionalist poetics in which marginal occupations – merchants, lawyers, and beggars – help to explain the relationship between divine intercession and human association. For the poet, however, the true test of human association is the beggar, because the beggar offers a conceptual model for thinking through the relationship between identification and discrimination. As B.7 unfolds, the poet becomes increasingly preoccupied with beggars, and in the C.9 revision, the beggar threatens to overtake the Pardon and become the whole poem, subsuming all questions about identity, association, and work.

In the B-text, the poet compares two approaches to almsgiving. According to authorities Cato and Peter Comestor, beggars who have no need to beg divert resources from the truly needy and defraud the giver in the process. With this approach, the onus is placed entirely on human agents to do the right thing: on the almsgiver to discriminate between false beggars and the truly needy and on the beggar to represent himself honestly. This approach contrasts sharply with the approach recommended by Jerome (attributed by Langland to Pope Gregory I): give to anyone who asks, because only God can discern true need. Givers, relieved of the burden of Judgement, can let God make the call, knowing that by giving in the first place they have secured themselves a place in heaven. Beggars continue to bear the burden of receiving alms, but in Langland's interpretation of "Gregory," all beggars are debtors, whether honest or not:

> For he that yeveth, yeldeth, and yarketh hym to reste,
> And he that biddeth, borweth, and bryngeth hymself in dette. . .   (7.78–79)

> [For he who gives, gives something up, and prepares his resting place,
> And he who begs, borrows, and brings himself into debt. . .]

Here as elsewhere, the poet uses metrical parallels (yeveth, yeldeth/yarketh vs. biddeth, borweth/bryngeth) to argue for moral equivalence: just as those who give alms in any capacity sacrifice their goods and score points in heaven, so those who beg for any reason, borrow, and bring themselves into debt. These lines effectively close the gap between false and honest beggars.

From the perspective of the giver, all beggars are the same: all beggars borrow, God provides surety for their debts, and God will refund the giver with interest, no matter to whom he gives. From the perspective of the beggar, all begging incurs a financial and spiritual debt, and beggars can count on God to absorb the debt only of those who demonstrate real need. And yet, insofar as God is willing to serve as their banker and judge, beggars exemplify the relationship between human and divine. The poet continues in B.7 with an admonition to beggars to be honest and content themselves with little ("Let usage be youre solas of seintes lyves redyng" [Get in the habit of consoling yourself with saints' lives] 7.85). He rails at vagrants who breed like animals – "But as wilde bestes with 'wehee' worthen uppe and werchen" (7.90) – and who mutilate their children to get more alms. These he distinguishes from those who have legitimate reasons not to work – the elderly, pregnant women, handicapped, and lepers – those people who, by suffering adversity meekly, are entitled not only to alms but also to divine forgiveness (7.102).

In his revision to the Pardon in C.9, the poet jettisons "Gregory," and lets stand Cato's advice to "take care to whom you give." Many scholars consider this revision, with its more uncompromising attitude toward beggars, to be evidence for the poet's tougher, more authoritarian stance in C. Significantly, though, the poet replaces "Gregory" with a new passage, which shows just how inadequate "Gregory's" attitude toward the poor really is: even as it argues against discrimination, it fails to reorient the giver ethically toward the needy. In C, Langland moves from Cato's advice to discriminate to a new passage, one of the most poignant descriptions of poverty ever written: the case of the poor neighbor. No one but God can know who deserves alms, but it is crystal clear to a worldly poet ("This I woet witterly, as the world techeth" [This I know for sure, as I have learned through experience] C.9.88) that the neediest are neighbors – "Woet no man, as y wene, who is worthy to haue; / Ac that most neden aren oure neyhebores" [No man knows, I think, who deserves to have [alms] / But those who are most needy are our neighbors] (C.9.70–71) – and it is to the plight of neighbors that "we nyme gode hede" [we should pay attention] (71).

The neighbor in this passage is not simply the *proximus/a*, the next-door neighbor, whose cow tramples on the garden. He or she is also, synonymously, the *vicinus/a*, a person with whom one has an ethical relationship, the one who, if your social equal, might stand bail for you in court or stir up trouble between your households, as Envy so often does: "I have a neghebore neigh me, / I have annoyed hym ofte ... Betwene mayné and mayné I make debate ofte" (B.5, 93, 97). But if the *vicinus/vicina* is an inferior, a poor cotter in a hut, he or she, however close, might be just out of view. Poor folk in "cotes" (C.9.72), who hold land in return for service, may appear to a landlord to be sufficient like himself: if they have skills ("craftes") to clothe and feed themselves (C.9.90), they might seem to have no need for alms. But the hardscrabble life of poor neighbors points to the insufficiency of all labor. If "craft" is one's only "catel" (income), it cannot cover all one's expenses, much less any treats beyond a farthing's worth of mussels on holidays (C.9.94–95). These cotters are proud, the poet explains. They identify *their* neighbors as those from whom they would like to conceal rather than reveal their adversity: they prefer "to turne the fayre outward, / And ben abasched for to begge and wollen nat be aknowe / What hem nedeth at here neyhebores at noon and at eue" [to give a good impression, / And are ashamed to beg and don't want it to be known / what they need from their neighbors, both day and night] (C.9.85–87).

Although the poet takes for granted the moral obligation of the rich to give to the poor, in this passage he importantly describes that obligation as an ethical posture: the rich can help the poor by recognizing their neighbors as neighbors, in asymmetrical relation: "These are almusse, to helpe that han suche charges / And to conforte such coterelles and lame men and blynde" [It is charitable to help those who bear such burdens / And to comfort such cotters and crooked and blind men] (C.9.96–97).[32] The case of the poor neighbor can thus be understood not only as a part of a larger ideological revision in C but also as a serious ethical interruption to B. The poet soon returns to his vigorous condemnation of panhandlers, layabouts, and vagrants, and he continues to uphold Piers's claim that forced labor, or law, or divine justice, will cure fraudulent begging. Yet the case of the poor neighbor nonetheless serves as a major reorientation toward the poor, if not the poet's last word on the subject.

In medieval England "face-to-face" encounters with the poor included a variety of practices, from street beggars asking for hand-outs, to largesse distributed at public events, to hospitality offered by the rich to a representative number of poor, such as indigent laypeople, scholars, and friars. The poet is particularly attentive to hospitality, no doubt because he was attached to a noble household. Later in C.9 the dreamer-narrator complains that he suffers in silence when lords and ladies patronize undeserving people, like profane minstrels or beggars with no spiritual ambition other than warming themselves on hot coals or eating a hunk of cheese (C.9.128ff.). He would rather that lords support the people he admires, God's minstrels, wanderers with spiritual credentials, who beg from no man (C.9.124–25b). Although such face-to-face encounters were indispensable to medieval culture, they present all kinds of problems for the poet. For one thing, they call on the giver to distinguish between those who need help and those who do not; for another, they give the wrong impression that those who do not beg are not struggling to meet basic needs.

Langland's poor neighbor offers a temporary reprieve from these ethical difficulties by stressing recognition, rather than discrimination or even identification. Furthermore, by stressing recognition, the poet describes the neighbor not just as any poor cotter but as a woman, and the poetic achievements of this passage have to do with its highly unusual portrait of female poverty. Both men and women are burdened with children and the chief lord's rent, and both have too many dependents and take in too little money (C.9.73, 91). But women's domestic work exemplifies the suffering of the neighbor because it is less observable by the rich:

> That they with spynnyng may spare, spenen hit on hous-huyre,
> Bothe in mylke and in mele, to make with papelotes
> To aglotye with here gurles that greden aftur fode.
> And hemsulue also soffre muche hunger,
> And wo in wynter-tymes, and wakynge on nyhtes
> To rise to the reule to rokke the cradel,
> Both to carde and to kembe, to cloute and to wasche,
> And to rybbe and to rele, rusches to pylie,
> That reuthe is to rede or in ryme shewe
> The wo of this wommen that wonyeth in cotes;
> And of monye other men that moche wo soffren,
> Bothe afyngred and afurste . . .   (C.9.74–85)

> [Whatever they earn from spinning, they spend it on the household,
> Both on milk and on meal, to make the gruel
> To satisfy their children who cry out for food;
> And they themselves also suffer much hunger,
> And woe in the wintertime, and waking up at night
> To rise, as a rule, to rock the cradle,
> Both to card, and to comb, to patch, and to wash,
> And to scrape, and to wind, and to pile rushes,
> That it is a pity to read or to show in rhyme,
> The woe of these women who dwell in huts,
> And of many other men who suffer much woe,
> Both hungry and thirsty . . .]

Poor female neighbors must take in extra spinning to pay for the milk and meal to feed their children. They endure hunger, cold, and sleepless nights. They ceaselessly comb wool and make candles. Their misery, somehow known to the poet but unknown to his readers, is the pitiful subject of

Figure 2. "Woman with a cradle." Jacques de Longuyon, *Les voeux du paon*. Pierpont
Morgan Library, MS G.24, f.10r. (Flemish, 1345–1355).

poetry, an alternative saint's life about poor women: "That reuthe is to rede
or in ryme shewe" [That pity is to read or show in rhyme] (*c*.9.82). Finally,
the woe of women neighbors stands in for the woe of neighbors as a whole.
By acknowledging women's work in the household, says the poet, a person
comes to recognize all his neighbors, both female and male.

Getting a new suit

In B.5–7 the group effort to win salvation is constantly impeded by the
difficulties of forming community. In the end, however, the poet reserves his
greatest sympathies for the group, and he describes community most affect-
ingly at the moments in which the folk flounder and the group model is
found wanting. For example, at the end of the Confession of the Sins, the
entire community joins together in prayer to God: "A thousand of men tho
thrungen togideres, / Cride upward to Crist and to his clene moder / To have

grace to go [to] Truthe – [God leve that they moten!]" [A thousand people then thronged together, / Cried upward to Christ and to his pure mother / To have grace to go to Truth, God believe that they might!] (5.510–12). They are accompanied by the saints on high, but dissolve almost immediately into confusion: "Ac there was wight noon so wys, the wey thider kouthe, / But blustreden forth as beestes over ba[ch]es and hilles" [But there was no person wise enough to know the way, / So they blustered forth like beasts over valleys and hills] (5.513–14).

Community is also sympathetic insofar as the identification with a common humanity mirrors acts of divine fellow feeling. As discussed above, human beings like Piers resemble God the Father when they discriminate between good people and bad. God, in turn, forges ethical bonds with human beings by imitating them: he sympathizes with the human condition and he empathizes with it through the Incarnation. God's radical identification with humanity through Christ's humanity is bound up in the helplessness of the community *qua* community, the lovable "groupiness" of the sinful and needy. Repentance's prayer at the end of Confessions of the Sins capitalizes on this crucial connection between group identification and divine empathy. The crowd who witnesses the Sins' confessions knows it can never make up the difference between intention and restitution. Robert the robber, for example, tearfully entreats God to recall the salvation of Dismus, the thief crucified next to Christ, who believed in him and so was saved. The community, however repentant, requires a supererogatory act of God, an act of mercy, which is always in excess of what people actually deserve. This supererogatory act – the conferring of grace on those who desire but can never earn it – underscores the disparity between divine and human justice.

Yet Repentance's prayer, aiming for grace, sketches a very different relationship between human sinfulness and divine mercy, positing a reciprocal relationship between God and humanity. Medieval devotional writing tended to emphasize Christ's pain on the cross at the hands of men, and called upon present readers to acknowledge Christ's willing sacrifice. God assumed human form and suffered death on the Cross in order to pay off the debt that humanity owed to him through Adam's original sin. In this view, human beings owe God endless gratitude for taking on human form, and their sympathy for Christ's suffering on the Cross is necessarily blended with the guilt they feel for sinning against a God who has sacrificed himself on their behalf. Middle English lyrics, like the one quoted below, plaintively express this mixture of pity and remorse:

Ihesu, for love þou bood so wo
þat blody stremys runne þe fro
þi whyte sydes woxen blw & blo –
Oure synnes it maden so, wolawo![33]

[Jesus, for love, you endured such woe
That bloody streams ran from you.
Your white sides grew black and blue –
Our sins made it so, woe is me!]

Langland is likewise interested in Christ's humanity and the relationships it construes between sympathy and identification, but in Repentance's prayer he dramatically reframes the associative bonds between God and man. The prayer argues that God, in fact, owes man through their shared humanity. If one emphasizes God's omnipotence, the power through which he created the world from nothing – "of naught madest aught" (5.482) – one ends up with a God who benevolently allows events to unfold (5.483), and who is unaffected by humanity even as he acts for everyone's good ("And al for the beste, as I believe"), turning Adam's original sin into a "happy guilt" (*felix culpa*) and "necessary sin" through the Incarnation (5.484a, from the Holy Saturday Liturgy). If, however, divine imitation is emphasized over divine omnipotence, the relationship between humanity and God looks quite different. In this view, God first made man in his own image during the Creation (5.482), and then remade himself in man's image during the Incarnation:

For thorugh that synne Thi sone sent was to this erthe
And bicam man of a maide mankynde to save –
And madest Thiself with Thi sone us synfulle yliche:
Faciamus hominem ad imaginem et similitudinem nostram; Et alibi,
Qui manet in caritate, in Deo manet, et Deus in eo;
And siththe with Thi selve sone in oure sute deidest
On Good Fryday for mannes sake at ful tyme of the day.   (5.485–89)

[Because of that sin your son was sent to the earth
And became man through a virgin in order to save mankind –
And made yourself with your son like to us sinful:
"We made man in our image and in our likeness; and elsewhere,
Who remains in charity, remains in God, and God in him";
And then, through your own son, you died in our suit
On Good Friday for man's sake at the appointed time.]

Indeed, when this argument is taken one step further, as it is here, it claims that this divine act of imitation fashioned a bond with humanity that exceeds the moment of the Redemption. God, by making himself through Christ like to sinful humanity ("us synfulle yliche") effectively assumed responsibility for people for all time. His fleshly identification with humanity created an indissoluble bond of kinship, quite literally through the flesh; as Repentance declares in the last lines of his prayer, "if it be Thi wille / That art oure fader and oure brother – be merciable to us / And have ruthe on these ribaudes that repenten hem soore" [if it is your will, / You who are our father and brother, be merciful to us, / And have pity on those losers who so earnestly repent] (5.502–04).

Finally, when taken to its logical extreme, imitation constitutes a reciprocal relation and a form of divine rather than human debt. In assuming humanity, God borrowed man's flesh, and man is consequently entitled to cash in. Christ owes humanity because he fought, died, and was resurrected in human form ("in oure sute deidest" [died in our suit; i.e., "in our garments" and/or "for our cause"]) (5.488); and "Thow yedest in oure sute" [you went forth in our suit] (5.497). As the writers of the gospels report, Jesus borrowed the "arms" of humanity to fight his most courageous deeds: "And al that Marc hath ymaad, Mathew, Johan, and Lucas / Of Thyne doughtiest dedes were doon in oure armes: / *Verbum caro factum est et habitavit in nobis*" [And according to everything that Mark, Matthew, John and Luke wrote, / Your most courageous deeds were done in our arms: / "The Word was made flesh and dwelt among us"] (5.500–01b). Although God paid the debt of original sin by dying in human form, his act of imitation became a kind of pure currency with which human beings could perpetually sue for mercy. For Langland, this reciprocal relationship between God and man, founded in divine imitation of humankind and in divine recognition of human need, is the ultimate form of community.

CHAPTER 4

Learning
(B.8–12)

"For we have no lettre of oure lif, how longe it shal dure"   (B.10.91)

Introduction

At the end of B.7, Piers receives a pardon from Truth on behalf of the community, and a priest offers to read and interpret it for him. The priest informs Piers that the pardon contains only two lines: those who have done well may look forward to eternal life in heaven, and those who have done evil are destined to eternal fire in hell. Exasperated by the priest or distressed by the pardon, Piers takes it upon himself to gloss this text: he tears the pardon in half and vows to pursue a life of prayer and penance on the model of the apostles:[1] "'*Ne soliciti sitis,*' he seith in the Gospel, / And sheweth us by ensamples us selve to wisse" ["Do not be solicitous," [Luke] says in the Gospel, / And shows us through examples how we should conduct ourselves] (7.127–8). The priest notes that Piers is educated and asks, "who lerned thee on boke?" (7.132), to which Piers responds with an intellectual autobiography calculated to provoke the priest: Abbess Abstinence taught him his "a.b.c." and Conscience taught him much more or better (7.136–37). To be literate, by any definition, is to write oneself into a moral life. Although Piers is ostensibly just a plowman, who relies on priests to instruct him in the faith, in fact he has built his miniature allegory from an educated priest's preaching materials: *abbatissa* and *abstinentia* are commonly among the first few entries in alphabetically ordered *distinctiones* books and concordances, biblical reference books for medieval preachers.[2] The priest mocks the plowman's pretensions to learning, and he and Piers debate with each other until the dreamer wakes up.

Although Piers disappears for a while, the poet does not abandon the idea, proposed by Piers, that the secret to salvation lies in the effort of people to work as a group. In passūs 8–12, however, the poet tackles

96

salvation theology from the perspective of teaching and learning.[3] This perspective is gained through the individual experience of a student, as opposed to the communal experiences of church, labor, pilgrimage, or marketplace, although the poet recognizes that learning, like salvation, is always about one's relationship to other people. This perspective also requires an inward turn, anticipated by Piers and his a.b.c. life, and characterized by the dreamer's exchanges with cognitive faculties, such as Thought, Wit, Reason, and Imaginatif, as well as with personifications of learning, such as Study, Clergy, and Scripture. Each one of these is understood to be an aspect of the dreamer's self, insofar as each one is an aspect of his learning life.

With this inward turn to learning, the dreamer is transformed from the passive viewer of the *Visio* into the protagonist of his own life. Like Piers in B.7, the dreamer, sometimes identified with the will, assumes a more confrontational attitude, which begins with his life as a student. In B.5–7, the dreamer merges with the crowd or watches from the sidelines: Will weeps after hearing Reason's sermon (5.61) and later, the dreamer peeps over the shoulders of Piers and the priest as they read the Pardon (7.108). Passūs 8–12, however, hearken back to an earlier scene of personified learning, Holy Church's instruction of the dreamer, who, as a student, engages and argues, is rebuked and humiliated, and whose early education has implications for later life: "'Thow doted daffe,'" says Holy Church, "'dulle are thi wittes. / To litel Latyn thow lernedest, leode, in thi youthe / *Heu michi quod sterilem duxi vitam invenilem!*'" ["You ignorant fool . . . Your wits are dull. / Man, you learned too little Latin in your youth" / 'Woe is me, what a useless life I led in my youth'"/ (1.140–1a; see 5.421–22). In passus 10, Dame Study, adopting a similar tone, berates Wit for teaching a fool like the dreamer (10.5–10). In passus 11, Scripture scorns the dreamer's position on baptism, and later in the passus, Reason reproves the dreamer for questioning the order of nature (discussed below). Imaginatif backs Reason up, reminding the dreamer that Adam lost Paradise when he meddled in divine affairs (11.414–17). The dreamer enters the fray, criticizing Reason for denying instinct to human beings (11.373–74), arguing with Scripture about baptism (10.343–45), and mocking the friars for their self-serving arguments (11.89–95).

The learning self is critical to this section of the poem. First, it allows the poet to explore the cruxes of salvation theology through the dreamer's life in education. Rather than presenting doctrine as catechesis, for example, the poet presents it as a series of intellectual, if not strictly academic topics: if baptism saves, how do we explain the case of the saved pagan? If charity is chief among the three virtues, faith, hope, and charity, how to explain the salvation of whores, pagans, and thieves? In this way, too, the dreamer becomes the protagonist of his own life through his desire to debate large questions concerning Christian salvation; likewise, his will to learn becomes both the structure and process of a moral life.

Secondly, the learning self allows the poet to pursue a formal resemblance between the cruxes of salvation theology and the social dynamics of teaching and learning.[4] A medieval life in higher education was characterized by dialectic, the public art of debating contrary positions. Literary representations of dialectic run the gamut from simple question-and-answer formats, such as Anselm of Canterbury's *Cur Deus Homo* [*Why God (Became) Man*] (*c.*1100), in which the student's objections are mere prompts for the master's arguments, to the *Fasciculi zizanorum* (*Bundles of Tares*), a record of debates that may have taken place at the University of Oxford in the later fourteenth century, where the reformist theologian John Wycliffe and his opponents debated among other controversial topics the nature of scriptural authority. It is where theology approaches dialectic that it can be grasped as a set of irreconcilable but equally viable positions: for instance, God may be portrayed as a strict gatekeeper (Matthew 25.12) or as a forgiving lord (Psalm 144.9). The apparent contradictions of these positions can be approached in a variety of ways: for example, as logical arguments (for example, the dreamer's parody of syllogistic logic at B.8.20–25); as theological "case studies," such as the virtuous pagan or the thief on the cross; and as examples or analogies (for example, life is like a boat, God is like a lord.).

Where theology approaches dialectic in *Piers Plowman* it produces emotional states which resemble the dynamic between teacher and student. When salvation theology is presented as a set of debatable positions, the result is an emotional rollercoaster: am I chosen or not? Am I capable or incapable of meriting eternal life? Is God merciful or just? For Langland, this either/or of salvation, the pendulum swing between salvation and damnation, hope and despair, is intrinsically bound up in the social dynamics of learning. In passūs 8–12, these dynamics reveal deep anxieties about pedagogical fitness having to do, for example, with the presumption of the student, the competence of the teacher, or the suitability of the subject for different audiences. Who is fit to learn, and in what contexts should knowledge be shared? How can scholarly debate be productive, and why does it devolve into carping and criticism? And most importantly, when does learning aid and when does it impede salvation?

One way of understanding B.8–12, then, is to observe that this section of the poem is less about formal education and its discontents than it is about forms of learning and their limits. This is not simply to say that human beings have a limited ability to understand God's plan or that learning only gets you so far, although the poem supports both positions. Rather, it is to say that how one approaches learning – as a student or teacher, as a preacher or critic, as a layman or cleric – and how one acquires or disseminates knowledge – through debate, cruxes, precepts, stories, dreams – determines one's ability to be saved. It is at the formal limits of learning where we trace the contours of a moral life.

The learning life

Ideally, the dreamer's entrance into learning should reveal something about the education of *Piers Plowman*'s mysterious poet. Langland motions to a range of specialized knowledge that few medieval or modern scholars could hope to master: liturgy, grammar, diplomatics, theology, even optics. It is doubtful that the poet, whose reformist ecclesiology resonates with some of the intellectual trends of 1370s Oxford, had no contact with university life. But if the poem alludes to many areas of specialized knowledge, it does not showcase the technical training of a university graduate. It is true that the poet developed some of his material, such as Piers's debate with the priest in B.7, from biblical commentaries, such as Hugh of St. Cher's commentary on the Psalms;[5] indeed, the composition of these scenes suggest the textual competence of a university-trained preacher. However, he does not affiliate his poem with a particular realm of learning the way a medieval scholar might typically do. He worries instead about the effects of education at all levels: he complains bitterly about parish priests who lack basic literacy (see 15.371–86), as well as about the misapplication of learning, as for example, in the case of the university friars, who try to dazzle layfolk with Trinitarian abstractions (15.70–79), or who spend too much time pursuing arcane theology and philosophy (20.273–76), and not enough time preaching to the laity. In fact, some of his most impressive feats of scholarly quotation and poetic translation are derived from introductory grammar texts and basic preaching materials. For example, in the scene in which the dreamer debates with the friars about the meaning of Dowel (8.6–26), it is thought that the poet borrowed his technique ("appellation") from William of Sherwood's elementary logic treatise, where he would have also found the distinction between kind wit ("naturalis scientia") and clergy ("sermoncinales scientia," or the arts of language that lead one to sacred scripture), so crucial to Imaginatif's defense of clergy in B.12.[6] The saying, "Heu michi quod sterilem duxi vitam iuvenilem" [Woe is me, what a useless life I led in my youth], quoted twice in *Piers Plowman* at dramatic moments of self-reproach but attested nowhere else in medieval literature, survives in a list of alphabetical proverbs in an English schoolbook (Manchester, John Rylands Library, Latin MS 394).[7] Patience's virtuosic translation of the definitions of poverty in B.14 originated with Vincent of Beauvais's thirteenth-century encyclopedia, the *Speculum historiale*, a major reference book for medieval writers of all stripes, including sermon-writers, chroniclers, and poets such as Gower and Chaucer. Anima's definitions of the soul in B.15.23–39, based on Isidore's *Etymologies*, lays out what Katharine Breen calls "sorry Latin," a glossary of heavily rubricated, undeclined Latin nouns, easily diagrammed, of the kind intended to educate lay readers with next to no Latin training.[8]

Langland draws upon a variety of learned texts, from elementary to scholarly, to construct a multilingual and versatile religious poetry. Interestingly, his most schematic presentations of learning gesture to, rather than recapitulate, the content of formal education. The poem's somewhat intimidating bid to comprehensive knowledge, for example, is inseparable from its main literary conceit, that it encompasses everything. This conceit takes forms both encyclopedic (for example, Anima's definitions of the soul) and spectacular (e.g., the multiple views of society in the Prologue). It is exemplified by Study's peculiar description of an academic curriculum in B.10, the heart of the poet's investigation of learning in B.10. Dame Study's syllabus models curriculum not as a specific course of study but as a form of learning that includes extracurricular pursuits both intellectual and vocational. She describes it as a catch-all of texts, disciplines, and *auctores*: the Bible, the Book of Wisdom, the Glossed Psalter; logic, law, "musons [measures] in Musik" (10.174); Plato, Aristotle, as well as "othere mo," whom she taught to argue (10.170–76). In other words, these items point to general apparatuses of learning rather than the objects or properties of disciplines. Study's syllabus features, for example, "Grammer for girles [children]" (10.177), "Geometry and Geomesie" (10.210), the magical arts, and tools for crafts, such as carpentry, carving, and masonry (10.179–81), perhaps Langland's homage to Hugh of St. Victor's *Didascalion* (*c.*1140), a classic treatise on education, which systematically explains the seven mechanical as well as the liberal arts.

A similar strategy is at work in the poet's casual lists of authorities. In C.12, for example, the poet/Trajan claims to be able to quote eleven hundred authorities on patient poverty, when in fact he only quotes the gospels:

Mo prouerbes y myhte haue of mony holy seyntes
To testifie for treuthe the tale that y shewe
And poetes to preuen hit: Porfirie and Plato,
Aristotel, Ennedy [in some manuscripts, Ouidius], enleuene hundred,
Tulius, Tolomeus – Y can nat tell here names,
Preueth pacient pouerte prince of alle vertues. . .   (C.12.170–75)

[I might quote more sayings from many holy saints
To attest to the truth of what I have been saying,
And poets to prove it: Porphyry and Plato,
Aristotle, Ennodius, eleven hundred,
Cicero, Ptolemy – I cannot recount all their names –
Prove patient poverty the prince of all virtues.]

This passage invokes the many and assorted collections of wisdom on different topics, compiled in all kinds of medieval manuscripts, such as the trilingual and versified "Prouerbes of diuerse profetes and of poetes and of oþur seyntes," compiled in the Vernon manuscript.[9] The first dated printed book in England was, unsurprisingly, the *Dictes and Sayings of Philosophers* (Caxton, 1477), a collection of sayings attributed to Homer, Plato, Alexander, Aristotle, and St. Gregory, among others. Langland's quick sketch of learned authority captures the compendiousness of proverbial citation, without actually reproducing any of its materials.

The many citations of "Cato" in *Piers Plowman* provide insight into how the poet uses formal learning to think about the forms and limits of learning. The *Distiches* attributed to Cato, a compilation of proverbs in Latin hexameter probably composed in the third or fourth century C.E., was the major textbook of Latin composition for schoolboys up to Benjamin Franklin. Like *Poor Richard's Almanac*, Cato's proverbs teach people how to feel and behave in a monotheistic "real world": how to suffer fools and poverty gladly, how to win friends and influence people, who to trust and what to avoid. Cato gave novice students a congenial mix of ethical and rhetorical training, and medieval writers fulsomely praise him. As one fourteenth-century translator exclaims, "gode grante vs grace. / to folow catouns trace!"[10] For some poets, however – those who loved him most – he signaled an all-too-familiar sententiousness, which gave a veneer of erudition to unexceptional thought. In the *Miller's Tale*, for instance, Chaucer famously makes fun of the cuckolded husband, John the carpenter, who "knew nat Catoun, for his wit was rude / That bad men sholde wedde his similitude" [Because he was unlearned, he did not know Cato's maxim which says that a man should marry someone like himself].[11] In this couplet, Chaucer uses knowledge of Cato to distinguish a clerk from a churl, while at the same time poking fun at proverbial good sense.[12]

Cato is quoted fondly and often in *Piers Plowman*, but in nearly every instance his authority is subordinated to his conventionality. This is not to say that the poet has gone beyond him in his studies – on the contrary, Cato remains very present in his thinking. Instead, he serves as a baseline of citation, signaling at once learnedness and its limits. For example, in *Piers Plowman*, Cato invokes an encyclopedic view of learning in which the opinions of various authorities are laid side by side, at the same time that he highlights the ethical disparities among them. Medieval Christian exegetes had recourse to different kinds of authorities: pagan and Christian, Old Testament and New. Each *auctor*, however, was freighted differently and could be used to different ends. Thus, in B.7, Langland weighs Cato's and the theologian Peter Comestor's (d. 1178) thoughts on discriminatory charity against the injunction to give indiscriminately, which the poet attributes to Pope Gregory I (7.71); at the end of the same passus, the dreamer pits Cato's warning against using dreams as evidence against the heavy-weight testimony of the bible in support of dreams (e.g., Joseph and Daniel) (7.150–52). Similarly, at 10.191 ff. Langland sets Christ's injunction to love one's enemies against Cato's pragmatic advice about friendship: if someone deceives you with words, you should do the same to him.

For Chaucer, Cato is "citation lite" because his wisdom is proverbial and therefore eminently citable, but also because he marks the intersection between learning and poetry. His proverbs are pithy, memorable, and, above all, translatable. His wit and sense are lightly transported from Latin hexameter to the English or French rhymed couplet or alliterative long line. At the beginning of B.12, in one of the few passages in *Piers Plowman* in which the poet talks about writing as a vocation, the dreamer tries to follow "Cato's trace" by claiming that "making" – the word that Chaucer reserves for his own literary endeavors – is time well spent. Imaginatif first introduces himself to the dreamer as the penitential faculty that helps people remember their past and imagine their future. Imaginatif then chides the dreamer for wasting his time – "thow medlest thee with makynge" [you mess around with poetry] (12.16) – when he ought to be reciting his Psalter and praying for other people's souls, namely those of his patrons ("and bidde for hem that yveth thee breed," 12.17). The dreamer cites Cato to excuse "making" as, at worst, a harmless, at best, a productive pleasure: as Cato told his son, make sure to mix up pleasure and responsibility ("*Interpone tuis interdum gaudia curis*" 12.22a). It makes sense that the poet would quote Cato at the very moment that his dreamer contemplates the authorial life. The dreamer's excuse is weak, to be sure, yet the link that Langland forges between citation and poetry gives his "making" an ethical force as good as any proverb. Cato's proverbs mark a child's entrance into learning, therefore providing the remedy for later self-reproach ("far too little Latin I learned in my youth"). He quotes Cato to remind us that poetic composition is a first foray into a realm of learning that may, in the end, prove to be redemptive.

Continuing education

Langland's quotations from Cato illustrate his preoccupation with learning as a form: learning confers identity and yields certain knowledge; at the same time, the contexts in which learning is displayed defines who one is and what one needs to know. The quotations from Cato also show that learning is key to the poet's imagining of a "life" not strictly his own. In his debate with the priest, Piers slyly rewrites autobiography as allegory: Abstinence taught him his alphabet and Conscience furthered his education. When Piers's a.b.c. life is placed within the wider frame of the dreamer's learning life, it becomes clear that B.8–12 borrows from two medieval biographical genres. The first is allegorical dream-vision typified by Guillaume de Lorris and Jean de Meun's instant classic, *Le roman de la rose* (*c.*1230–39), as well as by Deguileville's influential rewriting of the *Rose* as penitential allegory, the *Pilgrimage* trilogy (*c.*1330–55). The second is intellectual biography, best known from classic works such as Augustines's *Confessiones* (*Confessions*) (*c.*398) and Peter Abelard's *Historia calamitatum* (*History of [My] Calamities*) (*c.* 1132–33), and instanced in later medieval England by the biography of the mystic Richard Rolle (d.1349); and the autobiographical section of William Thorpe's *Testimony* (1409), an account of a Lollard preacher's interrogation by the Archbishop of Canterbury.

Both allegorical dream-vision and intellectual biography instruct the reader through the experiences of the narrator; both genres portray the narrator's life as an educable one, motivated by desire for knowledge, often derailed by that desire, and studded with moments of self-congratulation and self-reproach. In allegorical dream-vision, the dreamer, usually dull-witted but well-meaning, converses with personifications such as Reason or Old Age, who advise him how to attain a certain goal, such as salvation or seduction.[13] In medieval intellectual (auto)biography, the narrator, usually brilliant but headstrong, retells the story of his education, how he went to school, debated with and rejected his teachers, found a lifelong mentor or source of inspiration, and embraced a new life of knowledge, teaching, or spiritual perfection.

Both genres are highly conventional ways of imagining a life, but their conventions work differently. Allegorical dream-vision provides a mirror of human life and a generic process by which "everyman" should move from ignorance to knowledge or from lack to possession. It is a self-help genre that repays rereading and which, like the ritual of penance, assumes that the reader is always starting over. Intellectual autobiography is a pseudo-legal genre: it makes the case for an exemplary life, and it is authorized by the recorded details of a life.[14]

Langland draws imaginatively from these two genres in passūs 8–12. From allegorical dream-vision he borrows the character of the dreamer, who converses with personifications and is shuttled from one interlocutor to another: Thought agrees to be an intermediary between the dreamer and Wit (8.121–22); Study turns out to be Wit's wife and gives the dreamer tokens with which to approach Clergie and Scripture (10.158–59); the dreamer secures an audience with Clergie and Scripture through his connections with Wit and Study (10.223–25); the dreamer meets Reason and Imaginatif (11.334 and 408). As in similar allegories, Langland's dreamer has an identity – a pilgrim or wandering cleric – which compels him to seek out knowledge or experience, but he always remains, on some level, a personification, the driving force of the Will, the nickname of the poem's putative author. Thus, in passus 8, Thought introduces the dreamer to Wit as Will, the desire to act through reason (Wit), as well as a student requesting information about Dowel: "Here is Wil wolde wite if Wit koude teche hym" [This is Will, who wants to know, if Wit was able to teach him] (8.126). In the mirror of Middle Earth episode in B.11, Old Age and Holiness lament that the dreamer – or the Will, in this case, the sensual appetite – has cast off the governance of Wit in his pursuit of earthly pleasures: "'Alas, eighe!,' quod Elde and Holynesse bothe, / 'That wit shal torne to wrecchednesse for wil to have his likyng!'") ["Alas, oh!" said both Old Age and Holiness "That Wit should be so cast down, so Will can get what he wants"] (11.44–45). Like other medieval allegories, then, *Piers Plowman* charts the mental processes through which one acquires knowledge and learns how to choose for the good.

Piers Plowman departs significantly from other dream-visions, however. For one thing, the personifications in passūs 8–12 do not programmatically teach what they name. Wit neither defines wit, nor does he offer reliable information relevant to that faculty; the dreamer, though willful, is not consistently identifiable with the Will. Imaginatif exemplifies the medieval cognitive faculty the *vis imaginativa*, in the sense that he mediates between the knowledge gained from the physical world (kind wit or kind knowing) and Christian revelation, but he does not deal exclusively in images, as his name might suggest.[15]

Indeed, as the penitential faculty that he declares himself to be, helping the dreamer remember his past and make informed decisions about his future, Imaginatif conspicuously fails to get the poem "on the right track," recollecting for the reader his own spiritual progress. In the waking episode at the beginning of B.13, for instance, the dreamer, for the first time, remembers his dreams: how Fortune left him high and dry, how Old Age menaced him, how friars and priests betray the laity, and how Imaginatif revealed to him the workings of Kind [Nature, God the Creator] (13.5–20). One would expect that the moment the dreamer recalls his dreams, he would impose some order upon them, an exercise crucial for someone who is learning how to save his soul. But his recollections are not the reader's: the dreamer leaves out key characters like Trajan and Scripture, for example, and he attributes the vision of Kind to Imaginatif, when in fact it was Reason who was his guide. The dreamer's account of his own dreams is selective at best; at worst it is a failed penitential exercise.

Notably, too, this section of the poem does not offer the narrative resolution typically found in allegorical dream-visions. Readers may learn something, but the dreamer never reaches a moment of understanding consistent with the advice of his interlocutors; as Nicolette Zeeman cogently argues, B.8–12 do not trace the progress "from a less to a more informed or scholarly state of mind" but rather they enact "the dynamic of understanding and desire in the eager soul."[16] For Langland, cognition is merely one way of portraying a life in learning, and allegorical dream-vision is as a much a form of learning as it is an instance of it. At the beginning of B.11, Scripture's rebuke of the dreamer, "Many are called but few are chosen," thrusts the dreamer into the first of two inner dreams, where he sees, as if through a mirror, the whole course of his life, from lucky youth to wretched old age (5–60). This episode, a brilliantly compressed allegorical dream-vision, shows in miniature how allegory organizes a learning life.

From his second model, intellectual biography, Langland borrows the construction of an educable self within the social nexuses of teaching and learning. Examples can be found in the *vita* of the important mystic Richard Rolle in the *Officium et miracula* (*c.*1380?), probably written in preparation for Rolle's canonization, and in Thorpe's dissenting autobiography in his *Testimony*. Both texts record the moments in which their respective authors take charge of their education, making the learning life the place to fashion new ways of being. According to Rolle's biography, compiled by the nuns of Hampole sometime after his death in 1349, and partly modeled after

Bonaventure's *Life of St. Francis*, the young Rolle was funded to go to Oxford by Thomas Neville, Archdeacon of Durham. But when he turned nineteen, mindful of his death and always drawn to theology rather than secular study, Rolle decided to take up the life of a hermit rather than serve as a beneficed priest or estates administrator, as his family may have intended him to do. He persuaded his sister to give him two of her tunics, a grey and a white, which he cut and sewed until he had produced a costume in which – to his sister's horror – he took on the appearance of a hermit.[17] In his *Testimony*, written several decades later, William Thorpe, pressured by Archbishop Arundel to betray his Lollard colleagues, replaces his expected confession with a lengthy intellectual autobiography. According to Thorpe, his parents and friends spent a lot of money on his education to make him a priest. When he refused to take priestly orders, his kin "menaced" him until he came up with a compromise – that he be permitted to consult "wise priests" about the priestly office. His delighted parents, unaware that Thorpe meant Wycliffite scholars such as Philip Repington, agree to fund the enterprise. The result is a singular self, a professional dissenter who subverts expectations, and whose life in education is a sustained critique of the institutional priesthood.[18]

Like Rolle, Thorpe, and others, Langland's dreamer is an avid but willful learner, who reveres some teachers and questions others. Like him, too, he has an ambivalent relation to traditional institutions. He fitfully wakes into a society in which the conditions of membership include respecting superiors and refraining from criticism. He rejects these conditions and the abuse he receives drives him back from the frame of the poem into the dream: "And some lakkede my lif – allowed it fewe – /And leten me for a lorel and looth to reverencen / Lordes or ladies or any lif ellis" [Some people criticized my lifestyle – few accepted it – /And held me for a fool, and as the sort of person who hated to show reverence to / Lords or ladies, or anybody else] (15.4–6). Like Rolle, too, Langland's dreamer is perceived to be mad, his lunacy sometimes identifying him with exemplary nonconformists like St. Francis, who deserve the compassion of others because they display such admirable disregard for their own wellbeing (see "lunatyk loreles" at C.9.137). At other times, his lunacy, which drives him in and out of dreams, prevents him from achieving the clarity that self-knowledge ought to provide. He awakens from the third vision, for example, "witlees nerhande / And as a freke that fey were, forth gan I walke" [nearly out of my wits /And like a wild man began to roam] (B.13.1–2); and later, in passus 15, he reports that "my wit weex and wanyed til I a fool weere" [my wit waxed and waned until I become a fool] (B.15.3).

For Langland, as for Rolle and Thorpe, a life in learning revolves around key moments of interrogation, in which the narrator either commits to a vocation or chooses a new habit. In two "autobiographical" passages in *Piers Plowman*, the dreamer strenuously defends his life while, at the same time, reflecting upon the nature of a life in learning. In B.12, Imaginatif invites the dreamer to take stock of his life and change its course ("Amende thee while thow myght," 12.10). He urges the dreamer to abandon his "makings" and spend his time praying for patrons. The dreamer initially defends his making as a useful pleasure (see discussion above), but he quickly shifts gears, arguing that composition is necessary until someone explains to him the meaning of Dowel, or, presumably, when the poem itself provides adequate spiritual guidance.

In the second "autobiographical" passage in C.5, the dreamer is interrogated by Reason and Conscience, who accuse him, an able-bodied man, of shirking agricultural labor, as mandated by the Statute of Laborers (1351). Rather than providing a watertight defense of the author's life, as we might expect, the dreamer comically excuses himself with a fictive identity: he is too tall to stoop to labor. As he did with Imaginatif, the dreamer further defends himself by redefining what it means to live a productive life. Like Rolle and Thorpe, he was funded to go to school and discovered that a traditional university career was not the right road to a meaningfully spiritual life. Nowadays he "labors" with prayers and psalms for those who give him food, seeming to squander time by living a life of idleness, but actually investing boldly in his spiritual future by not conforming to social norms.

> When y yong was, many yer hennes,
> My fader and my frendes foende me to scole,
> Tyl y wyste witterly what holy writ menede
> And what is beste for the body, as the boek telleth,
> And sykerost for the soule, by so y wol contenue.
> And foend y nere, in fayth, seth my frendes deyede,
> Lyf that me lykede but in this longe clothes.
> And yf y be labour sholde lyuen and lyflode deseruen,
> That laboure that y lerned best therwith lyuen y sholde.
> *In eadem vocacione in qua vocati estis*   [Ephesians 4.1] (C.5.35–43a)

> [When I was young, many years ago,
> My father and my friends sent me to school,
> Until I understood truly the meaning of scripture,
> And what is best for the body, as the Book explains,
> And surest for the soul, which I will continue to follow.
> And truly, since my friends died, I never found,
> A life that suited me, except [the one] in these long clothes.

And if I must live by labor and earn my sustenance,
I should live by that labor that I learned best:
"In the same vocation in which you were called."]

His greatest hope is that his decision to live a life of exemplary nonconformity will result in a life worthy of being saved: "So hope y to haue of hym
that is almighty /A gobet of his grace, and bigynne a tyme / That alle tymes
of my tyme to profit shal turne" [So I hope to receive from Him who is
almighty /A gobbet of his grace, and reach a moment in my life / In which
all the periods of my life will turn to profit] (C.5.99–101). In this passage,
learning is a vocation taken up by people whose life-work is both a rejection
of traditional expectations of education, and whose notion of a self is
inseparable from the lifelong pursuit of knowledge.

However, where intellectual biography records a coherent and identifiable
self, forged in learning, Langland's dreamer is a pastiche of conventions. The
poet is less interested in developing a coherent life in learning than he is in
the literary markers of a learning life. One example of these markers is
singularity or "visible nonconformity." Like Rolle, for example, the dreamer
is distinctly dressed: in passus 8 he enters the third vision clothed in russet,
the cheapest and coarsest of cloths, which indicates a special condition, like
poverty, or a disposition, such as mourning or abjection. His costume also
recalls the first few lines of the poem, in which the dreamer has assumed the
guise of a sheep ("I shoope me into shroudes as I a sheep were"), and the
habit of a hypocritical hermit, "unholy of works" (Prol. 2–3).

Later in B.13, Hawkyn, an unflattering projection of the dreamer, is
described repeatedly as singular; dressed as a hermit, he submits to no
correction or rule: "And inobedient to ben undernome of any lif lyvynge;
/And so singuler by hymself as to sighte of the peple ... Yhabited as an
heremyte, an ordre by hymselve – Religion saunz rule and resonable
obedience / Lakkynge lettrede men and lewed men bothe" [And unwilling
to be criticized by any living person; /And, in his own opinion, so singular in
the eyes of others ... / Dressed as a hermit, in an order by himself – Religion
without rule and reasonable obedience; / Criticizing educated and ignorant
men both] (13.282–87). Singularity makes someone distinctive, but as the
dreamer's analysis of Hawkyn suggests, it is nearly impossible to be both
singular and praiseworthy. A singular person, simply by making himself
visible, is always on the verge of becoming a bragger, meddler, or hypocrite;
he is always exceeding, and therefore falling short of, that which he or she
ought to be. Rolle's mismatched costume, a "confusam similitudinem
eremitae" ("rough likeness to a hermit"), signals Rolle's rejection of

worldliness, and his invention of a creditable vocation. In *Piers Plowman*, that singular self remains provisional and incomplete: e.g., "*as I* a sheep *were*," "*in the habit of* a hermit unholy of works," "quod I *as a* clerc" (8.20), "*in manere of* a mendynaunt many yer after" (13.3) (my emphases).

The dreamer's singularity corresponds to another marker of intellectual biography: the irrepressible desire to correct others. In the third vision, the poet locates this desire between two oppositional terms, "suffraunce" and "lakking." By "suffraunce," he means integrity or practicing what you preach: suffraunce characterizes the preacher who submits himself to the word of God as disseminated by the institutional church (10.251–52); it also describes teachers who don't disparage others or seek redress. Says Thought, "[Ye wise], suffreth the unwise with yow to libbe, /And with glad wille dooth hem good" [(You wise), allow the unwise to live with you, /And with glad will do them good] (8.93–94, following 2 Corinthians 11:19). To suffer in this way is to follow the example of Christ, who made his life a treatise on suffering and taught his followers how to tolerate the ignorance and cruelty of others: "That theigh thei suffrede al this, God suffrede for us moore / In ensample we sholde do so, and take no vengeaunce / Of oure foes that dooth us falsnesse" [Even if [clerks] were to suffer all this, God suffered for us more /As an example that we should do the same, and take no vengeance / On our foes who do us wrong] (15.260–62). Importantly, to suffer is not simply to endure hardship or abuse; it is also to refuse to seek goods or revenge. A person who suffers is not moved by the behavior or possessions of others and, in social interactions, he is guided by an impartial love (15.173–75). The goal is to strike a balance between regard and disregard, to love sinners and yet maintain an uncritical attitude toward them.

Conversely, to criticize others is to engage in "lakking," a practice inimical to "suffraunce." Cato advises people to give as good as they get – if someone deceives you, you should do the same to them. But, as Dame Study points out, the gospel teaches the opposite, to turn the other cheek (10.191ff): "And alle that lakketh us or lyeth us Oure Lord techeth us to lovye" [Our Lord teaches us to love all those who criticize us or lie to us] (10.205). This tension between lakking and suffraunce presents some troubling questions for the dreamer, and presumably for the poet, who wrote many thousand lines of social critique.[19] How can a preacher suffer on the model of Christ and still take a stand against sin? Is reforming others a higher calling or is it really just "lakking" by a different name? As Clergy points out, a reformer who is guilty of sin runs the risk of turning reform into "lakking" and indicting himself in the process (10.261–62a). Later, in passus 15, Anima condemns the sins of the clergy, but he soon realizes that his criticism sounds suspiciously like "lakking," which is antithetical to true charity: "Neither he blameth ne banneth, bosteth ne preiseth, / Lakketh, ne loseth, ne loketh up sterne" [[Charity] neither blames, nor curses, nor boasts, nor praises, / Criticizes, nor looks askance] (15.252–53). "Suffraunce" and "lakking" act as formal constraints on the learning life. The role a person assumes as a teacher, preacher, or student, and his right to speak out in a given context, are determined by his ability to strike a balance between charity and criticism.

The tension between "suffraunce" and "lakking" comes to a head in B.11, a famously reflexive passus, in which the dreamer tries to figure out what being saved has to do with the desire to know everything about salvation. At the beginning of the passus, the dreamer experiences an "identity crisis": is he a reformer or a critic, a clerk or layman, saved or not, and is the poem itself an insider job, trafficking in clerical anti-clericalism? He criticizes those friars who would rather bury than baptize, the former being more lucrative (11.70–83), but he fears that the friars will admonish him in return for judging his brethren (11.90, citing Matthew 7.1 "*Nolite iudicare quemquam*"). Indignant, the dreamer consults Lewte (Equity), who agrees that true reform requires outspoken critics, and that laymen may feel free to criticize as they see fit, but clergy should maintain the discretion their profession demands (11.101–02). He cautions the dreamer, though, that the dreamer may be imperfect himself, and that he should consider the beam in his own eye before he judges the speck in another's (Matthew 7.3–5).

As Edwin Craun has recently discovered, this exchange between the dreamer and Lewte is derived from a genre of mainstream pastoral literature which Craun calls "critical ecclesiology." This literature encouraged the correction of superiors (for example, by a layperson of a priest, by a priest of a bishop, by anyone of general sinfulness), thereby distributing pastoral power within the community, while at the same time setting up the perimeters of public and private correction.[20] For Langland, this pastoral literature, invoked at a deeply fraught moment in the third vision, may have provided an excuse for a poem which speaks to a variety of audiences – friars, secular priests, bishops, and wealthy laymen – and whose dreamer inhabits a variety of communities – lay and clerical, manor and city, university and parish.

In the exchange between the dreamer and Lewte, the ethics of criticism further highlights the limits of the relationship between learning and salvation. Scripture concurs with Lewte that a critic should first evaluate himself, and she rebukes the dreamer for presuming to judge others when he is imperfect himself. Preaching the Parable of the Feast, at which many were called but few were chosen, she proposes that criticism excludes the critic from salvation, even in cases where the critic's intentions are perfectly good (11.111–14). Because no one is perfect, few can be saved, and thus the desire to correct only underscores the likeliness of exclusion from salvation. Scripture's rebuke throws the dreamer into paroxysms of "weer," a state of spiritual anxiety worthy of Augustine or Dante: "Al for tene of hir text trembled myn herte, /And in a weer gan I wexe, and with myself to dispute / Wheither I were chose or noght chose" [Distressed by her text, my heart trembled, /And I became perplexed and disputed with myself / whether I was chosen or not] (11.115–17). The dreamer's "weer" stems from a number of interrelated causes: the spiritual costs of criticizing others, the correctness of his position on baptism, and overwhelming fear of damnation.

In this scene, the poet juxtaposes the ethics of criticism with a spiritual problem about learning He explores this juxtaposition further in the vision of Kind which follows, in which the dreamer marvels at the wonders of the natural world:

> I seigh the sonne and the see and the sond after,
> And where that briddes and beestes by hir make thei yeden,
> Wilde wormes in wodes, and wonderful foweles
> With fleckede fetheres and of fele colours.
> Man and his make I myghte se bothe;
> Poverte and plentee, both pees and werre,
> Blisse and bale – bothe I seigh at ones,
> And how men token Mede and Mercy refused.   (11.326–33)
>
> [I saw the sun, and the sea, and then the sand,
> And how birds and beasts went forth with their mates:
> Wild snakes in the woods, and wonderful birds
> With flecked feathers of many colors.
> I could see both man and his mate,
> Poverty and plenty, peace and war,
> Bliss and bale – I saw them all at once,
> And how men accepted bribes and refused mercy.]

The dreamer wonders at the ingenuity of birds' nests, beyond the ken of any human artisan (11.344–49). This lyrical creation should lead the dreamer to the knowledge and love of God, and yet, as Zeeman has argued, for Langland's dreamer, nature is the site of both revelation and of alienation.[21] His vision of creatures moves him not to love the Creator (Kind), as it should, but rather to construct wrong-headed analogies between humans and animals: as the dreamer asks Reason a few lines later, if the gorgeous diversity of God's creation implicates both men and beasts, is it fair that they are held to different standards, with animals governed by instinct and human beings by free will? Reason objects to the dreamer's impertinent "lakking": "'Forthi I rede [the],' quod Reson, 'how rule thi tonge better, / And er thow lakke my lif, loke if thyn be to preise . . . / Ech a lif wolde be laklees – leeve thow non other'" ["Thus I counsel you," said Reason, "that you rule your tongue better / And before you criticize what I do, examine yourself . . . / Everybody would choose to be without fault – don't think otherwise"] (11.385–86, 389). Reason tells the dreamer that if he wants to be saved, he should draw a lesson from divine sufferance:

> And Reson arated me, and seide, "Recche thee nevere
> Why I suffre or noght suffre – thiself hast noght to doone.
> Amende thow it if thow myght, for my tyme is to abide.
> Sufferance is a soverayn vertue, and a swift vengeaunce
> Who suffreth moore than God?" quod he; "no gome, as I leeve.
> He myghte amende in a minute while al that mysstandeth,
> Ac he suffreth for som mannes goode and so is oure bettre".
>
> (11.375–81)

> [And Reason berated me, and said, "Don't bother yourself with
> Why I suffer or not – it has nothing to do with you!
> Reform yourself if you can, for my job is to wait.
> Sufferance is a sovereign virtue, and a swift vengeance.
> Who suffers more than God?" he said, "no one, as far as I know.
> He might instantaneously amend all that is amiss,
> But he tolerates [it] for man's good, and we are better off for it."]

Although God, through his suffering on the Cross, instantaneously erased the debt of original sin, he generally follows a non-interventionist policy. And just as God tolerates seeming inequities, so the dreamer should adopt an uncritical attitude both toward divine providence and toward fellow human beings. As Imaginatif explains, Adam ruled paradise until the day he "mamelede aboute mete and entremeted to knowe / The wisedom and the wit of God" [babbled about food and interfered in order to know / God's wisdom and purpose] (11.416–17). Likewise the dreamer's salvation is compromised by his intellectual hubris, which Imaginatif construes as criticism of the divine plan: "thow with thi rude speche / Lakkedest and losedest thyng that longed noght the to don" [you with your rude speech / Criticize and belittle things that have nothing to do with you] (11.418–19). If "lakking" undermines the learning life, it also resembles the way the first parents sought knowledge out of bounds.

In the mouths of lords

Learning, for the poet, is not just about being a trained cleric in relationship to other clerics, who live their lives inside or outside the university, enclosed or at large, in a chancery or a pulpit, who spar with friars or preach the fundamentals of the faith. Learning is also about being a clerk in close proximity to a lay lord, and, as I will argue, in B.9 and 10 the intimate relationship between lord and clerk imposes productive limits on the learning life. This relationship also forces the poet to reconsider the entertainment value of learned discourse. Throughout *Piers Plowman*, the poet frequently calls on an aristocratic audience ("ye lordes") to defend its prerogatives. He chastises lords and ladies for alienating land to monasteries (10.303–10; 15.321–24); he warns them to resist the flattery of friars (3.69–75); and he appeals to them to correct wayward clergy (15.562–65). The poet is sympathetic to clerks in the employ of wealthy laymen, who pray for benefactors, as the dreamer does for a living in B.12, or who are asked to extend hospitality to transients and freeloaders on their lord's behalf, a practice which the poet dissects in C.9. It is an unfortunate custom, he says, that those who serve in the retinues of lords and ladies give gold to minstrels, and he puts up with this practice, though he would much rather see the rich relieve holy men (C.9.131–36). Notably, however, it is in the section on learning (B.8–10) where lordship figures most prominently. These passūs foreground learning as a service to a lay lord, and imagine lordship as a form of intellectual work. As we will see, the relationship between lord and clerk enables new ways of thinking through big theological questions at the same time that it sets limits on learning about salvation.

The poem portrays the dreamer as an itinerant cleric, likely in minor orders, who is familiar with medieval academe but who, like Rolle in the *Officium*, has distanced himself from it. Like Rolle, too, the dreamer – and the poet – has a profound connection to the noble household. The poet continually returns to the ethics of singing for one's supper. He wants to know what audience to address, which subjects to speak about, and what it means to speak in error. These questions are located in the public intimacies of the hall, leading up to Conscience's feast in B.13, in which the dreamer, seated humbly at a side table with Patience, rails against a doctor of divinity who, honored on the dais, stuffs himself with blancmange. Significantly, the biblical parable that runs throughout this section of the poem is the Parable of the Feast (Matthew 22:2–14; Luke 14:16–24), in which a rich man (in Matthew, a king) plans a (wedding) feast, is spurned by his friends, and subsequently orders his servants to recruit guests from the streets. In Matthew, these recruits are both "good and evil," and at least one is underdressed for the occasion: many are called but few are chosen. In Luke's version, the street people are the poor, lame, and blind. Langland uses the parable to explore several interlocking subjects: the difficulty of winning heaven, the nature of true discipleship, and the importance of giving alms. At the same time, he uses the parable to think about the hall as a discursive space organized by the values of secular lordship: courtesy and prudence, magnanimity and freedom.

Langland's presentation of learning in the hall strikingly resembles that of his younger contemporary, John Trevisa, whose translations of major Latin works laid the groundwork for a vigorous English prose and who enjoyed the patronage of the powerful baron Thomas of Berkeley. Berkeley might have funded Trevisa's education at Queen's College, Oxford; later he employed him on the Berkeley estates, where Trevisa served as chaplain, eventually installing him as vicar of St. Mary's, Berkeley. One of Trevisa's original works is a treatise on translation, "The Dialogue Between a Lord and a Clerk" (*c*.1387), which served as the prologue to his translation of the *Polychronicon*, an influential Latin history. In the "Dialogue," a lord debates a clerk on whether it is fitting to translate the *Polychronicon* into English. The Clerk protests that the kinds of people who need to know the *Polychronicon* already know Latin and therefore do not require an English translation. The Lord replies that it is he, a lord, who arbitrates need, and he has deemed knowledge of the *Polychronicon* a basic one. Later, he reminds the Clerk that, throughout history, the transmission of learning – including biblical translations and theological treatises – has depended on the initiative of noble patrons. Learning, insists the Lord, is a noble service, underwritten by lords and performed by clerks.[22]

Like Trevisa, Langland considers learning to be a form of service and, also like Trevisa, he wonders what happens when a clerk introduces academic topics into the lay household: which topics make for appropriate dinner conversation? The poet tends to idealize monastic life and criticizes secular clerks like Trevisa who get sidetracked as administrators on estates and waste time arbitrating disputes ("lovedayes," 10.306), buying up property (a "lond buggere," 10.306), and riding and hunting (with "houndes at his ers," 10.308), the specialty of Chaucer's Monk. Langland believes that prayer and pastoral care are appropriate activities for all professional religious. Ideally, too, the religious life should be independent and stable, free from the constraints of patronage, travel, or family. The poet admires the friars' dedication to teaching but despises the competition for alms and social-climbing that characterizes mendicant life. At the same time, he finds it very difficult to imagine a life in learning outside of service and dependence.

In passus 10, Dame Study puts the question of secular learning, as it were, "on the table." She castigates clerks (like Wit) who throw pearls before swine, and who "lede lordes" (10.22) down the primrose path for personal gain rather than sharing true wisdom, which might go unrewarded. Such clerks flatter lords to line their own pockets, and they do so by drawing them into dangerous theological speculation. Theology is not appropriate dinner entertainment, nor is it appropriate for lay lords to style themselves theologians. Indeed, clerks commit a sacrilege when they encourage lords to discuss theological matters that do not concern them, and which, for Dame Study, even constitute an object of study in excess of Study proper: "The moore I muse therinne, the mystier it semeth" [The more I think about it, the mistier [theology] seems] (10.183). In the mouths of lords and their clerks, philosophical propositions start to sound suspiciously like jokes, as for example the Trinitarian riddle, "how two slowe the thridde":

Ac if thei carpen of Crist, thise clerkes and thise lewed,
Atte mete in hir murthes whan mynstrals beth stille,
Thanne telleth thei of the Trinite [how two slowe the thridde]
And bryngen forth a balled reson, and taken Bernard to witnesse,
And puten forth presumpcion to preve the soothe.
Thus thei dryvele at hir deys the deitee to knowe,
And gnawen God with the gorge whanne hir guttes fullen.   (10.51–57)

[But if these clerks and laypeople speak about Christ
For entertainment at dinner, when minstrels are still,
Then they tell a story about the Trinity, how two slew the third,
And they make specious arguments, and cite St. Bernard (of Clairvaux) as witness,
And they speak presumptively to make their case.
Thus they speak drivel at their dais when they discuss God,
And they gobble down God when their bellies are full.]

In this passage, intellectual presumption has become the currency of the hall; it is a form of excessive consumption that takes place when dinner is over and "mynstrals beth stille" (10.52). To speak inappropriately is to overeat, and such improper speech is like a ritual out-of-place, as if one were to gobble down the sacramental body of Christ ("thei . . . gnawen God with the gorge") (compare 10.66, 70).

The office of a lord, continues Study, includes the prudent management of entertainment. A lord should dine at home and in the hall, where he is in a position to be most generous to his retainers and to the poor; he should not "fare as a fithelere or a frere to seke festes" [Go like a fiddler or friar seeking feasts] (10.94). Likewise, if presumption means consumption of learning in excess of what the household requires, the lord should monitor the conversation at the dinner table. Household books, such as Robert Grosseteste's *Rules* or Walter of Henley's *Husbandry*, explain that lords maintain their honor when they administrate their estates effectively. To do so, they must familiarize themselves with all the services performed on their estates, from household accounting to the farrowing of pigs. Above all, a lord should supervise the services in the hall, from the ladling of the ale to the decibel of talk at the side tables. Grosseteste advises a lord or lady that he or she "be seated at all times in the middle of the high table, that your presence as lord or lady is made manifest to all and that you may see plainly on either side all the service and all the faults."[23] In *De regimine principum* (*On the Governance of Princes*), another text translated by Trevisa, Giles of Rome similarly urges his princely reader to take charge of the table, to suppress tales and jokes (in the French translation, "trop de paroles et trop de jangle"),[24] and to arrange that someone read aloud the customs of the realm, lives of saintly ancestors, and stories of great rulers.[25]

Lords and clerks, says Langland's Study, ought to discuss exemplary persons, whom medieval lords should strive to imitate. She gives the example of Tobit from the Book of Tobit, a secular lord praised for his obedience, almsgiving and patient suffering, who was often quoted in proverb collections and whose story was rendered into Anglo-Norman as *La vie de Tobie*.[26] Dame Study's ideal lord might have possessed a manuscript like Oxford, Jesus College MS 29, a thirteenth-century West Midlands manuscript, which contains several Anglo-Norman works, including Guillaume le Clerc's *Vie de Tobie*, as well as the early debate poem, the *Owl and the Nightingale*, and some English religious lyrics, among other texts.[27] Tobit was a man, says Dame Study, who, had good household values, who spent like a man, and didn't ask questions (10.85–89). "Swich lessons lordes sholde lovye to here / And how he myghte moost meynee manliche fynde" [Lords should love to hear these kinds of lessons / And how he might generously provide for the greatest household] (10.92–93).

As Trevisa would surely agree, it is good policy to flatter the intelligence of lords, but Langland is conflicted on this point: lords should not be encouraged to delve into matters that do not concern them, yet lordly attention to intellectual conversation gives learning both an occasion and a voice. From this perspective, the aristocratic hall, with its investments in service and performance, offers a way for English poetry to serve not only as a repository of Christian wisdom but also as a vehicle for theological debate outside the university. In this way, too, the poet's critique of presumption in the hall allows him to pursue theology as a poetic subject. In fact, as he shows in B.9 and 10, the minute you picture lords debating theology in the hall, you realize that moral theology relies upon frameworks of special interest to lay lords. Finally, putting theology in the mouths of lords exposes the limits of theological conversation, both the limits of what should be discussed, and the limits of the subject.

For example, the subject of evil in medieval Christian thought relies upon metaphors of wedlock, heredity, and generation. If medieval lords were, however outrageously, to debate the nature of evil, the debate would likely be shaped by their practical experiences with marriage. In B.9, for example, Wit delivers a long sermon on the nature of good and evil, a sermon sympathetic to the perspective of lay lords, and therefore exactly the kind of sermon the poet might be expected to criticize. Wit begins with the concept of "inwit" or the ability to make good moral choices, which he compares to the ability to consent in law: those who are empowered to consent are those who can protect themselves from the temptations of the devil, flesh, and world. Only those prohibited from consenting in law – the mentally ill, widows, and orphans, those who supposedly require the strong arm of a male guardian – are morally vulnerable (9.67–72). Wit's comparison between legal consent and free will is misleading; after all, many people who have the power to choose do not choose for the good, and an orphan who lacks the legal capacity to alienate land can nonetheless live a righteous life.

Clearly, Wit's sermon on good and evil is conditioned by the interests of his prospective audience, lay lords. Just as Wit is willing to conflate legal and moral consent, so he is keen to resist the more determinist strains of Christian doctrine, which he considers an affront to the dignity and freedom of lords. His solution is to make marriage and reproduction the explanation for the origins of evil. Wit first defines Dowel (doing well) as marriage solemnly contracted between a couple of the same status, whose union has been approved by their fathers and friends (9.115–16). Next he argues that if doing well is wedlock, doing evil must refer to poorly arranged marriages, and their unfortunate progeny, as for example, couples mismatched in age, character, or rank (9.155ff.). It is often the case, observes Wit, that children exhibit the same bad qualities as their parents, so evil must originate in marriage and procreation. The proof, he says, is written in the Psalms: "Of swiche synfulle sherewes the Sauter maketh mynde: *Concepit dolorem et perperit iniquitatem*" [Of such sinful wretches, the

Psalter makes mention, "The (sinner) has conceived sorrow and brought forth wickedness"] [Psalm 7:15] (9.122–22a). According to Wit, this model of sin is illustrated by biblical history before the Flood: because Cain, a fratricide, was conceived by his parents at the wrong time – during Eve's menses – he turned out badly, and what is more, he transmitted his sinfulness to future generations: "Here aboughte the barn the belsires giltes / And alle for hir forefadres thei ferden the werse" [Thus the child received the father's sins, /And everyone who came after fared the worse on account of their ancestors] (9.143–44). Only Noah's Flood could cleanse the cursed blood caused by Cain] (9.136).[28]

Theologically, Wit's sermon has some glaring problems. First, by reading salvation history through marriage, Wit has left out the main events in the history of sin: original sin and the Atonement. In his reading of Genesis, as mentioned above, Wit blames Cain's wickedness on intercourse during menstruation, but he passes over the first disobedience: Adam and Eve's overweening appetite for knowledge. If one reads the bible forward, as Wit does here, one might conclude that Adam and Eve's original sinfulness was transmitted "genetically" as bad character: Cain was just a bad seed from a rotten apple, whose corrupted genus was drowned in the Flood. But if one reads the bible "backward" through the Atonement, it becomes clear that all human beings are tainted by original sin. Thanks to the Atonement, a baptized infant starts with a clean slate – an idea often figured allegorically in medieval commentaries by the Flood[29] – although no one can subsequently choose for the good without divine aid. There is, in other words, a crucial difference between bad character (for example, a predisposition to commit fratricide), which may or may not be a family trait, and which may be prevented through arranged marriage, and original sin, which corrupted the ability of all human beings to produce righteous descendants, but which is *not* genetically inherited.

Wit admits that his version of antediluvian history (Cain to Noah), with its emphasis on the biological order of sin, contradicts the testimony of Christian scripture (9.145), which says that sin is *not* inherited through one's ancestors. Here Wit quotes the crucial verse from Ezekiel 18.20, "filius non portabit" [the son shall not bear [the iniquity of the father, nor shall the father bear the iniquity of his son]] (9.145b). Medieval theologians traditionally used this verse to describe the history of sin after the Atonement, when Christ had erased the debt of original sin, but Wit is unwilling to distinguish between original sin and moral character, because he is anxious to prove that history is no burden to lords. What happened in the past does not constrain the ability of people to choose in the present. Rather, history

profits noble layfolk: Genesis teaches them that, if they marry the right
people and have sex at the right times, they will not beget monsters. By
making this peculiar argument, Wit stresses the complicity of lordly values
and theological discourse. As Chaucer's Wife of Bath was so eager to prove,
the bible can be glossed through the practical experience of marriage.

The poet lets this lecture play out, but Wit's assumption that lords bring
something to the theological table surfaces once again and is met with firm
resistance. Dame Study rebukes Wit, complaining that lords, when they
hobnob with clerks, end up asking the wrong questions or "the whyes of
God almyghty" (10.124). Lords ask, for instance, why God allows sin to
exist, and why He "let" Adam eat the apple in the first place (10.107–14). Lay
lords and their retainers should not discuss such abstruse topics, however
much they seem to have a special purchase on them. Take original sin, for
example. Lords chafe at the burden of original sin because it seems to
undermine their freedom to choose for the good and, by association, their
freedom, their self-determination as members of a non-servile class. Lords
complain, for example, that spiritual heredity is unjust and muster specious
arguments against it:

> "Here lyeth youre lore," thise lordes gynneth dispute,
> "Of that ye clerkes us kenneth of Crist by the Gospel:
> *Filius non portabit iniquitatem patris* [Ezekiel 18.20]
> Why sholde we that now ben, for the werkes of Adam
> Roten and torende? Reson wolde it nevere!
> *Unusquisque onus suum portabit . . .*"   [Galatians 6.5] (10.111–14a)

> ["Here your teaching errs," these lords begin to dispute,
> "According to what you have told us Christ says in the Gospel:
> 'The son shall not carry the wickedness of the father.'
> Why should we who live now, on account of Adam's works,
> Be destroyed and tormented? It doesn't make sense!
> 'Each person bears his own burden'."]

In B.9, Wit quotes *filius non portabit* as a scriptural counterpoint to his own
argument that children inherit family traits; in doing so, he ignores the
implications of this verse for the doctrine of original sin. In the passage
quoted above, lords quote *filius non portabit*, in a slightly different context,
to refute the doctrine of original sin ("the werkes of Adam"). Like Wit, they
are concerned about their freedom: why should they be held accountable for
the sins of their ancestors? Are they not each of them responsible for
themselves? What lords refuse to grasp is a subtle point that medieval
theologians worked hard to make, that original sin is not something that

human beings inherit from Adam or from their ancestors; rather, it is a condition of unjust human nature. The Atonement alleviated the burden of original sin, but it put in its place a new understanding of how human nature is unjust as a result of the Fall. When we say that we do not bear the burden of our fathers, we mean only that the sins of our ancestors are not imputed to us: our father's sin is his own, and Adam is likewise responsible for his.

Still, it cannot be denied that the discourse of original sin is predicated on the idea of heredity: the goods, the character, and the merit or demerits that people inherit from their forebears. And medieval lordship, bound up with questions of inheritance and descent, cannot help but offer some valuable insight into the theology of sin. For instance, in his classic treatise *De conceptu virginali et originali peccato (On the Conception of the Virgin and Original Sin)*, Anselm of Canterbury concedes that ancestors influence their descendants even regarding the "goods of the soul." In one powerful statement, he writes,

> I do not deny that because of the positive merits of ancestors many and great benefits of body and of soul are imparted to their offspring. [Nor do I deny that] because of the sins of ancestors their children and grandchildren "unto the third and fourth generation," and perhaps even beyond, are scourged with various tribulations in this life and lose the goods – even goods of the soul – which they might have obtained through their ancestors, had these latter been just. (It would take too long to introduce examples of such cases here.) But I do maintain that original sin is present equally in all infants who are conceived naturally – just as the sin of Adam, which is the cause of infants being born in original sin, pertains equally to them all.[30]

In the final analysis, says Anselm, it is nearly impossible to divorce sinfulness from the moral or material inheritance received from ancestors. According to Dame Study, theological debate should be checked at the door of the aristocratic hall, yet, as *Piers Plowman* shows, the hall also establishes productive limits to learning about salvation. It warns of the dangers of learning out of place, of presumption and error, but it also highlights aristocratic values, like moral inheritance, from which Christian theology is derived. It is perhaps no surprise, then, that the hall is where Langland imagines an ideal learning at once morally fit and properly expressed, because it is there that a learned poet can perform.

Langland's fascination with learning in the hall recalls a story from the biography of Rolle in the *Officium et miracula*. In the story, a squire named John de Walton, whose sons recognize Rolle from Oxford, invites him to dinner, after hearing him give a sermon at a local church. Rolle refuses to enter the dining hall, waiting for an invitation to sit at the table. He quotes from Luke 14.10, "Friend, go up higher." When the squire discovers Rolle hiding out in an inferior room he places him above his own sons at the table ("armiger ipsum supra proprius filius collocavit ad mensam"), but disconcertingly, Rolle keeps such perfect silence at dinner that not one word proceeds from his mouth. Rolle tries to make a quick getaway after everyone has eaten, but the squire insists this is not customary behavior ("hoc non esse consuetudinis"), and pressures him to stay. When the meal is over, the squire, seeking to have a private colloquium with him, detains him until everyone else has gone and interrogates him, asking him whether he is the son of William Rolle. Reluctantly, Rolle discloses his identity, and the squire makes him a permanent houseguest, setting him up as a hermit in his own home, and providing him with clothing, food and all the necessities of life.[31] In this passage, Rolle's post-collegiate vocation takes shape with his refusal to engage in dinner conversation. He uses the conventions of the hall – the discourse expected of clerical guests – to call attention to his own specialness, his weird reticence making him the subject of an after-dinner conversation, i.e., the mutually flattering private exchange between himself and the squire.

Like Rolle, Langland is critical of these conversations, as much as he enjoys reporting them, and he, too, acknowledges that a clerical vocation, however outstanding, is always, in some way, indebted to patronage. In Luke, Christ advises his followers to choose the lowest seat at a feast. It is better to be raised than lowered in status: friend, go up higher! In this passage, Christ is talking about discipleship (to choose Christ is to lower oneself socially in order to be raised spiritually), but like Rolle, he is also talking about the value of noble service.

Throughout the poem the poet tries to define a learned discourse that is pedagogically and morally sound but at the same time supports the relationship between lord and clerk. Like Trevisa, he proposes the aristocratic hall as the site for such a discourse, a place where learning can be performed as a service to a lay lord. To be a guest of a medieval lord is to earn one's supper by performing for his pleasure. It is in the hall that the lord's meinée, his household officers and staff, are assembled and where he exercises lordly virtues; as the poet laments, "Elenge is the halle, ech day in the wike / Ther the lord ne the lady liketh noght to sitte" [Wretched is the hall, each day of the week / Where neither lord nor lady likes to sit] (10.96–97). It is in the hall, moreover, where the lord is judged for his generosity to members of his household and to itinerant religious, scholars, and the poor.

In passūs 8–10, the poet discovers in minstrelsy a trope for performance-as-service, and the figure for an ideal learning which is neither presumptive nor errant. Rather than banishing clerks from the hall, Langland proposes minstrelsy as an alternative to intellectual presumption and as an image for godly speech. For the poet, to be sure, minstrelsy is a questionable occupation, even a waste of resources that would be better spent on education or the poor. In the Prologue, the dreamer supposes that making people happy is fine as it goes – minstrels "geten gold with hire glee – synnelees, I leeve" (Prol. 34) – so long as "glee" does not devolve into total buffoonery (Prol. 35–37). In passus 13, however, Hawkyn acknowledges that minstrelsy by its very nature involves fiddling and farting, playing the pipe, and telling tall tales:

> Couthe I lye and do men laughe, thanne lacchen I sholde
> Outher mantel or moneie amonges lordes mynstrals.
> Ac for I kan neither taboure ne trompe ne telle no gestes,
> Farten ne fithelen at festes, ne harpen,
> Jape ne jogele ne gentilliche pipe,
> Ne neither saille ne saute ne synge with the gyterne,
> I have no goode giftes of thise grete lordes.   (13.229–35)

> [If I knew how to lie and make men laugh, then I, among the lord's minstrels,
> Would rake in both mantle and money.
> But because I can neither play drum or trumpet, nor recite *gestes*,
> Nor fart, nor fiddle, nor play the harp at feasts,
> Nor jest, nor juggle, nor pleasingly pipe,
> Nor skip about, nor tumble, nor sing to the guitar
> I have no good gifts from these great lords.]

As Hawkyn explains, minstrelsy is a suspect form of the active life, and he prides himself at being unsuccessful at it, receiving neither robes nor furred gowns from the many lords he serves.

The poet, too, insists that "lordes and ladies and legates of Holy Chirch" spend too freely on jesters, flatterers, and liars (13.422–23) when they ought to be helping poor people.

> Clerkes and knyghtes welcometh kynges minstrales,
> And for love of hir lord litheth hem at festes;
> Much moore, me thynketh, riche men sholde
> Have beggeres before hem, the whiche ben Goddes minstrales...
>   (13.437–40)

> [Clerks and knights welcome the king's minstrels,
> And for love of their lord hire them at feasts.
> That much more, it seems to me, rich men should arrange
> To have beggars before them, who are God's minstrels.]

At the same time, minstrelsy figures an ideal form of clerical service precisely because it does not exceed that which pertains to the hall. Minstrelsy was an integral part of the noble household throughout the later Middle Ages. In many great households, trumpeters announced courses or a guest's arrival; musicians played and sang during feasts, which were often followed by juggling, pageants, and poetic recitations. This kind of entertainment was distinguished from the religious services performed by chaplains, but the clerical staff were sometimes excellent performers in their own right and participated in household ceremonies. Although minstrels often traveled to other households, they tended to be identified with the household of one lord or lady and often wore his or her livery. They were sometimes very highly paid with cloaks, hoods, money, even property. In 1318 Thomas of Lancaster, for example, paid the large sum of £13 for five cloths to dress his minstrels.[32]

For the poet, minstrelsy is attractive, because it is a performance that fits its context: it is intrinsic to the ceremonial of the household and stays within the limits of what is deemed to be appropriate consumption. The poet complains that minstrels are overcompensated, whereas those who talk about Tobit, or the apostles, or Jesus's suffering are undervalued (10.30–36). And yet, he recognizes that minstrelsy helps conceptualize the values of the hall. In the *Officium*, Rolle's refusal to entertain his host kickstarts his new vocation as a hermit. Langland, too, finds it difficult to describe a moral alternative to learned conversation that is not a retreat from speaking or writing. For example, Wit defines Dobest as a person who "withdraweth hym by daye and by nyghte / To spille any speche or any space of tyme" [prevents himself night and day / From wasting any speech or amount of time] (9.97–98). And yet the poet places an ideal form of learning as service somewhere between the playing and silence of minstrels. When minstrels are still, clerical retainers make jokes about the Trinity and speculate wildly with their lords about the origins of evil. It is through the playing of minstrels, however, that the poet imagines a learned discourse properly performed.

This is a classic Langlandian strategy: to denigrate an occupation like minstrelsy, which seems on the face of it frivolous or deplorable, and then rehabilitate it for a new purpose. The poet complains that lay lords and their clerical retainers "konne na moore mystralcie ne musik men to glade / Than Munde the millere of *Multa fecit Deus*" [know no more minstrelsy nor music to make men happy / than Munde the miller knows of "God has done great things"] [Psalm 39:6] (10.43–44); that is, they don't know wholesome conversation any more than a peasant knows his psalms.

To waste speech, says the poet, is to be like a tavern-going minstrel with his untuned fiddle (10.155–56). By contrast, well-dispensed speech is "Goddes gleman" (God's player) and a "game of hevene" (9.102). Although true comfort comes not from musicians but from godly speech, minstrelsy offers the perfect metaphor for spiritually edifying discourse:

> Forthi I rede yow riche [th]at reveles whan ye maketh,
> For to solace youre soules, swiche minstrales to have –
> The povere for a fool sage sittynge at th[i] table,
> And a lered man to lere thee what Oure Lord suffred
> For to save thi soule from Sathan thyn enemy
> And fithele thee, withoute flaterynge, of Good Friday the storye,
> And a blynd man for a bourdeour or a bedrede womman
> To crie a largesse tofore Oure Lord your good loos to shewe.
>
> (13.442–49)

> [Therefore I counsel you rich, when you host parties,
> To invite the kind of minstrels who will comfort your souls:
> The poor man like a wise fool sitting at your table,
> And a learned man to teach you what our Lord suffered,
> In order to save your soul from Satan your enemy
> And perform for you, without flattering, the story of Good Friday,
> And a blind man for a jester or a bedridden woman
> To proclaim your reputation in front of Our Lord.]

Three "minstrels" comfort a rich man at his death: the poor man as a "fool sage," the learned man who instructs him through scriptural stories, and the blind and bedridden folk who proclaim his fame to God. If learning in the hall is a question of hiring the right "minstrels," then learning might have the ability to save.

Extreme learning

(Trajan)

In B.10, Scripture argues that rich men cannot win their "eritage in hevene" (341) without the grace and mercy of God. The dreamer, like a scholar, disputes against Scripture ("'*Contra*' quod I, 'by Crist! That I can repreve,'" 343) that baptism saves all Christians, but Scripture disagrees, arguing that baptism alone confers salvation only *in extremis*, among Saracens and Jews, in which case a non-Christian "for his lele bileve, whan he the lif tyneth, / Have the heritage of hevene as any man Cristene" [for his true belief, when he loses his life / Shall have the heritage of heaven, as much as any

Christian man] (10.347–48). Christians require something in addition to baptism, says Scripture: they need to perform works of charity, through which, by their example, they might convert the heathen.

Saracens and Jews are the first in a series of figures that test the extremes – the limits and constraints – of salvation theology. These test cases, which include the Roman emperor Trajan (98–117 CE), the thief on the Cross, and pre-Christian poets and philosophers such as Solomon and Aristotle, bear witness to God's mercy and justice. They show that God, through his absolute power (what he is capable of but refrains from doing) very occasionally overrides the system that he has designed through his ordinate power (what he has decreed). These cases thus define the norms as well as the exceptions of that system. For instance, the thief on the Cross, justified at the point of death, proves the saving power of faith and the efficacy of the New Law. At the same time, these exceptional figures may be used to change the norm or reveal inequities within the system. Why should a thief be saved? Do good works count for nothing? And is it fair that the Jews, who rejected Christ, should be automatically saved through baptism?

Exceptional figures, in other words, are critical points of intersection between theology and dialectic. They can be used to illustrate doctrine at the same time that they can be used to support conflicting and sometimes extreme positions. They are also forms of learning that test human knowledge about salvation. In legal terms, these figures might be called hard cases because they test the limits of doctrine and threaten to create new rules. At the same time, they are examples of theological equity, cases which expose the inadequacy of bodies of law in the attainment of justice. Finally, these exceptional figures, teetering on the brink of salvation, are figures with whom any sinner may sympathize, but especially the scholar, whose desire to learn coincides with his special need for grace.

In B.11, Scripture warns the dreamer that many are called but few are chosen, a verse that implies both the arbitrariness of divine selection and the obligation of human beings to perform good works. The dreamer is shaken by her warning but quickly recovers, placing his confidence once more in baptism. Baptism is attractive to him because it is both inclusive and irrevocable; it is a function of God's ordinate power and it therefore signifies an inviolable contract between God and humanity: Christ called everyone, says the dreamer, including the Saracens and Jews, and those who answered his call can never renounce their Christianity. The dreamer perversely compares baptism to un-freedom: just as a bondsman can never make a charter, or sell his property, without his lord's permission, so a baptized Christian can never act independently of God. Like a churl, a Christian can get into debt, even run away from "home," but the lord's men, Reason and Conscience, will eventually catch up to him and cast him into prison until he confesses his misdeeds (B.11.126). This analogy is meant to locate solace in abjection; and for many medieval writers, service, whether voluntary or compulsive, was a strain of piety from which Langland was not immune.

The Emperor Trajan abruptly interrupts the dreamer ("baw for bokes!" 11.140), contesting the idea that baptism is a precondition for salvation. According to the medieval book of saints' lives, the *Legenda aurea* (*The Golden Legend*, c.1260), Pope Gregory the Great (c.540–604), having learned that the Emperor Trajan avenged the death of a widow's son, prayed for the salvation of this virtuous pagan. Hearing Gregory's prayer, God agrees to save Trajan from the perpetual pain of hell.[33] Trajan's story, as an exceptional case, proves the absolute power of God to make exceptions within the system he has ordained, and testifies to his boundless mercy and to the intercessory power of his saints. But in medieval literature, the story also became an occasion to debate the fine points of Trajan's salvation: did a baptismal ritual, in fact, take place? Was Trajan brought back to life or did he remain in hell but cease to suffer pain? Through feats of clerical ingenuity, in other words, Trajan's case might illustrate the rule rather than serving as the exception that proves the rule.[34]

Exceptional figures like Trajan appealed to all kinds of writers, in part because of the interesting theological controversies provoked by these figures, and in part because of the perspective that they offered on Christian history. For example, *St. Erkenwald*, a late fourteenth-century alliterative poem about an Anglo-Saxon bishop, borrows some of the details of Trajan's story to dramatize the relationship between pre-Christian and post-Christian English history. In the poem, a miraculously preserved corpse is exhumed from the crypt of St. Paul's Cathedral. The corpse speaks, revealing that he was once a pagan judge in Celtic Britain, renowned for his virtue. Despite his illustrious career, however, his soul remains in darkness and his body intact. Upon hearing this speech, St. Erkenwald cries. His tears effectively baptize the judge, whose soul ascends to heaven and body turns to dust. In this story, the virtuous pagan defies the temporal limits of salvation by linking medieval England to its pagan past.

Unlike the *Erkenwald*-poet, Langland is uninterested in representing the ambiguities of Trajan's exceptional salvation; he is quite certain, in fact, that Trajan was saved. The poet is also strangely uninterested in the technicalities of the story, when Trajan lived with respect to Christ or Gregory, or what his redemption might have involved. Instead, he is intrigued with the way that exceptional cases like Trajan's serve as a form of learning:

Ac thus leel love and lyvyng in truthe
Pulte out of peyne a panynym of Rome.
Yblissed be truthe that so brak helle yates
And saved the Sarsyn from Sathanas and his power,
Ther no clergie ne kouthe, ne konnyng of lawes!   (11.161–65)

[And thus faithful love and living in truth
Pulled out of pain a pagan of Rome.
Blessed be the truth that so broke hell's gates
And saved the Saracen from Satan and his power,
About which no (Christian) learning can explain, nor knowledge of laws.]

In this passage Trajan claims that the exigencies of his case merit the creation of a new law: justification through works. He boasts that his "leel love and lyvyng in truthe" (11.161) unequivocally saved him from hell, giving scant credit to Gregory. But Trajan is arguing, too, that exceptionality dramatically redefines the relationship between learning and salvation. Line 165 ("Ther no clergie ne kouthe, ne konnyng of lawes") suggests that in exceptional cases like that of the virtuous pagan, rules stop being rules in the normal sense. Trajan is not arguing that "clergie" – Christian revelation, its institutions, rituals, and texts – does not matter. He is proposing, rather, that "clergie" refers to a traditional idea of learning in which there are exceptions that exist in order to confirm or refine the rules. "Clergie" also refers to a class of people – clerics – trained to understand the relation of exception to rule within a divinely ordained system, who, says Trajan, are missing the point of his case:

Love and leautee is a leel science. . .   (11.166)

[Love and equity is a loyal science]

"Lawe withouten love," quod Troianus, "ley ther a bene –
Or any science under sonne, the sevene arts and alle!"   (11.170–71)

["Law without love," said Trajan, "isn't worth a bean –
Or any body of knowledge under the sun, the seven arts and all!"]

For Trajan, to say that "lawe" and "science" mean nothing without love is to say that salvation *in extremis* upsets traditional learning by turning exceptions into exemplars. Trajan is an exception to the laws of salvation because he exemplifies love, both in his pity for the widow and Gregory's pity for him. Thus, it is the very suspension of a law that allows for the expression of the most basic Christian virtue, *caritas*, or love of God and neighbor.

Most importantly, in Trajan's case, to take exceptional instances as exemplary is radically to rethink the problem of inclusion that throws the dreamer into such a muddle. Baptism, the gift of grace through which God grants justification to faith, is temporally inclusive and atemporally exclusive. As the dreamer observes, all Christians, that is, all those living after Christ who believe in Christ and who enact that belief through the sacrament of baptism, enjoy the saving power of the Atonement:

> "For Crist cleped us alle, come if we wolde –
> Sarsens and scismatikes, and so he dide the Jewes:
> *O vos omnes sicientes, venite* . . . [Isaiah 55:1]
> And bad hem souke for synne save at his breste
> And drynke boote for bale, brouke it whoso myghte.
> Thanne may alle Cristene come," quod I, "and cleyme there entree
> By the blood that he boughte us with and thorugh bapteme after:
> *Qui crediderit et baptizatus fuerit* . . . ."   [Mark 16.16] (11.119–124a)

> ["For Christ called all of us to come if we wanted –
> Saracens, and heretics, and did the same with the Jews:
> 'O, all of you who thirst, come [to the waters] . . .'
> And bade them suck at his breast to save themselves from sin,
> And drink the remedy for suffering, enjoy it he who could.
> Then may all Christians come," said I, "And claim entrance there
> By the blood with which he bought us, and through baptism afterwards.
> 'He who believes and who is baptized [shall be saved]'."]

Jews, Saracens, and pagans who lived before Christ could not benefit from Christ's sacrifice, with the exception of those enlightened patriarchs and prophets who predicted his coming. Non-Christians like Trajan, who lived in a Christian era but did not choose Christ, are surely damned. In contrast to baptism, justification by works is temporally exclusive and atemporally inclusive: those who lived before Christ but performed good works are saved; conversely those in the Christian era who accept Christ but fail to act charitably are damned. In this sense, unbaptized Trajan is a perfect instance of an exception. But the emperor insists that his case is exemplary, not exceptional. It is an example of virtue but also of fellow feeling on the model of Christ; "bloody brethren" are those who share Christ's humanity, not baptism. In a poignant speech. echoing the dreamer's lines above, Trajan declares,

> For alle are we Cristes creatures, and of his cofres riche,
> And bretheren as of oo blode, as wel beggeres as erles.
> For at Calvarie, of Cristes blode Cristendom gan sprynge,
> And blody bretheren we bicome there, of o body ywonne . . .
>
> (11.198–201)

[For we are all Christ's creatures, and rich from his coffers,
And brethren as of one blood, beggars as well as earls.
For at Calvary, from Christ's blood, Christendom began to spring.
And there we became bloody brethren, won from one body.]

This amazing speech, with its emphases on universal salvation and human compassion, invokes the exemplary pathos of Gregory. The Pope was known for his capacity to be struck by situations and to challenge inequities. It was the Pope's compassion, moreover, that allowed him to create exceptions that transcend the limits of Christian time. Earlier in Gregory's story, the author of the *Golden Legend* recalls the famous story from Bede's *Ecclesiastical History* (*c*.731), in which the Pope sees young Anglo-Saxon slaves for sale in a Roman market and remarks upon their beauty. When he learns they are pagans, he sighs, noting the disjunction between inner stain and outward looks. When he hears they are called "Angles," he exclaims, "Good . . . they have the faces of angels and such men should be the fellow-heirs of the angels in heaven."[35] Gregory's pun on "angelices" shares something important with his prayer for Trajan: it expresses his desire to incorporate all people and races into the body of the saved. Gregory's gestures of sympathy reveal the common humanity of all people, even those out-of-step geographically, temporally, or racially with the Christian empire of which Rome is the center. Although Gregory fails to rescue the English slaves from slavery or hell, he proves that exceptionalism is an occasion for sympathy rather than for legality. Further, he shows that compassion can create an exceptional view of the world in which *everyone* has the chance to be saved.

As these stories about Gregory suggest, exceptionalism is inseparable from an affective response to the doctrine of salvation. This affective response is produced by both a fellow feeling toward those who are different and an overwhelming sense of inequity. It seems unfair that a just person would not be saved or a beautiful slave would be stained by original sin. For Gregory, the answer is not to change the law, for example, to waive the requirement of baptism. Rather the answer is to create an exception that showcases the importance of charity: the deeds of the virtuous pagan, the power of God to be merciful, and the pathos of Gregory. Trajan is exemplary not only because he cared about others but also because he became the object of divine and human compassion.

This display of charity by all three parties – God, Gregory, and Trajan – provisionally overcomes the distinctions created by Christian law. It also has implications for the way one learns about salvation. If Trajan is the exception that proves the rule, he also represents a form of learning in which the student is called upon to transcend the limits of self-identification. To identify with humanity on the model of Christ means helping those who are vulnerable, widows, orphans, and, most of all, the poor. As Trajan so eloquently explains, human beings are shadowed by Christ in the guise of a poor person: "For oure joy and oure [ju]ele, Jesu Crist of hevene, / In a pouere mannes apparaille pursueth us evere" [Our joy and our jewel, Jesus Christ of heaven / In a poor man's apparel pursues us ever] (11.185–86).

Trajan strongly connects with the poor for two reasons: first, because almsgiving demonstrates a feeling of shared humanity on the model of Christ, through which pagans like Trajan are (in rare instances) justified, and second, because poverty offers an approach to learning exemplified by exceptional cases. For the poet, there is no wider gulf than that between rich and poor, and to bridge that gulf is at once to affirm and rectify fundamental inequalities (11.196–97). To explain his radical identification with the poor, Trajan invokes Luke's version of the parable of the feast, which, in contrast to Matthew's, highlights charity rather than discipleship (Matthew 22:1–14; Luke 14:15–24). In Matthew's gospel, the King's guests are neighbors who refuse to come when called. In Luke, the guests are those most unlike the lord: the downtrodden, lame, and poor ("Ac calleth the carefulle therto, the croked and the povere," 11.191). Trajan simultaneously practices and benefits from the noble virtue exhibited in Luke. Giving to the poor is like praying for pagans and packs the same rhetorical punch: "And we his bretheren thorugh hym ybought, bothe riche and povere ... And every man helpe oother – for hennes shul we alle" [And we his brothers were bought through him, both rich and poor ... And every man should help the other, for hence shall we all go] (11.207, 210).

Trajan's exceptional case proves that salvation is likely for all because it is unlikely for some. As Imaginatif declares at the end of B.12: "*Salvabitur vix iustus in die iudicii; / Ergo – salvabitur*" ["Scarcely shall the just man be saved on the day of judgement / – so he shall be saved!"] (12.278–79, quoting 1 Peter 4:18). Medieval theologians tended to interpret *salvabitur vix iustus* as a comment on the difficulty of obtaining salvation, focusing, for example, on the gap between human and divine standards or the insufficiency of human justice without God's grace.[36] Heaven is challenging, and only God can make up the difference between what people can do and what they owe. Characteristically, Langland transports this verse into a very different context. In *Piers Plowman*, "vix" (scarcely, hardly) refers not to the human capacity to meet God's justice, but to a more extreme form of improbability, salvation without baptism. Trajan embodies the likelihood of salvation (through good works) through the extreme unlikelihood of his particular case (good works without baptism). In *Piers Plowman*, in other words, Trajan conflates the chosen few with the exceptionally saved. At the end of passus 12, the poet reiterates the idea that it is highly unlikely that an unbaptized person would ever be saved, however just. Humanity in Christ defines a Christian, not a universal, community: "Ne no creature of Cristes liknesse withouten Cristendom worth saved" [Nor may any creature of Christ's likeness be saved without Christendom] (12.276). As it turns out, however, it is the extreme unlikeliness of a pagan being saved that makes all salvation possible. Trajan raises the general hope that doing well will merit heaven.[37]

(Solomon and Aristotle)

Like the virtuous pagan, the case of the pre-Christian poets and philosophers – Solomon and Aristotle – tests the limits of salvation and the limits of learning. Trajan shows that God sometimes disregards his own laws in order to resolve inequities in human history. Like Trajan, Aristotle and Solomon beg questions about equity, but their cases tug especially hard on the heartstrings of medieval scholars: despite the fact that their learning complements, even supports Christian revelation, they were consigned irrevocably to hell. With Aristotle and Solomon, then, the question becomes, what is exceptional about damnation? Why are the just not saved, and if they are not saved, what, then, constitutes righteousness? Is it possible, for example, that Aristotle and Solomon were constrained by the very thing that would seem to recommend them, their learning? For the dreamer, baptism is a ready answer, for only baptism could have saved those pagans no matter how well they lived. He concludes in B.10 that it is easier to be saved as a sinning Christian (for example, the thief on the Cross, Mary Magdalene, or St. Paul) than as a wise pagan like Solomon (413ff.), and yet, as Langland shows, the problem cannot be resolved so easily. How does one understand one's own salvation if those commonly cited as authorities are condemned to hell? What would it mean to follow someone's words but not their works?

Many non-Christian philosophers and poets were fully integrated into medieval learning, and could be cited as authorities in a variety of contexts from Latin composition and moral instruction to biblical hermeneutics, physics, and theology. As discussed at the beginning of this chapter, Cato, though a pagan, was fundamental to medieval early education and synonymous in literary contexts with learned citation. Thus Scripture, arguing against worldly riches, cites Cato, St. Paul, and Solomon in rapid succession, summing up her argument as follows, "And patriarkes and prophetes and poetes bothe / Writen to wissen us to wilne no richesse" [And patriarchs, and prophets, and poets as well / Wrote to teach us not to follow riches] (10.338–39). In *Piers Plowman*, an important example of the integration of pagan learning is the "book of beasts," or information about the natural world collected by classical authors, such as Aristotle and Pliny, and bequeathed to medieval writers, who used this information to create similitudes, or moralizations of nature that illuminate Christian faith. The best-known moralization from the book of beasts – the proud peacock – is the one Imaginatif uses to argue for the value of pagan learning:

Ac of briddes and of beestes men by olde tyme
Ensamples token and termes, as telleth thise poetes,
And that the faireste fowel foulest engendreth,
And feeblest fowel of flight is that fleeth or swymmeth.
And that is the pecok and the pehen – proude riche men thei bitokneth.

                                                                    (B.12.235–39)

[But of birds and beasts men of olden times
Took examples and precepts, as these poets explain,
And that the fairest bird produces the foulest [flesh],
And is the bird least capable of flight, among those that fly or swim.
And that (bird) is the peacock, and the peahen – they symbolize proud rich men.]

As Imaginatif explains, this fine-feathered bird represents wealthy men, reverenced for their goods but unable to soar to heaven, grounded by their wealth on their dying day. Using one of Middle English poets' favorite puns, Imaginatif jokes that the peacock's "taile" [tale/tail], which drags it down to earth, is made entirely of sorrow (12.245). Like the peacock with its raucous voice – like the magpie but unlike the lark – a rich man's cries for mercy sound shrill in the ear of the Lord (12.251–52, 261); like the peacock's smelly, inedible flesh, a rich man's rank corpse contrasts sharply with the fragrant bodies of dead saints (12.256–58).

Imaginatif credits two sources for his moralization of the peacock, Aristotle (12.265) and "Avynet" (12.256), the latter possibly Avianus, the fifth-century fabulist, whose versified tales from Aesop were incorporated into medieval schooltexts.[38] In fact, Langland's moralization overlaps very little with this source, and it is likely that "Avynet" stands for a more general category – Latin verse with a Christian moral – just as Aristotle represents, in *Piers Plowman*, encyclopedic information about the natural world, useful in itself but also easily adopted to other interpretative systems.[39] Imaginatif's point is that the Christian moralization of creatures draws from material gathered by ancient writers. Yet his case for the salvation of ancient writers requires reading the "book of beasts" as a collective enterprise, in which it is actually quite difficult to separate the "exemples" and "termes" [examples and precepts] (12.236) collected by ancient authors from their latter-day moralizations.

The peacock belonged to a stock of literary imagery derived from a thousand-year old confluence of natural histories, Old Testament dietary laws, New Testament parables, biblical interpretation, and rhetorical treatises. Knowledge about animals circulated in the Middle Ages through the reception of Aristotle's *De historia animalium* (*The History of Animals*), translated into Latin by William of Moerbeke (*c.*1215–86). This treatise was transmitted, along with other classical texts, through various channels: Isidore of Seville's seventh-century encyclopedia, the *Etymologies*; Islamic and Jewish commentaries, and thirteenth-century encyclopedias, such as Vincent of Beauvais's *Speculum naturale* and Bartholomeus Anglicus's *De proprietatibus rerum*. Running alongside these scientific compendia was the bestiary, a collection of beasts inherited from late antiquity, often illustrated and nearly always moralized: the phoenix rises from its ashes, as did Christ in the Resurrection; the pelican revives her young with her own blood, just as Christ saves the faithful through his Sacrifice. The earliest version of the bestiary, the *Physiologus* (*The Naturalist*), composed in the second or third century, was attributed by later medieval writers variously to saints Basil and Cyrus, Ambrose and Jerome, even to Solomon and Aristotle. *Physiologus* formed the basis for later bestiaries, which were grouped by species.[40] The bestiary tradition, in turn, deeply enriched the homiletic repertoire, such as Thomas of Chobham's *Summa de arte praedicandi* (*Summary of the Preaching Arts*) (before 1236), as well as books of hours and psalters, such as the Queen Mary Psalter (c.1310–20), which boasts luxurious illustrations indebted to the bestiaries.

As Imaginatif's peacock amply shows, knowledge about animals inherited from antique writers provided a comprehensive language for Christian moralists; it also gave Langland a way to argue for the salvation of ancients writers. Imaginatif concludes from the peacock that the "great clerk" Aristotle deserves to be saved, even though we think we know he is damned to hell.[41]

> Aristotle the grete clerk, swiche tales he telleth;
> Thus he likneth in his logic the leeste fowel oute.
> And wheither he be saaf or noght saaf, the sothe woot no clergie,
> Ne of Sortes ne of Salamon no scripture kan telle.
> Ac God is so good, I hope that siththe he gaf hem wittes

To wissen us weyes therwith, that wisshen to be saved,
(And the better for hir bokes) to bidden we be ben holden
That God for his grace gyve hir soules reste;
For lettred men were lewed yet, ne were loore of hir bokes.

(12.265–73)

[The great clerk Aristotle tells such stories;
Thus he compares in his treatise the least little bird.
And whether he is saved or not saved, no learning can ascertain,
Nor record tell us [the fates of] Socrates or Solomon.
But God is so good, I believe that, since he gave them the wits
With which to teach us the ways, we who wish to be saved,
(And us the better for their books), we are bound to pray
That God in his grace give their souls rest;
For lettered men would still be ignorant,
If it were not for the lore of their books.]

In this remarkable passage, Imaginatif credits "[olde] lyveris" (12.131) not only with experiential wisdom ("kynde knowynges ... of diverse sightes," 12.136), but also with the total value of the comparison between human and animal: peacocks are like magpies; peacocks are like rich men. He concedes that pagan and Christian knowledge have different implications for Christian salvation, yet he shows, at the same time, that classification and moralization are part of the same project of fashioning similitudes: Aristotle "*likneth* in his logic, the leeste foule oute" (12.266), that is, he compares the properties of every creature.[42] Contemporary clerics are consequently better off than they otherwise would be ("better for hir bokes," 12.271), having received this learning from pagan writers. Pagan writers, in turn, are redeemed, not only because they helped shape Christian moral literature, but also because they made knowledge comprehensive through the act of comparison. They included everything down to the most insignificant bird: "Thus [Aristotle] likneth in his logic the *leeste fowel oute*" (12.266, my emphases). Granted, the knowledge they imparted was incomplete because they did not believe in Christ; but nonetheless they managed to bequeath to posterity a complete version of the natural world by accounting for every detail.

From this perspective, the book of beasts with its vast collection of similitudes resembles Gregory's universalizing impulse. Like Gregory, says Langland, we ought to pray for those not saved ("to bidden we be ben holden," 12.271), who are credited for the information in the book of beasts, and who discovered some worth in the most insignificant bird. Furthermore, as a telling revision in the C-text makes clear, if comparison is essentially an inclusive act, it is one that Langland extends to pagan writers as well. *Piers Plowman* B.12.265 ("Aristotle the grete clerk, swiche tales he telleth") is a metrically difficult line for several reasons: the second stressed syllable of the second half-line alliterates against metrical norms (i.e., ax/aa), and the first stressed syllable of the first half-line must alliterate on the third syllable of Aristótle for the line to scan correctly. In the C-text, the poet resolves these difficulties by adding a fourth line (C.14.193), thus deferring mention of Aristotle, and by replacing the first line B.12.265 ("Aristotle the grete clerk swiche tales he telleth) with a straightforward aa/ax line: "Thus porfirie and Plato and poetes monye" (C.14.189):

> Aristotle the grete clerk swiche tales he telleth;
> Thus he likneth in his logic the leeste fowel oute.
> And wher he be saaf or noght saaf, the soothe woot no clergie,
> Ne of Sortes ne of Salomon no scripture kan telle.   (B.12.265–68)

(See translation above.)

> Thus Porfirie and Plato and poetes monye
> Likneth in here logic the leste foul outen.
> And wher he be saef or nat saef, the sothe woet no clergie,
> Ne of Sortes ne of Salamon no scripture can telle
> Wher that they ben in hell or in hevene, or Aristotel the wyse...
>   (C.14.189–93)[43]

> [Thus Porphyry, and Plato, and many [other] poets
> Compare in their treatise every last little bird,
> And whether they be saved or not saved, no learning can ascertain,
> No record can tell us [the fate of] Socrates or Solomon –
> Where they are in heaven or in hell – nor of Aristotle the wise.]

In the revised passage, the poet extends the list of unsaved ancients for whom readers presumably should pray (Porphyry, Plato, Socrates, Solomon, Aristotle, and "poetes monye"), a list that appears in C to be infinitely expandable, its authors nearly interchangeable.

The "old livers," as Imaginatif calls them, are examples in contradictory ways: they are examples of good words and of bad works. The dreamer is forced to conclude that Aristotle and Solomon, despite their erudition, were profoundly un-exemplary: "And if I sholde werche by hir werkes to wynne me hevene, / That for hir werkes and wit now wonyeth in pyne – / Thanne wroughte I unwisly, whatsoevere ye preche!" [And if I, to win heaven, should follow their examples – / [of] those who now dwell in pain on account of their works – / Then I would be acting unwisely, whatever you may preach!] (B.10.386–88). If Trajan's exceptional salvation is taken as the

Figure 3. "Aristotle with his disciples." *Les diz moraulx des philosophes*. Cambridge, Harvard University, Houghton Library, MS Typ 0207, f.15. (Paris, 1400–1450).

norm (*salvabitur vix justus*), then the fates of Solomon and Aristotle suggest that learning constitutes a work that does not merit exceptional salvation.

Langland's investigation into the status of pre-Christian intellectual "work" begins with Wit's commentary on Noah's ark. The ark has always raised uncomfortable questions about equity; in *Piers Plowman*, for instance, Wit observes that however much humanity was tainted by Cain's sin, animals did not merit death (9.137–42). When the dreamer revisits Noah's ark in passus 10, he, too, is concerned about inequity, observing that the workmen who built the ark were drowned in the flood. We might expect the dreamer to gloss the workmen as pre-Christian authorities who helped lay the groundwork for Christian truth but were not saved through Christ. Peculiarly, the dreamer glosses the workmen, not as ancient poets and philosophers, but as contemporary clerks who do not practice what they preach: "Forthi I counseille yow clerkes, of Holy [Kirke] the wrights / Wercheth ye werkes as ye sen ywrite, lest ye worthe noght therinne!" [Therefore I counsel you clerks, the carpenters of Holy Church, / Perform your works as you see them prescribed, lest you amount to nothing] (10.411–12). The poet is grappling with two interrelated questions: if pre-Christian learning is not meritorious enough to justify exceptional salvation, should it be counted an unrighteous work? Further, if learning, as in the case of Solomon and Aristotle, can be understood as a work, does pre-Christian learning render *all* learning unrighteous, or at least a work with deadly constraints?

At this juncture, the poet might have reminded us that "old livers" were not perfect livers. Aristotle, for one, may have committed suicide. Solomon, though the reputed author of the Book of Wisdom (which sometimes included Proverbs and Ecclesiastes), was condemned by some writers for his adultery with the Queen of Sheba, and his subsequent idolatry. According to Langland's contemporary, John Gower, a medieval prince should study Solomon as a negative example of royal behavior.[44] For Langland, however, the significance of Solomon and Aristotle has to do not with behavior but with the spiritual costs of learning, and more specifically, the troubling gap between an author's citationality and his exemplarity.

The poet returns to this issue in Imaginatif's defense of the clergy in B.12. Imaginatif reproaches the dreamer for criticizing the clergy and reminds him that clerical learning – the written transmission of revealed truth – is indispensable for salvation:

> For as a man may noght see that mysseth hise eighen,
> Na moore kan no clerk but if he caughte it first thorough bokes.
> Although men made bokes, God was the maister,
> And Seint Spirit the samplarie, and seide what men sholde write.
>
> (12.99–102)

> [Just as a man cannot see who is missing his eyes,
> So a clerk knows nothing unless he has first read it in books.
> Although men made books, God was the master,
> And Holy Spirit the exemplar, and told men what to write.]

For Imaginatif, the value of clerical learning is highlighted by its opposite, kind wit, which in passūs 8–12 refers to both the natural ability to make sense of one's world and the wisdom provided by ancient thinkers whose salvation is in doubt. Medieval scholars recognized that the ancients were experts on kind wit, having laid the groundwork for a hermeneutics of Nature, a moral guide to the marvels ("selkouthes," "alle kynde sightes") of the natural world (12.132, 128). And just as all human beings rely on both received tradition and natural understanding, so Christian literates have recourse to two modes of learning: clergie and kind wit.

These might be regarded as complementary traditions. Both, for example, are mirrors of instruction (12.92ff.), and both are crucial to Christian witnessing: to behold any natural or supernatural wonder is to use one's kind wit (12.65ff.). As discussed above, however, the poet stresses the opposition between knowledge gained from pagan writers and those writers' spiritual status. For one thing, kind wit is incomplete without clergie: just as a blind man cannot wield his axe in battle (12.105–12), and just as a man thrown in the Thames cannot save himself if he has not learned to swim (12.160–69), so a "kyndewitted man" cannot be saved without Christian clerics to instruct him (12.107ff.). The poets and philosophers of old told moral tales about the natural world which helped save later Christians, but they are unlikely to have been saved themselves. Because "sapience," or the wisdom transmitted by Solomon and other ancient thinkers, is incomplete, it should be considered a worldly good ("catel"), which, if disassociated from Christian truth, becomes an encumbrance rather than an aid. Hence Imaginatif repeatedly associates riches and "kind wit," not only because ancient thinkers, like the rich, enjoyed their heaven on earth, but also because their knowledge was disassociated from Christian truth: "So catel and kynde wit acombreth ful manye; / Wo is hym that hem weldeth but he hem wel despende: / *Scient[es] et non facient[es] variis flagellis vapulab[un]t*" [So possessions and kind wit encumber very many; / Woe is he who wields them, unless he dispends them properly: / "Those who know (God's will) and do not act (according to it) will be beaten with many whips"] (12.55–56a, following Luke 12:47). According to Imaginatif, both the lack of knowledge and the refusal to put that knowledge into practice implicates the whole of world history, from Lucifer in hell to biblical figures like Solomon, Sampson and Job; to Greek and Roman scholars, such as Aristotle, Hippocrates, and Virgil; to Alexander the Great; to the fair Felice, the abandoned wife of romance hero Guy of Warwick; and the beautiful Rosamond, Henry II's doomed mistress (12.40–48).

To defend clerical learning at the expense of Solomon and Aristotle is not, however, to pass over the implications of their exceptional damnation. That God did not see fit to make exceptions for the ancients suggests that learning itself is somehow an obstacle because it is always incomplete. The dreamer deduces from Solomon's case, for example, that higher learning is not necessarily desirable: Christ gave the unlearned special powers to speak in front of kings, and St. Augustine himself, an academic hero, "the doughtieste doctour and devinour of the Trinitee" [The most impressive scholar and glossator of the Trinity] (10.452), wrote in the *Confessions* that the unlearned win heaven while wise men go to hell. The dreamer poignantly describes the salvation of these poor common laborers, whose faith pierces heaven with a Paternoster:

> Ne none sonner ysaved, ne sadder of bileve
> Than plowmen and pastours and povere commune laborers,
> Souteres and shepherdes – swiche lewed juttes
> Percen with a *Paternoster* the paleys of hevene
> And passen purgatorie penauncelees at hir hennes partyng
> Into the blisse of paradis for hir pure bileve,
> That inparfitly here knewe and ek lyvede.   (10.459–65)

[There are none sooner saved, nor more serious of belief
Than plowmen and shepherds and poor common laborers,
Shoemakers and shepherds – such ignorant nobodies
Pierce with a Paternoster the palace of heaven
And pass through purgatory without penance at their departure hence
Into the bliss of paradise, for their pure belief,
Who knew and lived here imperfectly.]

The lettered clergy get themselves in hot water, because they know what to do and do not follow through. It is incumbent on them to practice what they preach, an idea strongly reiterated throughout the poem. In this way, exceptional cases remind us that there is a constraint to all aids. Kind wit may be opposed to Christian learning ("clergie"), but both clergie and kind wit, as realms of acquired learning, might well be opposed to the "lowly grace" of simple layfolk, plowmen, and shepherds. Equally problematic is the ignorance of those laypeople who "inparfitly here knewe and ek lyvede" (12.465). For example if the clergy are identified with those prescient "pastors and poets" who attended the birth of Christ, and if laymen are identified with the rich men of Bethlehem asleep in their beds (12.143ff.), suddenly lay ignorance looks woefully incomplete.

Finally, as ancient writers show, if learning is the ultimate constraint, then everyone's salvation is exceptional in the sense that it is never a graspable rule. The inequity of the fate of old livers, of real concern to any learned person, means that if God is good, his ways are unknowable; even a person who seems to have deserved salvation is scarcely saved. Nor is it ever really possible to know who has been damned eternally to hell. In the final analysis, human knowledge is insufficient to explain divine mysteries. The dreamer quotes Solomon (against himself) on this point: "Ther are witty and wel libbynge, ac hire werkes ben yhudde / In the hondes of almyghty God" [There are those who are clever and live well, but their works are hidden / In the hands of almighty God] (10.430–31, quoting Ecclesiastes 9:1). As Imaginatif explains, Solomon and Aristotle were damned by the insufficiency of the learning that proved so important to later scholars, but people's salvation and damnation is finally unknowable. According to Imaginatif, they all deserve our prayers.

CHAPTER 5

Practice
(B.13–15)

"Thanne passe we over til Piers come and preve this in dede"
(B.13.133).

Introduction

In the third vision of *Piers Plowman* (B.8–12), the dreamer debates salvation theology with personifications of learning: Thought, Wit, Study, Clergie, Scripture, Reason, and Imaginatif. With each interlocutor, the dreamer tries to gauge the likelihood of his own salvation, and whether the plan of salvation is inclusive or exclusive, fair or unfair, proof of God's mercy or his justice. By connecting emotionally and intellectually with "old livers" – antique rulers, philosophers, and poets – the dreamer gains a purchase on his future while reaching back in time to those whose salvation is uncertain at best.

The dreamer's opening gambit in these passūs is to ask his interlocutors to define Dowel, Dobet, and Dobest (what it means to do well, better, and best), a line of questioning that continues into B.13. Each character he interviews has at least one good answer to the question, but Patience's answer in B.13 is the most succinct: "*Disce* and Dowel; *Doce* and Dobet; / *Dilige*, and Dobest" ["Learn" and Dowel; "teach" and Dobet; / "love (your enemies)" and Dobest] (13.138–39, from Luke 6:27). The Dowel triad promises a foolproof way of parsing the good life. At the same time it provides a literary form versatile enough to structure any expression, from the most compressed maxim, to a complete biblical episode, to an entire section of the poem. In B.19/C.21, for instance, Conscience uses the triad to organize Christ's life: Dowel represents the Incarnation; Dobet, Christ's teaching and miracles; and Dobest, Christ's death and the Atonement. Scribes of the B- and C-texts, perhaps inspired by B.19, used the Dowels as external markers in addition to, and often overlapping with, passus rubrics. Thus, in many C-text manuscripts, passūs 10–16 are labeled the

"*Vita* de Dowel"; passūs 17–19 the "*Vita* de Dobet"; and passūs 20–22 the "*Vita* de Dobest." In this C tradition, the rubrics shape the last two thirds of the poem into three periods of a holy life, or perhaps as three progressively better lives.[1] This is the enormous appeal of Dowel, that it can function both as verb and noun, describing both moral action (the dreamer or Christ did well), and persons or states (a good preacher = Dobet). The Dowel triad encapsulates this relationship between doing and being. For the poet and some of his early readers, moreover, Dowel held forth the possibility of an ideal form that correlates moral and literary practice.

The poem invites us to read the Dowel triad as a gloss on the *bona* of Truth's Pardon in B.7 – "Et qui bona egerunt ibunt in vitam eternam" [those who have done well will go to eternal life] (7.110a) – a line from the Athanasian Creed which suggests that a justice exists through which people can win heaven. As he tears the Pardon, Piers appears to reject this idea, and the dreamer eventually realizes with Piers that no human being can merit heaven by meeting God's standards – no one can ever merit condignly or deservingly – but rather, God in his goodness allows people to merit congruently, that is, in approximation of or in proportion to, divine justice.[2]

The two versions of the Pardon make a related point, as does the Trajan episode in a different way, that human righteousness is contingent upon Christian notions of time. Every Christian has the potential to be righteous because Christ redeemed humanity through the Atonement and created a system through which, with God's grace, people have the chance to do good works and earn heaven (as explained in the long version of the Pardon); and yet even a baptized Christian, unless he repents and amends his sin before death, might end up in hell (the short version of the Pardon).[3] These two admissions, that one cannot be righteous on one's own, and that virtue is partly a matter of timing, give rise to fervent prayer. At the end of B.7, for example, the poet prays that with the aid of divine grace he might be able "swiche werkes to werche" [to perform the kind of deeds] (7.199) that Dowel can disclose on his behalf at Judgement Day. Towards the end of B.12, Imaginatif concedes that the fate of the virtuous pagan can never be known, and the best we can do is pray for them (12.269–73). At the end of B.14, Hawkyn, regretting having lived past his baptism, cries for mercy: "So hard it is . . . to lyve and to do synne" (14.322).

The poet, however, is reluctant to abandon the idea of an intrinsic human goodness, an action or state that exemplifies it, and a literary practice capable of representing it. At the end of B.12, Imaginatif still hopes to find a justice ("truth") available to all peoples past and present, Christian or pagan, a justice that allows anyone to perform works that qualify as Dowel (12.288–89). Although drawn to extreme cases like the virtuous pagan, Langland rejects the idea that human beings can choose for the good without divine aid, or that human works can ever meet the standards of divine justice. Yet he repeatedly floats the Dowel triad to restart the conversation about what constitutes a virtuous life.

Piers Plowman B.13–15 is an extended meditation on virtuous practice, or how one might live well in deed and in this present life. These passūs are best remembered for two scenes – Conscience's dinner in B.13, a feat of allegorical brilliance, and the dreamer's encounter with the boisterous Hawkyn – but they are actually dominated by two very long speeches: Patience's sermon on patient poverty in B.14, and Anima's lecture on charity in B.15, in which he warns the English clergy to shape up or suffer correction by the secular arm. Both speeches are concerned with practice, or what it means to live a virtuous life, as well as with describing a temporality in which a virtuous life can be led. In his sermon to Hawkyn, Patience proposes patient, involuntary poverty as the best life, more deserving than riches and more comprehensible as a practice than poverty in spirit, although, as he shows, the two kinds of poverty are intimately related. Patience's defense of poverty gains momentum through a series of analogies between the lifecycles of humans and animals. In passus 15, Anima proposes that the best life is the one that imitates examples from the past; history, he explains, is a compendium of exemplary lives against which the lives of English clergy can be measured. The poet makes this case through a chronicle of historical saints, martyrs, and missionaries, who practiced what they preached and performed charity "in deed." These persons set an example for the present through self-denial, preaching, and miracle-working but, most wonderfully (and inimitably), by venturing their lives in pagan lands.

These two models of practice – patient poverty and historical exemplarity – are extremely attractive to the poet, in part because they are daunting and far-fetched, impossible for the average clerk or layman to perform. The poet is also drawn to these models because, like the Dowel triad, they raise important questions about the time of practice. Can a cleric, layman, bishop or king, live righteously in the present, or is the good life something to which one can only aspire, in a conditional future or an idealized past? Is virtuous practice by definition a categorical order or an irremediable state, like the faithful unlearned or hardworking poor, or is it an iterable form like penance, each repetition of which brings us closer to the solution to the problem of how to live a good life?

Such questions are, of course, explored elsewhere in the poem, for example, in the Plowing of the Half-Acre, where labor as a virtuous practice and spiritual metaphor depends quite literally on the season, whether people are hungry or not. They are further anticipated in B.11–12 by the poet's discussion of the exceptionally saved and damned for whom temporality is key to redemption. Passūs 13–15, however, contain some of the poet's most sustained experiments in thinking through the relationships between time, virtue, and practice. These passūs also get to the heart of Langland's poetic aspirations. For the poet, the difficult project of representing a virtuous practice is bound up in a poetics that compulsively pursues every form of life – animal or human, Christian or heathen, rich or poor, beggar or saint – as a potential moral exemplar.

Poor beasts

In *Piers Plowman* B.11 and 12, Imaginatif credits pagan philosophers, such as Aristotle, with knowledge of the natural world, knowledge that enabled medieval writers to bridge the Christian present and the pre-Christian past. In passus 12, he gives the example of the peacock, whose physical properties – gorgeous but useless feathers, raucous voice, stinking flesh – make it indispensable to Christian moralization: the peacock is like a rich man, who pays the price in the afterlife for his vanity and wealth. This knowledge of the natural world is key to the poet's imaginative work on behalf of unsaved pre-Christians: the act of moralizing properties recovers the temporal distance between Christian and pagan knowledge, while at the same time highlighting the spiritual divide between saved Christians and unsaved ancients. In B.14 the poet returns again to the "book of beasts" in order to undertake a different but equally radical project: a defense of involuntary material poverty as the best practice. In that passus, he pursues a series of analogies between men and beasts through which he argues for the intrinsic merit of the human poor. For the poet, the temporal similarities between the lives of animals and the poor argue for the merits of real human poverty.

Langland's interest in the temporalities of beasts begins even earlier, however, with Wit's treatise on the history of sin in B.9. In his discussion of Noah's ark, Wit pictures present-day animals protesting the two-by-two rule of the ark: "Beestes that now ben shul banne the tyme / That evere that cursed Caym coom on this erthe" [Beasts who are alive now should curse the time / That ever cursed Cain came on this earth] (9.137–38), as if to say, "why should we beasts pay for the sins of men?" To compare the perspective of humans and animals, as Wit does here, is an unusual move for a medieval poet to make. To do so is not just to pass up the opportunity to moralize (for example, the beasts in the ark symbolize the Christian faithful; the dove, which comes home to roost, is like the good preacher who ushers the faithful into the church), but further, it grants humans and animals a similar temporal experience, a sense of living together at the same time, and interpreting a common past. The dreamer might have objected that Wit is protesting the burden of human sin on behalf of those who lack immortal souls. Truly, to ignore such a crucial distinction between humans and animals, as Wit does, is to suggest that they share a moral history that can be "read" by all creatures.

In *Piers Plowman* B.14 the poet returns to this idea of shared temporal and moral experience. He proposes that the experiences of humans and animals are fundamentally alike, and further, that the best human practice becomes visible through comparisons between men and beasts. This proposition owes much to medieval Aristotelian encyclopedias, such as Bartholomaeus Anglicus's *De proprietatibus rerum* (*On the Properties of Things*) (*c*.1250), a compendium of information about the natural world: celestial properties, the body and its diseases, birds, animals, fish, seasons and gemstones, beverages and colors. Langland surely had access to the *Properties*, whether through a direct copy or through related literatures, such as preaching manuals. The Latin *Properties* was owned by most major medieval libraries, printed well into the Elizabethan period, and translated into several European vernaculars, including the English translation (1398) written by John Trevisa. Langland invokes the encyclopedic properties of animals to make a startling argument about human poverty and human merit: the best practice – involuntary poverty – is modeled by animals and read in the pattern of their lives.

Although Bartholomaeus wrote his encyclopedia as an aid to preachers struggling with biblical figures, he rarely moralizes information about the natural world in the way that Imaginatif, for example, moralizes the peacock. For Bartholomaeus, following Aristotle, what is instructive about creatures is their diverse physical properties and the various ways in which they can be grouped and compared. They can be classified generally (for example, farm animals are nutritious, wild animals are stringy) or specifically (for example, the bat is a hermaphroditic bird!). Not surprisingly, Bartholomaeus posits a hierarchy within all this diversity, with humans given pride of place, animals ranked above plants, and so forth. According to medieval theologians, such as William of Auvergne (d. 1249), even where animals resemble humans – for example, when they remember cruelty or care for their young – these qualities are merely effects of necessity. Instinct, however remarkable, does not attest to the moral intelligence that gives humans the power to choose for the good. But because Bartholomaeus is committed to comparing properties across species, he often brings species at different levels of the hierarchy into the same moral frame. In book 5 ("On the Human Body"), for example, he explains that all lions, like some humans, are wrathful, just as all sheep, like some humans, are meek.[4]

As this last example suggests, if human behavior is a function of properties shared by other creatures, it is possible to draw analogies between men and beasts that complicate traditional moral distinctions. For example, although medieval encyclopedists try to distinguish species through moral properties such as voluntarism, intelligence, and love, they inevitably blur those distinctions between species when compiling information about them. In his *Historia animalium* (*History of Animals*), the classic textbook of medieval natural history, Aristotle explains that some beasts, such as deer and bees, seek out company (*gregalia*), and some are loners (*solitaria*), such as vultures and wolves; man alone embodies a mixture of the social and the solitary. In the same section, Aristotle observes that among those creatures which seek out company, there are social creatures (*politica*) which have a common object in view (*commune . . . opus*), such as men, bees, wasps, ants, and cranes.[5] In *De civitate Dei* (*The City of God*, early fifth century), Augustine cites Aristotle's social and solitary creatures but carefully distinguishes man from the animals, not for man's degree of sociability but for the uniqueness of his common object: fellowship and its heavenly reward. Man chooses or loses heaven based on the quality of his moral society ("societatis unitas vinculumque concordiae"), established first as family affection between Adam and Eve. As Augustine explains further, because man was initially created through one man, Adam, rather than called into being *en masse* like other animals, man alone bridges the mortal life of animals (the world of appetites) and the immortal society of the angels (the world of the spirit).[6]

Bartholomaeus is keenly aware of Augustine's moral society. However, the encyclopedic drive to chart similarities across species sometimes obscures the special status of human fellowship. Bartholomaeus acknowledges, for example, that the theory that subtends the classification of animals makes humans unique: after rehearsing Aristotle's social and solitary animals, Bartholomaeus, following Augustine, repeats that, "among all animals, only man cannot live alone" ("inter omnia animalia homo non potest vivere solus"). But immediately he shuts down any meaningful discussion of human distinctiveness, adding that, in this respect, cranes, bees, and ants accord with man ("et grues et apis et formice communicant homini in hoc").[7]

This confusion about human distinctiveness can be blamed in part on the economy of the encyclopedia. But the collapse of moral difference occurs in *Piers Plowman* B.14 as well, and there the result is not ethical confusion, as we see in Bartholomaeus, but rather new possibilities about the way that value is assigned to human and animal lives. As argued below, the poet analogizes, rather than allegorizes, the relationship between men and beasts in order to describe the best human practice – patient, involuntary poverty. He does so by exploding the temporality of that analogy, how the time of practice – whether poverty, penance, or wealth – reveals something about its spiritual worth.

In *Piers Plowman*, the conversation about poverty begins with Hawkyn. In passus 13, Conscience, Patience, and the dreamer meet up with Hawkyn (*Activa Vita* in C) who professes to live a good life, supplying the community with wholesome wafers – loaves or cakes (with reference at 13.235–8 to the Eucharistic host) – and serving as a minstrel for little pay.[8] Hawkyn claims to be unconcerned with advancement; like the dreamer, he refuses to kowtow to his superiors, and he criticizes the Pope for failing to perform miracles. Like the dreamer, too, Hawykn is a drifter, disconnected from social institutions and, in his opinion, well positioned to critique them. Upon closer scrutiny, the dreamer notices that Hawkyn's coat is mottled with the stains and patches of the seven sins, and what first seems like a natural antipathy to corruption turns out to be mere meddling and contempt ("entremetten" and "lakking" 13.291, 287). Like Philosophy's dress in Boethius's *Consolation of Philosophy*, Hawkyn's coat is an exercise in reading – in his case, a chance to learn about sin by diagnosing the sinner. The more the dreamer examines the coat, the more deeply he perceives Hawkyn's sins, which expand to include every walk of the active life, from plowing, to begging, to retail.[9]

At the beginning of passus 14, Conscience and Patience step forward with a self-help program for Hawkyn, and Conscience advises him to wash his coat with the soap of penance (13.458–14.28). Patience offers a complement to penance, an alternative "liflode" [sustenance] to that purveyed by Hawkyn (14.32). Hawkyn scoffs at the idea that such a "liflode" could sustain anyone; it is just a bit of prayer, the *Paternoster* (Matthew 6:9–13, specifically, the verse "Panem nostrum cotidianum da nobis hodie" [Give us this day our daily bread]), but the dreamer describes it as "vitailles of grete virtues for alle manere beestes" [victuals of great virtue for all kinds of beasts] (14.38), and Patience proclaims it to be "liflode ynogh" [sufficient sustenance] (14.39). Patience's "liflode" is "ynogh" not because it is identical to the Eucharist, which, according to the biographies of some saints, could nourish indefinitely the body of a holy person.[10] Nor is it "ynogh" in a purely figurative sense, as when we talk about the "nourishing" or "sustaining" qualities of texts. For example, at Conscience's feast, Patience and the dreamer share a loaf of bread, along with drink and "other mete" made up of penitential verses drawn from the Psalms, while Conscience and Scripture dine upon the "sondry metes" of the gospels and patristics, and the doctor of divinity wolfs down real "mortrews and potages" with a bitter sauce of "*Post mortem*," or after-death aftertaste (13.37–54). In contrast, the materiality of Patience's "liflode" unhinges the metaphor between word and food. It sustains life insofar as it represents an attitude toward sustenance consonant with two statements in the *Paternoster*: patient subjection to the will of God the Creator ("Your will be done"), or a meekness that comes from the belief that God will provide the necessities of life ("*Give us* this day our daily bread"); and, alongside it, a total indifference to future need, following the example of the apostles, or what the poet calls elsewhere a "recklessness" ("Give us *this day* our *daily* bread") (my emphases).[11]

Patience continues in this mode, explaining that human beings should live on belief and love, just as animals live in the moment on the natural resources divinely ordained to them:

First the wilde worme under weet erthe,
Fissh to lyue in the flood, in the fir the criket,
The corlew by kynde of the eyr, moost clennest flesh of briddes,
And bestes by gras and by greyn and by grene roots,
In menynge that alle men myghte the same
Lyue thorugh leel bileue and loue, as God witnesseth:
Quodcumque pecieritis a patre in nomine meo . . . Et alibi, Non in
solo pane vivit homo, set in omni verbo quod procedit de ore Dei. . .
                                    [John 14:13, Matthew 4:4] (14.42–47)

[First the wild serpent under the wet earth,
Fish to live in the water, in the fire the cricket,
The curlew naturally by the air – the bird with the cleanest flesh –
And beasts by grass, and by grain, and by green roots,
As meaning that all men should do the same,
Live by loyal belief and love, as God witnesses:
"Who ever asks from the father in my name," and in another place: "Man lives not
  by bread alone but by every word that proceeds from the mouth of God."]

The scriptural quotations in Patience's speech link this passage to the "book of beasts" and specifically to moralizations, such as that of the *fulica* (curlew or coot), a kind of waterfowl.[12] Medieval bestiaries describe the *fulica* as an intelligent bird which stays in one place and abstains from dead flesh. In *Physiologus*, for example, the *fulica* is moralized *in bonum* as the type of Christian extolled by Patience in B.14, a person who does not run around seeking his own desires as Hawkyn does, but instead confines himself to that which is ordained by the church. Such a person demonstrates his faith in God to provide all that he needs, and his restraint is rewarded with the very thing that motivates it in the first place: spiritual food, or divine eloquence.

> So therefore every faithful man should maintain himself and live according to the will of God; he should not travel about running hither and yon, like heretics do; nor should he partake of worldly luxuries and bodily pleasures, like those birds who feed themselves with flesh ... Therefore wherever he encloses himself, God is: he makes [men of one manner] dwell in the house; and there he has the daily break of immortality; precious blood of Christ; refreshing himself with the feasts of saints and, "above honey and the honeycomb," the sweetest words of God: "For man shall not live by bread alone, but through every word of God."[13]

Patience's analogy, however, departs importantly from the moralizations of animals found in bestiaries. According to Patience, it is not simply that the properties of a particular beast, like the curlew, may be interpreted in such a way as to teach the right attitude toward God and food. Rather, taken together, all animals exemplify the right attitude toward God and food, because they all depend upon God to provide for them through the work of creation ("Your will be done," and see 7.125–30; 15.179, 276–306). As Patience explains, just as the Israelites lived for decades on manna in the desert, and just as the seven sleepers survived seven hundred winters without food, so all animals live in a perpetual present with a natural disregard for the future that human beings should emulate. All animals, human beings included, were created by God, and therefore all animals need God's grace. People, uniquely possessed of language, should express reliance on God as a spiritual attitude: "For thorugh his breeth beestes woxen and abrood yeden: / *Dixit et facta sunt, &c.* / *Ergo* thorugh his breeth mowen [bothe] men and beestes lyven, / As Holy Writ witnesseth whan men seye hir graces: / *Aperis tu manum tuam, et imples omne animal benediccione*" [For through his breath beasts grew and went forth:/ "He said and it was done," etc./ "Therefore" through his breath both men and beasts might live /As Holy Writ attests, when men say grace, / "You open your hand, and fill with blessing every living thing" (Psalm 144:16)] (B.14.60–62a).

Although Patience interprets the "liflode" of animals as the loyal belief and love that ought to govern human action ("In menynge that alle men myghte the same / Lyue," 14.46–47), it gradually becomes clear in B.14 that all animals model this attitude unconsciously, insofar as all animals must live on what God has ordained for them. This crucial move from allegory (the *fulica* symbolizes Christian obedience) to analogy (people should be more like the *fulica*) is anticipated by an encyclopedia like the *Properties*, which, by finding commonalities among species, tends to obscure moral differences between human and animal.

Patience, in his sermon, encourages Hawkyn to choose poverty in spirit, an attitude toward God and neighbor to which all people, not just the poor, can aspire. The idea is to divest oneself psychologically and materially from worldly care, in the style of St. Francis, and to trust entirely in God, following Christ's injunction in Matthew 19:21 to sell everything one has and give the money to the poor. In this respect, the poet does not question Patience's advice (and *Piers Plowman* primarily addresses readers who have something to give up in the first place). After all, this is Piers's decisive course of action in B.7 upon hearing the terms of the Pardon, that he will henceforth be not so busy about his "bely joy" (7.119), that he will eat his penance and seek his "liflode" (7.123) from God. As Piers poignantly exclaims, who but God feeds the starving birds in winter? (7.129–30). The sudden will to a life of poverty and prayer is what makes that life so striking, just as in the lovely lines in B.14 in which Patience compares voluntary poverty to a maiden who bravely chooses a love-match and "forsaketh / Hir fader and alle hire frendes" (B.14.265–66; on voluntary poverty, see Recklessness's speech at C.12.161ff.). But Patience's beast analogy suggests that if one were to compare the properties of all beasts – what God allots to animals as sustenance – one would reach a different conclusion, namely, that the essence of voluntary poverty is an involuntary state, in which humans live not on a prayer but, like the curlew, on air.

Patience's curious turn from allegory to analogy, and from voluntary to involuntary poverty, gives rise to two even more daring analogies between poor people and beasts, both of which compare the time in which humans and animals live in order to describe the best human practice. Hawkyn asks Patience whether patient poverty surpasses riches justly won and reasonably dispended, to which Patience responds by contesting the worth of riches in a spiritual economy. The rich, he says, are always already debtors. They have received their wages up front and therefore owe something when they die, a debt paid in hell. In a stunning image, Patience pictures a poor servant remonstrating with his lord for the wages due to him. The servant reminds the lord that the poor have earned their heavenly wages because they have suffered in advance on earth. In this sense, the servant says, the poor are like animals made "meke" and "milde" by winter, but given summer as their joyful reward:

> And seith, "Lo! Briddes and beestes, that no blisse ne knoweth,
> And wilde wormes in wodes, thorugh wyntres thow hem grevest,
> And makest hem wel neigh meke and mylde for defaute,
> And after thow sendest hem somer, that is thir souereyn ioye,
> And blisse to alle that ben, bothe wilde and tame.
> Thanne may beggeris, as beestes, after boote waiten,
> That al hir lif han lyved in langour and in defaute.
> But God sente hem som tyme som manere joye
> Outher here or elliswhere, kynde wolde it nere".   (14.111–19)

> [And [the servant] says, "Indeed, birds and beasts, which know no bliss,
> And wild snakes in the woods, you oppress them with winter,
> And make them virtually meek and mild for lack,
> And afterwards you send them summer, which is their utmost joy,
> And bliss to every one of them, both wild and tame.
> So may beggars, like beasts, expect their reward,
> Who lived all their lives with affliction and lack.
> Unless God sent them, at some point, some kind of joyful [reward],
> Either here or elsewhere, it wouldn't be natural!"]

We saw that Patience's first beast analogy ("First the wild serpent ...") trades on the philosophical gap between human will and animal instinct, and between a poor attitude and involuntary poverty. Beasts cannot help but rely on God to give them what they need, and people, in this respect, ought to try to be more like beasts. In the second, very beautiful comparison given above, Patience takes a more vertiginous turn, in which he directly compares the seasonal life of beasts to the lives of the Christian poor. If animals and poor people earn a different kind of "summer," they never-theless share the same worldly deprivations and capacity for joy. In this view, the likeness between human and animal experience argues for the intrinsic merit of the human poor: according to Patience, paupers may confidently sue God for their heavenly wages because affliction ("langor") and lack ("defaute") are natural properties of their condition, just as they are the natural properties of beasts. The unwilled hardship and unlooked-for joy experienced by both men and beasts make human poverty meritorious. Poverty, in this sense, is a continuous penance and an absolute good.

A few lines later, Patience, still railing against riches, revisits the "book of beasts" for the third and final time. In this passage, he places human and animals squarely in the same temporality, and with some surprising results. In the previous passage, the analogy between animals and poor people

seemed to fit well – the seasonal lives of beasts show what human beings
deserve in the afterlife because animals and poor people elicit pity in similar
ways. In the third passage, however, Patience reframes the analogy in such a
way as to make an even stronger case for the human poor. If the seasons of
beasts are compared to those of the human poor, the plight of poor people
suddenly seems far greater – for them both winter and summer are hard.
Now beasts start to resemble the rich who experience some seasonal joy,
enjoying their "summer" right here on earth:

> For muche murthe is amonges riche, as in mete and clothing.
> And muche murthe in May is amonges wilde beestes,
> And so forth while somer lasteth hir solace dureth.
> Ac beggeris aboute midsomer bredlees thei soupe,
> And yet is winter for hem worse, for weetshoed thei gange,
> Afurst soore and afyngred, and foule yrebuked
> And arated of riche men, that ruthe is to here.
> Now, Lord, sende hem somer, and som maner ioye,
> Heuene after hir hennes goyng, that here han swich defaute!   (14.157–65)

> [For there is much pleasure among the rich regarding food and clothing.
> And there is much pleasure in May among wild beasts,
> And as long as summer lasts their comfort continues.
> But beggars around midsummer eat without bread,
> And yet winter is worse for them, for wetshoed they walk,
> Awfully thirsty and hungry, and cruelly rebuked,
> And scorned by rich men, which is sad to hear.
> Now, Lord, send them summer, and some kind of joy,
> Heaven after their going hence, those who have such need here.]

The contrast between beasts, who experience some joy in summer, and the
human poor, who suffer year round, valorizes the plight of the poor, whose
righteousness is bound up in unalleviated physical suffering.

   In short, Patience's exhaustive comparisons between men and beasts
move the passus toward a full defense of (patient) involuntary poverty as
the most righteous human life. Importantly, too, this defense of real poverty
is achieved by comparing the time of humans and animals, whose lives
literally overlap. Lastly, and unexpectedly, Patience's beast analogies suggest
that the spiritual value of poverty can be measured, in part, by the feelings it
arouses in others. The poet expects that his readers will recognize that they
live in the same time as animals and the human poor, and that they can
sympathize accordingly. The poor are "afurst soore and afyngred, and foule
yrebuked," a line that recalls Langland's poignant description of poor
neighbors in C.9: "And hemselue also soffre muche hunger, /And wo in

winter-tymes . . . And of mony other men that moche wo soffren, / Bothe
afyngred and afurste" [And they suffer much hunger /And woe in
wintertime . . . /And [this is true] of many other men who suffer much
woe, / Both hungry and thirsty] (77–78, 84–85). It is easy to admire
spiritual athletes who voluntarily embrace a life of poverty, like the desert
Fathers, whose faith and asceticism Anima praises at length in B.15, or St.
Francis, whose life shadows Patience's sermon.[14] But poor people – like
virtuous pagans, like beasts in winter – provoke sympathy rather than
admiration, and in so doing they make a bold case for their own
redemption.

Poor comparisons

With Patience's analogies between human and animals, Langland explores
the time of practice, and identifies real poverty (unwilled and unrelieved) as
the essence of spiritual poverty. But he has not yet exhausted the possibilities for representing the virtue of poverty, and he relentlessly pursues every
implication of the argument for the poor. For example, although Patience
commends involuntary poverty for being an abject and unwilled condition,
he also gives it a moral agency and rhetorical power. In the Middle English
verse rendition of Deguileville's *Pilgrimage of the Life of Man*, a likely source
for *Piers Plowman*, Patient Poverty explains to Impatient Poverty that "Ther
may no thyng a man avayle; / (What maner thyng that euere it be,) / But it
be doon of volunte" [Nothing may avail a man / (Whatever it may be) /
Unless it be done willingly].[15] Langland would agree with Deguileville that
all moral action proceeds from the will (*voluntas*), and that poor people, if
they want their poverty to count as virtue, should accept it without
complaint. However, in his thought experiment about poverty in B.14,
the poet explodes the difference between the *voluntas* of intention and the
voluntas of condition: it is precisely when poverty is non-elective and reflects
a permanent condition that it merits heavenly reward.

According to Patience, moreover, involuntary poverty, as a permanent
condition, lays claim to a peculiar agency. In 14.202–73, for example, he
explains how different aspects of real poverty work to counteract each of the
seven sins. To be a truly virtuous practice, poverty must be patient, yet it
naturally wards off vice. It is nearly impossible for the poor not to do well
because they are habitually downtrodden and therefore much less susceptible to sin than the rich are. A poor man must be subservient, not proud; he
cannot afford to speak in anger; his gluttony is limited ("for his rentes wol
nought recche" [because his income won't stretch] (14.231)); the contest

between a poor man and avarice is like a "lovely layk" [amusing game] (14.244) between a David and a Goliath, the giant swatting at a "petit thyng" (14.243), who reaches only to his navel.

In this way, involuntary poverty, as an unchanging state, acquires an agency seemingly at odds with the helplessness of the poor. Earlier in the passus, Patience imagined an improbable situation, a poor servant arguing with his lord for the wages still due to him. Similarly, in the treatise on the seven sins summarized above, the unalterable situation of poverty is what allows poverty's merit to be asserted so strongly. The poor can make a claim for heavenly reward as bold as any beggar's request for alms: "Thanne may beggeris as beestes, after boote waiten, / That al hir lif han lyued in langour and in defaute" [Then beggars, like beasts, may expect their reward, / Who lived their whole lives with affliction and lack] (14.116–17). Earlier the poet reviled the boisterous beggar with his pack on his back (Prol.40–42, and 6.213); by B.14, however, the beggar has come to represent the spiritual works (*opera*) of real poverty:

> For the riche hath muche to rekene, and right softe walketh;
> The heighe wey to heveneward ofte riche letteth:
> *Ita [in]possibile diviti* [Matthew 19:23–24]
> Ther the poore preesseth bifore, with a pak at his rugge –
> *Opera enim illorum sequuntur illos* – [Revelation 14:13]
> Batauntliche as beggeris doon, and boldeliche he craveth,
> For his poverte and his pacience, a perpetuel blisse:
> *Beati pauperes: quoniam ipsorum est regnum celorum.* [Matthew 5:3]
>
> (211–15)

> [For the rich man has much to account for, and so he treads very lightly;
> The highway to heaven often obstructs the rich:
> "Thus it is (im)possible for a rich man [to enter the kingdom of heaven]."
> There the poor man leads the way, with a pack at his back –
> "For their works will follow them" –
> Forcibly, as beggars do, and boldly he asks,
> For his poverty and his patience, a perpetual bliss:
> "Blessed are the poor, for theirs is the kingdom of heaven."]

Poverty, says Patience, quoting Vincent of Beauvais's *Speculum historiale*, is an *odibile bonum*, a hateful good or virtue in disguise, etc. (14.276ff.), a passage which Chaucer puts in the mouth of the wise old woman in the *Wife of Bath's Tale*, and which Langland typically narrativizes into "a little vignette of action," turning passive verbs into active: "Selde sit poverte the sothe to declare, / Or as justice to jugge men enjoyned is no poore . . .

Remocio curarum" [Seldom does Poverty sit to deliver a verdict, / Nor are poor people appointed justices to judge other men ... "Removal of cares"] (287–88, 290b).[16] For a medieval cleric, poverty might have served as an exercise in paradox, at the same time as it served as an exercise in imitation: a "poor" attitude is only an impression of what is taken to be poor people's natural humility. But poverty, for Langland, is also a moral experiment in personification, assigning both agency and choice to those whose virtue is to possess neither.

If the merit of poverty is identified with the natural condition of the poor – if involuntary lack is the essence of patient poverty – then the rich must be categorical sinners. This is an intolerable position for the poet, which he tries hard to correct. Patience explains that if every Christian is a laborer, the poor man receives his payment after his work is done, that is, when his tribulation on earth has earned him his heavenly reward. The rich man, by contrast, receives his pay in advance and must work it off in Purgatory. Patience never clarifies whether the "work" in question is suffering or refraining from sin and doing good deeds. If the work is suffering, then plainly the rich, through no fault of their own, can never hope to earn heaven.[17] If the work of salvation means refraining from sin and doing good deeds, then the salvation of the rich starts to look suspiciously like that of a Trajan or an Aristotle, slimly possible, however unattested, says Patience, by legends of the saints ("by holy seintes bokes" 14.155).

This section of the poem was the site of a notable revision, a revision that further underlines the tension in the poem between a poor attitude and real poverty. The revision also shows that the literary practice to which the poet was most committed was reiteration, the constant re-launching of a proposition or an analogy, even if doing so meant sacrificing ideological coherence. In the C-text, Patience moves smoothly from an unqualified condemnation of wealth ("So Y sey by yow ryche: hit semeth nat that ye sholle / Haue two heuenes for youre here-beying") [So I say to you rich, it doesn't look like you'll receive two heavens in exchange for your time here on earth] (C.16.8–9) to the third beast analogy, in which beasts are compared unfavorably to rich men enjoying their "summer" ("Muche murthe in May is amonge wilde beestes") (B.14.158/C.16.10). In the B version, however, the poet ripped these passages apart – or, in C, he stitched them together – inserting a provision for the rich so vaulting that it approaches an *impossibilium*:

Ac if ye riche have ruthe, and rewarde wel the poore,
And lyven as lawe techeth, doon leaute to alle,

Crist of his curteisie shal conforte yow at the laste
And rewarden alle double richesse that rewful hertes habbeth.
And as an hyne that hadde his hire er he bigonne,
And whan he hath doon his devoir wel, men dooth hym oother bountee –
Yyveth hym a cote above his covenaunt – right so Crist yyveth hevene
Both to riche and to noght riche that rewfulliche libbeth;
And alle that doon hir devoir wel han double hire for hir travaille –
Here foryifnesse of hir synnes, and hevene blisse after.   (B.14.145–154)

[But if you rich have pity, and reward the poor well,
And live as law teaches, deal fairly with all,
Christ in his courtesy will comfort you at the end,
And reward with double riches all those who have compassionate hearts.
And like a servant who received his pay before he began,
And when he has done his work well, men give him an extra tip –
Give him a coat above his contract – in this way Christ gives heaven
Both to rich and to not-rich who live compassionately;
And all those who do their work well will have double pay for their efforts –
Here, forgiveness for their sins, and later, heavenly bliss.]

In this new passage, those servants entrusted in advance with their wages –
that is, the rich – earn a spectacular reward, provided they live "rewfulliche"
[compassionately, sorrowfully], a reward that pushes the limits of God's
mercy by allotting them two heavens, double riches, double pay, and, in a
phrase that resonates with medieval service, a "coat above his contract." In
this analogy, the rich become a rich person's dream servants, so zealous in
their duties they deserve an extra gift. Although Patience has been arguing –
and will continue to argue – that real poverty, as an involuntary condition,
constitutes the best life, in this passage he posits service as an alternative
rubric under which both rich and poor can prove themselves righteous: the
poor may be like animals, but the rich are like their own servants. This
passage, by giving the rich their own virtuous temporality – the time of
faithful service – allows even the rich the possibility of doing well.

One might be tempted at this point to criticize Langland for yoking the
rhetorical force of poverty to an argument that has little to do with the
alleviation of the suffering of the poor. As David Aers argues, for example,
although Langland exposes the moral shortcomings of the new fourteenth-
century "work ethic" in the Plowing of the Half-Acre, and although he
advocates a radical identification with the poor in B.11 (where Trajan
commiserates with the plight of poor people) and again in B.14, he stops
short of offering a solution to real poverty.[18] Langland's contribution,
however, is to devise a poetics capable of producing a range of ethical
stances and of constructing simultaneous models of human righteousness.

In B.14, the device is analogy, and specifically the comparison of the physical and moral properties of species. At the heart of this ethical poetics is a belief in the transformative power of material poverty, a kind of poverty that not only guarantees the poor a special purchase on salvation but also fuels the poet's thinking about poverty in spirit and the salvation of the rich. The poet cares about social justice, and yet his main concern is not the eradication of poverty in fourteenth-century England any more than it is the compassionate treatment of animals. Among other things, the eradication of poverty would obviate the need for sympathetic charity, which is, for Langland, the foundation of morality. Rather, as the "double hire" passage shows, the poet cares about the ways that analogies between humans and animals, rich and the poor, penitents and paupers, lead to a practice worthy of heaven.

The example of the past

At the beginning of this chapter, we saw that the Dowel triad describes the best life practice in two ways: as a continuous state and as a repeated or progressive action. From this perspective, Dowel points to a central concern of the poem, the time of practice, or the moment, pattern, or era in which a meritorious life can be led. In *Piers Plowman*, the time of practice has particular significance for the clergy, who claim special status and are meant to set an example for everyone else. In B.9–11, the Dowel triad seems to conform roughly to the tripartite division of the estates: Dowel = laity, Dobet = clergy, and Dobest = lords, temporal or spiritual. Dowel clearly distinguishes those who follow the basic tenets of Christianity from those who instruct others in the faith. Thus Wit explains that to Dowel is "to drede God" and follow the law (9.204), implying that one can do well simply by performing the role of a credulous and obedient layperson. Similarly, Clergy tells the dreamer that Dowel represents belief in the articles of the faith, as proper to the laity in their presumed simplicity. In Wit's definition, however, Dobet and Dobest propose two different models of clergy: Dobet refers to those preachers and teachers who humbly practice what they preach, while Dobest refers to those who "bryngeth adoun the mody" [bring down the proud] (9.205), i.e., those who make it their business to protect the faithful and stamp out corruption. According to Clergy, Dobet means living what you teach, whereas Dobest means combating sin in a larger arena: "Thanne is Dobest to be boold to blame the gilty, / Sythenes thow seest thiself as in soule clene" [Then is Dobest to be bold (enough) to denounce the guilty, / When you see yourself to be clean in (your own) soul] (10.258–59).

These two roles, Dobet and Dobest, need not be mutually exclusive. In theory, someone who strives for perfect integrity – a Thomas Becket or, centuries later, a Thomas More – might land the job of reformer; conversely, a reformer should have a reputation for piety. Two problems immediately present themselves, however. The first problem, discussed in the previous chapter, has to do with what the poet calls "suffraunce": if the perfect cleric is a preacher, the perfect preacher not only practices what he preaches but also maintains an uncritical attitude toward other people. But how can someone who never criticizes blame the guilty? The second problem has to do with the language of reform: the minute you identify a reformer you expose the shortcomings not only of the reformer, but also of the clerical estate as a whole. To give someone moral authority is to imagine all the ways the professional religious compromise their estate: through sycophancy, as when they flatter lords and cast pearls before swine; through ignorance, like those "overskipperis," who don't know how to sing or read psalms (11.309,13),[19] or recite good verses or compose letters (15.385); and, worst of all, through hypocrisy. After defining Dobest, Clergy cautions, "Forthi, ye correctours, claweth heron, and correcteth first yowselve!" [Therefore, you correctors, listen up, and correct yourselves first!] (10.283, and see 266–68).

In short, to speak of Dowel, Dobet, and Dobest, is to hold up a mirror to the contemporary clergy, while at the same time inviting all readers and listeners to participate in clerical reform. One of the poet's objectives is to find a time and a place where integrity and reform can be reconciled. In B.15 he makes a radical proposition, that universal Christian history and specifically, the history of conversion, is the place where the best clerical practice can be found.

Towards the end of B.13, the poet returns to one of his favorite topics: entertainment at feasts, and the conduct of lords in the hall. The rich expect every day to be a holiday, so they surround themselves with "fool-sages, flatereris and lieris" (13.423). A lord would be better off patronizing three other "minstrels": the poor man as a "fool sage sittynge at th[i] table" (13.444), a learned man to instruct him, and a blind man in the jester's place (13.436–57). Conscience's feast is an exemplary instance of lordly conduct. No host could be more gracious than Conscience, who attends to every guest while encouraging scholars and paupers to discourse on morality. The doctor of divinity, though a glutton and bore, ably defines Dowel for the company, as he who does what clerks teach, Dobet as he who teaches others, and Dobest as he who does what he says and preaches (13.116–18). At Conscience's urging, Patience, a poor pilgrim, also defines the Dowel triad as learn (*Disce*), teach (*Doce*), and love one's enemies (*Dilige*) (13.137–39). Patience subsequently glosses Dobest, explaining that if someone were systematically to imply the injunction to love one's enemies, he would make a world of difference, overcoming all dissention and disunity and convincing Western leaders to abide by his judgment: "Patientes vincunt" [The patient overcome] (13.172a).

At this point, decorum breaks down. The doctor of divinity sneers at Patience's gloss: no one person could make peace between the pope and his enemies, or between two Christian kings! (13.173–79). Conscience reacts differently. He is moved by Patience to mourn his sins and announces to the company that he will join Patience in pilgrimage to seek the world ("Frendes, fareth wel!") (13.181) like a new recruit signing up for a crusade. Clergy is skeptical about Conscience's plans: does he simply long for adventure? Clergy volunteers to teach him scripture instead, but Conscience insists he would rather have Patience any day than half of Clergy's books (13.189–202). By the end of the episode, however, Conscience and Clergy make up, promising to collaborate in the future on the kind of diplomatic enterprises that Patience described earlier, such as negotiating peace and converting the heathen. Conscience boasts to Clergy that, with Patience's help, "'Ther nys wo in this world that we ne sholde amende, /And conformen kynges to pees, and alle kynnes londes / Sarsens and Surre and so forth alle the Jewes – / Turne into the trewe feith and intil oon bileve'" ["There is no woe in this world that we would not amend /And we would compel kings and every type of lord to make peace. /And we would convert Saracens, and Syria, and likewise all the Jews to the true faith and to one belief"] (13.208–11). For the poet, converting the infidel – a task that would require infinite patience! – is the very demonstration of Patience's injunction to Dobest, or "love one's enemies."

It is through this conversion initiative, summed up by Conscience's missionary trip to Syria, that the poet will imagine the best clerical practice. Conscience and Patience's pilgrimage is primarily, of course, a penitential, inward journey: Patience assures Conscience that he has "vitalles" [victuals] to sustain them both in the "hungry countrees" (13.220) of unkindness and greed (13.216). The poet is invested, however, not only in allegories of penance, but also in the narrative that underwrites penitential allegory: the story of worldwide Christian reform and the universal history of Christian salvation, which encompasses every period, nation, and corner of the earth. Just as Patience's test of spiritual poverty is real poverty, so Anima's test of a "pilgrim's" mettle is whether he can convert unbelievers in foreign lands. As B.15 shows, the fantasy at the center of *Piers Plowman* is that Christianity will triumph, both in the soul and in the world. The auxiliary fantasy in B.15 is that history is a reliable guide to Christian charity, as well as a compendium of great deeds against which the conduct of contemporary English clerks can be measured. This is by no means to say that Langland expects English priests to abandon their parishes and head for Jerusalem; on the contrary, he wants them to keep themselves and their parishioners morally fit at home. Rather, it is to say that the poet imagines an ideal practice, the unification of word and deed, through universal Christian history, whose past and future lies in the conversion of the world.

At the beginning of B.15, the dreamer meets Anima or the soul, who lectures to him on the nature of charity. For Anima, charity means total integrity, as represented by preachers who teach with examples and by example on the model of Christ. Unfortunately, integrity is a harder thing to detect than hypocrisy, and Anima makes good on his promise to write a "muche bible" [huge volume] (15.89) of clerical offences against charity. Some clerics, like the dreamer, have an excessive appetite for knowledge, which does them a "double scathe" [double harm] (15.59): the more they know, the more they have to live up to what they know. Bad, too, are the preaching friars who delve into theological abstractions ("materes unmesurables") (15.71) and deny the laity basic pastoral care such as the Ten Commandments, the seven deadly sins, and the five wits. Worst of all are the members of that "inparfit preesthode" (15.95) – a phrase that would resonate with Lollard (heretical) writings on spiritual election – who, even when they speak well, set bad examples for the laity (15.108–10).

If charity's opposite, hypocrisy, is evident in the conduct of clerks, when and where can true charity be found? At what time and in which place do words and works conform? The dreamer confesses that though he has witnessed many acts of compassion, he has only glimpsed charity imperfectly reflected in his own self:

"Clerkes kenne me that Crist is alle places;
Ac I seigh hym nevere soothly but as myself in a mirour:
Hic [vidimus per speculum] in enigmate, tunc facie ad faciem." (15.161–62)

[Clerks teach me that Christ is in all places:
But I have never truly seen him except in my own reflection:
"Here [we see through a glass as if] in an enigma, then [we will see] face to face".]

Charity, says the dreamer, or, in other words, Christ as the embodiment of charity, is only imperfectly reflected in ordinary people. Charity is an *enigma*, says the dreamer, quoting the famous line from Corinthians 1.13.[20] As one modern scholar has argued, the rhetorical force of Corinthians 1.13 lies not just with the familiar *per speculum* ("through a glass") but also with *in enigmate* (mysteriously, or as an enigma). In classical rhetoric, an *enigma* usually refers to a small puzzle or riddle, a local trope that mixes what is known with what is seemingly mysterious. It took a master theologian like St. Augustine of Hippo to see the potential of *enigma* to become a "trope of tropes," one that might address larger and more abstract philosophical ideas about figuration. Thanks to Augustine, *enigma*, insofar as it expresses a relationship between likeness and unlikeness, became the core trope of typology, signifying human history and its mysterious fulfillment in Christian time. From one perspective, people are radically unlike God because, in a fallen world, humanity falls short of divinity, while, from another perspective, people are radically like God through Christ's humanity.[21] This is the *enigma* of identity and faith in an Augustinian worldview.

Langland's dreamer contends that charity is an *enigma*, by which he means that we can never tell whether someone's words and works agree because true charity in Christ exceeds everything people know about human goodness. But if Christ's humanity – imperfectly reflected in the self (*per speculum*) – bridges the gap between God and man, might it not be possible to discern the intention of others and praise or damn them accordingly? In fact, says Anima, true charity *is* manifest in history, and therefore can be known historically through Piers the Plowman, or Jesus Christ in human time, in Anima's cryptic phrase: *"Petrus, id est, Christus"* [Peter, that is Christ] (15.212), Petrus (Piers's Latin name) signifying both Christ's apostle, St. Peter, to whom Christ entrusted the Church, and Piers's alter ego as Christ. In B.13 Conscience claims not to know the right definition of Dowel, but he is sure he will know it when he sees it, when Piers the Plowman proves it in deed (13.133). With *"Petrus, id est, Christus"* Anima says something very similar: Piers the Plowman represents the historical incarnation of charity, from the life of Christ through the institutional church founded by St. Peter, the first Pope. Just as importantly, Piers the Plowman represents that historical perspective that allows charity to be identified in the first place. No earthly creature can judge the intention of another; even those with higher learning can discern nothing beyond what words and works reveal (15.198), yet "Piers the Plowman parceyveth moore depper / What is the wille, and wherfore that many wight suffreth" [Piers the Plowman perceives more deeply / What the will is, and for what reason anyone suffers] (15.199–200). These lines, however mystifying, invite us to think about charity as an historical and a historiographical phenomenon: it is exemplified by persons in time and documented in writings about the past.

In this way, history offers an alternative discourse of clerical reform, a *speculum historiale*, which, in its supposed completeness and transparency, serves as *Piers Plowman*'s specular Other. From the dramatic line, "*Petrus, id est, Christus*" (15.212), Anima's lecture on clerical transgression becomes a sprawling history, populated with ascetics, martyrs, missionaries, and saints. According to universal Christian history, all sorts of people have performed charity "in deed": "For I have seyen [Charity] in silk and som tyme in russet, / Bothe in grey, and in grys [gray], and in gilt harneis ... I have yseyen Charite also syngen and redden, / Riden and rennen in raggede wedes" [For I have seen (Charity) in silk, and sometime in russet, / In shades of gray, and in gold trappings ... I have also seen Charity sing and teach / Ride and go in ragged clothes] (15.220–21, 225–26). Anima's history includes martyr kings; early saints Anthony, Egidus, and Mary Magdalene, the latter who, according to the *Golden Legend*, lived without food for thirty years in the desert; apostles Peter, Paul, and Andrew; leaders of religious orders, Francis, Dominic, Benedict, and Bernard of Clairveaux; the sixth-century missionary Augustine of Canterbury, and the murdered archbishop, Thomas Becket.

In this way, B.15 resembles any number of medieval universal chronicles. Langland might have been particularly impressed, however, by the recent success of the *Polychronicon*, a Latin universal chronicle in seven books compiled a generation earlier than *Piers Plowman* by Ranulph Higden. The *Polychronicon* draws on dozens of chronicles, encyclopedias, exegetical works, and saints' lives, which Higden syncretized and abridged. What makes the *Polychronicon* different from other universal histories is the way in which it subordinates universal Christian history to English history. Although it professes to be history of all times and places – biblical, Roman, papal, imperial – as it approaches the fourteenth century, its trajectory becomes increasingly English. In his third prologue to the *Polychronicon*, which tries out different organizational schemes, Higden explains that one way to organize time after Christ is through the conquests of the British Isles: it is for this reason that his fourth book covers the life of Christ to the coming of the Anglo-Saxons; the fifth book covers the Anglo-Saxons to the coming of Danes; the sixth book the Danes to the Norman invasion; and the seventh the Normans through the reign of Edward III. Later medieval writers saw Higden's innovation as an invitation to translate (Latin) monastic historiography into vernacular contexts and national histories, such as royal genealogies, religious polemic, versified bibles, and biblical drama.[22] *Piers Plowman* B.15 operates like a *Polychronicon* in miniature. Although it traces the contours of universal Christian history, it features an all-star English cast, beginning with the Anglo-Saxon kings Edward and Edmund, the great missionary to the Anglo-Saxons, St. Augustine of Canterbury, and, in some *Piers* manuscripts, Thomas Becket, killed in 1170 by Henry II's henchmen. The poet's emphasis on English characters suggests that the history of Christian charity comes into focus through a national English chronicle.[23] As will become clearer below, Langland's Englishing of universal history is key to his vision of clerical reform.

According to Higden, the role of historical writing is to model good deeds for the present and, for Langland, no example of charity is more manifest than Christ's. Throughout the course of history, exemplary persons suffered like Christ: the desert fathers patiently starved, and martyrs, like Peter and Paul, were tortured and imprisoned (15.269–306). Christ showed his followers how to submit to ignominy and pain:

> For wel may every man wite, if God hadde wold hymselve,
> Sholde nevere Judas ne Jew have Jesu doon on roode,
> Ne han martired Peter ne Poul, ne in prison holden.
> Ac he suffrede in ensample that we sholde suffren also,
> And seide to swiche that suffre wolde that *Pacientes vincunt.*   (15.263–67)

> [For every man should know well, if God himself had wanted it,
> Neither Judas nor Jew would have had Jesus crucified,
> Nor would they have martyred Peter or Paul, or held them in prison.
> But he suffered in example that we should also suffer,
> And said to those who would suffer that "the patient overcome".]

Christ and his apostles, through their exemplary submission, set records for great deeds; most spectacularly, through the Atonement, Christ showed how suffering could be an efficacious act and an outstanding example of dying for one's beliefs.

In Langland's view in B.15, no deed is greater and more worthy of imitation than converting others to Christianity. At Conscience's feast, discussed above, Patience explains that to do best, to love your enemies, is to achieve Christian unity on a grand scale or, in other words, *"Patientes vincunt"* (the patient overcome); this is the mission that Conscience and

Clergy hope to carry out one day. It is by converting others, moreover, that Christ reconciled Dobet and Dobest, suffering and reform. According to Anima, clerks who spread the gospel faithfully imitate Christ's example by obeying his command to go out into the whole world and preach, "*Ite in universum mundum et predicate*" (15.491). The eleven apostles, says Anima, turned the whole world to the right belief; nowadays the institutional Church has "so manye maistres – / Preestes and prechours, and a pope above" (15.439–40) that it should be a relatively simple matter to convert "alle manere men" (15.439). All preachers, of course, should take the high road and guide others through their good example. A person's soul is lacking "that seeth no good ensaumple / Of hem of Holi Church that the heighe way sholde teche / And be gide, and go bifore as a good banyer" [who sees no good example / from those [representatives] of Holy Church who are supposed to teach the high way / And be guides and go in front like a good banner] (15.433–5). To be truly exemplary, however, is to realize this metaphor literally and sally forth to win Christian souls.

In the good old days, the British Isles were themselves the site of exemplary preaching and conversion: Augustine of Canterbury, dispatched to "heathen lands" (England and, more controversially, Wales) by Pope Gregory I, baptized the king and converted that whole territory "To Crist and to Cristendom, and cros to honoure" (15.446). Crucially, says Anima, Augustine won over the Anglo-Saxons through miracles rather than through a great deal of preaching (15.448). Although the medieval clergy must set good examples "by hire wordes and werkes" (15.477), charity in deed is exemplified not only by sermonizing but also by the great deeds that underwrite sermons, such as the miracles wrought by Christ and his apostles. Anima repeats a story from the gospels about a rich man who fed his guests not with wild game but with chickens so tame that they came when he whistled (15.461ff.). So, says Anima, today's clerks should whistle to "rude men" with good examples, just as Christ performed miracles to woo Christian souls: "with wederes and with wondres he warneth us with a whistelere / Where that his wil is" (15.482–83) [with weather and with wonders he warned us with a whistler / What it was he wanted].

This seems like a tall order for the average preacher – surely setting a good example need not be demonstrated in miracles! But Anima's history is not just a compendium of worthy deeds but also a plan of action so tough that present-day clerics cannot hope to live up to its standards. It is nothing less than an indictment of the contemporary clergy who, by not practicing what they preach in their parishes and dioceses, have essentially ceased to follow the great examples of their forbears, who worked miracles and converted the masses.

For the poet, the most damning proof that latter-day clerics are not doing their duty is the existence of Islam. In the past, high-ranking clerics took risks and traveled far to win souls, but nowadays "What pope or prelate now parfourneth that Crist highte – / *Ite in universum mundum et predicate* [*evangelium omni creaturae*]?/ Allas, that men so longe on Makometh sholde bileve!" [What pope or prelate now performs what Christ commanded – / "Go into the whole world and preach [the gospel to every creature]"?/Alas, that men continue to believe in Mohammed!] (15.490–91, from Mark 16:15). The worst offenders, says Anima, are those metropolitan (titular) bishops who hold sees *in partibus infidelium* [in the territory of the infidels] but do not fulfill the duties that pertain to their titles. It was common practice in the Middle Ages to assign bishops to non-residential sees in order to provide auxiliary bishops for busy dioceses, or to find places for prelates of defunct dioceses in once-Christian cities. After Saladin captured Bethlehem in 1187, for example, the Bishop of Bethlehem was invited to live in Clamecy, France, which remained the seat of the Bishopric of Bethlehem for nearly six hundred years. For the poet, this universal failure has particular resonance for the reform of the English clergy: bishops who bear Syrian titles, he complains, should not be scampering around England, sanctifying altars and encroaching upon the rights of priests to hear confession (15.527–28). They should be preaching the faith in the cities of their titles.

At the beginning of B.15, the dreamer jokes with Anima that just as Anima has many names (for example, Conscience, Reason, Love), so bishops have many titles: "'Ye ben as a bishop,' quod I, al bourdynge that tyme, / 'For bisshopes yblessed, thei bereth manye names / – *Presul* and *pontifex*, and *metropolitanus*, /And other names an heep, *episcopus* and *pastor*'" ["You're like a bishop," I said, just joking around, / "because ordained bishops bear many names – / *Leader* and *promoter*, and *metropolitan*, / And a host of other names, *overseer* and *shepherd*"] (15.40–43). The joke is that those with multiple appellations can never live up to all of them. Likewise, those prelates with titular sees, who "bere bisshopes names of Bethleeem and of Babiloigne" (15.509), present the most egregious case of hypocrisy, because they bear these titles in name only.

> So manye prelates to preche as the Pope maketh –
> Of Nazareth, of Nynyve, of Naptalym and Damaske.
> That thei ne wente as Crist wissith – sithen thei wilne a name –
> To be pastours and preche the passion of Jesus,
> And as himself seide, so to lyve and dye:
> *Bonus pastor animam suam ponit* [*pro ovibus*].   [John 10.11] (15.492–96a)

[(There are) so many prelates available to preach, whom the Pope has created –
Of Nazareth, of Ninevah, of Naphtali, and Damascus.
(It's a shame) that they don't follow Christ's lead – since they want the title –
To be pastors and preach the passion of Jesus.
For as he said himself, and lived and died by these words,
"A good pastor gives his life (for his sheep)."]

The Muslims living in these cities, apparently waiting to be converted, are a reproof to the pope who appointed the bishops in the first place (15.508). After all, says Anima, Christ himself was a "*metropolitanus*" (15.515) sent to the Holy Land by the "hye kyng of hevene" (15.510) to convert the people there; in doing so, he set an example to all those who wrongly believe that titular sees merely commemorate the glory days of Latin Christendom. The failure of titular bishops to reside in the cities of their titles, and the concomitant failure of Christianity to resist the incursions of Islam, amount to a rejection of Christian history, of Christ's example, and of every saint who spread the faith "In Inde, and in Alisaundre, in Ermonye, in Spayne," and who, in those foreign places, died (15.520–21).

But the failure of the institutional church to live up to the example of Christian history implicates more than just its leaders; for the poet, the resilience of Islam implicates the whole English clergy, whose practice is temporally and geographically out of step with the past. For medieval writers, historical *exempla* tend to work equally well as models of good behavior and as moralizations of virtue or vice. As such they can be used either to exhort people to imitate literally the deeds of their forebears or to condemn sin more generally. Anima forces history to do double-duty in his version of the apocryphal story of Mohammed, taken originally from the *Golden Legend*. According to this story, Mohammed, a Christian cleric denied promotion, headed for the Middle East and conned the people of Syria into accepting a new religion with him as their Messiah. In a travesty of Pentecost (in which the Holy Spirit descends upon the apostles in the form of a dove), Mohammed trained a dove to eat corn from his ear so when he preached, his audience would believe a divine messenger was speaking to him. Anima moralizes this story with a lesson for "Englisshe clerkes":

> And siththe Oure Saveour suffred the Sarsens so bigiled
> Thorugh a Cristene clerk acorsed in his soule –
> Ac for drede of the deeth I dar noght telle truth
> How Englisshe clerkes a colvere fede that Coveitise highte,
> And ben manered after Makometh, that no man useth trouthe.
>
> (15.411–15)

Figure 4. "Mohammed preaching." Giovanni Boccaccio, *De casibus virorum illustrium*,
trans. Laurent de Premierfait. Bibliothèque nationale de France, MS Français 226, f. 243.
(Paris, before 1450).

[And thus our savior allowed the Saracens to be beguiled
Through a Christian clerk, cursed in his soul.
But for fear of death I dare not tell the truth:
How English clerks feed a dove called Covetousness
And behave just like Mohammed, with the result that no one has integrity any
 more.]

As long as Islam continues to hold sway, all Christian clerks, it seems, are
implicated in Mohammed's deception. But English clerks who live in the
here and now of the poet's address – as opposed to the there and then of the
Middle East – are doubly implicated. English clerks are greedy hypocrites
like Mohammed because they fail to do what Mohammad did so well:
convert people. What is more, Mohammed, for Langland a pseudo-
prophet, converted unbelievers through the kind of trick that English
clerks, like Augustines of yesteryear, ought to perform as real miracles.[24]

 Anima's call to English clergy to convert the infidel is, of course, an
impossible mandate, not only because it requires ordinary preachers to play
the part of latter-day missionaries, but also because it strategically ignores
the difficulties of such a project. If the history of Christianity is supposed to
be triumphant and universal, insofar as it conflates universality with

geography it is bound to disappoint. For two centuries the Crusades had united Western lords and clergy in the effort to establish an earthly Jerusalem under Christian control, but by the mid thirteenth century, the Latin Kingdom of Jerusalem and the strategic ports adjoining it had returned to Muslim hands. By the mid fourteenth century, Western Christendom was bordered on the east by the Ottoman Turks, who had incorporated most of the former Byzantine Empire into the Dar al-Islam. The former Latin kingdom of Jerusalem and a large swathe of Christian and Jewish holy sites in the Middle East were controlled by the powerful Mameluke dynasty, who had beat back the Crusaders in the previous century and whose kingdom now stretched from Egypt to the Caucasuses.

Langland's strategy of imagining clerical reform through the Christian conversion of Islam recalls that of the author of *Mandeville's Travels* (*c*.1360), which survives in approximately three hundred manuscripts, including several manuscripts containing *Piers Plowman*. Mandeville's narrator, who identifies as English, claims to document his itinerary through personal experience. In truth, like *Piers Plowman* B.15, *Mandeville's Travels* draws from collections of saints' lives like the *Golden Legend*, as well as from encyclopedias, chronicles, Wonders of the East stories, and other travel narratives of the kind bound in the massive *Piers* manuscript Cambridge University Library Dd.i.17, which also contains an English Mandeville, a Latin *Polychronicon*, a Marco Polo, a *Gesta Machometi*, and many other works about English history, world travel, and Islam. Like *Piers Plowman*, B.15, *Mandeville's Travels* is a variation on universal history, recorded as one person's travels to the Middle East and beyond. Its success was due, in part, to its lively synthesis of these diverse materials, but also to the way that it handles the monumental failure of Western Christianity to spread the gospels through preaching or conquest, or even to fulfill the minimum requirement of safeguarding pilgrims traveling to the Holy Land.

In the prologue to the *Travels*, Mandeville declares his purpose to show Western Christians the best route to Jerusalem, which he hopes will be reclaimed one day from Islam. He professes to have detailed knowledge of the Holy Land, having served as a mercenary to the Great Sultan. Purportedly, the Sultan not only granted him privileged access to Christian holy sites but also, according to Mandeville, conversed with him in private audience. He reports that the Sultan was eager to discuss comparative religions: as Mandeville knowledgeably observes, the Koran accepts Christ as a prophet, retells the story of the Annunciation, and anticipates the Last Judgement. Surely, says Mandeville, because "als mykill as [Muslims] ga þus nere oure faith in þir pointes and many oþer, me think þat mykill þe titter and þe lightlier þai schuld be conuerted till oure lawe thurgh preching and teching of Cristen men" [for as much as (Muslims) approach our faith in these points and many others, it seems to me they could be more readily and easily converted to our religion through the preaching and teaching of Christian men].[25] The Sultan admits that the only obstacle to their conversion is the bad behavior of Christians. This behavior has been reported to the Sultan by his spies. "Your priests," says the Sultan, "seruez noȝt Godd duely in gude liffyng, as þai schuld do. For þai schuld giffe to lewed men ensaumple of gude liffyng, and þai do euen þe contrary; for þai giffe þam ensaumple of all wikkidness" [do not duly serve God in good living, as they should do. For they should give to unlearned men an example of good living, and they do the opposite; for they give them an example of total wickedness] (compare to *Piers Plowman* B.15.567ff.).[26] As a result, the laity commit the seven sins, which the Sultan elaborates in Langlandian detail: they frequent taverns instead of churches, they lie, swear, fornicate, and cheat.

Like Mandeville, Anima insists that Muslims and Jews, as monotheistic peoples, are always on the cusp of conversion: "And sith that thise Saracens, scribes and Jewes / Han a lippe of our bileve, the lightloker, me thynketh, / Thei sholde turne, whoso travaile wolde and teche hem of the Trinite:/ *Querite et invenietis*" [And since these Saracens, scribes and Jews /Are on the brink of belif, it seems to me it would be quite easy / To convert them, if somebody would make the effort to teach them about the Trinity: / "Seek and you shall find [them]"] [Matthew 7:7] (15.500–02). In Anima's account, their conversion to Christianity requires only the presence of preachers with geographical imagination, willing to fulfill their duties as bishops of "Nazareth, of Nynyve, of Neptalym, and Damaske" (15.493). Like Mandeville, Langland wants to have it both ways: he views the conversion of the infidel as clear proof of Christian valor, and at the same time, an assignment easily discharged. According to the *Travels*, if you interview any Muslim about his faith, he will promptly recite his Creed, like any good Christian.

> And, if a man ask þam of þaire beleue and how þai trowe, þai answere and saise, "We trowe in Godd, þat made heuen and oþer thinges of noght, and withouten him es na thing made. And we trowe þe day of dome schall comme, whare ilk man schall hafe his mede after his disserte. We trowe also verraily þat all es sothe þat Godd has spoken thurgh þe mouthes of his haly prophetez, whils þai welk in erthe."[27]

> [If any man ask them what is their faith and what they believe in, they answer thus and say: "We believe in God, who made heaven and other things from nothing. And without him nothing is made. And we believe that the day of

doom will come, when every man shall have his reward according his deserts.
And we also believe truly that everything is true which God has spoken
through the mouths of his holy prophets while they walked on earth."]

Apparently, major differences in belief systems can be overcome not only by
theological similarities by also by a catechistic sameness. Langland echoes
Mandeville's conviction: non-Christians are so ready to accept Christianity
that they are only a macaronic half-line away from reciting the Apostolic
Creed:

And sithen that the Sarsens and also the Jewes
Konne the firste clause of oure bileve, *Credo in Deum patrem omnipotentem,*
Prelates of Cristene provinces sholde preve, if thei myghte,
Lere him litlum and litlum *Et in Jesus Christum filium,*
Til thei kouthe speke and spelle *Et in Spiritum sanctum,*
And rendren it and recorden it with *remissionem peccatorum,*
Carnis resurreccionem et vitam eternam, amen. (15.606–11a)

[And since the Saracens and the Jews, too,
Understand the first clause of our belief, "I believe in God the omnipotent father,"
Prelates of Christian provinces should see to it, if they can,
[That they teach] them little by little, "And in [his] son Jesus Christ,"
Til they can speak and declaim, "And in the Holy Spirit,"
And recite it and write it [along] with "remission from sins,
The resurrection of the Body and eternal life, amen."]

Anima makes the task of the medieval preacher look like a *fait accompli*.
Why do today's clerics not measure up to the example of the apostles if the
conversion of the infidel is no harder than teaching the Creed to boys in
school or to the laity in confession? With a nudge in the right direction,
Saracens, Jews, and everyone else will soon learn to "rendren it and
recorden." Learning the Creed is simply a matter of acquiring a few Latin
phrases, and this passage shows just how easy it is by making the subjects of
Christian belief the objects of English verbs ("konne," "lere," "speke and
spelle," "rendren it and recorden"), and assimilating them to alliterative
meter.[28] At present, to be sure, Jews and Saracens believe only in God the
omnipotent father (the first line of the Creed), but if Christian clergy taught
them the mysteries of the Incarnation, Atonement, and Resurrection, they
would surely pick up the rest, little by little. In the end, teaching and
conversion would be of one accord, and the conduct of the clergy transparent to its critics.

If universal Christian history is a model for present-day clerks, if it
teaches them to go forth and perform true charity by converting the infidel,
what happens to English clerks who do not fulfill history in deed, and who

do not recognize themselves in history's mirror? On the one hand, Anima seems to be saying that the best clerical practice is, by its very nature, anachronistic. English priests should practice what they preach, but they certainly cannot be expected to conform to examples of twelfth-century metropolitans or early English missionaries. If, in an ideal world, priests should act historically, then perfect integrity is always outmoded. Modern-day English clerks should imitate Christ both by preaching (Dobet) and by venturing their lives (Dobest), and yet they are necessarily confined to the space and time of fourteenth-century England, whose parishes are crowded with secular priests and friars jockeying for titles, benefices, and alms. In *Piers Plowman*, the distance between past and present deeds, and between Syria and England – a distance so striking in the triumph of Islam – makes Anima's crusading call a function of national religious reform.

On the other hand, the poet is eager to make fourteenth-century England an historical testing ground for an ideal practice, and he does this through the figure of Thomas Becket.[29] According to the poet, medieval England's most popular saint, Archbishop of Canterbury Thomas Becket is an example ("forbisne," 15.526) and mirror to all prelates because he died protecting the rights of the church from the encroachments of Henry II, a notorious non-crusader; in so doing, he took England back in time and turned it into a foreign country where martyrs could die defending their faith: "Amonges unkynde Cristene for Cristes love he deyede / And for the right of al this reume and alle reumes Cristene" [Among unnatural (or unsympathetic) Christians, he died for Christ's love /And for the justice of this and all Christian realms] (15.523–24). This is the ideal England for an exemplary clergy, a land exoticized by martyrs such as those who died for their faith "In Inde, and in Alisaundre, in Ermonye, in Spayne" (15.520). Today's clergy, in their greed and ambition, follow the example not of Becket but of the Knights Templar (mentioned at B.15.537), a crusading order, who in 1312 were dispossessed and suppressed by the French king, their leaders tortured and burnt at the stake. This is something of the fate that the poet predicts for the English clergy, for their own good: if they cannot imitate Augustine or Becket, if they do not cultivate great deeds on their native soil, they will themselves be dispossessed by the secular arm, which, in the absence of resolute bishops, must take up the burden of Dobest.

In another textual tradition not thought to be original to the B-text,[30] the poet's ethical demand to convert the infidel is transformed into a call for clerical disendowment at home. In these lines, which anticipate the proto-Protestant reformer John Wycliffe's theories about dominion, the violence that subtends the rhetoric of conversion (and is inherent in the paradox

Patientes vincunt) is visited on an English clergy doomed to failure. The Emperor Constantine should never have endowed the church with temporal possessions, and it is the duty of secular lords, those who know their history, to strip them away as they see fit: "Taketh hire landes, ye lordes, and let hem lyve by dymes; / If possession be poison and inparfite hem make, / Good were to deschargen hem for Holy Chirches sake /And purgen hem of poison, er moore peril falle" [Take their lands, you lords, and let them live on tithes; / If possession is poison and makes them imperfect, / It would be good to unburden them for Holy Church's sake /And purge them of the poison, before greater peril happen] (15.563–66). According to these lines, if a perfect practice exists, and if a virtuous temporality may begin anew, it will be in the very near future, in a radically reformed England.

CHAPTER 6

Belief
(B.16–18)

"Youre wordes arn wonderfulle"   (B.17.24)

Introduction

In the last chapter, we saw that the poet's call for missionaries is the outcome of the poem's turn to history. Throughout the poem, the poet accuses clerics of failing their constituencies; they are grasping and sycophantic, illiterate or abstruse. In B.15, Langland recommends lay reading of history as the path to clerical reform. Secular lords should encourage clergy to act "historically": to remodel their lives on those of the saints, and to imitate their ecclesiastical forebears, who ventured their lives converting non-believers. In passūs 16–18, the poet continues to take an historical approach to faith, but his focus shifts from universal history to biblical narrative. Together these passūs make a thrilling "prequel" to passus 15: at the beginning of passus 16, the dreamer enters an inner dream in which he beholds the Garden of Eden, the Fall, and the birth of Christ. Flanked by Old Testament figures Abraham and Moses, the dreamer races down the road of gospel time until he reaches Jerusalem in passus 18, where he beholds the Crucifixion and the harrowing of hell.

Piers Plowman is not charged with converting the heathen: the poem is too diffuse to win new souls, however much it forecasts the Christian conquest of the world as its own narrative end. But neither does the poet's call to convert the heathen merely recycle a Western Christian fantasy that the walls of Islam will one day be breached and the Jews converted or cast out. Instead, it reveals a poem deeply engaged with the long history of belief. Like *Mandeville's Travels* and like many other texts from this period, *Piers Plowman* locates the proper discussion of belief on the road through the sacred past – a road littered with believers and non-believers, witnesses to and deniers of Christian faith.

Like many medieval writers, Langland would agree that religious conviction is inseparable from belief in narrative. Faith means believing in a sequence of events, as in the first chapter of Genesis in which God says, "let x or y be done," and we are told, mysteriously, "it was so." Faith in God also means accepting an historical logic as, for example, a typological reading of history in which the biblical past figures all future pasts (for example, Abraham was prepared to sacrifice Isaac, just like God sacrificed his only-begotten Son). In *Piers Plowman* B.16–18 the poet explores this relationship between belief and history, or between what one believes and the expression of that belief in sacred narrative. In these passūs, belief and history go hand in hand: confessions of the faith pave the way for a triumphant retelling of salvation history; conversely, sacred narrative is built out of declarations of belief. Finally, in rehearsing the story of the sacred past, the poet takes his most daring leaps of theological and poetical imagination.

The long history of belief

At the beginning of B.16, the dreamer pretends not to grasp the meaning of charity, though it has been explained to him several times already: "Ac yit am I in a weer what charite is to mene" [But I am still confused about the meaning of charity] (16.3). Anima responds with a thickly allegorical description of the Tree of Charity, a tree that sprouts leaves of faithful words and blossoms of obedient speech in the garden of the Heart. The dreamer longs to see the tree; he would give up all other food for the chance to taste its fruit (16.10–11). Anima assures him that Piers tends the tree, and upon hearing Piers's name, the dreamer falls into a love-swoon and into the poem's second inner dream. There he beholds the tree, propped up by the three staves of the Trinity and laden with delicious fruit.

At first glance, the Tree of Charity seems to be a standard allegory about human morality, not unlike Wit's castle of Dowel, which protects the lady Soul from a rapacious devil-knight. The difference is that the Tree of Charity is rooted in the long history of salvation and attests to the saving power of biblical narrative. The dreamer begs Piers to pull down a branch so he can taste an apple, but as Piers reaches for it, it shudders, and the apples drop into the hands of the Devil waiting to gather them up (B.16.73–85). The fruit growing on the Tree signifies the moral "fruit" borne by a righteous person steadfast in faith, while also recalling the fruit of the Garden of Eden, which tempted the first parents with knowledge out of bounds (compare B.11.415–20). But the Tree of Charity does something else as well: it reveals the historical operations of charity. The apples snatched up

by the Devil are none other than the holy men, the patriarchs and prophets
("Adam and Abraham and Ysaye the prophete, / Sampson and Samuel, and
Seint Johan the Baptist," 16.81–82) who witnessed the faith before its
revelation but languished in hell until the coming of Christ.[1] At stake in
this scene, in other words, is not just the dreamer's moral education but also
his induction into sacred narrative.

As the apples fall from the Tree, the dreamer tumbles down the rabbit
hole of history. Piers and the Trinity mobilize to recover their human "fruit"
through the incarnation of Christ, whom the poet describes as a choice fruit
himself, ripening in Mary's womb in fulfillment of the prophecies. From
this point the narrative unfolds into a life of Christ, laid out like a series of
miniatures, beginning with the Annunciation to the Virgin and the conception of Jesus, who, in Langland's version, matures into a knight tough
enough to fight the fiend (16.101–02). Piers the Plowman, representing
Jesus's human nature, notes that the time is ripe to teach Jesus the "leche-
craft" he needs to work miracles. Jesus reforms prostitutes, heals the sick,
raises Lazarus from the grave, multiplies the fishes and loaves, castigates the
money-changers, and prophesies the fate of the Temple. This sketch of
Christ's life deftly covers the highlights of the Gospels, ending with the Last
Supper (Maundy Thursday) and the Crucifixion (Good Friday), gorgeously
described as chivalric warfare:

> Jesus was his name
> That on the Friday folwyng for mankynde sake
> Justed in Jerusalem, a joye to us alle.
> On cros upon Calvarie Crist took the bataille
> Ayeins deeth and the devel, destruyed hir botheres myghtes –
> Deide, and deeth fordide, and day of nyght made. . .   (16.161–66)

> [Jesus was his name
> Who, on the Friday after, for mankind's sake,
> Jousted in Jerusalem, a joy to us all.
> On the cross at Calvary, Christ joined the battle
> Against death and the devil, destroyed the might of them both –
> Died, and killed death, and turned night into day.]

The dreamer wakes from his swoon, rubs his eyes, and begins to search far
and wide for Piers. Through the dreamer's quest for Piers, which ends with
Christ's joust in Jerusalem, the poet retells salvation history in order, from
select Old Testament figures (Abraham and Moses) to a fuller account of the
New Testament (beginning with the Good Samaritan), followed by magnificent renderings of the Crucifixion and the harrowing of hell in B.18, and

concluding with Christ's Resurrection on Easter Sunday. The opening image of the Tree of Charity thus shows how charity can be apprehended through sacred narrative. On God's part, charity can be understood as God's continuous interaction with humanity through the patriarchs and prophets, and ultimately through Christ, which turns human history into a story about divine love as well as a story about sin and loss. On the poet's part, charity means the ability to sustain a long story about divine immanence, replete with witnesses to the faith, and centered on the life and death of Christ.

To be sure, *Piers Plowman*, with all its fits and starts, makes for a frustrating narrative. In B.16–18, however, the poet embraces the long narrative poem as a form of true charity and a record of the faith. Specifically, in B.16–18, the poem makes contact with one of its ostensible genres, vernacular biblical narrative. Although the poem contains many and diverse genres, when viewed through the lens of B.16–18, it starts to resemble a biblical compendium: most of the gospels and psalms could be pieced together through the quotations; B.1 briefly outlines the history of sin, from Adam to Cain to Judas (1.63–70), followed by a dramatic account of the Fall of Lucifer; B.9 recounts, eccentrically, the lineage of Cain and Noah's ark; B.11 describes the earthly paradise and, briefly, the Fall of Adam and Eve.

As a biblical compendium or virtual bible, the poem has much in common with thirteenth- and fourteenth-century texts that retell scripture in pieces. For example, the many temporal markers in B.16–18 (for example, "Til it bifel on a Friday, a litel before Pasqe. / The Thursday before, there he made his cene" [Until it happened on a Friday, right before Easter. / The Thursday preceding, he had arranged his supper there] (16.139–40) link the poem to *temporale* literature, collections of sermons containing biblical readings for the moveable feasts of the liturgical year, such as Robert of Gretham's Anglo-Norman *Mirroir* (c.1250) and its Middle English translations, or the Middle English *Northern Homily Cycle* (early fourteenth century). Both of these works contain biblical quotation, translation, and paraphrase taken from the readings assigned for each Sunday.

As a version of the bible, *Piers Plowman* also takes a page from *sanctorale* literature, collections of sermons for saints' days, such as the *Legenda aurea* (c.1260, referenced in B.15.269) or the early Middle English *South English Legendary* (compiled c.1280). Although *sanctorale* collections revolve around the lives of saints, they frequently incorporate *temporale* material pertaining to Christ's life. Additionally, *sanctorale* collections sometimes contain stories related to the apocryphal Gospel of Nicodemus, Langland's source for the harrowing of hell episode in B.18. These stories, in turn, contain *vitae*, which comprehend all of salvation history. One such life, which may have inspired Langland's Tree of Charity, is the sweeping tale "De Sancto Ligno" ("On St. Cross") or "De Inventio Crucis" ("On the Discovery of the Cross"), which traces the Cross's journey through biblical time and space.[2] Sometimes fused with the story of the Cross is the "Life of Adam and Eve," a strange saga recounting Adam's quest for divine forgiveness, from his expulsion from Paradise to his deliverance from hell.[3] These apocryphal *vitae* provided material for B.16–18 as well as a pattern for the poem as a whole. *Piers Plowman*, the last two thirds of which some scribes labeled the *vitae* of Dowel, Dobet, and Dobest, embodies this idea of a *vita* as a life story that encompasses all history – a biographical *summa* of Christian time.

Temporale* and *sanctorale* collections gave rise to fourteenth-century vernacular texts capable of retelling the bible on a massive scale. An important example from Northern England is the hulking *Cursor mundi (Runner of the World, c.*1300), which reached 30,000 lines of verse. The *Cursor mundi* arranges its vast materials more or less chronologically, materials drawn from the collections mentioned above as well as from preaching handbooks and from Peter Comestor's *Historia scholastica* (*c.*1170). Another example of a vernacular bible is the biblical cycle plays, which dramatize salvation history from Creation to Doomsday. The cycle plays flourished in fifteenth-century York, Wakefield, Chester, and East Anglia; the York cycle, boasting over fifty individual pageants, may have reached its final form as early as 1376, when Langland was completing the B-text of *Piers Plowman*.

These biblical literatures represent the "omnibus" version of salvation history, a history that places the bible in the largest possible frame.[4] Omnibus bibles do not distinguish between canonical scripture and apocrypha, or between text and commentary, and they emphasize narrative appeal – miracles, deeds, speeches – over textual fidelity. In this sense, these texts are governed by assumptions about scripture very different from those that informed the English Wycliffite bible and later Protestant bibles. The translators of the Wycliffite bible (fl.1380s–1390s) claimed to address the needs of their readers by reconstructing a pristine text, purged of scholastic error, and is rendered into a straightforward English prose.[5] By contrast, the authors of omnibus scriptures, whether writing in Latin or a vernacular, claim to serve their readers through the hugeness and comprehensiveness of their projects.

For the author of the *Cursor mundi*, for example, the length and scope of his biblical poem amount to a form of narrative conquest, or what he boldly calls "overrunning":

Sum maner þing is good to knawe
Þat done was in þe olde lawe
Bitwixe þe olde lawe & þe newe
How crist vs bote bigan to brewe
I shal ȝou shewe bi myn entent
Soþely of hir testament
Al þis world ar þis book blynne
Wiþ cristis helpe I shal ouer rynne
And telle sum geste principale.[6]

[It is good to know something about those things
That were done in the Old Law,
[And] between the Old Law and the New.
How Christ began to brew a remedy for us,
It is my intention to show you,
Truly from their testimony.
Before this book ends, with Christ's help
I shall overrun the whole world,
And relate an important story.]

In this passage from the Prologue, the poet states his goal to tell a "principle geste," a foundational story, the arc of which traces the history of the world. He describes biblical narrative as a series of chivalric exploits and his own biblical narration as imperial warfare on behalf of Christianity (see Matthew 24:14). At the end of the Prologue, the poet explains that he has even taken his title from this notion of "overrunning": "Cursur o werld man aght it call, / For almost it ouer-rennes all" [One ought to call [this poem] the "Runner of the World" because it nearly overruns everything].[7]

Piers Plowman B.16–18, which is clearly modeled after this literature, boasts much more highly wrought poetry than does a poem like the *Cursor mundi*, but it follows some of the same principles that guide other omnibus versions of the bible. For one thing, it subordinates scripture to salvation history, cutting and pasting biblical stories into a long history of belief. For another thing, *Piers Plowman* makes a virtue out of comprehensiveness. In B.16–18, the poet assembles extra-biblical materials dispersed across biblical literature – the Tree of Charity, the debate between the Four Daughters of God, likely derived from Robert Grosseteste's *Chasteau d'amour*; and the harrowing of hell episode taken from the *Gospel of Nicodemus*. Further, in his rendition of Christ's life and death, the poet continually calls attention to his all-consuming overrunning narrative, a narrative that reflects upon, even if it is not specifically identified with, *Piers Plowman* as a whole. It is a narrative which threatens to roll on indefinitely. The dreamer wakes up at the end of B.18, on Easter Sunday, but the salvation history he has experienced spills over into subsequent passūs: B.19 summarizes Christ's life once more as the story of Dowel, this time followed by a brief history of the institutional church, the Antichrist, and the signs of the Apocalypse, leaving off the final scene in true omnibus bibles, the Last Judgement.

In its most capacious form, medieval biblical narrative features a succession of characters who attest to the Christian faith. Likewise *Piers Plowman* B.16–18 presents salvation history as a gallery of witnesses: Piers, Abraham, Moses, the Good Samaritan, the Four Daughters of God, and Book. Looming large among these witnesses are the forerunners, patriarchs, and prophets like Abraham and Moses, who predicted Christ's coming or professed Christian doctrine in advance of its revelation in the New Testament. Born too early in the history of salvation, these men are doomed to hell, but their lives, like their souls, are redeemable through Christ because they believed in the faith. These men are indispensable to Christian history because they make the history of salvation an ongoing story about faith: through them, for example, biblical interpretation can be rewritten as biblical narrative. In Genesis 20, Abraham welcomes three strangers in the desert, who turn out to be divine messengers, interpreted by medieval exegetes as the three Persons of God. In omnibus bibles this interpretation is often rehistoricized through the figure of Abraham, who actually identifies the messengers as the Father, Son, and Holy Spirit. Similarly, in B.16.223–30, belief in the Trinity is reabsorbed into the biblical narrative from which it was initially taken, becoming part of Abraham's life story.[8]

Interestingly, in *Piers Plowman*, the forerunners double as historical witnesses and as personifications, that is, embodiments of the virtues that they espouse (i.e., Abraham/Faith and Moses/Hope). Their double identity, in turn, reflects back on the peculiar role of the forerunner. Forerunners not only play a meaningful role in history but they also embody the relationship between narrative and belief, their prescient belief in Christ making them a constituent part of sacred narrative. The dreamer asks Moses/Hope if the Ten Commandments are efficacious, and Moses confirms that they are: "For though I seye it myself, I have saved with this charme / Of men and of wommen many score thousandes" [For though I say it myself, I have saved with this charm / A great many thousands of men and of women] (17.18–19). Abraham/ Faith chimes in:

"He seith sooth," seide this heraud, "I have yfounde it ofte.
Lo! here in my lappe that leeved on that charme –
Josue and Judith and Judas Macabeus,
And sixti thousand biside forth that ben noght seyen here!"   (17.20–23)

["He speaks truth," said this herald, "I have seen it often.
Lo! Here in my lap [are] those who believed in that charme –
Joshua, and Judith, and Judah Maccabee,
Yes, and sixty thousand besides them who are not named here!"]

In Abraham/Faith's bottomless lap are forerunners too numerous to see, incalculable witnesses to the faith, who, along with Moses's thousands, populate salvation history.

These figures are also indispensable because they enfold Christ's life into the long history of belief, a history which supports the view of a triumphant Christianity of the kind that Patience and Conscience envision in B.13 and Anima predicts in B.15. This history rolls backwards to Eden and forward to the saints, consuming everything in its wake (13.165–172, 207–11; 15.220 to end). In the liturgical calendar, the "short" history of Christ's life begins in Advent, the four weeks preceding Christmas; the "long" history begins on Septuagesima Sunday, the first Sunday of the seventeen-day preparation for Lent.

The Old Testament readings for Septuagesima are taken from the first few chapters of Genesis: Creation, Adam and Eve, the Fall, and the story of Cain and Abel. Subsequent Sundays cover Noah, Abraham, Isaac, Jacob, and Moses. Medieval homilies for Septuagesima Sunday endorse the long history of belief by showing that the dominion of the Church depends upon the fullness of its reckoning. The gospel reading for that day is the parable of the vineyard (Matthew 20:1–16), in which a householder hires men to labor in his vineyard, offering to pay the same wages to those who join up late as the wages paid to those who have worked since morning. Several homily collections, including the *Middle English Mirror* and the *Northern Homily Cycle* coordinate the Old and New Testament readings for this Sunday through an imperialist historiography: all of Christ's "workers" deserve the same reward if the times of the day (morning, midday, evening) are read as epochs of salvation history, and if the workers are glossed as the patriarchs, prophets, and apostles: Adam to Noah = morning, Noah to Abraham + Abraham to Moses = midday; Moses to Christ = evening. At the end of the "day," Christ himself comes to harrow hell and judge the world, and his apostles come too, to show people the way. The vineyard, in this reading, is Holy Church, which has spread all over the world and will continue to grow until the last holy man has been saved.[9] Thanks to the forerunners, then, sacred narrative can be structured into historical periods, and thanks to their spiritual labor, salvation history assimilates all human time, converting the time of labor – the hours clocked in the vineyard – into the time of Christian history.[10]

Very similarly, in *Piers Plowman*, Abraham/Faith and Moses/Hope call attention to an overrunning narrative at the same time that they structure the history of belief: Abraham represents pre-Mosaic Law, Moses represents post-Mosaic law, and, idiosyncratically, in Langland's triumvirate, the Good Samaritan represents the New Law in a post-Christ era. And just as the poet used the forerunners to underscore the relationship between narrative and belief, so he uses them to emphasize the saving power of sacred narrative. Sacred narrative restores a fallen humanity through the life of Christ, but it also rehabilitates narrative more generally. A sufficiently long history of salvation, stuffed with characters and stories, solves the problem of incompleteness, which is always a condition of narrative and, in a Christian scheme, a condition of human history.

Langland makes this point in his brilliant revision of the parable of the Good Samaritan. On the highway to Jerusalem, Abraham/Faith, Moses/ Hope, and the dreamer encounter the Good Samaritan "ridyng ful rapely the right wey" [riding very fast down the right way] (17.50). The Good Samaritan stops to help a half-dead man or *semivif*, "naked as a nedle," who has been attacked by thieves [Luke 10:25–37] (17.54–57), but Abraham/ Faith and Moses/Hope lose their nerve and flee the scene. Later, they try to talk to the Good Samaritan as he speeds towards Jerusalem, but they soon fall away, as if in a race, and only the dreamer manages to catch up. The dreamer accuses Abraham/Faith and Moses/Hope to the Samaritan, but the Samaritan excuses them, explaining that, in the case of poor *semivif*, something drastic is required, not aid on a human scale but a major intervention through the bloody sacrifice of Christ. Neither Faith nor Hope can cure the sick man, says the Samaritan, "withouten the blood of a barn [child] born of a mayde" (17.94). Certain events must take place before Abraham and Moses can retroactively assume their duties as "forster" and "hostiler," guiding folk through the spiritual wilderness (Faith) and sheltering those whose faith is weak (Hope) (17.113–24).

Notably, in this scene, the poet has sutured the parable of the Good Samaritan to the narrative of the forerunners: first, he has added the Good Samaritan to the roster of "runners" traveling posthaste down the road to Jerusalem; second, he has allegorized the three runners as the theological virtues of faith, hope, and charity. These changes affect the way we read sacred narrative. From the perspective of the institutional church, the parable of the Good Samaritan is a tale about supersession: the Jews were overthrown by Christ's followers, who, unlike the Jews, grasped the spirit of the law that the Jews had passed down. In Langland's version of the parable, the supersessionist reading implicates Old Testament Jews as well (see Chapter 7): Abraham and Moses stand for the Jewish priests in the parable who, when put to the test, fail to obey the golden rule – "love God and your neighbor" – by helping the half-dead man. Yet the poet, by allegorizing the forerunners as theological virtues, invites us to read the parable another way, through the long history of belief. Without Christ the testimony of the patriarchs and prophets would be meaningless, and in this way Christ can be said to replace those who came before him. At the same time, substitutions always occur when what is deemed to be partial is exchanged for what is deemed to be complete, and when what is lesser is exchanged for what is greater. This is the thrust of the famous quotation from I Corinthians from which the poet has derived his Faith, Hope, and Charity:

> Charity never falls away: whether prophecies shall be made void, or languages shall cease, or knowledge shall be destroyed. For we know in part, and we prophesy in part. But when that which is perfect shall come, that which is in part shall be done away ... Now we see through a glass as an enigma; but then face to face. Now I know in part; but then I shall know even as I am known. And now there remain these three: faith, hope, and charity, but the greatest of these is charity. (I Corinthians 13:8–13)[11]

By enlisting the Good Samaritan in the ranks of the forerunners and by allegorizing all three, Langland has matched the second part of the passage, which lists the theological virtues, faith, hope and charity, to the first part, which talks about prophecy before Christ. Although charity is the greatest virtue, exceeding the other two virtues to which it is compared, all three are critical and remain together on the right side of the Redemption. The superlative virtue of charity, in other words, has a pre-history, just as virtue in general is always a proposition about time. Likewise, though Abraham and Moses appear to be inadequate to the task of Christian history, in fact, as theological virtues they straddle both sides of the divide, proving themselves to be critical to the writing of sacred narrative.

In B.16–18 the poet tries his hand at an overrunning narrative, and in doing so, he associates his poem with biblical literature in the vernacular, like the *Cursor mundi*. He also signals his commitment, however belatedly, to writing a long narrative poem. One of the signs of the poem's

self-identification with vernacular biblical literature is its use of romance
tropes. Many vernacular religious writers from the thirteenth century
advertised their texts as "productive Others to secular romance."[12] The
author of the *South English Legendary*, for instance, promises to give his
audience what they really want:

> Men wilneþ muche to hure telle of bataille of kynge
> And of kniȝtes þat hardy were þat muchedel is lesynge
> Wo so wilneþ muche to hure tales of suche þinge
> Hardi batailles he may hure here þat nis no lesinge
> Of apostles & martirs þat hardy kniȝtes were . . .

> [People greatly desire to hear stories of royal battles,
> And of knights who were hardy; these stories contain much falsehood.
> Woe to those who greatly desire to hear tales about such matters!
> Here, one can hear [stories] about tough battles, which contain no falsehood,
> About apostles and martyrs, who were hardy knights. . .][13]

In the same vein, the *Cursor mundi*-poet brags that his poem will remedy
the age-old problem of literary taste: folks would rather listen to secular
romance than to sacred scripture, so enthralled are they by heroes like
Alexander, Julius Caesar, Brutus, King Arthur, Sir Gawain and Sir Kay,
Charlemagne and Roland, as well as by famous lovers like Tristan and
Isolde.[14] The *Cursor mundi*-poet plans to substitute his massive religious
poem for such "lemmon" poetry, swapping the Mother of God for the
traditional female love-object, and recounting the heroic doings and deeds
found in scripture.[15]

Piers Plowman, written several generations after the *Cursor mundi*, does
not apologize for being a long religious poem in English, nor does it worry
about rehabilitating chivalry for religious narrative. But like the *South
English Legendary* and the *Cursor mundi*, *Piers Plowman* borrows romance
tropes in order to sustain a compelling narrative about Christian faith. For
Langland, the origin of narrative is the desire for salvation, and the purpose
of narrative is to explore that same desire.

Not surprisingly, the central trope of Langland's biblical romance is the
joust. Christ, the greatest of knights, plans to fight Death, the greatest of foes,
in a much-publicized tournament in Jerusalem. All history before Christ is
the journey to see that one-time-only event to which the forerunners look
forward with bated breath. Finally, Christ himself arrives in Jerusalem:

> Barefoot on an asse bak bootles cam prikye,
> Withouten spores other spere; sprakliche he loked,
> As is the kynde of a knyght that cometh to be dubbed,
> To geten him gilte spores on galoches ycouped. . .   (18.11–14)

[Barefoot on an ass's back, shoeless [he] came riding,
Without spurs or spear; sprightly he looked,
As do knights who come to be dubbed,
To win gilded spurs on slashed shoes.]

A few lines later, we are told that Christ is dressed in his noble armor, his "gentries" (22), his "helm and in his haubergeon" (23), and the "paltok" (25) and "armes" (22), he has borrowed from Piers (that is, his human nature). Like Launcelot bearing Sir Terry's shield at the famous Assumption tournament in Malory's *Le Morte D'Arthur*, Christ's costume disguises his true identity or his divine nature: he is "sembable to the Samaritan, and somdeel to Piers the Plowman," "as is the kynde of a knyght" (18.10,13). Christ is a knight because, despite his humble guise, he is no victim of circumstance. At the same time, Christ looks like a knight, because he is, to all appearances *only* human – bootless (18.11), because he has not yet received the trappings of knighthood, but also, seemingly, bootless (useless, without remedy) in the face of death. After his death on the Cross, Christ "duels" with the blind Longinus, the Jews' "champion chivaler" (18.99), who has been duped into stabbing Christ's body with his lance. Like other outstanding knights Christ turns out to be as good a healer as he is a fighter, restoring Longinus's sight with his own blood in one of the poem's best lines, "The blood sprong doun by the spere and unspered the knyghtes eighen" [the blood sprang down along the spear and opened the knight's eyes] (18.86). The female characters in these passūs are likewise described as characters from courtly romances. In B.16, the Virgin Mary accepts "hendliche" (courteously) Gabriel's announcement that she is pregnant with Jesus, after which Jesus is said, erotically, to "jouke in hir chamber" (rest in her chamber) before his joust on the Cross (92). In B.18, Peace calls Christ/Love her "lemman" (beloved), and recites poetry about her spiritual consummation in Christ (181–86). These, of course, are allegories of romance: scripture is like a romance because Christ is like a knight who fights, heals, and loves. But a poet who dabbles in allegories of romance proves himself capable of writing a straight-up romance, in other words, of satisfying his audience's desire for stories about love and war while drawing their attention to religious matters.

In B.16–18, Langland highlights something else about the relationship between narrative and desire: the desire both to prolong a story and to bring it to completion belongs to sacred and secular narrative alike. These twinned desires or, very simply, anticipation, fuel the long history of belief. In B.16–18, anticipation belongs first and foremost to the forerunners, and drives the diplomatic narrative of Abraham/Faith and Moses/Hope, Christ's herald and his messenger. In the Prologue to *The South English Legendary* (called the *Banna sanctorum*, the *Proclamation [or Banners] of the Saints*), the narrator explains that a strong king always assigns a vanguard to precede him in battle – archers, crossbowmen, and trumpeters (the patriarchs and prophets), as well as a standard-bearer (John the Baptist), who carries the royal banner in front of him. A strong king also deploys a rearguard (the saints and martyrs) to defend the army from behind.[16]

Langland borrows the trope of the royal procession in B.16–18, but he expands it into a diplomatic, rather than a military procession. Like the vanguard in the Prologue to the *South English Legendary*, Abraham and Moses stretch forth the history of salvation between Paradise and the Crucifixion. As members of Christ's entourage, they witnessed his former "guest appearances" in human history, he has sent them on official business, and now they expectantly await his arrival. In the middle of Lent, the dreamer meets Abraham/Faith, who introduces himself as herald looking for a knight. Abraham/Faith recounts his life to the dreamer (following Genesis 17–18, 22) as a series of previous encounters with this knight, a great lord with whom he has exchanged "trewe toknes" (16.230). To prove his love for this lord he nearly sacrificed his own heir, Isaac, and he ordered his whole household ("Myself and my meynee") (16.236) to shed blood, that is, through circumcision. Abraham/Faith feels secure in his relationship with his lord, who has granted him and his heirs "Lond and lordshipe and lif withouten ende" (16.240). This lord will surely redeem all the patriarchs and prophets from the devil's custody ("poukes pondfold," 16.264), laying down his life as guarantee for theirs. Abraham/Faith longs for redemption but also for reunification with his lord: "And thus I seke hym ... for I herde seyn late / Of a buyrn that baptized hym – Johan Baptist was his name – / That to patriarkes and to prophetes and to oother peple in derknesse / Seide, that seigh here that sholde save us alle / *Ecce Agnus Dei* ..." [Therefore I seek him ... for I have heard tell lately / of a man who baptized him – John the Baptist was his name / Who said to the patriarchs, and prophets, and other people in darkness, / that he saw the one who will save us all / "Behold the lamb of God"] (16.249–52a, John 1:29).

Further down the road, the dreamer meets Moses/Hope, a "spie" or messenger, who bears the Ten Commandments as letters patent:

> "I am Spes, a spie," quod he, "and spire after a knight[17]
> That took me a maundement upon the mount of Synay
> To rule alle reames therewith – I bere the writ here"...   (17.1–3)

["I am *Hope*, a spy," said he, "and [I] seek after a knight
Who gave me a mandate on Mount Sinai
With which to rule all realms – I have the writ here."][18]

The dreamer asks about Moses's writ, whether it is sealed, and if he can read it, if it is not sealed closed. Moses explains that he is looking for the lord who issued the document, who owns the seal, and who will authorize the writ as letters patent, that is, as open letters with their characteristic hanging or pendant seal: "I seke hym that hath the seel to kepe – /And that is cros and Cristendom, and Crist theron to honge" (17.5–6). Moses/ Hope, Christ's messenger searching for his lord, holds the Redemption in diplomatic suspension: just as the truth of the Old Testament is contingent upon the New Testament, so the authority of Moses's writ depends upon a seal which will hang from the parchment, engraved with an image of – or perhaps resembling as it dangles – Christ hanging from the Cross. The event that Moses so keenly desires – the sealing of the writ, the Crucifixion of Christ – will bring this narrative to an end and redemption to humankind: "And whan it is asseled so, I woot wel the sothe / – That Luciferis lordshipe laste shal no lenger" [And when it is sealed in this way, I know well the truth / That Lucifer's lordship shall last no longer] (17.7–8).

This diplomatic procession appears similarly in a much earlier text with a long shelf-life, the *Ancrene Wisse* (*Guide for Anchoresses*), a handbook written for women recluses in the first quarter of the thirteenth century. The *Ancresse Wisse* was geared toward noble women who had renounced marriage and allowed themselves to be enclosed for life. The author tries to help his female audience reconcile their impoverished social life with a rich spiritual life, and he encourages them to redirect their desire for a worldly husband to a new lover, a king, Christ. The anchoress should picture herself as a lady receiving the mission of a great king who seeks her as his lover: Christ the King sends the forerunners before him with private letters ("leattres isealet") to woo his bride and prepare her for his arrival; eventually Christ himself comes with letters patent, an open letter, publicly declaring his love:

> Earst, as a mon þe woheð, as a king þet luuede a gentil poure leafdi of feorrene londe, he sende his sonden biuoren, þet weren þe patriarches ant te prophe[te]s of þe Alde Testament, wið leatrres isealet. On ende he com him-seoluen, ant brohte þe Godspel as leattres iopenet; ant wrat wið his ahne blod saluz to his leofmon, luue gretunge forte wohin hire wið ant hire luue wealden.[19]

[First, like a man who woos you, as a king who loved a poor noble lady from a far-off land, to whom he sent his messengers before him, who were the patriarchs and the prophets of the Old Testament, with sealed letters [i.e., private letters]. In the end he came himself, and brought the Gospels as letters patent and wrote with his own blood greetings to his beloved, love greetings with which to woo her and win her love.]

This romance with Christ, a miniaturized version of the overrunning narrative, is charmingly realized in Langland's version of the Four Daughters of God. Truth doubts the veracity of the Atonement, but Mercy reminds Truth that Peace has a privileged correspondence with her lover, Love: "Love hath coveited hire longe – leve I noon oother / But he sente hire som lettre, what this light bemyneth" (18.168–69) [Love has desired her for a long time – I don't believe otherwise /And he has sent her some letter about what this light means]. "Lo, here the patente" (18.185), exclaims Peace a few lines later, brandishing the telltale letter.

Yet, in *Piers Plowman*, the longing for Christ and the expectation of fulfillment primarily belong not to a female subject but to the advanced party of male retainers who precede their lord and await his coming. They are incomplete without him, but their claims to fulfillment are based on prior affinity; they understand the chain of events like no one else. As the author of the *Ancrene Wisse* later explains to his female readers, Old Testament prophets model a relationship between human beings and God because they were present at God's earlier interventions in history and can testify to his love. This male relationship with God exceeds the heterosexual intimacy the author imagines for his female reader. After giving several examples from the Old Testament of Christ's love, the author of the *Ancrene Wisse* asks his female reader, "Nes þis wið luue ibunden? Hwet wult tu mare? Luue is his chamberleng, his conseiler, his spuse, þet he ne mei nawt heole wið, ah teleð al þet he þencheð. In Genesy: *Num celare potero Abraham que gesturus sum?*" [Is this (are these acts of intervention) not bound with love? What more do you want? Love is [Christ's] chamberlain, his counselor, his spouse, from whom he cannot conceal anything, but to whom he reveals all his plans. In Genesis: "Can I hide from Abraham that which I intend to do?"][20]

What is the role of Piers, then, in Langland's biblical narrative? Piers, forever the object of the dreamer's desire, finally re-emerges in B.16. Throughout the poem, he plays different roles in different contexts. In passūs 5–7, he exemplifies the obedience of those folk who try to fulfill divine commandments in a fallen world; this was the version of Piers that fifteenth- and sixteenth-century readers found especially compelling.[21] In passus 18, Piers embodies the human nature of Christ, or what Christ acquires for himself in order to effect the redemption of humanity. Later, in B.19, he becomes Christ's proxy in the world, or the authority that Christ delegates to the institutional church through the apostle, Peter. Passūs 16–18 further help us see why Piers's appearances are so sporadic, and why he is either remote to the point of absence or so fully present that he makes the dreamer swoon. Piers, it turns out, expresses a major principle of medieval religious narrative: a story worth telling is one in which history continually repeats itself, although not necessarily in regularly marked intervals. A story worth telling is a story in which the incursions of the divine are trans-formative, as in the Redemption, but also recurrent, as for example, via prophecy or miracle. From this angle, the dreamer's love-swoon for Piers in passus 16 is not just a deepening of his dreaming life but also a kind of forerunning, the longing for an object incarnated in history.

Affecting theology

In 1215, Pope Innocent III convoked the Fourth Lateran Council, in part to drum up enthusiasm for a fifth crusade. All sorts of church business was conducted at the Council. One item on the agenda was the arbitration of theological positions, such as the condemnation of Abbot Joachim of Fiore's accusation against Peter Lombard, that Lombard, by arguing for a common essence uniting the three Persons of the Trinity, was positing a fourth aspect of the Godhead. Modern scholars tend to remember Fourth Lateran for Canon no.21, which decreed that every person who has attained the age of reason (7–8 years old) should make annual confession to a priest. This canon had far-reaching consequences for vernacular religious litera-ture: over the next 150 years, it generated an outreach program for confessors and parish priests charged with the spiritual instruction of lay people. *Piers Plowman* can certainly be seen as a very sophisticated outcome of that program.

Also important to *Piers Plowman*, however, is Canon no.1, which con-tains a new profession of Trinitarian belief compiled from the Apostolic and Athanasian Creeds. Canon no.1 concludes by stating that the doctrine of the Trinity has been revealed to Christ's servants throughout the course of time: "This Holy Trinity in its common essence undivided and in personal properties divided, through Moses, the holy prophets, and other servants, gave to the human race at the most opportune intervals of time the doctrine of salvation."[22] Or, in other words, Trinitarianism is self-evident because it is embedded in the history of the church. History and belief are, again, mutually constitutive discourses; the history of the church is made up of witnesses to the faith and, *vice versa*, belief in the articles of the faith allows the institutional church to be written. As we will see below, the inventiveness of Trinitarian expression in B.16–18 is enabled precisely by the biblical history in which it is situated.

The Prologue to the *Cursor mundi* argues something similar to Canon no.1, that belief in the Trinity is the *sine qua non* of sacred narrative. The Trinity, says the poet, is the ground of salvation history:

> But no werk wel laste may
> Wiþoute good grounde to laste ay
> þerfore þis werke I wol founde
> On a selcouþ studfaste grounde
> That is þe holy trinite
> That al is made of his bounte.
> Furst at him self I sett my merk
> And aftir to telle of his hond werk.[23]

> [But no work may last long
> Without a good, enduring foundation.
> Therefore I will found this work
> On a truly steadfast ground,
> Which is the Holy Trinity,
> From whose bounty all is made.
> First, I set my mark at him,
> And then afterwards I tell of his handiwork.]

Trinitarianism similarly supplies a foundational theology for *Piers Plowman*. Like the *Cursor mundi*, B.16–18 portrays the Trinity as the creative force of salvation history and the ground of sacred narrative. The dreamer, noting the three staves propping up the Tree of Charity, observes that they measure equal length and even appear to come from the same plant (16.57–59). Piers gruffly discourages the dreamer from pursing a theological angle, but in fact he has just explained to the dreamer that the three staves represent the Trinity: the power of God the Father, the wisdom of God the Son, and the Holy Spirit, through whose grace the soul can freely resist the temptations of the flesh, Devil, and world (16.60–67). These staves support the soul against temptation both in the Garden of Eden and in every subsequent age. They also work together historically to effect the Redemption of fallen humanity: as the Devil absconds with the fruit, Piers sets after him armed with the three staves; or, in other words, Christ redeems humanity through the Incarnation, an event made possible by the collaboration of the Trinity: "*Filius* by the Faderes wille and frenesse of *Spiritus Sancti*, / To go robbe that rageman and reve the fruyt fro hym" ["Son" through the will of the Father, and through the freedom of the "Holy Spirit", / To go rob that ragman [devil] and steal the fruit from him] (16.88–89).

Langland's Tree of Charity episode was likely inspired by the "Discovery of the Cross"/"Life of Adam and Eve" stories mentioned above. In these stories, Adam's son Seth places three seeds from the forbidden fruit under the tongue of his dying father. The seeds sprout into three trees of remarkably equal height whose sacred wood, centuries later, becomes the building materials for the Cross. As the history of salvation unfolds, the three trees are continually identified as Trinitarian symbols: Moses recognizes them as tokens of the Trinity and buries them at Mount Tabor; David, impressed by their beauty, encloses them in a holy garden; Solomon later discovers them while building the Temple; the Jews eventually find them and make them into the Cross; finally, Constantine's mother, St. Helena, forces Judas's descendants to reveal the location of the buried Cross.[24] In these narratives, as in B.18, the three trees offer a sure foundation for sacred narrative, binding epochs of salvation history with revelations of the faith.

Trinitarianism is also a foundational theology for *Piers Plowman* because it constitutes the doctrine of salvation given to the human race at "opportune intervals of time" or in other words, the way that doctrine is embedded in the history of the church. In this view, it is not surprising that Abraham/Faith is a great expositor of the Trinity and a mouthpiece for a theologically adventuresome vernacular poetry. He tells the dreamer that he has been appointed herald to a great lord (Christ) who wears a blazon of the Trinity, three Persons in one God: "Thre leodes in oon lyth, noon lenger than oother, / Of oon muchel and myght in mesure and in lengthe. / That oon dooth, alle dooth, and ech dooth bi his one" [Three people in one body, one no bigger than the other, / Of one size and might, in measure and in length. / What one does, all do, and each one does by himself] (16.181–83).

As a herald, Abraham/Faith is trained to read coats of arms, a duty he stirringly discharges in B.18 when, looking out a window, he spots Jesus the jouster entering Jerusalem: "Thanne was Feith in a fenestre, and cryde, '*A! Fili David!*'/As dooth an heraud of armes whan aventrous cometh to justes" [Then Faith was in a window, and cried, "Oh! Son of David!"/As a herald of arms does when adventurers come to the jousts] (18.15–16). Medieval heralds were important not only in tournaments, where armorial bearings played a crucial ceremonial role, but also in warfare, where they were used to identify prisoners and the dead. In this sense, heralds, like forerunners, are both witnesses and interpreters: they testify to a lord's identity and construe for others the symbols with which he represents himself.

Figure 5. "Trinitarian shield." William Peraldus, *Summa vitiis*. British Library, Harley MS 3244, f.28r. (England, 1255–1265).

In Abraham/Faith's reading of Christ's blazon, credic language promises to be something like heraldic grammar, transparent and regular, easily diagrammed. In fact, his definition of the Trinity may have reminded some of the poem's early readers of the *scutum fidei* (shield of the faith) a popular image in medieval art, illustrating perfect symmetry among the Persons of the Trinity, and perfect balance between equivalence and distinctiveness. To take a well-known example, a thirteenth-century copy of William Peraldus's *Summa de vitiis* (*Treatise on the Vices*, before 1250) displays a huge knight battling a facing page of vices. The knight bears a shield painted with his coat of arms, a blazon of the Trinity, an image used to this day to teach the Athanasian Creed.

The shield depicts a larger triangle divided into three smaller triangles of equal size. On the sides of the exterior triangle we read that the Father is not identical to the Son; the Son is not identical to the Holy Ghost; and the Holy Spirit is not identical to the Father. The sides of the three interior triangles, connected by "Deus" at the midpoint, prove that the Father is equal to the Son, and the Son to the Holy Ghost, and all three equal to God.

As a herald, Abraham/Faith considers his description of the Trinity to be a noble service. From the perspective of literary history, his Trinitarianism reflects a major task of English verse in this period: to communicate simply and directly the articles of the faith. This is a task that *Piers Plowman* repeatedly takes up, especially in B.17, where the Trinity is defined several times.[25] Elsewhere in the poem, Clergy declares belief in the Trinity to be basic to lay morality (i.e., Dowel), and he explains the Trinity in the most technical language he can muster: "Thre proper persones, ac nought in plurel nombre, / For al is but oon God and ech is God hymselve: / *Deus Pater, Deus Filius, Deus Spiritus Sanctus* / God the Fader, God the Sone, God Holy Goost of bothe . . ." (10.239–42).[26] Clergy is careful not to deviate too far from the Latin Creed: he defaults to a Latinate vocabulary ("proper persones," "plurel nombre"); he hews to a Latin syntax (compare "ac nought" and "al is but" to the Latin "non . . . sed" construction in the Latin Creed); and he excavates from the Latin Creed an alliterative metrics which appears to support the logic of Trinitarian theology – the three alliterated staves in each line correspond to the same word: *Deus Pater, Deus Filius, Deus Spiritus Sanctus*/<u>God</u> the Fader, <u>God</u> the Sone, <u>God</u> Holy Goost of bothe.[27]

However, for Abraham/Faith, Christ's faithful servant, Trinitarian theology has the potential to be something more than a rote expression of belief. It has the potential to generate a theology of the affections or a theology that teaches people how to love God and neighbor by analyzing the relationships among the three divine Persons. In B.16, Abraham/Faith compares the Trinity to lordship and to marriage, and in B.17, the Good Samaritan compares the Trinity to a hand and then to a candle. These beautiful analogies exploit the emotional life inherent in the idea of divine Personality, and they do so by upsetting the balance between the three Persons emphasized by Clergy, the Latin Creed, and the *scutum fidei*. If the job of medieval English verse is to create a vernacular capable of explaining the mystery of three Persons in one God, Trinitarianism, by positing a divine community of three, points to ineluctable asymmetries among the three Persons – the inequalities of power within the Godhead, and the lack or loss in one Person with respect to another. For this reason, translating Trinitarian theology into English verse might mean preserving the balance between Persons *or* it might mean experimenting further with asymmetry. Langland admires the Creed but he also pushes its limits, extracting from the theology on which it is based a complex of affections, both human and divine.

Abraham/Faith begins by comparing the Trinity to a lord. He is, after all, supremely qualified to parse divine lordship: he has circumcised his whole household at the request of his divine Lord. God, says Abraham, is a lord, but God, he says a few lines earlier, is also *like* a lord because lordship is fundamentally plural, defined by its instruments and effects:

So thre bilongeth for a lord that lordshipe cleymeth:
Might, and a mene [his owene myghte to knowe],
Of hymself and of his servaunt, and what suffreth hem both.
So God, that gynnyng hadde nevere, but tho hym good thoughte,
Sente forth his sone as for servaunt that tyme,
To ocupien hym here til issue were spronge –
That is, children of charite . . .   (B.16.191–97)

[A lord who claims lordship requires three things:
Might, and an intermediary [or servant], through which to know his own might,
His own might, and the might of his servant, and what both of them experience.
Likewise God, who never had beginning, but as it seemed right to him,
Sent forth his Son like a servant that time,
To keep himself busy here [in the world] until issue was produced –
In other words, the children of charity . . .]

In this passage, the poet describes lordship as tripartite and reflexive: it requires might but also an intermediary or mediator ("mene"), through which a lord comes to know his own power and that of his servant (or "meinie": servants, members of the lord's household), as well as what both of them, the lord and his servant, experience ("suffreth") as a result (i.e., what the lord's power achieves in the world). By analogy, God the Father sent forth his servant, Christ, as his representative in the world until he had achieved his object: loving-kindness, or the "children of charite," or the Holy Spirit. This complex analogy is essentially a brief treatise on lordly power: a lord sends forth his servant – the instrument of his command – to do his bidding; in so doing, the lord accomplishes his object at the same time that he comes to know his own power reflexively. God the mighty Father similarly creates in the plural through the con-certed effort of Persons, who perform different roles but act as one God. The analogy further shows what it means for Christ to serve as a mediator between God and man, just as a servant serves as a mediator when he represents his lord in the world.[28]

The problem with it is that, in order to represent the social intimacies of divine power, it unsettles the balance between the three Persons. The Athanasian Creed plainly states that power pertains equally to all three Persons, and that power is constitutive of all three Persons: "likewise the Father is Lord, the Son Lord, and the Holy Spirit Lord; And yet they are not three Lords but one Lord."[29] Langland has likely taken the lord–servant analogy, at least indirectly, from St. Augustine's *De Trinitate* (*on the Trinity*) which, following St. Paul, explains that the Son is said to be the servant of the Father, not because he is less in nature but rather because he is less in fashion (*habitus*): God takes on different forms of the same nature in order to accomplish different objectives with respect to human salvation.[30] Augustine's distinction between nature and fashion is critical for two reasons: first, because it restores the coequalness of the three divine Persons – which the lord–servant analogy, central to Paul's preoccupations with freedom and servitude, threatens to undermine – and secondly, because it affirms the omnipotence of a deity who, within his nature, knows no subjection. In B.16, however, Langland reactivates the very analogy that Augustine tried to shut down, and he shows in the process that the plurality of power that pertains to human lordship is, in fact, quite different from that which pertains to divine lordship. A servant is an instrument of the lord precisely because he does not possess the same status and authority as the lord. It is by virtue of his inferiority that the servant can act as mediator or proxy, making the power of his lord manifest in the world. As Augustine knew well, it is important to recognize figures of speech for what they are: rhetorical devices, not theological arguments. His goal in *De Trinitate* was to describe the divine nature as precisely as possible. In contrast, Langland, by restoring the lord–servant analogy, sacrifices theological precision, and, in doing so, opens up worlds of affection between the three Persons of the Godhead, stressing mutuality, hierarchy, and intimacy.[31]

From the "children of charite," Abraham/Faith segues into a second Trinitarian analogy: the analogy of the family. The life of man, says Abraham/Faith, is a "tokenynge of the Trinity" and the source of all analogy. Consequently, the three states of marriage represent the Trinity: wedlock, widowhood, and virginity. But wedlock, insofar is it is procreative, can represent the whole Trinity by itself. Like the first family – Adam, Eve, and their children – the Persons of the Trinity originate in one Person, God the Father:[32]

Adam, oure aller fader; Eve was of hymselve,
And the issue that thei hadde it was of hem bothe,
And either is otheres joye in thre sondry persones,
And in hevene and here oon singuler name.   (16.205–08)

[Adam, the father of us all; Eve came from him,
And the children that they produced came from both of them,
And all three are each others' joy in three different persons,
And in heaven and here one singular name.]

Although the Father is said to be made through nothing, the Son is said to be begotten "from the Father," and the Holy Spirit is said to "proceed" from both Father and Son, doctrinally speaking, it is crucial to assert that none of the three Persons of the Trinity is created in the same way as creatures are.[33] What happens, then, when the Trinity is compared to the first family? For one thing, the emphatic non-createdness of the three Persons of the Trinity is collapsed into human procreation: the Son is "of the Father," like Eve is "of" Adam's rib, and their children come from both of them just as the Holy Spirit is said to proceed from both the Father and the Son. Although Abraham/Faith's analogy is not a theological treatise (and in C.18.228, the poet emphasizes that the likeness between the Trinity and the human family is merely a similitude), it nevertheless targets a point of theological vulnerability, suggesting that divine generation, what the Trinity achieves within itself, is fundamentally like human creation, or what the Trinity achieves in the world. The upshot is that the relationships between the three Persons look like affective relationships of love, pleasure, and pain. Like the nuclear family, says Abraham/Faith, the Persons of the Trinity are bound by joy, a joy that can be imagined through postlapsarian procreation. Like Adam, Eve, and their children, the Trinity knows joy through the reflexive feelings of its own self-creation.

The poet would not deny that the three Persons of the Trinity are uncreated and, in that respect, coequal. Marriage, however, turns out to have an irresistible explanatory power, and human procreation helps to explain the emotional bonds within the Godhead. Additionally, marriage explains what it means for God to feel bereft. Abraham/Faith explains that if you were to adjust the analogy of the family from the nuclear family (father, mother, children) to states of matrimony (wedlock, widowhood, virginity), God the Father clearly represents matrimony because it is through the procreative "might" of a married couple that children come into being (B.16.211). For Abraham/Faith, the Son represents not celibacy or virginity but widowhood, or the aching loss that God feels when he voluntarily becomes a creature, knowing loneliness and death: "The Sone, if I it dorste seye, resembleth wel the widewe: / '*Deus meus, Deus meus, ut quid dereli-quisti me?*'/ That is, creatour weex creature to knowe what was bothe" [The Son, I dare say, closely resembles the widow: / "My God, my God, why have you forsaken me?" / That is to say, the Creator became the created so he could understand both] (16.213–15). The poet has taken this quotation from the liturgy of Good Friday, a service suffused with the theme of Christ's suffering.

Langland's description of Christ as an inconsolable widow exemplifies his affective theology: it shows what God experiences inwardly, within the divine community of three, at the same time that it shows how God extends himself outward to creation through the life and death of Christ. The comparison between Christ and the widow suggests further that God experiences emotional distress as part of the divine nature: by extending himself from one to three Persons, God knows both intimacy and loss. Abraham/Faith has come a long way from the theological precision of the Athanasian Creed or the mathematical concision of the *scutum fidei*. The question driving his analogies is not how can God be said to be at once singular and plural, or how can the three divine Persons be said to be distinct but equal, but more movingly, how does one describe the constellations of intimacy and interdependence within the Godhead?

Langland's literary experiment in Trinitarian theology reaches a climax in the Good Samaritan's sermon. At the beginning of B.17, the dreamer pretends that Abraham and Moses represent different creeds, and asks the two patriarchs whether he should believe in Abraham/Faith's testimony – faith in the Trinity – or in Moses/Hope's testimony – "love God and your neighbor" (17.35–36), carved on a rock-hard writ. After all, the Ten Commandments, though a staple of medieval catechism, do not mention a triune God. The dreamer puts the same question to the Good Samaritan at 17.125ff.: should he believe in the Trinity or in "Love God and neighbor," for surely true faith can be summarized as one principle? The Good Samaritan reconciles the two tenets through the metaphors of the hand and the taper, which explain how the Trinity is the perfect illustration of theology as charity. The Persons, as a community of three, teach us how to love God and neighbor. The Samaritan, like a good preacher, tells the dreamer that if his own conscience or heretics with arguments should cause him to doubt his faith, he should show them his hand. The Trinity, in this powerful image, is like faith itself: it performs one's belief through the body. In the exquisite passage that follows, the Samaritan explains that the Trinity is like a hand with different parts: clenched, it becomes a mighty fist (symbolizing the Father); unfurled, its fingers grope and "taste," like knowledge itself ("that touched and tastede at techynge of the pawme," 17.148, symbolizing the Son/Word); the sensitive palm allows the fingers to unclench or unfurl (symbolizing the Holy Spirit). But just as the fist, fingers, and palm make up one hand, so the three Persons of the Trinity hold the whole world within themselves. As in the American spiritual, Langland's Trinity "Halt al the wide world withinne hem thre – / Both wolkne and the wynd, water and erthe, / Hevene and helle and al that ther is inne" [Holds all the wide world within the three of them, / Both the sky and the wind, water and earth, / Heaven and hell and what lies therein] (17.160–62).

The Samaritan's hand demonstrates both the power of faith and the creative force of the Trinity. It also argues for the interdependence of the community of three. As the Samaritan explains, not only is each Person necessary to the operations of the Godhead, the function of the Holy Spirit being more nebulous than those of the Father or Son, but also each Person is insufficient without the other. In his *Metalogicon*, the philosopher John of Salisbury (*c*.1120–1180), writing about human society, talks about how the Trinity, the plural and creating God, has ordered the parts of the world in such a way that each part requires the other:

> For the creative Trinity, the one and true God, has so ordered the parts of the universe for the sake of a more firmly joined connection and protective charity that each one requires the assistance of the others and a defect in one is repaired by the others, insofar as each individual part is like a member of the other individual parts.[34]

The Trinity, in its plurality, models and orders a diverse human society, though unlike human society, the Trinity is not fundamentally deficient (the Son, for example, does not exist because the Father needs help). Using his own hand as a prop, the Good Samaritan reads the neediness of the created world, which makes mutual aid necessary, back into the Trinity itself. And he does so, importantly, by diagnosing the hurt and lack experienced by the Godhead. If the palm of the hand (the Holy Spirit) should be "ymaymed or ypersed," wounded stigmata-like, the fist could no longer close, and the fingers would fail to grope or grasp: "For the fyngres that folde sholde and the fust make, / For peyne of the pawme, power hem failleth / To clucche or to clawe, to clippe or to holde" [For the fingers, which are supposed to fold and make a fist, / Lose all ability, on account of the palm's pain, / To clutch or to claw, to grab or to hold] (17.187–89). Conversely, says the Samaritan, now speaking of himself, if my fingers were broken ("toshullen") but my palm was unharmed ("withoute maleese"), I still might manage to help myself in various ways "though alle my fyngres oke [ache]" (17.192–95). Naturally, the Good Samaritan does not believe that God is aggrieved, or that any Person can be physically hurt. His point about the Trinity is that God, in his plurality, models loving-kindness, and in that sense belief in the three Persons is the beginning of human ethics. The Holy Spirit, the essence of divine and human "kyndenesse," is the common denominator of the God–God and human–God relationship. A person should love his neighbor because everyone is made in God's image; he who hurts another person also "hurts" God or, in the poet's striking phrase, "priketh God as in the pawme" (17.199).

The metaphor of the candle or taper similarly affirms the sanctity of life by showing how each individual is made in the image of the triune God. The torch is the Father, the wick the Son, and the flame the Holy Spirit. A candle will not give light if it lacks any of those things, just as the Persons of the Trinity are equally God and equally interdependent. And if the Holy Spirit, the embodiment of charity in the world, is likened to the light that shines from a candle, to quench that light is to cause enormous suffering. Thus, concludes the Samaritan, sinning against the Holy Spirit is like murdering a good man, who is the embodiment not only of the Holy Spirit (the light), but of the Trinity as a whole (the candle):

> For every manere good man may be likned to a torche,
> Or ellis to a tapur, to reverence the Trinity;
> And whoso morthereth a good man, me thynketh, by myn inwit,
> He fordooth the levest light that Oure Lord lovyeth.　　　(17. 278–81)

> [For every sort of good man may be compared to a torch,
> Or else to a taper, in honor of the Trinity;
> And whoever murders a good man, it seems to me,
> He extinguishes the dearest light that our Lord loves.][35]

When a man sins against God, it only "semeth that he greveth / God that he grypeth with" [seems that he grieves / God with whom he grapples] (17.202–3), and yet the harm done to the Godhead, which the Good Samaritan asks the dreamer to imagine – a harm which reflects through analogy the harm that people inflict on each other – is intrinsic to belief in the Trinity. In the analogies of the hand and taper, the divine nature, or the interdependence between three Persons, rests on this notion of divine suffering. The harm experienced by the Godhead argues for the existence and necessity of three Persons while, at the same time, linking human morality to the divine community of three.

In B.9–10 and then again in B.15, the poet worries about the dissem-
ination of learning to the laity, and identifies Trinitarian theology as the
boundary between good and bad preaching. At the end of B.15, however,
Anima proposes belief in the Trinity as the gateway to universal conversion:
if only Saracens and Jews would learn the Creed! In this way, Trinitarianism
establishes the limits of clerical learning, suggesting directions that the poem
itself might take: in one direction, the poem moves toward scholastic
obscurities; in the other it moves toward the rote expression of belief.
Throughout *Piers Plowman*, however, the poet manages to talk quite a bit
about theology in creative and sometimes very emotional ways: in B.9–10,
he reports the arguments about original sin supposedly bandied about by
lords and clerks; in B.16 and 17, as we have just seen, he offers an extended
and moving analysis of Trinitarianism; in passus 18, he stages a rousing
debate concerning two of the most important subjects in Christian theology, the justice of the Redemption and the necessity of the Atonement.
These subjects, firmly embedded in sacred narrative, make the poet's
experimental theology a function of an ambitious vernacular poetics.

Beautiful reasons

In B.18, the dreamer, wandering wet-shoed, falls asleep in Lent to dream of
Jesus's death and resurrection. In this passus, the poet limits himself to the
formal divisions that *Piers Plowman* promises but hardly ever delivers. The
length of the passus conforms to the length of a dream (vision 6), and B.19
and 20 will repeat this pattern. In B.18, too, action is neatly marked by
liturgical time – the dramatic events that take place in B.18 correspond to
the liturgical events of Holy Week, from Palm Sunday. This link between
narrative and liturgical orders further connects the dreamer's vision to his
experience of waking life. Having once more grown dissatisfied with the
world, he wants desperately to sleep, and when he finally does, he dreams of
children singing hymns of praise: "Gloria, [laus et honor]" and "Hosanna
[in excelsis Deo]," sung in procession on Palm Sunday. At the end of the
passus, the dreamer wakes to the caroling of the Four Daughters of God and
bells sounding Easter Mass, both in his dream-world and in his waking life.

Here, too, at long last, within the context of the Easter liturgy, is a vision
of Christ on the Cross. Christ, a noble "prikiere" (18.25), comes riding to
Jerusalem disguised in Piers's "armes" to fight the devil and win back the
"fruit" stolen from the Tree of Charity. As discussed above, Christ's joust, a
trope taken from romance, paints the Crucifixion as the valiant act of a
knight rather than the passive suffering of a victim. Christ's death on the

Cross also invokes epic in its most condensed form, in which the cosmic forces of Good and Evil face off in the great battle. As Abraham/Faith says, Calvary can be radically simplified to a dispute between Life and Death: Christ as Life, fighting for the life of humankind against Death, or the devil, humankind's spiritual slayer:

> Deeth seith he shal fordo and adoun brynge
> Al that lyveth or loketh in londe or in watre.
> Lif seith that he lieth, and leieth his lif to wedde
> That, for al that Deeth kan do, withinne thre daies to walke
> And fecche fro the fend Piers fruyt the Plowman,
> And legge it ther hym liketh, and Lucifer bynde,
> And forbite and adoun brynge bale-deeth for evere:
> *O Mors, mors tua ero, [ero morsus inferne]!*   (18.29–35a)

> [Death says he shall annihilate and bring down
> All that lives or looks, in land or in water.
> Life says that he lies, and lays down his life as proof,
> That, whatever Death tries to do, in three days he will walk
> And fetch from the fiend the fruit of Piers the Plowman,
> And call it what he wants, and bind Lucifer,
> And destroy and bring down bitter-death for ever:
> "O Death, I will be your death, [Hell, I will be your sting]!"]

From here, the poet launches into an account of the Crucifixion: the trial before Pilate, the taunting and scourging of Christ, the crown of thorns, the vinegar mockingly proffered to Christ, the natural phenomena that occurred at his death (solar eclipse, earthquake, dead men rising), and the blind Longinus who, coerced by the mob, stabs Christ's body with his spear and miraculously recovers his sight when blood sprays into his eyes. This ingeniously compact summary recalls medieval ivories, with their dense narration and finely etched details.[36] What stands out from Langland's version, however, is not a blow-by-blow account of Christ's suffering, as might be expected, but a starkly drawn battle between life and death. Even the moment of Christ's death is majestically spare: "'*Consummatum est,*' quod Crist, and comsede for to swoune, / Pitousliche and pale as a prison that deieth / The lord of lif and of light tho leide hise eighen togideres" ["It is finished," said Christ, and began to swoon, / Piteous and pale like a prisoner who is dying; / Then the Lord of Life and of Light closed his eyes [or "cast them upwards"]] (18.57–59).

Medieval literature and art are replete with depictions of the tortured Christ, with Mary and her companions mournfully arrayed, the narrator or patron kneeling among them or watching from the sidelines. For the medieval spectator, Christ's body – perforated with wounds and "peynted al blody" (*Piers Plowman* B.19.6) – might serve as a goad to penance, his loving sacrifice highlighting the worshiper's sins. Alternatively, Christ's crucified body might serve as a screen for spiritual reflection. The English mystic Julian of Norwich (1342–1416) says in her *Shewings* that she prayed for three things: a mental image of the Passion, bodily sickness with which she might share in Christ's suffering, and three "wounds" (contrition, compassion, and steadfast longing).[37] Spiritual athletes, like St. Catherine of Sienna (1347–1380), chose other ways of linking Christ's suffering to their own lives, for example, through acts of self-denial such as fasting, or extreme acts of charity, like caring for lepers. As the modern scholar Caroline Bynum has so influentially argued, Christ's body, abject and feminized, offered a way for medieval women to identify with the deity through their own self-inflicted suffering.[38]

These traditions of representing Christ's suffering do not seem to have had an impact on *Piers Plowman*. As many readers have noticed, the poet's description of Christ battling the forces of darkness in B.18 recalls much earlier portrayals of Christ as a triumphant warrior, as in Anglo-Saxon elegies like the much-cited example of the *Dream of the Rood* (c.1000), in which the Cross recounts its role in Christ's battle on Calvary: "Rod wæs ic aræred ahof ic ricne cyning, / heofona hlaford hyldan me ne dorste. / Þurhdrifan hi me mid deorcan næglum" [I was the cross raised up; I lifted the rich king, / Lord of the heavens; I dared not bend, / They drove through me with dark nails].[39] To be sure, a poem like the *Dream of the Rood* shares a very important idea with later medieval lyrics, that created beings, like the Cross, are capable of sharing in Christ's experience. The medieval liturgy, too, assured continuity between earlier and later religious poetry, as for example, the battle hymns written in honor of the Cross by the sixth-century bishop Venantius Fortunatus, which were sung for centuries at Passiontide ("Royal banners go forth") and Good Friday ("Sing, my tongue, the glorious battle").[40] Hymns like these skillfully combine pity for Christ's suffering with awe for his glorious deeds.

Piers Plowman, however, departs from later medieval passion literature in its nearly exclusive emphasis on the warrior Christ. And it does so, at the critical moment, by underlining its own metrical form, the alliterative long line. Modern scholars speculate whether fourteenth-century alliterative poems such as *Piers Plowman* descended from Anglo-Saxon alliterative poetry, despite some significant metrical differences between them. Did fourteenth-century poets deliberately revive an earlier poetry, or had Old English meter simply gone off the radar, preserved in oral poetry or in written English prose? Or might alliterative poetry have been reconstituted from medieval Latin prose? Whatever the case, it is conceivable that a later poet like Langland might view alliterative poetry – whether he considered it to be archaic or modern – as a repository of heroic depictions of Christ. The stunning last line of passus 18, with its Anglo-Saxon lexis and stress patterns, encapsulates this warrior aesthetic in an unmistakably Old English form. The dreamer, electrified by his vision, orders his wife and daughter to pray to the Cross. Sounding not a little like the *Beowulf*-poet, he exclaims about the Cross, "May no grisly goost glide there it shadweth!" [May no grisly ghost go where it casts its shadow] (18.433).

Because the image of the suffering Christ looms so large in later medieval literature, its absence in *Piers Plowman* feels like an omission. David Aers accounts for this absence as follows: he argues, against Bynum, that the emphasis in the later Middle Ages on Christ's humanity and specifically on the way Christ's humanity could lead to practices of self-inflicted suffering, was neither the only available model for thinking about Christ in this period, nor was it especially subversive, as Bynum would have it. For Aers, the truly subversive *imitatio Christi* in this period is exemplary teaching, a major focus of Wycliffite writings. According to Aers, the Wycliffites' focus on teaching as the best imitation of Christ's humanity is fully anticipated by Langland, who drew from the recesses of Christian piety a powerful alternative to mainstream representations of Christ.[41]

Teaching and preaching are major topics in *Piers Plowman*, without a doubt. As discussed in Chapter 5, the poet's concerns about preaching explain his missionary zeal in B.15, which, in turn, leads him to articulate a really subversive position: the disendowment of professional religious (15.547ff.). To appreciate the poet's innovations, however, we need not credit him with a proto-Reformist perspective, insisting, for example, that his emphasis on good preaching is a corrective to cultic excess. For one thing, B.18 does not exist in a vacuum but participates in a dense cultural field. The heart-stopping line "The lord of lif and of light tho leide hise eighen togideres" (see above) is so affecting, in part, because it evokes more graphic images of Christ's death. Furthermore, if the poet shies away from cultic iconography – the tortured Christ or the grieving Virgin – he is wholly engaged with some of the emotional issues that underwrite medieval depictions of Christ's humanity: vulnerability, mutuality, pain, and loss. In B.17, the poet's sustained attention to divine Personality shows not that he is disinterested in Christ's humanity, but rather that he is committed to representing the presence of God in the human condition. A writer who refuses to represent divinity inevitably highlights God's absence and extreme otherness. Conversely, a writer who represents divinity, as Langland does in B.17 and 18, runs the risk of compromising God's absolute power by ascribing feelings to him, constraining him in time and space. Trinitarianism pulls in both directions. On one end, it asks us to refuse representation in order to preserve the integrity of the Godhead (as in the Creed); on the other, it invites us to think about God as a complexly social being whose sympathetic incursions into human affairs – what makes God representable in human terms – is modeled by relationships among the divine community of three.

A similarly emotional and deeply poetical engagement with theology takes place in B.18, the story of Christ's death and his resurrection. The subject of this passus is the Atonement, the reconciliation between God and man through Christ's sacrifice on the Cross, and the redemption from hell. As the main event in the history of salvation, the Atonement makes the "ineffable and infinite" suddenly "finite and historical," and as such it raises the question of the relationship between representation and theology.[42] For example, one challenge presented by the Atonement is finding a language sufficiently moving or grand to capture the significance of the event. For medieval writers, a related challenge was to explain the theological reasons for spiritual redemption: why did God have to become man in order to save humanity from the devil (and endure pain and death in the process), and how was he justified in redeeming humanity in the first place?

In *Piers Plowman*, the poet meets the aesthetic and rhetorical demands of the Atonement by stitching together several "witnessing" scenes – the testimony of the patriarchs and prophets, the debate between the Four Daughters of God, and the quarrel between the devils in hell – in order to create a poetic field rich enough to explain salvation theology. Passus 18, as a result, is a veritable grab bag of "reasons" recited by different speakers – Abraham, Truth, Righteousness, Mercy, Peace, Lucifer, and Christ. These speakers reel off arguments for and against the Atonement/Redemption which come from different legal and ethical systems: from the codes of medieval warfare, a liege lord (Christ) should pay ransom to the enemy for the lives of his men (the souls in hell); from criminal law, a king (Christ) has the right to forgive a felon (humanity); from medicine, poison is an antidote to poison; from property law, a person (the devil) acquires rights over property (souls) that he has occupied for a long time; but, from proverbial wisdom, those who beguile deserve to be beguiled (the devil, in the guise of a snake with a woman's face, tricked Adam and Eve into eating the apple, and so he should be tricked by God who disguised himself as a man); and finally, from the Old Testament, the principle of reciprocal or commutative justice or "an eye for an eye and a tooth for a tooth" (through whatever means the devil won the souls of men, so he should be forced to give them up).[43]

These strands of argument come from very different places, but the poet weaves them into a poetics of fittingness, a poetics capable of expressing the logic of the Redemption and Atonement by accounting both for the rightness of Christ's actions and for the balance restored to the cosmos and to history when God became man. In his triumphant speech to Satan, Christ declares,

> *Dentum pro dente et oculum pro oculo.*
> *Ergo,* soule shal soule quyte and synne to synne wende,
> And al that men hath mysdo, I man, wole amende it
> Membre for membre [was amendes by the Olde Lawe],
> And lif for lif also – and by that lawe I clayme
> Adam and al his issue at my wille herafter.
> And that Deeth in hem fordide, my deeth shal releve,
> And both quyke and quyte that queynt was through synne.
>
> (18.341–47)

> ["A tooth for a tooth and an eye for an eye."
> "Therefore" a soul shall pay for a soul and a sin go to sin,
> And all that men have done wrong, I, a man, shall amend it.
> Member for member was the satisfaction meted out by the Old Law,
> And life for life also – and by that law I claim
> Adam and all his descendants to be at my will from now on.
> And that which Death destroyed in them, my death will restore,
> And both revive and repay what was drowned through sin.]

This is what might be called a rhetorical poetics, a poetics which is persuasive, not because it constructs coherent, well-developed arguments (as *ergo* would imply), but because it takes fittingness – what is proper, necessary, or congruent – to be the ground of argument. The two biblical verses that run through this passage, and through B.18 as a whole, are "Dentrum pro dente et oculum pro oculo" (Exodus 21:22–27) and "mors ero mors tua" (Hosea 13:14), the latter given in Latin at 17.112b and 18.35b.[44] At first glance, these two verses could not be more different. The first verse, about just punishment (a "mirror" justice), is a rule of law or prescriptive tag for human societies; the second verse, about the triumph of life over death, refers to divine, not human conduct, and is a classic example of literary paradox. In the speech quoted above, Christ cites these two verses in order to yoke together different reasons for the Atonement, the punishment of the devil, and the redemption of man. In doing so, he wreaks havoc on the idea of reciprocal justice by making himself the third party (Christ, by sacrificing himself, pays man's debt to the devil – "dentrum pro dente" – through his own life – "ero mors tua"). This passage also shows that syntactical or metrical fittingness is sufficient to unite different theological frameworks. Just as one tooth or eye is set in apposition to the other, so death is set in apposition to death, member to member, life to life, and soul to soul.

Although many medieval theologians talk about the Redemption in terms of its fittingness – its properness and its symmetry – Anselm of Canterbury, in his landmark work *Cur Deus Homo* (*Why [did] God [become] Man?*, late eleventh century) proved himself master of the discourse. Anselm recognized that the logic of the Redemption, the reasons why humanity needed to be saved through the sacrifice of Christ, constitutes for human beings the very beauty of the Atonement:

> As death had entered the human race by man's disobedience, so it was fitting [*opportet*, "it was necessary"] that by man's obedience life would be restored. And, as sin, which was the cause of our condemnation, had its origin from a woman, so the author of our righteousness and salvation would be born from a woman. And so also [was it fitting] that the devil, who had conquered man by tempting him to taste of the tree, should be conquered by man in the suffering on the tree which man bore himself. There are many other things also, which, if we carefully examine them, give a certain ineffable beauty [*ineffibilem quondam ... pulchritudinem*] to our redemption as accomplished in this manner.[45]

According to Anselm, logic merely helps to represent the beauty of the Redemption, a beauty actually impossible to express in language, yet what he shows in this passage, in fact, is that the beauty of the Atonement can be expressed through the artful arrangements of words and phrases, which mimic the logic of theological argument. In this passage the logic of the Redemption is articulated by the symmetries of language, and specifically through a series of relative and purpose clauses, which emphasize syntactical and narrative balance. Arranged on either side of a series of adverbs ("sic," "ita," "ut") are appositions of active and passive verbs ("vincerat"/ "vinceretur"), repetition of key words ("a femina"/ "de femina"), and accusative constructions cleverly reworded ("per gustum ligni" vs. "per passionem ligni"). Anselm would have been sympathetic to Albert Einstein, who, writing about the Field Equation of General Relativity [$R\mu\nu - \frac{1}{2} g\mu\nu R$], praised the "incomparable beauty" of the theory, by which he was referring both to a phenomenon outside of language, and to the symmetry of the symbolism he had invented to describe it.

Anselm's beautiful reasons were transmitted to later writers through compilations such as the *Legenda aurea* (*The Golden Legend*). The *Golden Legend*, the anthology of saints' lives compiled by Jacobus de Voragine, included all kinds of useful information for preachers in addition to stories about the saints. In the section called the "Passion of the Lord," for instance, Voragine lists every reason he can find for the Redemption, in no apparent order. Voragine cares about the sheer volume of reasons that can be assembled in one place, united primarily by their fittingness, by which he means their congruency (*congruitas*) and their rightness rather than their necessity. For example, some of his schemas have to do with the circumstances of the Redemption narrative, i.e., at what time and place and through which manner Christ redeemed man ("congruitas autem attenditur ex parte temporis, ex parte loci et ex parte modi").[46] What is important to these schemas is that the circumstances of the Crucifixion balance out the circumstances of original sin. So, just as Adam was created and then sinned on a Friday in March at midday, so Christ was crucified on a Friday at March at midday; where Christ died, Adam, too, was buried. Or again, one can convey the amazing congruity of the Redemption ("secondo fuit congruentissimus ad curandam morbum") through catalogs of similarities and contraries ("per similia et per contraria"). Thus, from Voragine's list of similarities, just as Adam was made in the image of God, so Jesus was the image of God; just as through a woman folly was shown, so by a woman wisdom was born. Adam was naked in Eden; Christ was naked on the Cross. Death came through a tree, life through the Cross, and so forth. Voragine counters this list of similarities with a list of contraries: for example, Adam sinned through pride and gluttony, but Jesus saved mankind through humility.[47]

In passus 18, Langland draws upon Voragine's storehouse of reasons and, like Voragine, he privileges congruency over necessity. The fittingness of the Redemption can be demonstrated not through logical steps, from which one is forced to conclude that the salvation of man through Christ's incarnation and sacrifice was the only possible course of action, but rather through an associative symmetry, a series of demonstrations of how, through the Redemption, balance is restored to the God–man relationship and to sacred narrative. In the process, however, the poet manages to recover Anselm's beautiful reasons or the idea that theological arguments, pleasingly placed, can express the ineffable beauty of the Redemption. Langland accomplishes this by translating the rhetoric of Redemption theology into alliterative poetry. He shows in the process that English poetry is not only capacious enough to handle theological argument, but stylistically competent to express theology as art.

There are many spectacular examples of this technique in B.18. In the debate between the Four Daughters of God, for example, the lovely maidens, Mercy and Truth, walk toward each other across a portentous terrain. Truth is amazed by what she sees ("Ich have ferly of this fare," 18.125) – the light at hell's gates – but Mercy assures her that such wonders signify the redemption of humanity. Patriarchs and prophets have often preached about this day,

> That *man shal man save* thorugh a maydenes helpe,
> And that was tynt through *tree, tree* shal in wynne
> And that *deeth down borughte, deeth shal releve.*
>
> (18.138–40, my emphases)

> [That man shall save man through a maiden's help,
> And that which was lost through a tree, a tree shall regain,
> And that which death brought down, death shall deliver.]

These three lines contain three different "reasons" for the Redemption and Atonement: a man will be saved though a man; what was lost through a tree (of knowledge), a tree shall redeem (the Cross); that which Death (the devil, eternal death in hell) brought down, the death (of Christ) shall redeem. With each reason, the poet tries out a different syntactical solution, ingeniously ranged across the alliterative long line. In the first line, 138, he has enclosed the main "argument" in the first half-line (a man shall save man, hence God needed to take human form), with the apposite words (man/ man) conforming to the alliterated staves. The poet has placed supporting information in the second half-line (Christ was conceived through the Virgin). In lines 139 and 140, the poet arrays his arguments symmetrically around the caesura with the caesura doing the logical work of Latin adverbs *ut, ita,* or *sic.* In line 139, the poet fashions a chiasmic structure for his argument: the two apposite words that constitute the argument (tree/tree) are contained in the last and first metrical feet on either side of the caesura ("through tree, / tree shal"). In line 140, he has set the two halves of the "argument" in parallel on either side of the caesura ("that deeth down brought . . . deeth").

A similar example can be found in Christ's victory speech. The devils in hell are discussing the legality of the Redemption when Christ knocks on the door. Lucifer asks the perilous question, "who's there?" (*qui est iste?*). He and Christ subsequently take part in a call-and-response taken from Psalm 23, which was recited as an antiphon at Lauds on Holy Saturday (and which is represented in some versions of the Gospel of Nicodemus). In this passage, bilingualism brilliantly captures the back-and-forth of the Latin liturgy:

> Eft the light bad unlouke, and Lucifer answered,
> "*Quis est iste?*
> What lord artow?" quod Lucifer. The light soone seide,
> "*Rex glorie,*
> The lord of might and of mayn and alle manere vertues –
> *Dominus virtutum.*
> Dukes of this dymme place, anoon undo thise yates,
> That Crist may come in, the Kynges sone of Hevene!" (18.315–21)

> [Then the light asked that [the door be] unlocked, and Lucifer answered,
> "'Who is it?'
> What lord are you?" said Lucifer. The light answered straightaway,
> "'The King of Glory,'
> The Lord of might and main and all kinds of virtues –
> 'The Lord of virtues.'
> Dukes of this dim place, unlock these gates,
> So that Christ may come in, the King of Heaven's son."]

Finally Christ bursts into hell, gathers up his followers, and delivers a rousing speech which confirms the devils' suspicions that Christ is, in fact, both man and God, acting with perfect justice. In this speech, the fittingness of the Redemption, the way that that sequence of events both contains and transcends all reasons, is proof of Christ's victory:

> And I, in liknesse of a leode, that Lord am of hevene,
> Graciousliche thi gile have quyt – go gile ayein gile!
> And as Adam and alle thorugh a tree deyden,
> Adam and alle thorugh a tree shal turne to lyve.
> And gile is begiled, and in his gile fallen. (18.357–61)

> [And I, who am Lord of heaven, in the likeness of a person
> Have graciously defeated your guile – go guile against guile!
> And just as Adam and everyone died through a tree,
> Adam and everyone through a tree shall turn to live.
> And guile is beguiled and has succumbed to its own guile.]

In this passage, Christ collapses three different arguments: first, he deliberately tricked the devil by assuming the likeness of a man ("go gile ayein gile"); second, the logic of the Redemption turns on narrative balance – Adam, and all human beings, suffered death and will be redeemed through a tree, that is, through Christ's sacrifice on the Cross; third, according to proverbial wisdom, guile will be defeated by guile ("ars ut artem falleret"), a saying derived from Cato, which was traditionally associated with the Good Friday liturgy. Together these fitting reasons build a speech for Christ, but they also model a theologically accomplished poetry. No wonder that, for Geoffrey of Vinsauf, author of the most important medieval treatise on Latin composition, the *Poetria Nova* (*c*.1200), Christ's speech to the devil models the best in poetic tropes. Geoffrey writes, "'Since human virtue was, thus, one with God's virtue, therefore it is necessary that, just as the enemy overthrew man, he be overthrown by man himself; that just as the enemy won by means of a Tree, he be conquered by the same; that whom he captured through a trick, he should be captured by.' Thus spoke the Son."[48]

Running through these arguments for the fittingness of the Redemption is the notion of experience, both the personal experience of the actors in the Redemption (Adam, Lucifer, God, sinners) and the experiential wisdom that makes formulations of congruity possible (for example, guile will be defeated by guile; poison is an antidote to poison). In a passionate rejoinder to her sisters, Truth and Righteousness, who doubt the Redemption, Peace explains that God became man and man fell from grace for the same reason: so that they could appreciate the good. Those unfortunate souls in hell were placed there for their own benefit, so that they, too, might understand contrary things:

> For hadde thei wist of no wo, wele hadde thei noght knowen;
> For no wight woot what wele is, that nevere wo suffrede,
> Ne what is hoot hunger, that hadde nevere defaute. (18.204–06)

> [For had they not known about woe, they would not have known weal,
> Because no person knows what weal is, who has never suffered woe,
> Nor what hot hunger is, who has never had lack.]

Peace makes contraries the ground of experience and the foundation of divine reason: no one can understand life without the sure knowledge that all living things perish, and no one can know day without night and *vice versa*. Similarly, Adam learned to appreciate his Edenic joy when he lost it. In Peace's theology, governed by the experience of contraries, God, who "woot of alle joye" (18.224) voluntarily enlarged his experience of the world by submitting himself to human form ("suffrede to se the sorwe of deyng," 18.214), just as Adam, involuntarily through sin, enlarged *his* experience of the world by becoming mortal, knowing sorrow and death. This idea, that experience benefits all parties – even God recommends and knows intimately the experience of contraries – gives some respite from the barrage of argument and from the doldrums of history (see 18.202–28 and especially

205–16). Ultimately, experience, couched in the language of fittingness, moves salvation theology away from the operations of justice and mercy, of right and offense, and toward the reciprocal acts through which God and people gain knowledge about the world and about each other.

We saw that Langland's collection of arguments for the Atonement, which drives the debate between the Four Daughters of God and between the devils and Christ, amounts to a poetics of fittingness. Christ is so persuasive when he speaks to the devils because he has at his disposal so many beautiful if sundry reasons, culled from a number of discourses, which, taken together, mirror the appropriateness – as well as the justice – of human salvation. In this view, Atonement theology is a deeply satisfying collection of truisms about law, narrative, and behavior, which, in *Piers Plowman*, is rendered into literary art through an enterprising alliterative poetics.

Importantly, moreover, the proverb is the basic unit of this poetics. Proverbs convey a certain learned artistry at the same time that they proclaim the value of collective experience. And proverbs, so familiar in their concision, tend to sound banal in everyday contexts but they also induce enormous feeling when the stakes are high. Indeed, the very climax of B.18 – Peace's reconciliation with her quarrelling sisters – revolves around the poet's gorgeous translation of a Latin proverb, taken from a collection of proverbs called the *Liber parabolarum*, a popular schooltext attributed to the late twelfth-century author Alain de Lille. This proverb, which encapsulates the passus's many arguments for the Atonement and Redemption, turns out in translation to be a species of love poetry, an affecting lyric with which Peace restores friendship among her sisters and summons the divine love that motivated the Atonement in the first place. The poet calls the proverb a "note of poesie" ("a small bit of poetry set to music" or perhaps, "an example of literary ornament") and expands it into four English lines:

> Thanne pipede Pees of poesie a note:
> "*Clarior est solito post maxima nebula Phebus;*
> *Post inimicitias clarior est et amor.*
> After sharpest shoures," quod Pees, "moost shene is the sonne;
> Is no weder warmer than after watry cloudes;
> Ne no love levere, ne lever frendes
> Than after werre and wo, whan love and pees ben maistres"...
>
> (18.410–14)

> [Then Peace piped a note of song:
> "'Brighter is the sun Phebus after the greatest clouds;
> After enmity, love is brighter.'

After the sharpest showers," said Peace, "most bright is the sun;
No weather is warmer than after watery clouds;
Nor is love dearer, nor friends dearer,
Than after war and woe, when love and peace are masters."]

Peace's proverb summarizes her larger argument about the Atonement: that God allowed man to sin and die, and that God assumed human form to redeem man from sin and death, so both God and man might experience the opposite of what they formerly knew. But her virtuosic translation of the proverb moves Atonement theology from *ratio* to *amicitia* by exploding the proverb's antitheses: "After sharpest shoures," "no weder warmer than," "no ... levere, ne lever," and "Than after werre and wo."

Langland's beautiful reasons, simultaneously rhetorical and poetical, tease out the emotion that underlies theological argument. Geoffrey of Vinsauf considers the difficulties and pleasures of the composition process: it is not easy to find the word that fits a metaphor, but when you do, it is a huge relief. Nor is it easy to strike a balance between seriousness and pomposity, or between clarity and ornament. But when you finally achieve balance in writing, you successfully reconcile opposing forces of language. Geoffrey supports this point about writing with a proverb that echoes both Alain de Lille and medieval Redemption theology: "So opposites mingle; but they pledge peace, and enemies stay on as friends."[49] Langland's beautiful reasons show how an English poetics can perform the work of Latin rhetoric, and in the process, fashion a truly literary theological vernacular.[50]

CHAPTER 7

Institutions
(B.19–20)

"Cometh with me, ye fooles, / Into Unite Holy Chirche" (20.74–75)

Introduction

The last two passūs of *Piers Plowman* return the poem to irresolution and experiment. At the end of B.18, with church bells tolling and the Four Daughters caroling, the poem seems to have reached its apogee and discovered its lost plot. The triumphant art of B.18, its dramatization of the Redemption, required a partial surrender to biblical narrative or the long history of belief, beginning with the Edenic Tree of Charity and ending with the risen Christ. More of Christian history remains to be written, however, namely, the founding of the church, the Apocalypse, and the Last Judgement. By treating the first two events but not the third B.19–20 moves the poem away from narrative resolution and throws its dreamer back onto a landscape of spiritual uncertainty and social critique. In the heady last lines of B.20, when Unity-Holy Church has been breached and Contrition lies comatose inside, Conscience abandons the community and vows to keep searching for Piers:

> "By Crist!" quod Conscience tho, "I wole bicome a pilgrym,
> And walken as wide as the world lasteth,
> To seken Piers the Plowman, that Pryde myghte destruye,
> And that freres hadde a fyndyng, that for nede flateren
> And countrepledeth me, Conscience. Now Kynde me avenge,
> And sende me hap and heele, til I have Piers the Plowman!"
> And siththe he gradde after Grace, til I gan awake. (20.381–87)

> ["By Christ!" said Conscience then, "I will become a pilgrim,
> And walk to the ends of the earth
> To seek Piers the Plowman, who might destroy Pride,
> And arrange a stipend for friars, who flatter for need

211

And who dispute with me, Conscience. Now may Kind avenge me,
And send me luck and health, until I have Piers the Plowman!"
And then he cried after Grace, until I woke up.]

Conscience's desire to traverse messianic time overtakes the dreamer's desire in the Prologue to see and understand everything, and Conscience's longing for Piers gestures to a future that will remain unwritten in *Piers Plowman*. As Vance Smith argues, the poem's ending does not recuperate its beginning, as one might expect of a medieval treatise, sermon, or dream-vision. The poem does not conclude, for example, with the dreamer yawning besides the brook where he first fell asleep, or the poet addressing his readers and his God, as does one of his imitators, the author of *Pierce the Ploughman's Crede*, who signs off with an admonition and a prayer. It would fall to *Piers* scribes to make a "good end" to the poem, like the scribe of the Westminster manuscript (an A–C text), who recycled materials from the first two passūs to make a pious ending, or the "John But" scribe, who fashioned a coda to the A-text out of rumors of the author's death.[1] Instead, Langland takes his ending not from the beginning but from the middle of the poem, from Conscience's feast in B.13, where Conscience, struck to the heart, ditches his guests to join Patience in pilgrimage (see 13.181, "Frendes, fareth wel"). His dramatic exit from the hall is justified both by Patience's defense of the unsolicitous life, a life in which one relies on God to provide (B.14), and by Anima's call for English missionaries to the Holy Land (B.15). The poet may not have recuperated the poem as an entire work, but by keeping the middle in sight, he has redeemed the impulse to wander which first set the poem into motion.

If passūs 19–20 are left to one side, however, the poem reaches a satisfying conclusion at the end of B.18 with the Redemption and the dreamer's devotions at Easter Mass. Recently, Lawrence Warner has offered an attractive argument to support this idea: if, as most scholars agree, C is an authorial revision of B, the original B-text did not extend to passus 19 and 20. Rather, scribes copying Langland's B-text ("ur-B"), sometime after the poet had put C into circulation, copied C.21 and C22 (B.19 and B.20) to complete their B manuscripts. Among B-texts, B+C 21/22 alone survived.[2] Warner's most persuasive evidence has to do with the surprisingly few changes from B.19/20 and C.21/22 in comparison to the rest of the C revisions. Completing one version with another was common practice among *Piers* scribes: seven A-texts are finished off with C-texts, suggesting that medieval scribes were more invested in completeness than in preserving the integrity of what modern scholars judge to be authorial or unified versions.[3] That the poet thought to add two more passūs to C is surely significant: these last two passūs amount to a final statement of sorts, whether or not they originally appeared in B. However, if Warner's thesis is correct, Langland once deemed B.18 an appropriate end to his poem, resolving all experiment and indecision in Christ's life and death.

Whether or not B.19 and 20 turn out to be original to B, they behave something like revisions. The C-text sometimes comes across as the more formally and ideologically conservative text, as if the poet as reviser tacked to a new political wind.[4] This version is less tolerant of vertiginous leaps and jagged transitions. Most significantly, the C-reviser excises passages and whole scenes, which some medieval readers, especially after the 1381 Peasants' Revolt, might have thought controversial, such as the Coronation episode (B Prologue) in which a lunatic, angel, goliard, and commune presume to counsel the king, and Piers's tearing of the Pardon in B.7, an act which recalls the rebels' destruction of documents in London.[5]

It is questionable, however, that radicalism or conservatism can adequately characterize any stage in the poem's composition.[6] For one thing, the time of literary revision and the time of political upheaval or cultural change are never fully synchronous; for another, the C-text introduces two daring pieces of new writing. The first of these is C.5, the dreamer's defense of his life in which he insists he is no runaway or wayward laborer of the kind that later fourteenth-century statutes were designed to locate and punish. Rather, he is a trained cleric of no particular order, once funded by friends to attend school, now uncertainly located but cleared for take-off to spiritual points unknown.[7] The second piece is C.9, the revision to the Pardon episode, which massively reframes major topics such as poverty and charity and which, with its giddy praise of "lunatic lollers" (people who have madly, joyfully, renounced worldly care), reclaims the Wycliffite heresy and its "Lollard" adherents from official ecclesiastical disinformation.[8] It may be, too, as Warner suggests, that scribes revising B with C manuscripts were responsible for introducing controversy, such as the call for clerical disendowment in B.15.556–68, a position which, after the 1380s, was associated with Wycliffism. Even if the disendowment passage was preserved, not introduced in C, the poet's politics in C are fairly cutting edge.[9]

Regardless of whether B.19 and 20 were added to B from C – that is, whether they were conceived as C-text revisions and added to B, or whether they were retained in C from B in a relatively unrevised state – they show that the lines between versions should not be too sharply drawn. And yet, as this chapter argues, these last two passūs behave like revisions because they offer a new revisionary perspective on the poem, as if the poem itself were already something of an institution. With these passūs, the poet invents an institutional writing, in which his techniques and preoccupations become legible – even conventional – with respect to his poem.

Institutional poetics

Most strikingly, in B.19–20, the poet establishes poetic units by matching passus to dream. Typically, in medieval dream-visions, like *Pearl*, the dreamer falls asleep once, at the beginning, and all subsequent allusions to dreaming and writing refer back to that original moment: I dreamed, I woke, I wrote down what I dreamed. The moment in which the dreamer falls asleep, often luxuriously in his own bed, is the moment most likely to be illustrated precisely because it is not repeated – it is truly initial – as, for example, the portrait of the sleeping dreamer perched in the illuminated capital of the Prologue in Corpus Christi College, Oxford, MS 201, f. 1. By contrast, Langland's dreamer, like a prophetic Joseph or Daniel, dreams many dreams after the first. Successive dreams reveal either a strangely casual or a deeply compulsive attitude toward dreaming.

From passus 18, however, the poet begins to mark his multiple dreams as formal poetic units, a pattern which becomes visible with the addition of B.19 and 20: passūs 18, 19, and 20 contain one dream apiece; in passūs 18 and 19 passus and dream are nearly conterminous, as if the poet had belatedly discovered the dream-unit as his basic building block. Dreaming, in B.19, also creates narrative continuity in ways unanticipated by earlier passūs (cf. B.13.1–20). At the end of passus 18, the dreamer, roused by Easter bells, orders his family to go to church and pray to the Cross. In the first few lines of B.19, the dreamer recounts this waking episode, this time linking his ritual devotions both to the act of writing and to the transcription of the dream: "Thus I awaked and wroot what I hadde ydremed, /And dighte me derely and dide me to chirche / to here holly the masse and to be housled after" [Thus I woke and wrote what I had dreamed /And dressed up and went to church / To hear the whole mass, and, afterwards, to receive the Eucharist] (19.1–3). At the end of B.19, the dreamer wakes up and writes his dream down – "And I awakned therwith, and wroot as me mette" [And following that, I awoke and wrote what I dreamed] (19.485). "Til I gan awake," the very last words of the poem, links poem to passus to dream.

Additionally, in these last two passūs, the poet invents an institutional writing through copious self-reference. Passūs 19–20 are a veritable digest of the Prologue to passus 7. The description of the gifts of grace distributed to the community in B.19, for example, recasts the quantifier formula ("some . . . some") with which the dreamer first envisions the field of folk in the Prologue, lines 20–34: "Some [wyes] he yaf wit, with wordes to shewe . . . And some he kennede craft . . . and some he lered to laboure . . . and some to dyvyne and divide . . . And some to compace craftily . . ." etc. [Some men he gave wit, to expound with words, some he taught a profession . . . and some he taught to labor . . . and some to infer and divide . . . And some cleverly to conspire] (19.230–52). If this community of skills in B.19 seems less fractured than the Prologue's errant folk, it is because the poet has projected the field of folk onto a different present, onto the origins of the church, a mass reeducation program, as opposed to the contemporary now of social satire when "Somme putten hem to the plough" but "somme putten hem to pride" (Prol. 20, 23).

In such re-visionary moments the poet tends to dial down discord in order to amplify self-reference. For instance, in B.19, Piers enters the scene as an agricultural laborer and an estates middleman between human beings and God. As Grace's reeve and registrar, Piers makes sure that people pay what they owe ("Redde quod debes"), but his task is more straightforward than it was in the *Visio*, detached from the manorial relations and social conflict that plagued B.6. And just as Piers, in the Plowing of the Half-Acre, conjures up Hunger as a form of crowd control, so Conscience summons Kind (Nature) to scare people into penance and keep sin at bay. Kind's Malthusian solutions are, like Hunger's, merely temporary, but unlike Hunger, Kind is not an occasion for ethical wrangling but rather a formidable weapon against Antichrist.

The invention of an institutional writing – by which I mean the poem's formal recognition of its own techniques – is intricately bound up with the subject of B.19–20, the career of the earthly church, and it is activated through stories of institutional origins. A good example is the passage in B.19 about the relationship between foundational virtues and political rights, which is essentially a rewriting of the coronation episode of the B. Prologue. In this debate, Grace allegorizes the four cardinal virtues – justice, prudence, temperance, and fortitude – as the seeds of the good life which Piers will sow with the Old and New Testaments. In textbook Langlandian style, the poet acknowledges that the cardinal virtues, which, ideally, lay the groundwork for a perfect society, can also be used to cover up unethical behavior. The poet calls attention to this mismatch between foundational virtues and virtue in practice, as he does in the Prologue, by including voices usually marginal to political debate. A brewer interrupts, declaring he will not be ruled by justice because he wants to cheat customers, and a vicar, in a fit of bad-tempered ignorance, misreads the cardinal virtues as ecclesiastical dignitaries (cardinals) who, in his opinion, poorly represent the church. The vicar's perverse reading of "cardinal" recasts the cautious etymological joke in the B Prologue, where the poet reproves corrupt Roman cardinals, who ought to be the "closing gates" (*cardinales*) of virtue (B. Prol.100–12). To this cacophony in B.19 the poet adds the opinions of those entrusted with power. A lord, for example, distorts the cardinal virtues in order to justify a repressive manorial economy: in contrast to Piers's divine stewardship, the lord orders his henchmen to seize from his tenants whatever goods the auditor says they owe: "With *Spiritus Intellectus* thei toke the reves rolles, /And with *Spiritus Fortitudinis* fecche it – wole [he, nel he]," [with the "Spirit of Intellect" [i.e. reason, discernment] they took the reeve's rolls. / And fetched it with the "Spirit of Fortitude" – whether he was willing, or no] (19.467–68.) A king, speaking for absolutism, injudiciously defines *Spiritus Iusticie* as the God-given right to take what he wants from his people.

In this scene, the poet does not simply recycle earlier techniques, which have come to look quintessentially Langlandian over the course of the poem; he also, importantly, recognizes an affinity between revisionary writing and institutional history. At the intersection of the two stands the authorial persona, whom the poet resurrects at the beginning of B.20. Throughout *Piers Plowman*, the poet projects onto the dreamer a persona of indeterminate status, a person who, in his need and itinerancy, resembles a vagrant, pilgrim, or friar, i.e., someone whose life is by definition irregular. By revisiting this persona at the end of the poem, Langland confronts some of the problems inherent in authorial revision and in the institutionalization of irregular lives.

At the beginning of B.20, for example, the dreamer, hungry and comfortless in his waking life, faces his own Need. His encounter with Need is nothing less than the encounter with his own self as a person, a person who seeks aid and who, therefore, feels constant pressure to justify his life. In this sense, Need, who speaks in a reflexive third person ("So Nede, at greet nede, may nymen as for his owene" [So Need, when in great need, may take (something) as if it were his own], 20.20), is the personification of one's ethical relationship to oneself and to other people. Need, in other words, is how one represents one's self to oneself as Other ("there I am, that person in need"), obviating the need for personal pronouns such as "he", "she", or "I." At the same time, the reflexive character of Need captures the sickening quality of both self-justification and literary re-vision. As Need says approvingly about himself, "For nede maketh nede fele nedes lowe-herted" [For Need necessarily makes the needy feel humble] (20.37). The repetition of the word "need" in this difficult line (translated literally, "For need makes need feel needs low-hearted") conveys at once the feeling of insufficiency that, for the poet, is the basis for Christian morality, and the total self-absorption necessary to a person's defense of his life and work.[10] This pathological quality of Need is important, too, because it highlights the ethics of institutional writing. Need figures one's relationship to oneself and to other people at the same time that it refers to the processes through which an author justifies his or her work and makes it recognizable to readers.[11]

Need promises the dreamer the justification he seeks, a justification indistinguishable from a moral principle and as weighty as a sanction. In C.5, the dreamer, interrogated by Reason and Conscience, admits that he has neither the skill nor the physique with which to labor, nor, as a cleric, does he have an order on which to hang his hat. Like a tramp without a passport, or friar without a license, the dreamer desperately needs an excuse for the life he leads. In the Need episode in B.20, which anticipates C.5, in the order of revision, and follows from C.5, in the order of the poem, the dreamer wonders where his next meal lies, but once again he lacks an excuse for a life of itinerancy and poverty more than he lacks food.[12] Need assures the dreamer that his very neediness excuses a life of roaming and begging. According to Need, for instance, the dreamer resembles Christ on the Cross, exemplary in his dispossession. In a gorgeous expansion of Luke 9.58/Matthew 8:20 ("Foxes have holes and birds have nests, but the Son of Man has nowhere to lay his head"), Need imagines Christ in mourning for his own homelessness and that of all humanity.

> So he was nedy, as seith the Book, in manye sondry places,
> That he seide in his sorwe on the selve roode,
> "Bothe fox and fowel may fle to hole and crepe,
> And the fissh hath fyn to flete with to reste.
> Ther nede hath ynome me, that I moot nede abide
> And suffre sorwes ful soure, that shal to joye torne".   (20.42–47)

> [He was so needy, as the Book says, in so many respects,
> That, in his sorrow, he said, on the selfsame Cross,
> "Both the fox and the fowl may flee and creep into their holes,
> And the fish have fins with which to swim to their rest,
> Yet need has seized me, so that I must need endure,
> And suffer acute sorrows, which will one day turn to joy."]

Need, however, is a shaky ground on which to build a defense because what makes him praiseworthy – the way he portrays the self in terms of material lack– is also what threatens to discredit him. After all, the self in need is a self that constantly demands relief. For Langland, this contradiction is embodied by the mendicant friars, whose lifestyle he admires in theory, but whose shrewd defenses of their own poverty (they "glosed the gospel as hem good liked," Prol. 60) he finds to be self-serving and exploitative.[13] By the end of the poem, the friars' pernicious need actually drives Conscience out of Unity and over the edge of the poem. An accomplished orator like the friars, Need's defense of need shows how self-regard can be morally problematic. According to Need, for instance, the dreamer's neediness epitomizes the cardinal virtue of temperance, which, says Need, is the trustiest tool in the spiritual kit, superior to the three other virtues, which go to unhappy extremes: fortitude overshoots its mark, justice can be too arbitrary or high-handed, and prudent men trust too much in their own abilities (20.23–33a).

Even more troubling is the way that Need defines himself as a thing that replaces human aid and personal responsibility. Need, accountable only to himself, acts like legal surety, and provides his own counsel: "Coudestow noght excuse thee," he asks the dreamer, "as dide the kyng and othere . . . that thow nome na more than nede thee taughte, /And nede ne hath no lawe, ne nevere shal falle in dette?" [Could you not excuse yourself, just as the king and others did . . . that you took no more than Need taught you, / And Need has no law, nor shall ever fall in debt?] (20.6, 9–10). Like a stand-in, or a pledge, like any legal custom (20.13 ff.), Need is a cover for something, something that one can offer on one's own behalf. Even if a person has no money to make a purchase, "Nede anoon righte nymeth hym under maynprise" [Need legitimately stands [literally "seizes" or "takes"] bail for him] (20.17). To have no law, claims Need, is a law in itself: it is an excuse to help yourself when there is no one to help you. More dubiously, this law unto himself warrants immoral actions such as stealing, which for Need, passes for natural law ("lawe of kynde," 18): "So Nede, at gret nede, may nymen as for his owene, / Withouten conseil of Conscience or Cardynale Vertues – / So that he sewe and save *Spiritus Temperancie*" [So Need, at time of great need, may take something as if it were his own, / Without consulting Conscience or the Cardinal Virtues, /As long as he follows and supports the spirit of temperance] (20.20–22).

In sum, the conversation between Need and the dreamer offers a comment on the relationship between institutional writing and literary revision: insofar as the latter seeks justification in the former, the author is never entirely off the hook.

Apocalypse now

At the beginning of passus 19, the dreamer falls asleep during Easter Mass at a local church, where he beholds Piers the Plowman – Jesus in human form – "peynted al blody" and parading the cross in front of the people. Shifting gears from parochial devotions to ecclesiastical history, the dreamer asks Conscience to name the figure before him: is this Jesus the jouster or Piers the Plowman? Conscience tells the dreamer he must distinguish God in human form (i.e., Jesus/Piers) from the risen Christ. The dreamer waxes disputatious with Conscience, arguing that one name, Jesus, should suffice. Conscience explains that Jesus's names designate separate but mutually supporting roles. He goes on to explain that a plurality of names is necessary to grasp the significance of Jesus's victory over death, or what it meant for him to declare his sovereignty at a critical juncture in history. A knight commands respect, a king dubs knights, but only a conqueror redistributes property, proclaims new rules, and upsets the status quo (makes "lordes of laddes," 19.32). Like a conqueror, Jesus as Christ made free men of his followers and "lowe churls" of the "gentil" Jews who despised him. Nowadays, Jews worldwide are subjected, like churls, to taxes and restrictions: "as wide as the world is, wonyeth ther none / But under tribut and taillage as tikes and cherles" [As wide as the world is, none of them dwell / Except under tribute and taxes, like curs and churls] (19.36–37).

These disquieting lines about the dispersal and subjugation of the Jews reveal the institutional stakes of the poem's re-vision. Recalling the very last lines of the poem, in which Conscience declares he will "walken as wide as the world lasteth" (20.382), and the first lines of the Prologue, in which the dreamer tells how he "Wente wide in the world, wondres to here" (Prol.4; and see also 19.335–37), this line about the worldwide subjugation of the Jews reminds us that the literary desire to survey the world and the spiritual desire to wander unchecked are supported by a firm belief in Christian dominion. Langland's belief in a worldwide Christian dominion, fueled by Anima's universal chronicle in B.15 and proclaimed at the beginning of B.19 with Christ's conquest, gives the poem's involuted narrative a larger structure which passūs 19 and 20 bring to the fore.

Although Conscience's description of Christ's victory as a species of world conquest gives the poem a discernible structure, it also shuts down one of the possibilities of a worldwide Christianity – universalism – or the geographical and temporal inclusion of non-Christians. This possibility animated the theological debates in B.11–12, where the poet considered the possibility of everyone's salvation – Jews, Muslims, pagan scholars,

Roman emperors, and the rich. It also anchored the poet's reformist history in B.15–18, where he imagines Jews and others playing different roles in an "omnibus" version of Christian history: as goads to modern missionaries, or, in the case of the Jews, as witnesses to the faith, or markers of Old and New Testament time. In these passūs, universalism is not identical to the conviction that non-Christians deserve to be saved or even tolerated; it is, instead, a proposition about the limits of God's mercy or what it means for people to participate in a saving narrative in which identity and status are subject to change. Universalism is also an exhortation to Christians to act charitably by extending the boundaries of self-identification, whether to pagans or the destitute. From this perspective, Conscience's explanation of Christ's conquest, which irrevocably alters the status of Jews from nobles to churls, contradicts the universalist theory at the poem's intellectual center and undermines the universalist practices critical to the poem's literary imaginary, such as almsgiving, evangelism, crusade, and even dream-vision.

This closing down of universalism in B.19 is anticipated by Abraham/ Faith, a time-traveler, who castigates the Jews for not recognizing Christ during Christ's lifetime ("And ye, lurdaynes, han ylost . . ." B.18.102–09).[14] According to Abraham/Faith, Jews after Christ suffered a reversal of status because they committed a "villany" by rejecting Christ, testifying to their intrinsic and inescapable churldom. The Jews lost, in other words, not simply because they happened to be on the wrong side of conquest, but because history, as it pertained to them, became untraversable, cordoned off by status and hierarchy, crime and punishment. Mandeville, in his *Travels*, tells a well-known story about Alexander the Great, at whose prayer God shut up the people of Gog and Magog or the Ten Lost Tribes in the Caspian hills (Caucasus Mountains). As Mandeville explains, these Jewish tribes will break out during the reign of Antichrist, when they will join forces with contemporary Jews, who have been learning Hebrew for that purpose.[15] Like Mandeville, Conscience and Abraham portray Christian belief in a bounded era and on the inexorable march to the apocalypse where enemies must be definitively unmasked.

Conscience's rejection of the Jews in B.19 is consonant with medieval Christian hermeneutics, in which Jews participate in two overlapping narratives, one of continuation and fulfillment – Jews before Christ, such as Abraham and Moses, prophesized the Christian era – and the other of contradiction and replacement – truth as Jews think they know it has been contradicted by Christian revelation and consequently, Jews have been replaced as God's chosen people. As *Piers Plowman* scholars have observed, the supercessionist move from the first hermeneutic to the second, and from inclusion to exclusion, is the price that must be paid for narrative progress, if the poem is to move forward from biblical history to the Church Militant.[16] Just as critical to this move is the isolation of Jews from other non-Christian groups. When Jews are lumped together with other non-Christians, such as ancient pagans or latter-day Muslims, as they are in B.15, they benefit from universalism: they witness the faith or stand ready to convert to Christianity. Conversely, where the category of "non-Christians" is reduced to "Jews," universalism with its multiple temporalities tapers off into a strictly linear history culminating in the apocalypse. This teleology is not actually necessary for *Piers Plowman* to exist, but the supercessionist turn at B.19 heralds a new and final trajectory both for Christian history and for the poem.

Significantly, what is lost for the Jews in Conscience's treatise on conquest, universalism, is gained for England, which becomes, in B.19–20, the site of total war and total reform. In his universal chronicle in B.15, Anima oscillates between an international view of Christianity, characterized by conversion and crusade, and a national view, characterized by the reform and disendowment of English clergy on English soil: "Taketh hire landes, ye lordes, and let hem lyve by dymes" (15.563). As we saw in Chapter 5, the poet's radical reform of the English clergy is deliberately anachronistic and disorienting. According to Anima, English clergy should be more like sixth-century missionaries, ready to die in heathen lands, which England and Wales once were. And yet, if the poet's plan for reform is deliberately impractical (its real purpose being to reform the clergy rather than sending them abroad), it nevertheless claims the geographical space of England as the *terra nova* of Christian imperialism.

Likewise, in B.19–20, the poet creates a distinctly English version of the Church Militant, this time in opposition to the papacy and to the Holy Roman Empire. A vicar sardonically warns cardinals to "helden hem stille" with Jews in Avignon (19.425–26), referring to the "Babylonian Captivity" (*c*.1305–77) in which Clement V removed the papal see to France, where he and his successors recruited Jewish craftsmen and financiers to help build the papal compound. The vicar, no perfect cleric, proceeds to compare the "inparfit" Pope (432) unfavorably to Piers the Plowman, whom he wishes could be crowned "Emperour of al the world" (431). Although Piers, in this section of the poem, represents a version of the pope, the vicar's desire to substitute Piers for the pope resonates with longstanding English anti-papal sentiments. The vicar's nomination of Piers also makes an English claim to a secular Christian empire represented by the Holy Roman Emperor, the official

Protector of the church who, in the later Middle Ages, was almost always elected from a German or Czech house (but could theoretically be a French prince). His nomination of Piers also, importantly, entails a leap of social as well as political imagination. It assumes that the bid for a worldwide Christianity, a Christianity whose only obstacle is the corruption of its clerics, may be made by an English plowman who embodies the apostolic origins of the papacy better than any contemporary pope.

Conscience's treatise on conquest ushers in a new history of Christianity, the history of the Church Militant or the timeline of the church on earth from the life of Christ, his ministry, and death, through the institution of a community of believers fortified with virtues and grace in their ongoing struggle against sin. B.19.68–199 retells the story of Christ's life (already narrated in B.18) in an elegant redaction of the gospels, chronologically ordered from the birth of Christ to the last lines of the Apostolic Creed, which predict the Last Judgement: "And [Christ will] demen hem at domesday, bothe quyke and dede – / The goode to the Godhede and to greet joye, /And wikkede to wonye in wo withouten ende" [And [Christ will] judge them at doomsday, both the living and the dead – / The good [will go] to the Godhead and to great joy, /And the wicked will dwell in woe without end] (19.197–99). This redaction is structured by the poem's own terms, Dowel, Dobet, and Dobest: as a child, a "fauntekyn ful of wit," Christ did well; as he grew older and performed miracles, he did better; with the Crucifixion and Resurrection, he did best.

The story of Christ's life in passus 19 forms a diptych with the story of the apocalypse in passus 20. These last two passūs chart the history of the church on earth – its members, leaders, values, and rules – culminating in an apocalypse in which the church's best work, providing a bulwark against evil, is sabotaged by Antichrist and his followers. That the poem ends with a present-day apocalypse, rather than with Judgement Day, points not to finality but to re-vision.[17] Apocalyptic writing is inherently retrospective; it gives the feeling of déjà vu, that we are reliving events, only now with a keener sense of their significance and a heightened awareness of their horror. It is also proscriptive, either prophesying events to come or dramatizing events formerly prophesied. In B.19–20, apocalyptic writing reflects back on the work of the poem, as if the poet's sporadic warnings about the future (e.g., Prol.65–67) have paved the way for a literary apocalypse. The apocalypse now of passus 20, by situating the breakdown of the church in the poem's version of England and the failure of its institutions, plays up the revisionary character of these last two passūs. In a rewriting of the Meed episode, for example, Avarice invades Westminster Hall, where he corrupts justice and the ecclesiastical courts and converts "Cyvyle [law] into Symonye" (20.137). Antichrist's gifts to his followers – chief among them the friars, whose greed is "yvele ... yholde in parisshes of Engelonde" (20.280) – further evokes Meed's liberality in the king's court: "Freres folwede that fend, for he gaf hem copes, /And religiouse reverenced hym and rongen hir belles" [Friars followed that fiend, because he gave them cloaks, /And religious orders reverenced him and rung their bells] (20.58–59).

Apocalyptic writing deals primarily with institutions: kings and usurpers, popes and anti-popes, latter-day movements, the breakdown of traditional orders, natural disasters, legions and empires, monuments and war. In *Piers Plowman*, apocalyptic writing gives the poet the chance to describe a final battle, which is simultaneously the final battle between Church and Antichrist and the allegorical conflict between good and evil waged within every soul. Langland's apocalyptic showdown is funny and affecting by turns, exploiting both the literary resources of alliterative warfare and the seductiveness of apocalyptic writing. In the ranks of the opposing armies, for example, poet has enlisted an array of Langlandian personifications: natural forces (Fortune, Kind), sins (Lechery, Pride), worldly temptations (Comfort, Revel), generic persons (lord, lady), bodily afflictions (Elde), and faculties of the soul (Conscience). A lord, looking for an easy way out, calls for Comfort to bear his banner: "The lord that lyved after lust tho aloud cryde /After Confort, a knyghte, to come and bere his baner. /'Alarme! Alarme!' quod that lord, 'ech lif kepe his owene!'" [Then the lord who followed his own desire called out / For Comfort, a knight, to come and bear his banner: / "On guard! On guard!" said that lord, "every man for himself"] (20.90–92). But before minstrels can pipe or heralds announce the lists, the pleasure-loving folk are confronted by formidable foes: Elde, old age, in the vanguard of the opposing army, who carries the banner before Death, followed by Kind with his battery of pestilences, which crush everything in their wake.

> Deeth cam dryvynge after and al to duste passhed
> Kynges and knyghtes, kaysers and popes.
> Lered ne lewed, he lefte no man stonde
> That he hitte evene, that evere stired after.
> Manye a lovely lady and [hir] lemmans knyghtes
> Swowned and swelted for sorwe of Dethes dyntes.   (20.100–05)

[Death came driving after and dashed all to dust:
Kings and knights, emperors and popes,
Learned men and laymen. He left no man standing,
Whom he hit with full force, that might ever move after.
Many a lovely lady and [her] lover knights
Swooned and perished for sorrow of Death's blows.]

For the Christian community nothing short of total reform at every level can prevent the coming of Antichrist. Disease, old age, and death exist to remind people of their mortality and to check mortal sin. And still, these ravishing lines remind us that apocalyptic literature, with its laments for fallen glory, its attention to bodies, and to the ravages of war and plague, can also be powerfully seductive. In the prologue to the *Decameron*, Giovanni Boccaccio describes the devastations of the Black Death in Florence in 1349, which left some survivors – even single young women – to their own devices, some of them alone in empty houses mourning the dead, others fleeing for country homes where they might distract their companions with titillating tales. Boccaccio begins his account of the first day with his own kind of seduction, an *ubi sunt* lament for his fellow citizens who once possessed great wealth, physical beauty, and certified health: "Oh, what noteworthy families, what vast patrimonies, what conspicuous fortunes were left without any rightful heir! How many brave men, how many lovely ladies, how many graceful youths, who even Galen, Hippocrates or Aesculapius would have said were completely healthy, ate in the morning with their relatives, friends, and acquaintances, and then that same evening dined with their ancestors in the other world!"[18]

In B.20 Langland parodies the attractions of apocalyptic literature in a hilarious reenactment of the dreamer's mid-life crisis from B.11 (the Mirror of Middle Earth). Life enters into combat with Elde, only to realize that no one can resist old age. Life rides off to Revel, "a riche place and a murye" (20.181) with Elde at his heels, and the dreamer blunders into their path. Elde savages the dreamer, leaving him bald, toothless, gouty, and sexually dysfunctional, until his wife sees no further use for him: "For the lyme that she loved me fore, and leef was to feele – / On nyghtes, namely, whan we naked weere – / I ne myghte in no manere maken it at hir wille, / So Elde and he[o] it hadde forbeten" [For the limb for which she loved me, and desired to feel – / Namely, on nights when we were naked – / I could not in any way make it do what she wanted, / So much had she and Old Age beaten it to a pulp] (20.195–98).

Body-building

Langland's attempt to describe the church's moments of origin and its founding principles – the ways in which it establishes community and performs spiritual work, rewards and punishes, and defends itself against its worst enemies – all of this self-consciously "institutional art" seeks its substance in physical structures, in bodies and buildings, and most spectacularly in Piers's barn called Unity or Holy Church. Piers has diligently sown the seeds of cardinal virtues, and Grace advises him to build a house to store his ripe crops. Piers insists that Grace provide the timber, and together he and Grace build a barn. The timber is the Cross and crown of thorns, Christ's blood is the mortar, and the roofing is Holy Writ:

> "By God! Grace," quod Piers, "Ye moten gyve tymber,
> And ordeigne that hous er ye hennes wende."
> And Grace gaf hym the cros, with the croune of thornes,
> That Crist upon Calvarie for mankynde on pyned;
> And of his baptisme and blood that he bledde on roode
> He made a manere morter, and mercy it highte.
> And therwith Grace bigan to make a good foundement,
> And watlede it and walled it with hise peynes and his passion,
> And of al Holy Writ he made a roof after,
> And called that hous Unite – Holy Chirche on Englissh.   (19.322–31)

> ["By God, Grace!" said Piers, "You must give the timber,
> And set that house in order, before you depart."
> And Grace gave him the Cross, with the crown of thorns,
> On which Christ suffered on Calvary on behalf of mankind;
> And of his baptism and blood, which he bled on the Cross,
> He made a kind of mortar, and called it mercy.
> And next Grace began to make a good frame,
> And wattled it and walled it with his pains and his passion,
> And afterwards, he made a roof of all Holy Writ
> And called that house Unity – Holy Church in English.]

In this passage, Piers's barn has become a sanctuary built of holy relics and sacred text, and the steady allegory further supports the materiality of the building. Conscience counsels all Christians to seek refuge in Unity and dig a great moat around it, which all manage to do, with the exception of a prostitute, a juryman, and a summoner, recalling the strategies of exclusion at the end of B.5, where a prostitute and pardoner lose confidence in Piers's allegorical pilgrimage (19.371–73; 7.639–42). Conscience praises the diggers for their penitential labor and offers the consecrated host to those who have made amends.

The building called Unity – barn, sanctuary, reliquary, fortress – represents both the institutional church, besieged by Antichrist, and the human soul, manned by Conscience, assaulted by sin, and saved by the penance meted out by the church. In both aspects, as church and soul, this building is constructed with a view to its ruin, and it is the apocalypse itself, with its emphasis on destruction, that gives Unity its peculiar solidity – and vulnerability. It is the combination of solidity and vulnerability, deep-seated corruption and resolute materiality, that makes Unity such a crucial figure for the poet's institutional poetics.

Langland's apocalypse borrows heavily from William of Saint-Amour's *De periculis novissimorum temporum* ("On the Dangers of the Final Days," *c.*256), which identifies the perfidy of the friars as a sign of the times and the harbinger of Antichrist. Saint-Amour's treatise became a blueprint for an anti-fraternal criticism (and later, anti-Lollard polemic), condemning the insidious movement of the friars, who wander aimlessly, invade parishes, penetrate homes, and impose on the hospitality of others. In Langland's version of anti-fraternal apocalypticism, the dreamer wends his way to Unity, where Conscience stands constable. Antichrist and his minions storm the barn, and Conscience appeals to the clergy for help. The friars readily answer his call, but they "kouthe noght wel hir craft" (20.231), so Conscience forsakes them at first. Need, who knows the friars better than anyone, advises Conscience to keep them out for good and leave them poor: "Lat hem be as beggeris, or lyve by aungeles foode!" [Let them be beggars, or live by angels' food!] (20.241), but Conscience, always the good host, laughingly disregards Need's advice, promising to feed and clothe the friars in Unity (20.249).

Conscience's courtesy, however, proves to be Unity's undoing. As Contrition lies wounded, Conscience sends for a healer with the "sharp salve" of penance, but other people barricaded in Unity request Friar Flatterer instead, a physician with a gentle reputation. Though Conscience knows no better physician than Piers the Plowman (20.321–22), he graciously accedes to the general demand. Sir Penetrans-Domus arrives, and Peace the porter recognizes him as one of those silver-tongued friars who penetrate homes with their eloquence and impregnate the women inside. Conscience, too, is reluctant to admit him, but "Hende Speech" (courtesy) intervenes. The friar is admitted to Contrition, whom he treats so gently that Contrition falls into a stupor. In this scene, the poet charmingly leavens his apocalyptic narrative with the anti-fraternal satire from which it was initially derived. The friars are both the enemy within who bring about the catastrophic end of the earthly church and a charlatan order, eager for hand-outs, who take advantage of their credulous hosts. The physical structure of Unity gives these two narratives common ground; it also ingeniously restores the poem to one of its literary forebears, the allegorical dream-vision *Le roman de la rose*. In the *Rose*, the young male narrator, after 17,000 lines and with the help of characters like Fair-Seeming and Courtesy, seduces a virginal Rose who has been locked in a fortified tower. For Langland, the infiltration of the tower and the rape of the Rose in the *Roman de la rose* accounts for the seductiveness of a poetics of apocalypse and reform. Conversely, Langland's apocalyptic narrative affiliates *Piers Plowman* with a famous allegorical poem (the *Rose*) and an institution of medieval literary culture.

In *Piers Plowman*, the substance of institutional writing is finally located in physical structures, erected and demolished, zealously guarded but susceptible to harm. If Unity-Holy Church, the physical site of apocalyptic imagining, takes its cue from anti-fraternal satire and other literary seductions, it also refers back to that ultimate institutional body, the body of Christ. As Jill Mann has suggested, Sir Penetrans-Domus's infiltration of Holy Church can be read as a travesty of the harrowing of hell in B.18, where Christ's grim knock tells the devils inside that he is not everything he seems (18.260 ff.). [19] The penetration of Unity-Holy Church by the friars also recalls the gorgeous description in B.19 of Christ's visit to his apostles following the Resurrection, taken from John 20. In this passage, Christ enters the home where his apostles are gathered in order to prove to the doubting Thomas that he lives after death. The door is locked and barred – in Langland's version, emphatically so – yet Christ miraculously passes through; just as miraculously, Thomas passes his hands through Christ's side and grips his fleshly heart:

> And as all thise wise wyes weren togideres
> In a hous al bishet and hir dore ybarred
> Crist cam in – and al closed, both dore and yates –
> To Peter and hise apostles, and seide, "*Pax vobis*"
> And took Thomas by the hand and taughte hym to grope,
> And feele with hise fyngres his flesshliche herte. . .   (19.166–71)

> [And when all these wise men were gathered together,
> In a house locked up and their door barred,
> Christ came in – and all was closed, both door and gates –
> And to Peter and his apostles, he said, "Peace unto you"
> And took Thomas by the hand and taught him to grope
> And feel with his fingers his fleshly heart.]

Figure 6. "Doubting Thomas." *Gough Psalter*. Oxford, Bodleian Library, MS Gough. liturg.8, f.50v. (English, 1300–1310).

The seemingly secure home of the apostles, the sexually charged language of spiritual healing and the yielding of body and flesh together resemble the friar's abuse of Conscience's courtesy and the undermining of his stronghold. Both episodes, in different ways, substantiate the structures of the institutional church by dramatizing its violability, so key to a poetry of piety and reform.

Within twenty years of the publication of the C text, *Piers Plowman* would generate a number of imitations, including *Mum and the Sothsegger*, *Richard the Redeless*, and *Pierce the Plowman's Creed*, all alliterative, reform-minded poems which Helen Barr has aptly labeled the *Piers Plowman* tradition.[20] No doubt Langland's cultivation of an institutional writing in B.19–20 helped make it possible for subsequent poets to write in a Langlandian tradition.

Notes

CHAPTER 1 INTRODUCTION

1. For an assessment of the biographical evidence, see Hanna, *William Langland*, pp. 1–10.
2. On the Reformers' reception of *Piers Plowman*, see Kelen, *Langland's Early Modern Identities*; King, "Robert Crowley's Edition," and Hailey, "Robert Crowley and the Editing of *Piers Plowman*."
3. Barr, *Signes and Sothe*, p. 9.
4. Quotations are taken from Schmidt's edition of B, Pearsall's edition of C, and Schmidt's parallel edition of ABC, where noted, with reference to Kane and Donaldson's edition of B and Russell and Kane's edition of C (translations are my own). Passūs numbers refer to the B-text unless otherwise indicated. Unfortunately, this study could not take advantage of Vaughan's new edition of the A-text. All citations from the bible are to the Douay-Rheims edition of the Vulgate.
5. See Middleton, "'Kynde Name,'" and Simpson, "The Power of Impropriety."
6. Middleton, "Acts of Vagrancy."
7. See Alford, "The Design of the Poem," and Kerby-Fulton, "*Piers Plowman*," p. 520.
8. Mann argued controversially that A might have been a later version redesigned for a particular audience. See Horobin, "The Scribe of Rawlinson 137"; Mann, "The Power of the Alphabet"; Kane's response to Mann, "An Open Letter to Jill Mann"; and Warner, *Lost History*, pp. 2–4.
9. See Burrow, "Langland Nel Mezzo del Cammin."
10. Kerby-Fulton, "*Piers Plowman*," p. 521.
11. See Rigg and Brewer, eds., *Piers Plowman: the Z version*, and Kerby-Fulton, "*Piers Plowman*," pp. 518–19.
12. Barr, *Signes and Sothe*, p. 7.
13. Justice, *Writing and Rebellion*, ch. 3.
14. Debates on scribal vs. authorial authority for the rubrics are summarized by Alford, "The Design of the Poem," pp. 30–31; Kerby-Fulton, "*Piers Plowman*," pp. 514–15; and Galloway, *Penn Commentary*, pp. 19–20.
15. See Lawton's illuminating discussion in "Alliterative Style."

16. For helpful taxonomies of alliterative meter, with reference to *Piers Plowman*, see Duggan, "Notes on the Metre of *Piers Plowman*," Schmidt's appendix to his edition of the B-text, pp. 506–8, and his *Clerkly Maker*, ch. 2, and M. Smith, "Langland's Alliterative Line."

17. Duggan, in "The Shape of the B-Verse," discusses the problem of distinguishing the practices of poets from those of scribes. See also his "Notes on the Metre of *Piers Plowman*" and "Meter, Stanza, Vocabulary, Dialect."

18. Smith, "Langland's Unruly Caesura."

19. Again see Duggan, "Notes on the Metre of *Piers Plowman*," and "The Shape of the B-Verse."

20. Duggan, "Notes on the Metre of *Piers Plowman*."

21. M. Smith argues further in "Langland's Alliterative Line" that modulation in *Piers Plowman* reflects the distance in all poetry, as in music, between versification and meter. As J. Smith argues in "The Metre Which Does Not Measure," the way we understand the continuity or discontinuity of a tradition depends on the way we understand relationship between norms and deviation, and between literary language and ordinary speech.

22. Hanna, "Defining Middle English Alliterative Poetry," p. 51.

23. Lawton, "The Idea of Alliterative Poetry," Cornelius, "The Rhetoric of Advancement" and "The Latin *Cursus* and Middle English Alliterative Verse," presented at the 4th International Conference on *Piers Plowman* (Philadelphia, 2007).

24. Lawton, "The Unity of Middle English Alliterative Poetry."

25. On evidence for Langland's authorship of *William of Palerne*, see Warner, "Langland and the Problem of *William of Palerne*."

26. *The Riverside Chaucer*, ed. Benson, p. 287, lines 42–43.

27. See Hanna and Lawton's introduction to their edition of the *Siege of Jerusalem*.

28. Except for Cotton Nero A.x, no surviving manuscript of alliterative poetry does not contain other items, so there is no evidence that readers of alliterative poetry constituted a "regional block" or even a "textual community" (Lawton, "The Diversity of Middle English Alliterative Poetry," p. 149).

29. Horobin and Mooney, "A *Piers Plowman* Manuscript by the Hengwrt/Ellesmere Scribe"; Horobin, "Adam Pinkhurst" and "In London and opelond"; Scase, "Two *Piers Plowman* C-Text Interpolations"; and Kerby-Fulton, "Langland 'in his Working Clothes.'"

30. As M. Smith writes, "as a multilingual, clerical, poet, [Langland] was committed to a loose, flexible style of versification, enabling the thematic reconfiguration of the normative metrical markers, stress and alliteration" ("Langland's Alliterative Line," p. 165).

31. Machan, "Language Contact in *Piers Plowman*."

32. See Steiner, "Commonalty and Literary Form."

33. Edited by Wenzel, in *Preaching in the Age of Chaucer*, ch. 21. Both Brinton and Langland might have known this exemplum from Nicole Bozon, *Les contes moralisés*, ed. Smith and Meyer, no. 121.

34. Somerset, "Al þe comonys with o voys atonys."

35. Lawler, "*Piers Plowman.*"
36. Alford, "The Role of the Quotations," and Allen, "Langland's Reading and Writing."
37. Higden, *Polychronicon*, ed. Babington and Lumby, bk 1, ch. 59.
38. See Butterfield's interesting comments on this pun in Anglo-Norman, the relationship between "English notions of freedom and French identity," and the literary layerings of continental and insular French ("Chaucerian Vernaculars," pp. 34–37).
39. For example, Bozon's French and Latin collection, *Les proverbes de bon enseignement*, ed, Thorn, or the trilingual "Proverbes of diverse profetes and of poetes and of othur seyntes" in the Vernon manuscript.
40. More subtle are the moments in which the poet constructs an English sentence from French grammar. For example, in several instances, the poet uses the absolute possessive "his owene," as in the somewhat puzzling expressions, "each lif to knowe his owene" (each person to know his own) (Prol. 122) and "wite wel his owene" (look to himself, or look out for himself?) (Prol. 208, and see 20.92). The use of the pronoun "own" as an absolute possessive, as opposed to a possessive determiner (e.g., his own life, a room of her own), is much more common in medieval French, and especially in law French, than in Middle English, perhaps because of the slippage between possession ("propre") and property ("propre," "propres," or "propries").
41. *Grosseteste, Le chasteau d'amour*, ed. Cooke, p. 4, lines 24, 26–27, 43.
42. Olson, "Geoffrey Chaucer"; Trigg, *Congenial Souls*, Bowers, *Chaucer and Langland*, and Grady, "Chaucer Reading Langland."
43. Cooper, "Langland's and Chaucer's Prologues," and Mann's classic book *Chaucer and Medieval Estates Satire*.
44. Deguileville, *The pilgrimage of the lyfe of the manhode*, ed. Henry, lines 8–12.
45. *The Wars of Alexander*, ed. Duggan and Turville-Petre, p. 178, lines. 5784–89.
46. *St. Erkenwald*, ed. Peterson, in *The Complete Works of the Pearl Poet*, p. 326, lines 57–64.
47. Hanna, *London Literature*; Lindenbaum, "London Texts and Literate Practice"; and Barron, "William Langland: A London Poet."
48. Bozon, *Le char d'Orgeil*, in *Deux Poemes*, ed. Vising, p. 24, lines 445–47.
49. See Steiner, "Naming and Allegory."
50. *Alliterative Morte Arthure*, in *King Arthur's Death*, ed. Benson, rev. edn, Foster, lines 26–47. Of course, listing places is not only an alliterative phenomenon. In *La lettre de l'empereur Orgeuil*, Bozon gives a brief biblical history of pride, listing key players Lucifer, Adam, Cain, Saul, David, and Holofernes, followed a few lines later by key places in England where pride was in evidence: Lewes, Evesham, Northampton, Winchester, Chesterfield, Gloucester – i.e., places where important battles took place in the 1260s Barons' Revolt. In a later version of the poem, Pride (Orgeuil) also invades Scotland, Wales, and England, and then France, Normandy, and Burgundy (in *Deux Poemes*, ed. Vising, p. 64, lines 33–65b).

CHAPTER 2 VALUE

1. On medieval Boethius see Lerer, *Boethius and Dialogue*; Dwyer, *Boethian Fictions*; Wetherbee, "The *Consolation* and Medieval Literature"; Minnis, *Chaucer's "Boece"*; and Nauta, "The *Consolation*: the Latin Commentary Tradition, 800–1700."

2. Boethius, *The Consolation of Philosophy*, trans. Walsh, pp. 2–3.

3. Galloway, "*Piers Plowman* and the Schools"; Alford, "Langland's Learning"; and this volume, Chapter 4.

4. Galloway, *The Penn Commentary*, pp. 150–56, discusses Langland's debts to Deguileville and *Le roman de la rose*. On the influence of Deguileville on English poets, see Steiner, *Documentary Culture*, chs. 1 and 3; and Kamath, "Naming the Pilgrim."

5. Deguileville, *The pilgrimage of the lyfe of the manhode*, ed. Henry, p. 8.

6. *Ibid.*, pp. 3–4.

7. Boethius, *The Consolation of Philosophy*, trans. Walsh, p. 6.

8. On women and the medieval classroom, see Hanna, "School and Scorn"; Enders, *The Medieval Theater of Cruelty*, pp. 129–59; Curry Woods, "Boys Will Be Women" and "Weeping for Dido"; Curry Woods and Copeland, "Classroom and Confession"; and Copeland, *Pedagogy, Intellectuals and Dissent*.

9. Raskolnikov, "Promising the Female."

10. See Nolan, "The Fortunes of *Piers Plowman*."

11. Boethius, *The Consolation of Philosophy*, trans. Walsh, p. 18, lines 5–12. The heavy stress of the original Latin poem (in adonics) better conveys the effect: "Si mare uoluens / turbidus Auster / misceat aestum, / uitrea dudum / parque serenis / unda diebus"). Latin from www9.georgetown.edu/faculty/jod/boethius/jkok/list_t.htm.

12. On medieval prosimetrum, see Eckhardt, "The Medieval *Prosimetrum* Genre"; Butterfield, "*Aucassin et Nicolette* and Mixed Forms"; and Johnson, "Chaucer and the Consolation of *Prosimetrum*."

13. See Gasse, "The Practice of Medicine" and Bishop's study of medieval literature and medicine, *Words, Stones, and Herbs*.

14. Brown, ed., *Religious Lyrics of the xvth Century*, no. 206, p. 163, lines 16–18.

15. Friedman, *Orpheus in the Middle Ages*, and Blumenfeld-Kosinski, *Reading Myth*.

16. Atkinson, "An Early Fourteenth-century French Boethian Orpheus."

17. "Dic allegorice quod Orpheus, filius solis, est Christus, filius dei patris, qui a principio Euridicem .i. animam humanam per caritatem & amorem duxit ipsamque per specialem prerogativam a principio sibi coniunxit. Verumtamen serpens, diabolus, ipsam novam nuptam .i. de novo creatam, dum flores colligeret .i. de pomo vetito appeteret, per temptationem momordit, & per peccatum occidit, & finaliter ad infernum transmisit. Quod videns Orpheus Christus in infernum personaliter voluit descendere & sic uxorem suam .i. humanam naturam rehabuit, ipsamque de regno tenebrarum ereptam ad superos secum duxit, dicens illud Canticorum .ii. 'Surge, propera amica mea & veni.'" Bersuire, *Metamorphosis Ovidiana*, fol. lxxxv. The Latin

passage and English translation are given in Friedman, *Orpheus in the Middle Ages*, pp. 127–28.

18. *Riverside Chaucer*, ed. Benson, p. 35, line 770.
19. http://auchinlick.nls.uk/mss/horn.html, lines 102–08, adapted from Wiggins's transcription (Auckinlick MS).
20. *Piers Plowman* is not the first English text to use the word "meed" in the context of bribes of corruption. It had long been a common complaint that people abuse their authority or betray other people's trust in order to gain "meed" or compensation. But *Piers Plowman* is the first full exploration of meed as the subject and object of human desire.
21. In *The Complete Works of the Pearl-Poet*, ed. Waldron, lines 1513 and 1515.
22. Horobin, "Reconsidering Lincoln's Inn 150."
23. Giancarlo, *Parliament and Literature*, ch. 5.
24. Fowler, "Civil Death and the Maiden."
25. Note the shift from plural to singular pronouns at 2.99ff.
26. See Steiner, "Naming and Allegory."
27. For example, Ormrod, "Who Was Alice Perrers"; Trigg, "The Traffic in Medieval Women"; and Robertson, "Measurement and the 'Feminine.'" See also Kennedy, *Maintenance, Meed, and Marriage*.
28. All citations from William of Malmesbury, *Gesta Regum Anglorum*, ed. and trans. Winterbottom and Thomson, p. 757, v. 418.5.
29. In C, the King takes a harder line, threatening to make an example of Meed by enclosing her in the notorious Corfe Castle, Dorset, should she not abide by his advice. See Galloway, *The Penn Commentary*, pp. 306–07.
30. See Wallace, *Premodern Places*, pp. 46–48. I thank Prof. Wallace for sharing his essay, "Chaucer, Langland, and the Hundred Years' War" in advance of publication.
31. Briggs, *Giles of Rome's "De regimine principum"* ch. 1, and Somerset, *Clerical Discourse*, ch. 3.
32. Giles of Rome, *De regimine principum*, 2.2.7, henceforth *DRP*.
33. *Ibid.*, 2.3.20.
34. *Ibid.*, 1.2.23.
35. Genet, ed., *Four English Political Tracts of the Later Middle Ages*, p. 187.
36. Insofar, however, as labor can be repoliticized through labor statutes, as it will be in the Hunger episode in B.6, it, too, will come under scrutiny and ultimately will be discarded by the poet as a way to imagine the nation.
37. D. V. Smith, *Arts of Possession*, p. 72.
38. See *Wynnere and Wastoure*, ed. Trigg.
39. Williams, "Boethius Goes to Court."
40. As Giancarlo explains, this scene is probably meant to represent a high session of parliament rather than a session of king's bench, because it culminates in debate rather than in a single judgement (*Parliament and Literature*, 195); for additional scholarship on *Piers Plowman* and parliamentary politics in this period, see Steiner, "Commonalty and Literary Form."
41. *DRP*, 2.2.20–21 and 2.1.24.

42. *DRP*, 2.3.19, 3.2.18. See Horrox's account of medieval courtiers in "Caterpillars of the Commonwealth?"

43. Compare to Baldwin, "The Historical Context," based on her important book, *The Theme of Government*, which argues that Langland's solution in this passage is an absolutist solution to the problems of government and, as such, an apolitical solution (83).

CHAPTER 3 COMMUNITY

1. See Davlin, "*Petrus, id est, Christus*," p. 288.

2. Justice, "The Genres of *Piers Plowman*"; Lawton, "The Subject of *Piers Plowman*"; Middleton, "Narration and the Invention of Experience"; and D. V. Smith, *The Book of the Incipit*.

3. See Adams, "The Reliability of the Rubrics," and "Langland's *Ordinatio*"; Alford, "The Design of the Poem"; Burrow, "The Structure of *Piers Plowman*"; Benson and Blanchfield, *The Manuscripts of "Piers Plowman."*

4. The text of the Creed can be found in Denzinger, *Enchiridion Symbolorum*, nos. 75–76, pp. 41–42.

5. Quotation in Dobson, *Peasants' Revolt*, 375, taken from Walsingham's *Historia Anglicana*. See Barr, *Socioliterary Practice*, ch. 5, for an interesting discussion of these verses, and see Freedman's excellent survey of medieval attitudes toward the peasantry, *Images of the Medieval Peasant*.

6. Aers, *Chaucer, Langland and the Creative Imagination*, esp. ch. 1; Kaye, *Economy and Nature*; and Little, *Religious Poverty and the Profit Economy*.

7. See Swanson, *Indulgences in Late Medieval England*, and Rubin, *Charity and Community*. As Rubin explains, the terms of the indulgence often reflect the priorities of the bishop assigning them (indeed the very state of being needy could earn an indulgence). Bishop Fordham of Ely (1388–1425) gave over a third of his indulgences to the sick and destitute, while other Ely bishops focused more on rewarding charitable giving, supporting religious houses, funding public works, or even ransoming prisoners (pp. 266–68).

8. See Steiner, *Documentary Culture*, ch. 3.

9. Modern criticism of this scene is extensive. Influential essays include Woolf, "The Tearing of the Pardon"; Carruthers, "The Tearing of the Pardon"; Lawton, "*Piers Plowman*: On Tearing – And Not Tearing"; Scase, "Writing and the Plowman"; and Steiner, *Documentary Culture*, ch. 3.

10. See Lawler, "The Pardon Formula in *Piers Plowman*"; and Adams, "Langland's Theology."

11. Baldwin, *The Theme of Government*; Fowler, "Civil Death and the Maiden"; Kantorowicz, *The King's Two Bodies;* Pollock and Maitland, *The History of English Law*, vol. 1., esp. ch. 2, pt. 13, "The King and the Crown," pp. 511–26; also Stokes, *Justice and Mercy*.

12. Steiner, *Documentary Culture*, pp. 102–3.

13. See the fascinating case studies in Barron and Burgess, ed., *Memory and Commemoration*; also Daniell, *Death and Burial*; and Rubin, *Charity and Community*.
14. *The Book of Margery Kempe*, ed. Windeatt, bk 2, ch. 68, pp. 311–12.
15. Rappaport, "On the Obvious Aspects of Ritual," in *Ecology, Meaning, and Religion*, pp. 173–221.
16. Myrc, *Instructions for Parish Priests*, ed. Peacock, pp. 34–35, lines 1107–36.
17. See Curry Woods and Copeland, "Classroom and Confession," esp. pp. 386–94.
18. Rappaport, "On the Obvious Aspects of Ritual," p. 193.
19. *Fasciculus Morum*, ed. Wenzel, p. 631.
20. *Riverside Chaucer*, ed. Benson, p. 303, lines 489–91.
21. See generally, Wenzel, *The Sin of Sloth*, and more specifically, Aquinas, *Summa Theologica*, vol. 3, pt. 2.2, qu. 35, esp. art. 3.
22. *Riverside Chaucer*, ed. Benson, p. 528, bk 3, line 1092.
23. Mann, "Troilus' Swoon." On gesture in medieval literature, see Burrow, *Gesture and Looks*.
24. Rappaport, "On the Obvious Aspects of Ritual," p. 95.
25. Malory, *Works*, vol. III, ed. Vinaver, bk 20.
26. Froissart, *Chroniques*, eds. Ainsworth and Diller, bk I, ch. 123, pp. 549–50.
27. Malory, *Works*, vol. III, ed. Vinaver, bk 19, p. 1152.
28. Christ later uses "bloody brethren" to distinguish between those who are and are not baptized (18.376–79).
29. See Middleton, "Acts of Vagrancy"; Aers, "*Vox Populi*"; Hilton, *Bond Men Made Free*; Dyer, "Social and Economic Background."
30. See Bennett, "The Curse of the Plowman"; Kirk, "Langland's Plowman"; Pearsall, "Poverty and Poor People"; Frank, "The Hungry Gap"; and Dyer, "*Piers Plowman* and Plowmen."
31. See Robertson, *The Laborer's Two Bodies*, chs. 1 and 2.
32. Following Levinas, "The Proximity of the Other," in *Alterity and Transcendence*, trans. Smith. See also Scott, "*Piers Plowman*" and the Poor."
33. *Religious Lyrics of the XIVth Century*, ed. Brown, p. 112, no. 89, lines. 17–20.

CHAPTER 4 LEARNING

1. For bibliography on the Pardon episode, see Chapter 3, n. 9.
2. Allen, "Langland's Reading and Writing," p. 355; Kaske, *Medieval Christian Literary Imagery*, pp. 33–40; and Rouse and Rouse, "Biblical Distinctions."
3. As Simpson has observed, the first vision of the poem represents political discourses, the second vision, penitential discourses, and the third vision, discourses of education (*Introduction to the B-Text*, pp. 83–84).
4. Following recent discussions of medieval *habitus*, see Holsinger, *The Premodern Condition*, ch.3, and Breen, *Imagining an English Reading Public*, esp. chs. 2 and 5.

5. Allen, "Langland's Reading and Writing," and Alford, "The Role of the Quotations."
6. Galloway, "*Piers Plowman* and the Schools," pp. 91–92.
7. Cannon, "Langland's *Ars Grammatica*" and "The Middle English Writer's Schoolroom."
8. Breen, "Langland's Literary Syntax," esp. pp. 4–8 (forthcoming).
9. In *Minor Poems of the Vernon Manuscript*, vol. 1, ed. Horstmann, pp. 522–53.
10. "Cato's Morals," in *Cursor mundi*, parts 3–4, ed. Morris, 1674 (Appendix iv).
11. *Riverside Chaucer*, ed. Benson, p. 68, lines 3227–8.
12. Mann, "'He knew Nat Catoun'"; Cannon, "Langland's *Ars Grammatica*" and "The Middle English Writer's Schoolroom."
13. Spearing, *Medieval Dream Poetry*, ch. 1.
14. On medieval intellectual biography, see Copeland, *Pedagogy, Intellectuals, and Dissent*, part 2 and "Premodern Intellectual Biography"; Kerby-Fulton, "Authority, Constraint, and the Writing of the Medieval Self."
15. On Imaginatif as a cognitive faculty see Minnis, "Langland's Imaginatif," Harwood, "Imaginative in *Piers Plowman*," and Kaulbach, "The *Vis Imaginativa*." For a trenchant recent study of Imaginatif, the imaginative faculty, and the acquisition of knowledge in the poem, see Karnes, "Will's Imagination."
16. Zeeman, "*Piers Plowman*," p. 202.
17. *Officium et miracula*, ed. Woolley, pp. 23–26. See generally, Watson, *Richard Rolle*.
18. In *Two Wycliffite Texts*, ed Hudson, Copeland, "William Thorpe," and Steiner, *Documentary Culture*, ch. 6.
19. See Simpson, "The Constraints of Satire," and Steiner, *Documentary Culture*, ch. 4.
20. Craun, *Ethics and Power*, esp. ch. 3.
21. Zeeman, "*Piers Plowman*," esp. pp. 164–87.
22. See Steiner, "Radical Historiography."
23. "e vus memes tutes oures en miliu seez del haute table, ke vostre presence a tuz uvertement[cum seignur ou dame aperge, e ke vous overtement] puissez de une part e de autre ver tuz e le servise e le defautes" (Grosseteste, *The Rules of Robert Grosseteste*, in *Walter of Henley and Other Treatises on Estate Management and Accounting*, ed. and trans., Oschinsky, pp. 402–03).
24. *Li livres du gouvernement des rois*, ed. Molenaer, p. 267.
25. Giles of Rome, *De regimine principum*, 2.3.20. See Trevisa, *The Governance of Kings and Princes*, ed. Briggs, Fowler, *et al.*, pp. 285–86 (Latin original supplied for this section in this edition).
26. See, for example, Bozon, *Les proverbes de bon enseignement*.
27. According to Cartlidge, MS 29 likely also contained the poem "Will and Wit," a poem which anticipates *Piers Plowman*, and which still survives in the sister manuscript to Jesus MS 29, London, British Library, MS Cotton Caligula A. ix (Cartlidge, "The Composition and Social Context").

28. This account is different in C, following the *Vita Adame et Eve* tradition; here Adam and Eve do wrong by having sex during a period in which they are doing penance.

29. See, for example, St. Ambrose's interpretations of baptism in *De mysteriis*, 3.10–11, in *Sancti Ambrosii Opera, pars VII*, ed. Faller, pp. 92–93.

30. "Non nego propter merita bona parentum, filiis multa et magna beneficia corporis et animae impendi, et propter peccata parentum filios et nepotes usque in tertiam et quartam generationem, et forsitan ultra, diversis tribulationibus in hac vita flagellari, et ea perdere bona etiam in anima, quae forsitan per illos consequerentur, si justi essent; quorum exempla nimis longum est hic inserere. Sed dico peccatum originale in omnibus infantibus conceptis naturaliter aequale esse: sicut peccatum Adae, quod est causa cur nascantur in illo, ad omnes pertinet aequaliter" (*Liber de conceptu virginali et originali peccato*, ch. 24, PL 158:0459B). Translation adapted from *On the Conception of the Virgin*, in *Anselm of Canterbury*, vol. 3, trans. Hopkins and Richardson, 174.

31. *Officium et miracula*, ed. Woolley, pp. 25–36.

32. Woolgar, *The Great Household in Late Medieval England*, pp. 26–29.

33. Jacobus de Voragine, *Legenda aurea*, ed. Graesse, "De Sancto Gregario," ch.4, pp. 196–97.

34. See Grady, *Representing Righteous Heathens*, Whatley, "Heathens and Saints"; Hill, "Universal Salvation"; and Watson, "Visions of Inclusion."

35. Bede, *Ecclesiastical History*, ed. and trans. Colgrave and Mynors, II.i. 132–35.

36. Following I Peter 4:18: "Et si iustus vix salvabitur, impius, et peccator ubi parebunt?" [And if the just man can scarcely be saved, where do the impious and sinner appear?]. See, for example, Bede, *Super epistolas catholicas expositio, In primam epistolam Petri*, IV.18, in *Bedae Venerabilis Opera, pars II*, ed. Laistner, 255, and Peter Lombard, *Commentarius in Psalmos Davidicos*, Psalm 6.12 [PL191:0105D].

37. At the end of B.12 the poet gives a litany of alternative "extreme" positions inspired by Trajan, for example, that one can be baptized through fire or blood, as well as by water at the font; and that integrity itself is a kind of faithfulness, and therefore a quality that merits eternal reward.

38. "Avynet" is not mentioned in C, and the identity of the "poet" responsible for the peacock is more ambiguous in that version. See Mann's *From Aesop to Reynard*.

39. Allen, *Ethical Poetic*, p. 205.

40. The texts of *Physiologus* do not always include the peacock, but notably, the non-standard version of the Latin *Physiologus*, misattributed to St. Epiphanius (*c*.310–400), contains nearly all the material in *Piers Plowman*, B.12, most significantly, Langland's moralization of the peacock as rich men, whose massive tail and leaden feet keep them earthbound, and whose deathbed cries go unheeded by the Lord. http://library.uvic.ca/site/spcoll/physiologum/commentary/txt_physiologus.htm

41. See Trevisa's defense of Aristotle's life in his translation of Higden's *Polychronicon*, ed. Babington and Lumby, 3.24.

42. The Middle English verb "liknen" often translates the Latin "assimilare," to make like, or to compare. *MED*, s.v.² "liknen."
43. Langland may be referring to Porphyry's *Isogogue*, a commentary on the introduction to Aristotle's *Categories*, translated by Boethius.
44. Gower, *Confessio amantis*, in *Complete Works* ed. Macaulay, 7.4476–89.

CHAPTER 5 PRACTICE

1. For the manuscript traditions of these external markers, and debates about their scribal or authorial origins, see this volume, Chapter 1, n. 14, and Chapter 3, n. 3.
2. Simpson, "*Piers Plowman*": *An Introduction*, 76, pp. 122–23. For discussions of Langland's relationship to Augustinianism and Pelagianism, see Adams, "Langland's Theology" and "Piers' Pardon and Langland's Semi-Pelagianism"; Woolf, "The Tearing of the Pardon"; and Aers's reassessment of later medieval Augustinianism, *Piers Plowman* in *Salvation and Sin*, ch. 4.
3. For the theology of the Pardon episode, see Lawler, "The Pardon Formula in *Piers Plowman*," and Steiner, *Documentary Culture*, ch.3.
4. Bartholomaeus Anglicus, *Liber de proprietatibus rerum Bartholomei anglici*, bk 5.
5. Aristotle, *De historia animalium*, trans. William of Moerbeke (1215–86), ed. Beullens and Bossier, vol. IX, bk. I, pt.I, pp. 8–9.
6. Augustine, *De civitate Dei, libri XI–XXII*, bk 12, ch. 22, CCSL 48, p. 380.
7. Bartholomaeus Anglicus, *Liber de proprietatibus rerum*, bk 18, ch. 1.
8. For scholarship on Hawkyn, see Staley, "The Man in Foul Clothes" and Watson, "Pastoral Theology."
9. Alford argues that, for medieval writers, to conform was to discover one's true self; conversely to be singular – to labor under the delusion that one is self-modeled rather than contingent – was to lose oneself altogether ("The Scriptural Self").
10. For examples and discussion, see Bynum, *Holy Feast, Holy Fast*, pp. 73 and 78, 113–49.
11. See Gillespie, "Thy Will De Done," Watson, "Pastoral Theology," and Clopper on Patience and the Franciscans in '*Songes of Rechlessness*,' esp. chs. 5 and 6.
12. In English bestiary literature, the curlew is usually associated with the Latin *coturnix*, the bird that gave manna to the Israelites in the desert. See Spearman, "Langland's 'Corlew'."
13. "Sic ergo omnis homo fidelis secundum dei uoluntatem conseruatur et uiuit; non huc atque illuc per diuersa oberrans circumuolat, sicut faciunt haeretici; nec saecularibus desideriis ac uoluptatibus delectatur corporalibus, sicut illae uolucres quae carnibus uescuntur … Ibi ergo se continet, ubi dominus: Inhabitare facit unanimes in domo; et ibi habet quotidianum panem immortalitatis, potum uero pretiosum sanguinem Christi; reficiens se sanctis epulis et, super mel et fauum, suauissimis eloquiis domini: Non enim in solo pane uiuit homo, sed in omni uerbo dei" (*Physiologus Latinus Versio B*, ed. Carmody, ch. 22, "*Fulica*", p. 39). See also Guillaume le Clerc's Anglo-Norman bestiary, and

especially his entry on the *fulica*, based on the *Physiologus*, which resonates with *Piers Plowman* B.12 (*Le Bestiare Divin*, ed. Hippeau, pp. 254–56).

14. The poem seemingly offers up a kind of medieval ecocriticism or an "alternative model of human interaction with other living species," such as that represented by St. Francis (Kiser, "The Garden of Saint Francis," p. 231). In the case of St. Francis, whose compassion for animals was legendary, sympathy for animals goes hand in hand with his rejection of mercantile values and his radical identification with all creatures. In *Piers Plowman*, however, pathos works differently than it does in biographies of the saint. See also Kiser, "Animal Economies" and "Chaucer and the Politics of Nature."

15. Deguileville, *The Pilgrimage of the Life of Man*, ed. Furnivall, trans. Lydgate, lines 22710–12.

16. Lawler, "*Piers Plowman*," p. 154.

17. In Patience's increasingly vexed analogy, just as the rich have joy on earth and not in heaven, so the rebel angels, who once had joy in heaven, now reside in hell with Lucifer (B.14.121–24).

18. Aers, "*Piers Plowman*: Poverty, Work, and Community" in *Community, Gender, and Individual Identity*, pp. 20–72.

19. See Holsinger, "Langland's Musical Reader."

20. Alford, "The Role of the Quotations," and Allen, "Langland's Reading and Writing."

21. Cook, "The Figure of Enigma."

22. On the currency of the *Polychronicon* in fourteenth-century England, see Galloway, "Latin England," Lavezzo, *Angels on the Edge of the World*, ch.3, and Steiner, "Radical Historiography."

23. Compare C.12.170–75, a catalog of saints and ancients who embodied the virtues of patient poverty.

24. The Mohammed legend can be found in "De sancto Pelagio papa," in Jacobus de Voragine, *Legenda aurea*, ed. Graesse, 827–31, ch.181. See Mula, "Mohammed and the Saints," on Mohammed in medieval hagiography.

25. *Mandeville's Travels: The Egerton Version*, ed. Warner, ch.15, p. 68.

26. *Ibid.*, ch.15, p. 69.

27. *Ibid.*, ch.15, p. 68.

28. As Zieman points out, the most significant prayers in medieval Christianity underwent a process of nominalization in which the first few words are "converted into material entities with which one can interact" (*Singing the New Song*, p. 136).

29. See Warner, "Becket and the Hopping Bishops."

30. See Warner, *Lost History*, ch.3.

CHAPTER 6 BELIEF

1. See Cole, "Trifunctionality and the Tree of Charity."

2. *Inventio Sancti Cruci* is summarized in *Cursor mundi*, ed. Morris, vol. 1, parts 3–4, pp. 1240–51, lines 21627–846.

3. See *Canticum de Creatione* in *The Apocryphal Lives of Adam and Eve*, ed. Murdoch and Tasioulas, and *Sammlung altenglischer Legenden*, ed. Horstmann.

4. As Lawton sketches out so brilliantly in "The Bible" and "Englishing the Bible: 1066–1549"; see also Morey's informative *Book and Verse*.

5. See Ghosh's introduction to *The Wycliffite Heresy*.

6. *Cursor mundi*, ed. Morris, part. 1, p. 15, lines. 115–23.

7. *Ibid.*, p. 23, lines 267–68.

8. See Kirk, "Langland's Narrative Christology."

9. "Dominica vi post Epiphanium," from *The Middle English "Mirror,"* ed. Blumreich, pp. 95–96. The *Northern Homily Cycle* has a more elaborate scheme: Adam–Noah, Noah–Abraham, Abraham–Moses, Moses–David, David–Jesus, Jesus to the present. The Anglo-Norman version divides this scheme into canonical hours (see *The Middle English "Mirror,"* ed. Duncan and Connolly, pp. 122–23).

10. Sermon for Septuagesima Sunday, *Northern Homily Cycle*, ed., Thompson, pp. 83–92, esp. lines 143–164. The author of the *Northern Homily Cycle* observes that Saracens and Jews ought to be included in this scheme if the history of the church is to be a narrative of world dominion. What a shame, he says, echoing *Piers Plowman* B.15, that the pope does not send preachers to convert the Saracens!

11. "Caritas numquam excidit sive prophetiae evacubuntur, sive linguae cessabunt, sive scientia destruetur. Ex parte enim cognoscimus et ex parte prophetamus. Cum autem venerit quod perfectum est, evacubitur quod ex parte est … Vidimus nunc per speculum in aenigmate: tunc autem facie ad faciem. Nunc cognosco ex parte: tunc autem cognoscam sicut et cognitus sum. Nunc autem manent fides, spes, caritas, tria haec: major autem horum est caritus."

12. Hanna, *London Literature*, p. 151.

13. *The South English Legendary*, ed. D'Evelyn and Mill, p. 3, lines 59–63.

14. *Cursor mundi*, ed. Morris, part 1, pp. 9–11, lines 1–26.

15. *Ibid.*, lines 69–110. The Middle English translation of Robert de Gretham's Anglo-Norman *Miroir ou les Évangiles des Domnées* likewise proposes itself as a wholesome alternative to "romaunces & gestes" (*The Middle English Mirror*, ed. Duncan and Connolly, p. 3, lines 15–18).

16. *The South English Legendary*, ed. D'Evelyn and Mill, pp. 2–3, lines 34–57 ff.

17. A linguistic pun on the Middle English verb "spirian" (to search for) and the Latin verb "spirare" (to breath, to yearn).

18. For a detailed analysis, see Steiner, *Documentary Culture*, pp. 115–18.

19. *Ancrene Wisse*, ed. Millett, 7.2, p. 146.

20. *Ibid.*, p. 154.

21. On the Protestant reception of *Piers Plowman* see Kelen, *Langland's Early Modern Identities*.

22. "Haec sancta trinitas secundum communem essentiam individua, et secundum personales proprietates discreta, per Moysen et sanctos Prophetas, aliosque famulos suos juxta ordinatissimam dispositionem temporum, doctrinam humano generi tribuit salutarem" (*Acta et decreta sacrorum conciliorum*

recentiorum, ed. Granderath, 106). English translation adapted from http://www.ewtn.com/library.

23. *Cursor mundi*, ed. Morris, pp. 15–17, lines 125–32.
24. See n. 3 and n. 4 above.
25. For comparison, see B.17.127–28 and 17.165.
26. In "Langland's Unruly Caesura," Smith observes that these lines are punctuated differently in different manuscripts, some scribes emphasizing the rhythmically double form of the alliterative line, some emphasizing the triadic phrasing of the Creed.
27. Compare to the language of the Athanasian Creed: "Ita Deus Pater, Deus Filius, Deus Spiritus Sanctus; et tamen non tres Dii, sed unus est Deus." Latin text of "Symbolum 'Quicumque' pseudo-Athanasianum" is taken from *Enchiridion Symbolorum*, pp. 41–42. nos. 75–76.
28. For another example of Langland's "service" piety, see the dreamer's description of baptism as unfreedom at B.11.127–37.
29. "Ita Dominus Pater, Dominus Filius, Dominus Spiritus Sanctus; et tamen non tres Domini, sed unus est Dominus."
30. Augustine, *De Trinitate*, ed. Mountain with Fr. Glorie, I.vii.35. "Est ergo dei filius deo patri natura aequalis, habitu minor. In forma enim serui quam accepit, minor est patre: in forma autem dei in qua erat etiam antequam hanc accepisset, aequalis est patri."
31. Compare this passage with the "*Faciamus*" passage in B.9.38–45, in which Wit explains how performative speech works through the three Persons of the Trinity.
32. There are several excellent studies of *Piers Plowman* and marriage, including Tavorima, *Kindly Similitude*, Galloway, "Intellectual Pregnancy," and Davis, "On the Sadness of Not Being a Bird."
33. "Pater a nullo est factus nec creatus, nec genitus;/Filius a Patre solo est: non factus, nec creatus, sed genitus; Spiritus Sanctus a Patre et Filio, non factus, nec creatus, nec genitus, sed procedens." [The Father is made from nothing, neither created nor generated; the Son is from the Father alone, not made, not created, but begotten; the Holy Spirit is from the Father and the Son, not made, not created, but proceeding.]
34. "Sic enim ad firmioris nexus compagem et caritatis custodiam uniuersitatis partes creatrix Trinitas Deum unus et uerus ordinauit, ut alterius operes altera indigeret, et altera defectum suppleret alterius, dum sunt singula quasi singulorum membra." John of Salisbury, (*Metalogicon*, 1.i., ed. Hall, pp. 12–13), translation adapted from Nederman and Forhan, eds., *Medieval Political Theory*.
35. The taper metaphor is a composite of two Trinitarian metaphors common in medieval religious literature, the sun and the candle.
36. Just for example, the Dormeuil Diptych (Paris, c.1375), in The Thomson Collection, Art Gallery of Ontario. http://www.ago.net/agoid107358
37. Julian of Norwich, *Shewings*, ed. Crampton, ch.2.

38. Bynum, *Holy Feast, Holy Fast*. For a recent study of emotion and female piety, see McNamer, *Affective Meditation*.
39. Mitchell and Robinson, eds., *A Guide to Old English*, p. 260, lines 44–46a.
40. See Harbert, "Langland's Easter."
41. See Aers, "Christ's Humanity."
42. Kirk, "Langland's Narrative Christology."
43. Marx, *The Devil's Rights*, ch.1.
44. As Furrow notes, this is Latin not just for scholars but for those who are "conversant in the clichés of [their] culture," those who, like many a modern reader, can recognize but can't fully explain E=mc² ("Latin and Affect," p. 37).
45. Anselm of Canterbury, *Cur Deus Homo*, 1.iii. "Oportebat namque ut sicut per hominis inobedientiam mors in humanum genus intraverat, ita per hominis obedientiam vita restitueretur; et quemadmodum peccatum, quod fuit causa nostrae damnationis, initium habuit a femina, sic nostrae justitiae et salutis auctor nasceretur de femina; et ut diabolus, qui per gustum ligni quem persuasit, hominem vincerat, ita per passionem ligni, quam intulit, ab homine vinceretur. Sunt quoque alia multa quae studiose considerata ineffabilem quamdam nostrae redemptionis, hoc modo procuratae, pulchritudinem ostendunt" [PL158.0364C]. English translation adapted from *Anselm of Canterbury*, vol. III, ed. and trans. Hopkins and Richardson, pp. 52–53.
46. See this volume, Chapter 3, n. 17.
47. Jacobus de Voragine, *Legenda aurea*, ed. Graesse, ch. 53, pp. 229–30. Voragine takes much of his material from Augustine's *De doctrina Christiana*, but has greatly amplified it with other sources.
48. "'Quia sic erat una / Cum virtute Dei virtus humana, necesse / Est igitur, sicut hominem prostravit, ab ipso / Sternatur; sicut a lingo vicit, et inde / Vincatur; laqueo quem fecit, eo capiatur.'/ Filius haec." (Geoffrey of Vinsauf, *Les Arts Poétiques*, ed. Faral, p. 243, lines 153–58.) Kopp's translation, which I quote in the text, can be found in *Three Medieval Rhetoric Arts*, ed. Murphy, p. 86.
49. See *Three Medieval Rhetoric Arts*, 63. "Sic se contraria miscent,/Sed pacem spondent hostesque morantur amici" (Geoffrey of Vinsauf, *Les Arts Poetiques*, ed. Faral, p. 223, lines 834–35).
50. Watson, "Censorship and Cultural Change."

CHAPTER 7 INSTITUTIONS

1. Middleton, "Making a Good End," and Smith, *The Book of the Incipit*, especially "Making Beginnings" and "The Book That Makes Itself."
2. Warner, *Lost History*, esp. ch. 4.
3. See Horobin's description of Harley 3954, a *Piers Plowman* manuscript which changes course midstream from a longer (B) to a shorter version (A) ("Harley 3954"). The scribes of Huntington MS 114 and the Ilchester manuscript (University of London Library, MS slv88), appear to have had access to key C passages before Langland had figured out how to incorporate them into

B. See Kerby-Fulton's neat summary of scribal reception in *"Piers Plowman,"* pp. 515–20, and generally, Hanna's indispensable *William Langland.*

4. See Benson's digest of biographical criticism in *Public "Piers Plowman,"* esp part 1, *"Piers Plowman* and Modern Scholarship." The classic work is Donaldson, *"Piers Plowman": The C-Text and Its Poet.*

5. Aers, *"Vox Populi"* and Lindenbaum, "London Texts and Literate Practice."

6. See Scanlon's perceptive comments on the difference between "conservative" and "traditional" as applied to medieval texts ("Kings, Commons, and Kind Wit," pp. 197–98).

7. Middleton, "Acts of Vagrancy."

8. See Cole, *Literature and Heresy in the Age of Chaucer,* chs 2 and 3.

9. Gradon, "Langland and the Ideology of Dissent"; Hudson, *The Premature Reformation,* pp. 398–408; and Warner, *Lost History,* ch. 3.

10. Paxson, "Sick of Allegory," and Fradenberg, "Needful Things."

11. See Kim, "Hunger, Need, and the Politics of Poverty," and Crassons, *The Claims of Poverty,* ch.1.

12. Middleton, "Acts of Vagrancy."

13. For different approaches to Langland and the friars, see Kerby-Fulton, *Reformist Apocalypticism,* p. 146, and Clopper, *"Songes of Rechelesnesse."*

14. Simpson identifies the historiographical impulse as the hidden element beneath Langland's attitude to Judaism. As he explains, there is an historical moment at which the Jews cease to bear the mark of faith: the Crucifixion, the moment at which their denial of Christ's divinity is unambiguously expressed (*"Piers Plowman": An Introduction,* p. 158).

15. *Mandeville's Travels,* ed. Seymour, p. 193.

16. See Narin van Court's application of Boyarin's notion of "supercession" to *Piers Plowman* in "The Hermeneutics of Supercession." See also Adams, "Langland's Theology," Ames, *The Fulfillment of the Scriptures,"* and Goldstein, "'Why calle ye hym Crist'."

17. For literature on *Piers Plowman* and apocalypse, see Bloomfield, *"Piers Plowman" as a Fourteenth-Century Apocalypse,* and Kerby-Fulton, *Reformist Apocalypticism.*

18. "O quante memorabili schiatte, quante amplissime eredità, quante famose ricchezze si videro senza successor debito rimanere! Quant valorosi uomini, quante belle donne, quanti leggiadri giovani, li quali non che altri, ma Galieno, Ippocrate o Esculapio avrieno giudicati sanissimi, la mattina desinarono co' loro parenti, compagnie e amici, che poi la sera vegnente appresso nell'altro mondo cenarono con li loro passati!" (Boccaccio, *Il Decameron,* ed. Rossi) (translation from *Decameron,* trans. Nichols, pp. 13–14).

19. Mann, International *Piers Plowman* Society meeting, Oxford, 2011.

20. See Barr's introduction to *Signes and Sothe.*

Bibliography

ABBREVIATIONS

Series and reference works

EETS: *Early English Text Society; ES: Extra Series, OS: Original Series*
CCSL: *Corpus Christianorum. Series Latina.*
CSEL: *Corpus Scriptorum Ecclesiasticorum Latinorum*
CCCM: *Corpus Christianorum Continuatio Mediaevalis*
MED: *Middle English Dictionary,* ed. Hans Kurath and Sherman M. Kuhn (Ann Arbor, 1952–2001). http://quod.lib.umich.edu/m/mec/.
PL: *Patrologiae Cursus Completus. Series Latina,* ed. J. P. Migne, 221 vols. (Paris, 1844–65). http://pld.chadwyck.co.uk/.

Journals

ChR: The Chaucer Review
ELH: *English Literary History*
JEGP: *Journal of English and Germanic Philology*
MÆ: *Medium Ævum*
NMR: *New Medieval Literatures*
PQ: *Philological Quarterly*
SAC: *Studies in the Age of Chaucer*
YLS: *Yearbook of Langland Studies*

CLASSICAL AND MEDIEVAL SOURCES

Acta et decreta sacrorum conciliorum recentiorum. Ed. Theodor Granderath. Freiburg, 1890.
Ambrose, *Sancti Ambrosii Opera.* Ed. Otto Faller. *CSEL* 73. Vienna, 1955.
Ancrene Wisse: A Corrected Edition. Ed. Bella Millett. *EETS OS* 326. Oxford, 2008.
Anselm of Canterbury. *Cur Deus Homo* [*PL* 158].
  Liber de conceptu virginali et originali peccato [*PL* 158].

Anselm of Canterbury. Ed. and trans. Jasper Hopkins and Herbert Richardson. 2nd edn. Toronto, 1975.

The Apocryphal Lives of Adam and Eve. Ed. Brian Murdoch and Jacqueline A. Tasioulas. Exeter, 2002.

Aristotle. *De historia animalium.* Trans. William of Moerbeke, ed. Pieter Beullens and Ferdinand Bossier. Leiden, 2000.

Atkinson, Keith. "An Early Fourteenth-Century French Boethian Orpheus," *Parergon*, 26, 1980 pp. 1–52.

The Auchinleck Manuscript. Ed. David Burnley and Alison Wiggins. National Library of Scotland. Version 1.1, 2003. http://auchinleck.nls.uk

Augustine. *De civitate Dei, libri XI–XII.* Ed. B. Dombart and A. Kalb. *CCSL* 48. Turnhout, 1955.

   De doctrina Christiana. Ed. J. Martin. *CCSL* 32 (Index, ser. A). Turnhout, 1982.

   De Trinitate, libri XV. Ed. W. J. Mountain with Fr. Glorie. *CCSL* 50–50a, 2 vols. Turnholt, 1968.

Bartholomaeus Anglicus. *Liber de proprietatibus rerum Bartholomei anglici.* Strasbourg, 1485.

Bede. *Bedae Venerabilis Opera, pars II.* Ed. M. L. W. Laistner. *CCSL* 121, Turnhout, 1983.

   Ecclesiastical History of the English People. Ed. and trans. Betram Colgrave and R. A. B. Mynors. Oxford, 1969.

Bernardus Silvestris. *Cosmographia*, Ed. Peter Dronke. Leiden, 1978.

Bersuire, Pierre. *Dictionarium seu repertorium morale fratris Petri Berchorii*, 3 parts. Paris, 1521–22.

   Metamorphosis Ovidana Moraliter . . . explanata, Paris, 1509; Basel, 1543; with introduction and notes by Stephen Orgel, New York, 1979.

Boccaccio, Giovanni. *Decameron.* Trans. J. G. Nichols. London, 2009.

   De casibus virorum illustrium. Tutte le opere di Giovanni Boccaccio, vol. IX. Ed. Vittore Branca. Milan, 1983.

   Il Decameron. Ed. Aldo Rossi. Bologna, 1977.

Boethius. *Consolatio Philosophiae.* Ed. James J. O'Donnell. Bryn Mawr, 1984. Online. Available at: www9.georgetown.edu/faculty/jod/boethius/jkok/list_t.htm.

   The Consolation of Philosophy. Trans. Patrick Gerard Walsh. Oxford, 1999.

The Book of Margery Kempe. Ed. Barry Windeatt. New York, 2000.

Bozon, Nicole. *Deux poemes de Nicholas Bozon: Le char d'Orgeuil. La lettre de l'empereur Orgueil.* Ed. Johan Vising. Goteburg, 1919.

   Les contes moralisés de Nicole Bozon. Ed. Paul Meyer and Lucy T. Smith. Paris, 1889.

   Les proverbes de bon enseignement. Ed. A. Chr. Thorn. Lund, 1921.

Brown, Carleton, ed. *Religious Lyrics of the XIVth Century.* Oxford, 1924.

   Religious Lyrics of the XVth Century. Oxford, 1939.

Chaucer, Geoffrey. *The Riverside Chaucer.* 3rd edn, ed. L. D. Benson. Boston, 1987.

The Complete Works of the Pearl Poet. Ed. Malcolm Andrew *et al.* trans. Casey Finch. Berkeley, 1993.

Cursor mundi: the cursur o the world, a Northumbrian poem of the xivth century in four versions. Ed. Richard Morris. *EETS* 57, 59, 62, 66, 68, 99, 101. London, 1874–93.

Deguileville, Guillaume de. *The pilgrimage of the lyfe of the manhode.* Ed. Avril Henry. 2 vols. *EETS OS* 288. London, 1985.

The Pilgrimage of the Life of Man. Ed. F. J. Furnivall, trans. John Lydgate. *EETS ES* 83. London, 1904.

Enchiridion symbolorum, definitionum et declarationum de rebus fidei et morum. Rev. edn, ed. Heinrich Denzinger. Rome, 1976.

Fasciculus Morum: A Fourteenth Century Preacher's Handbook. Ed. and trans. Siegfried Wenzel. University Park, PA, 1989.

Froissart, Jean. *Chroniques.* Ed. Peter F. Ainsworth and George T. Diller. Paris, 2001.

Genet, Jean-Philippe, ed. *Four English Political Tracts of the Later Middle Ages.* London, 1977.

Geoffrey of Vinsauf. *Poetria Nova,* in *Les Arts Poétiques du 12e et 13e siècle,* Ed. E. Faral. Paris, 1924, pp. 194–262.

Poetria Nova, in *Three Medieval Rhetorical Arts.* Ed. James Murphy, trans. Jane Baltzell. Berkeley, CA, 1971. pp. 27–108.

Giles of Rome. *De regimine principum.* Rome, 1607.

Gower, John. *The Complete Works of John Gower.* Ed. G. C. Macaulay. 4 vols. Oxford, 1899–1902.

The Major Latin Works of John Gower. Trans. Eric Stockton. Seattle, 1962.

Grosseteste, Robert. *Chasteau d'amour.* Ed. M. Cooke. London, 1852.

The Middle English Translations of Robert Grosseteste's "Chateau d'amour," Memoires de la Societe Neophilologique de Helsinki 32. Ed. Kari Sajavaara. Helsinki, 1967.

The Rules of Robert Grosseteste, in *Walter of Henley and Other Treatises on Estate Management and Accounting.* Ed. and trans. Dorothea Oschinsky. Oxford, 1971.

Guillaume le Clerc. *Le Bestiare Divin.* Ed. M. C. Hippeau. Paris, 1852.

Guillaume de Lorris and Jean de Meun. *Le roman de la rose.* Ed. Daniel Poirion. Paris, 1974.

Higden, Ranulf. *Polychronicon Ranulphi Higden monachi Cestrensis: together with the English Translations of John Trevisa and of an Unknown Writer of the Fifteenth Century.* Ed. C. Babington and J. R. Lumby. 2nd edn, London, 1964.

John of Salisbury. *Metalogicon.* Ed. J. B. Hall. *CCCM* 98. Turnhout, 1991.

Julian of Norwich. *The Shewings of Julian of Norwich.* Ed. Georgia Ronan Crampton. Kalamazoo, MI, 1994.

King Arthur's Death: The Middle English Stanzaic Morte Arthur and Alliterative Morte Arthure. Ed. Larry D. Benson. rev. edn. Edward E. Foster. Kalamazoo, MI, 1994.

Langland, William. *Piers Plowman: A New Annotated Edition of the C-Text.* Ed. Derek Pearsall. Exeter, 2008.

Piers Plowman: A Parallel-Text Edition of the A, B, C, and Z Versions, Schmidt, A. V. C. ed. London, 1995.

Piers Plowman: The A-Version. Ed. George Kane. London, 1960.

Piers Plowman: The A-Version. Ed. Miceál F. Vaughan, Baltimore, MD, 2011.

Piers Plowman: The B-Version. Ed. George Kane and E. Talbot Donaldson. London. rev. version, 1988.

Piers Plowman: The C-Version. Ed. George Russell and George Kane. London, 1997.

Piers Plowman: The Z-Version. Ed. A. G. Rigg and Charlotte Brewer. Toronto, 1983.

The Vision of Piers Plowman: A Critical Edition of the B-Text, 2nd edn. Ed. A. V. C. Schmidt. London, 1995.

The Lay Folks' Catechism. Ed. Thomas Frederick Simmons and Henry Edward Nolloth. *EETS OS* 118. London, 1901.

Li livres du gouvernement des rois: a Thirteenth-Century French Version of Egidio Colonna's Treatise "De regimine principum." Ed. S. P. Molaenaer. New York, 1899.

Lombard, Peter. *Commentarius in Psalmos Davidicos* [*PL* 191].

Malory, Thomas. *The Works of Sir Thomas Malory*, vol. III. Ed. Eugene Vinaver. Oxford, 1967.

Mandeville's Travels. Ed. M. C. Seymour. Oxford, 1967.

Mandeville's Travels: The Egerton Version. Ed. George F. Warner. Ann Arbor, MI, 1982.

The Middle English "Mirror." Ed. Thomas Gibson Duncan and Margaret Connolly. Heidelberg, 2003.

The Middle English "Mirror." Ed. K. M. Blumreich. Turnhout, 2002.

Minor Poems of the Vernon Manuscript. Ed. Carl Horstmann. 2 vols. *EETS OS*, 98, 117. London, 1892.

Myrc, John. *Instructions for Parish Priests*. Ed. Edward Peacock. Whitefish, MT, 2004.

Nederman, Cary J., and Kate Langdon Forhan eds. *Medieval Political Theory – A Reader: The Quest for the Body Politic*. New York, 1993.

Nicholas of Lyre. *Biblia sacra cum glossis, interlineari et sacra ordinaria, Nicolai Lyrani Postilla*, 7 vols. Lyons, 1565.

Northern Homily Cycle. Ed. Anne B. Thompson. Kalamazoo, MI, 2008.

Officium et miracula of Richard Rolle, of Hampole. Ed. Reginald M. Wooley. New York, 1919.

Physiologus Latinus Versio B, Editions preliminaries. Ed. Francis Carmody. Paris, 1939.

The "Piers Plowman" Tradition: A Critical Edition of "Pierce the Ploughman's Crede," "Richard the Redeless," "Mum and the Sothsegger," and "The Crowned King." Ed. Helen Barr. London, 1993.

Sammlung altenglischer Legenden. Ed. Carl Horstmann. Heilbronn, 1878.

Sancti Epiphanii ad Physiologum. Antwerp, 1638, digital facsimile and transcription at http://library.uvic.ca/site/spcoll/physiologum/commentary/txt_physiologus.htm.

The South English Legendary. Ed. Charlotte D'Evelyn and Anna J. Miller. *EETS OS* 235, 236, 244. London, 1956–59.

Thomas of Chobham. *Summa de arte praedicandi.* Ed. F. Morenzoni. Turnhout, 1988.

Trevisa, John. *The Governance of Kings and Princes: John Trevisa's Middle English Translation of the "De regimine principum" of Aegidus Romanus.* Ed. Charles F. Briggs, David C. Fowler *et al.* New York, 1997.

— *On the Properties of Things: John Trevisa's Translation of Bartholomaeus Anglicus "De proprietatibus rerum"* Ed. M. C. Seymour. 2 vols. Oxford, 1975.

Two Wycliffite Texts: The Sermon of William Taylor 1406, The Testimony of William Thorpe 1407. Ed. Anne Hudson. *EETS OS* 301. Oxford, 1993.

Voragine, Jacobus de. *Legenda aurea.* Ed. Georg Theodor Graesse. Whitefish, MT, 2010.

Walsingham, Thomas. "Historia Anglicana," in *The Peasants' Revolt of 1381.* Trans. R. B. Dobson. London, 1970.

The Wars of Alexander. Ed. Hoyt N. Duggan and Thorlac Turville-Petre. Oxford, 1989.

Wenzel, Siegfried. ed. *Preaching in the Age of Chaucer.* Washington, DC, 2008.

William of Malmesbury. *Gesta Regum Anglorum: The History of the English Kings.* Ed. and trans. R. M. Thomson and M. Winterbottom. Oxford, 1998.

Wogan-Browne, Jocelyn, *et al.* eds. *The Idea of the Vernacular: An Anthology of Middle English Literary Theory, 1280–1520.* University Park, PA, 1999.

Wynnere and Wastoure. Ed. Stephanie Trigg. *EETS* 297. London, 1990.

MODERN SCHOLARSHIP

Adams, Robert "Editing and the Limitations of *Durior Lectio*," *YLS*, 5, 1991, pp. 7–15.

— "Langland's *Ordinatio*: the *Visio* and the *Vita* Once More," *YLS*, 8, 1994, pp. 51–84.

— "Langland's Theology," in *A Companion to "Piers Plowman,"* ed. John A. Alford. Berkeley, CA, 1988, pp. 87–114.

— "The Reliability of the Rubrics in the B-Text of *Piers Plowman*," *MÆ*, 54, 1985, pp. 208–31.

— "Piers's Pardon and Langland's Semi-Pelagianism," *Traditio*, 34, 1978, pp. 367–418.

Aers, David. *Chaucer, Langland, and the Creative Imagination.* London, 1980.

— "Christ's Humanity and *Piers Plowman*: Contexts and Political Implications," *YLS*, 8, 1994, pp. 107–25.

— *Community, Gender and Individual Identity: English Writing 1360–1430.* London, 1988.

— "Representations of the Third Estate: Social Conflict and its Milieu around 1381," *Southern Review (Australia)*. 16, 1983, pp. 335–49.

— *Salvation and Sin: Augustine, Langland, and Fourteenth-Century Theology.* Notre Dame, IN, 2009.

Sanctifying Signs: Making Christian Tradition in Late Medieval England. Notre Dame, IN, 2004.

"*Vox Populi* and the Literature of 1381," in *The Cambridge History of Medieval English Literature*, ed. David Wallace. Cambridge, 1999, pp. 432–53.

Alford, John, A. 1988. "The Design of the Poem." In *A Companion to "Piers Plowman"*, ed. Alford, Berkeley, CA, pp. 29–65.

"Langland's Learning," *YLS*, 9, 1995, pp. 1–17.

"Literature and Law in Medieval England," *Publications of the Modern Language Association*, 92, 1977, pp. 941–51.

"*Piers Plowman*": *A Glossary of Legal Diction*. Cambridge, 1988.

"*Piers Plowman*": *A Guide to the Quotations*. Binghamton, NY, 1992.

"The Role of the Quotations in *Piers Plowman*," *Speculum*, 52, 1977, pp. 80–99.

"The Scriptural Self," in The *Bible in the Middle Ages: Its Influence on Literature and Art*, Levy, Bernard S. ed. Binghamton, NY, 1992, pp. 1–21.

Alford, John, A., ed. *A Companion to "Piers Plowman."* Berkeley, CA, 1988.

Allen, Judson Boyce. *The Ethical Poetic of the Later Middle Ages.* Toronto, 1982.

"Langland's Reading and Writing: *Detractor* and the Pardon Passus," *Speculum*, 59, 1984, pp. 342–62.

Ames, Ruth. *The Fulfillment of the Scriptures: Abraham, Moses, and Piers.* Evanston, IL, 1970.

Baldwin, Anna P. *A Guide to Piers Plowman.* Basingstoke, Hampshire, 2007.

"The Debt Narrative in *Piers Plowman*," in *Art and Context in Late Medieval English Narrative: Essays in Honor of Robert Worth Frank*, ed. Robert R. Edwards. Cambridge, 1994, pp. 37–50.

"The Historical Context," in *A Companion to "Piers Plowman*," ed. John A. Alford. Berkeley, 1988, pp. 67–86.

The Theme of Government in "Piers Plowman" Cambridge, 1981.

Barney, Stephen A. *The Penn Commentary on "Piers Plowman,"* vol. v, C Passus 20–22; B Passus 18–20. Philadelphia, 2006.

Barr, Helen. *Signes and Sothe: Language in the "Piers Plowman" Tradition.* Cambridge, 1994.

Socioliterary Practice in Late Medieval England. Oxford, 2001.

Barron, Caroline M. *London in the Later Middle Ages: Government and People, 1200–1500.* Oxford, 2004.

"William Langland: A London Poet," in *Chaucer's England: Literature in Historical Context*, ed. Barbara A. Hanawalt. Minneapolis, MI, 1992, pp. 91–109.

Bennett, Judith M. "The Curse of the Plowman," *YLS*, 20, 2006, pp. 215–26.

Benson, C. David. *Public "Piers Plowman": Modern Scholarship and Late Medieval English Culture.* University Park, PA, 2004.

Benson, C. David and Blanchfield, Lynne S., *The Manuscripts of "Piers Plowman": The B-Version.* Woodbridge, Suffolk, 1997.

Bishop, Louise. *Words, Stones, and Herbs: The Healing Word in Medieval and Early Modern England.* Syracuse, NY, 2007.

Bloomfield, Morton *"Piers Plowman" as a Fourteenth-Century Apocalypse*. New Brunswick, NJ, 1962.

Blumenfeld-Kosinski, Renate. *Reading Myth: Classical Mythology and Its Interpretations in Medieval French Literature*. Stanford, CA, 1998.

Bowers, John M. *Chaucer and Langland: The Antagonistic Tradition*. Notre Dame, IN, 2007.

The Crisis of Will in "Piers Plowman." Washington, DC, 1986.

"Piers Plowman and the Police: Notes Towards a History of the Wycliffite Langland," *YLS*, 6, 1992, pp. 1–50.

Breen, Katharine. *Imagining an English Reading Public 1150–1400*. Cambridge, 2010.

Brewer, Charlotte. *Editing "Piers Plowman": The Evolution of the Text*. Cambridge, 1996.

Briggs, Charles F. *Giles of Rome's "De regimine principum": Reading and Writing Politics at Court and University c.1275-c.1525*. Cambridge, 1999.

Burgess, Clive and Barron, Caroline M. eds. *Memory and Commemoration in Medieval England*. Donington, 2010.

Burrow, J. A. *Gestures and Looks in Medieval Narrative*. Cambridge, 2002.

"Langland Nel Mezzo del Cammin," in *Medieval Studies for J. A. W. Bennett*, ed. P. L. Heyworth, Oxford, 1981.

Langland's Fictions. Oxford, 1993.

"The Structure of *Piers Plowman* B xv–xx: Evidence from the Rubrics," *MÆ*, 77, 2008, pp. 306–12.

Butterfield, Ardis. *"Aucassin et Nicolette* and Mixed Forms in Medieval French," in *Prosimetrum: Cross-Cultural Perspectives on Narrative in Prose and Verse*, ed. Joseph Harris, Joseph and Karl Reichl. Cambridge, 1997, pp. 67–98.

"Chaucerian Vernaculars," *SAC*, 31, 2009, pp. 25–51.

The Familiar Enemy: Chaucer, Language, and Nation in the Hundred Years War. Oxford, 2009.

Bynum, Caroline Walker. *Holy Feast, Holy Fast: The Religious Significance of Food to Medieval Women*. Berkeley, CA, 1987.

Cable, Thomas. *The English Alliterative Tradition*. Philadelphia, 1991.

Cannon, Christopher. "Langland's *Ars Grammatica*," *YLS*, 22, 2009, pp. 1–25.

"The Middle English Writer's Schoolroom: Fourteenth-Century English Schoolbooks and their Contents," *NMR*, 11, 2009, pp. 19–38.

Carruthers, Mary. *The Book of Memory: A Study of Memory in Medieval Culture*. Cambridge, 1990.

"Piers Plowman: the Tearing of the Pardon," *PQ*, 49, 1970, pp. 8–18.

Cartlidge, Neil. "The Composition and Social Context of the MSS Jesus College Oxford 29 (11) and BL Cotton Caligula A.ix," *MÆ*, 66, 1997, pp. 250–69.

Chism, Christine. *Alliterative Revivals*. Philadelphia, 2002.

Clopper, Lawrence. "Langland's Markings for the Structure of *Piers Plowman*," *Modern Philology*, 85 no. 3, 1988, pp. 245–55.

"Songes of Rechelesnesse": Langland and the Franciscans. Ann Arbor, MI, 1997.

Cole, Andrew. *Literature and Heresy in the Age of Chaucer*. Cambridge, 2008.

"Trifunctionality and the Tree of Charity: Literary and Social Practice in *Piers Plowman*," *ELH*, 62, 1995, pp. 1–27.

Coleman, Janet. *Medieval Readers and Writers: 1350–1400*. New York, 1981.

Cook, Eleanor. "The Figure of Enigma: Rhetoric, History, Poetry," *Rhetorica: A Journal of the History of Rhetoric*, 19 no. 4, 2001, pp. 349–78.

Cooper, Helen. "Langland's and Chaucer's Prologues," *YLS*, 1, 1987, pp. 71–81.

Copeland, Rita. *Pedagogy, Intellectuals, and Dissent in the Later Middle Ages: Lollardy and Ideas of Learning*. Cambridge, 2001.

"Pre-Modern Intellectual Biography," in *The Public Intellectual*, ed. Helen Small. Oxford, 2002, pp. 40–61.

"William Thorpe and His Lollard Community: Intellectual Labor and the Representation of Dissent," in *Bodies and Disciplines: Intersections of Literature and History in Fifteenth Century England*, ed. Barbara Hanawalt and David Wallace. Minneapolis, MN, 1996, pp. 199–222.

Cornelius, Ian. "Cultural Promotion: Middle English Alliterative Writing and the *Ars Dictaminis*" PhD diss., University of Pennsylvania, 2009.

"The Rhetoric of Advancement: *Ars dictaminis, Cursus*, and Clerical Careerism in Late Medieval England," *NML*, 12, 2010, pp. 287–328.

Crassons, Kate. *The Claims of Poverty: Literature, Culture, and Ideology in Late Medieval England*. Notre Dame, IN, 2010.

Craun, Edwin. *Ethics and Power in Medieval English Reformist Writing*. Cambridge, 2010.

Cropp, Glynnis. 2005. "The Occitan *Boecis*, the Medieval French Tradition of the *Consolatio Philosophiae* and Philosophy's Gown," in *Etudes de Langue et de Littérature Médiévales offertes à Peter T. Ricketts à l'occasion de son 70e anniversaire*, ed. A. Buckley and D. Billy. Turnhout, pp. 255–66.

Curry Woods, Marjorie. "Boys Will Be Women: Musings on Classroom Nostalgia and the Chaucerian Audience(s)," in *Speaking Images: Essays in Honor of V.A. Kolve*, ed. Robert F. Yeager and Charlotte C. Morse. Asheville, NC, 2001, pp. 143–66.

"A Medieval Rhetoric Goes to School – and to the University: The Commentaries on the *Poetria nova*," *Rhetorica: A Journal of the History of Rhetoric*, 9, 1991, pp. 55–65.

"Weeping for Dido: Epilogue on a Premodern Rhetorical Exercise in the Postmodern Classroom," in *Latin Grammar and Rhetoric: From Classical Theory to Medieval Practice*, ed. C. D. Lanham. New York, 2002, pp, 284–94.

Curry Woods, Marjorie and Copeland, Rita. "Classroom and Confession," in *The Cambridge History of Medieval English Literature*, ed. David Wallace. Cambridge, 1999, pp. 376–406.

Daniell, Christopher. *Death and Burial in Medieval England*. London, 1998.

Davis, Isabel. "On the Sadness of Not Being a Bird: The Representation of Abraham and Late Medieval Marriage Ideologies in William Langland's *Piers Plowman*," in *Medieval Domesticity: Home, Housing, and Household in Medieval England*, ed. P. J. P. Goldberg, and Maryanne Kowaleski. Cambridge, 2008.

Davlin, Mary Clemente. "*Petrus, id est, Christus*: Piers the Plowman as The Whole Christ," *ChR*, 6 no. 4, 1972, pp. 280–92.

Dobson, R. B. *The Peasants' Revolt of 1381*. London, 1983.

Donaldson, E. Talbot. *"Piers Plowman": The C-Text and Its Poet*. New Haven, CT, 1949.

Duffy, Eamon. *The Stripping of the Altars: Traditional Religion in England, 1400–1580*, 2nd edn. New Haven, CT, 2005.

Duggan, Hoyt N. "Metre, Stanza, Vocabulary, Dialect," in *A Companion to the "Gawain" Poet*, ed. Derek Brewer. Cambridge, 1997, pp. 221–42.

"Notes on the Metre of *Piers Plowman*: Twenty Years On," in *Approaches to the Metres of Alliterative Verse*, ed. Judith Jefferson and Ad Putter. Leeds, 2009.

"The Shape of the B-Verse in Middle English Alliterative Poetry," *Speculum*, 61, 1986, pp. 564–92.

Dwyer, Richard. *Boethian Fictions: Narratives in the Medieval French Versions of the "Consolatio philosophiae."* Cambridge, MA, 1976.

Dyer, Christopher. "*Piers Plowman* and Plowmen: A Historical Perspective," *YLS*, 8, 1994, pp. 155–76.

"The Social and Economic Background to the Rural Revolt of 1381," in *The English Rising of 1381*, ed. R. H. Hilton and T. H Ashton. Cambridge, 1984, pp. 9–42.

Eckhardt, Caroline. "The Medieval *Prosimetrum* Genre (From Boethius to *Boece*)," *Genre*, 16, 1988, pp. 21–38.

Enders, Jody. *The Medieval Theater of Cruelty: Rhetoric, Memory, Violence*. Ithaca, NY, 1999.

Fowler, Elizabeth. "Civil Death and the Maiden: Agency and the Conditions of Contract in *Piers Plowman*," *Speculum*, 70, 1995, pp. 760–92.

Fradenburg, Louise O. "Needful Things," in *Medieval Crime and Social Control*, ed. Barbara Hanawalt and David Wallace. Minneapolis, MN, 1999, pp. 49–69.

Sacrifice Your Love: Psychoanalysis, Historicism, Chaucer. Minneapolis, MN, 2002.

Frank, Robert W. "The 'Hungry Gap,' Crop Failure, and Famine: The Fourteenth-Century Agricultural Crisis and *Piers Plowman*," 1990, *YLS*, 4, pp. 87–104.

Freedman, Paul H. *Images of the Medieval Peasant*. Stanford, CA, 1999.

Friedman, John Block. *Orpheus in the Middle Ages*. Syracuse, NY, 2000.

Furrow, Melissa. "Latin and Affect," in *The Endless Knot: Essays on Old and Middle English in Honor of Marie Boroff*, ed. M. Teresa Tavormina and R. F. Yeager. Cambridge, 1995, pp. 29–41.

Galloway, Andrew. "Intellectual Pregnancy, Metaphysical Femininity, and the Social Doctrine of the Trinity in *Piers Plowman*," *YLS*, 12, 1998, pp. 117–52.

"Latin England," in *Imagining a Medieval English Community*, ed. Kathryn Lavezzo. Minneapolis, MN, 2003, pp. 41–95.

The Penn Commentary on "Piers Plowman," vol. 1. Philadelphia, 2006.

"*Piers Plowman* and the Schools," *YLS*, 6, 1992, pp. 89–107.

"Writing History in England," in *The Cambridge History of Medieval English Literature*, ed. David Wallace. Cambridge, 1999, pp. 255–83.

Gasse, Rosanne. "The Practice of Medicine in *Piers Plowman*," *ChR*, 39 2004, no. 2, pp. 177–97.

Ghosh, Kantik. *The Wycliffite Heresy: Authority and the Interpretation of Texts*. Cambridge, 2002.

Giancarlo, Matthew. *Parliament and Literature in Medieval England*. Cambridge, 2007.

Gillespie, Vincent. "Thy Will be Done: *Piers Plowman* and the Paternoster," in *Late Medieval Religious Texts and Their Transmission*, ed. A. J. Minnis. Woodbridge, Suffolk, 1994.

"Vernacular Theology," in *Oxford Twenty-First Century Approaches to Literature: Middle English*, ed. Paul Strohm. Oxford, 2007.

Given-Wilson, Christopher. *Chronicles: The Writing of History in Medieval England*. London, 2004.

Goldstein, James. "'Why calle ye hym crist, sithen Iewes called hym Iesus?': The Disavowal of Jewish Identification in *Piers Plowman* B Text," *Exemplaria*, 13, no. 1, 2001, pp. 215–55.

Gradon, Pamela. "Langland and the Ideology of Dissent," *Proceedings of the British Academy*, 66, 1980, pp. 179–205.

Grady, Frank. "Chaucer Reading Langland: The House of Fame," *SAC*, 18, 1996 pp. 3–23.

"*Piers Plowman*, *St. Erkenwald*, and the Rule of Exceptional Salvation," *YLS*, 6 1992, pp. 61–86.

Representing Righteous Heathens in Late Medieval England. New York, 2005.

Green, Richard Firth. *A Crisis of Truth: Literature and Law in Ricardian England*. Philadelphia, 1998.

Poets and Princepleasers: Literature and the English Court in the Late Middle Ages. Toronto, 1980.

Hailey, R. Carter. "Robert Crowley and the Editing of *Piers Plowman* (1550)," *YLS*, 21, 2007, pp. 143–70.

Hanna, Ralph III. "Alliterative Poetry," in *The Cambridge History of Medieval English Literature*, ed. David Wallace. Cambridge, 1999, pp. 263–84.

"Defining Middle English Alliterative Poetry," in *The Endless Knot: Essays on Old and Middle English in Honor of Marie Boroff*, ed. M. Teresa Tavormina and Robert Yeager. Cambridge, 1995, pp. 43–64.

London Literature: 1300–1380. Cambridge, 2005.

Pursuing History: Middle English Manuscripts and Their Texts. Palo Alto, CA, 1996.

"School and Scorn: Gender in *Piers Plowman*," *NMR*, 3, 1999, pp. 213–27.

William Langland. Aldershot, 1993.

Hanna, Ralph and Lawton, David eds. *The Siege of Jerusalem EETS OS 320*. Oxford, 2003.

Harbert, Bruce. "Langland's Easter," in *Langland, the Mystics and the Medieval English Religious Tradition: Essays in Honour of S.S. Hussey*, ed. Helen Phillips. Cambridge, 1990, pp. 57–70.

Harwood, Britton J. "Imaginative in *Piers Plowman*," *MÆ*, 44, 1975, pp. 249–63.

Hewett-Smith, Kathleen M., ed. *William Langland's Piers Plowman: A Book of Essays*. London, 2001.

Hill, Thomas. "Universal Salvation and its Literary Context in *Piers Plowman* B.18," *YLS*, 5, 1991, pp. 65–76.

Hilton, Rodney. *Bond Men Made Free: Medieval Peasant Movements and The English Rising of 1381*. New York, 2003.

Holsinger, Bruce. "Langland's Musical Reader: Liturgy, Law, and the Constraints of Performance," *SAC*, 21, 1999, pp. 99–141.

"Lyric Inventions: The Short Poems," in *The Yale Companion to Chaucer*, ed. Seth Lerer. Yale, 2006, pp. 179–212.

The Premodern Condition: Medievalism and the Making of Theory. Chicago, 2005.

Horobin, Simon. "Adam Pinkhurst, Geoffrey Chaucer, and the Hengwrt Manuscript of the *Canterbury Tales*," *ChR*, 44, 2010, pp. 351–67.

"Harley 3954 and the Audience of *Piers Plowman*", in *Medieval Texts in Context*, ed. Graham D. Caie and Denis Renevy. New York, 2008, pp. 68–84.

"'In London and opelond': The Dialect and Circulation of the C Version of *Piers Plowman*," *MÆ*, 74, 2005, pp. 248–68.

"Reconsidering Lincoln's Inn 150," *MÆ*, 77, 2008, pp. 30–53.

"The Scribe of Rawlinson 137 and the Copying and Circulation of *Piers Plowman*," *YLS*, 19, 2005, pp. 3–26.

Horobin, Simon and Mooney, Linne R. "A *Piers Plowman* Manuscript by the Hengwrt/Ellesmere Scribe and Its Implications for London Standard English," *SAC*, 26, 2004, pp. 65–112.

Horrox, Rosemary. "Caterpillars of the Commonwealth? Courtiers in Late Medieval England," in *Rulers and Ruled in Late Medieval England: Essays Presented to Gerald Harriss*, ed. R. E. Archer and Simon Walker. London, 1995, pp. 1–15.

"Service," in *Fifteenth-Century Attitudes: Perceptions of Society in Late Medieval England*, ed. Horrox. Cambridge, 1997.

Hudson, Anne. *The Premature Reformation: Wycliffite Texts and Lollard History*. Oxford, 1988.

Jefferson, Judith and Putter, Ad, eds. *Approaches to the Metres of Alliterative Verse*. Leeds, 2009.

Johnson, Eleanor. "Chaucer and the Consolation of *Prosimetrum*," *ChR*, 42 no. 4, 2009, pp. 455–72.

Justice, Steven. "The Genres of *Piers Plowman*," *Viator*, 19, 1988, pp. 291–306.

Writing and Rebellion: England in 1381. Berkeley, CA, 1994.

Justice, Steven, and Kerby-Fulton, Kathryn, eds. *Written Work, Langland, Labor, and Authorship*. Philadelphia, 1997.

Kamath, Stephanie A. Viereck Gibbs. "Naming the Pilgrim: Authorship and Allegory in Guillaume de Deguileville's *Pèlerinage de la vie humaine*," *SAC*, 32, 2010, pp. 36–56.

Kane, George. "An Open Letter to Jill Mann about the Sequence of the Versions of *Piers Plowman*," *YLS*, 13, 1999, pp. 7–33.

Kantorowicz, Ernst. *The King's Two Bodies: A Study in Mediaeval Political Theology*. Princeton, NJ, 1957.

Karnes, Michelle. "Will's Imagination in *Piers Plowman*," *JEGP*, 108, 2009, pp. 27–58.

Kaske, Robert. *Medieval Christian Literary Imagery: A Guide to Interpretation*. Toronto, 1988.

Kaulbach, Ernest. "The *Vis Imaginativa* and the Reasoning Powers of Ymaginatif in the B-Text of *Piers Plowman*," *JEGP*, 84, 1985, pp. 16–29.

Kaye, Joel. *Economy and Nature in the Fourteenth Century: Money, Market Exchange, and the Emergence of Scientific Thought*. Cambridge, 2000.

Kelen, Sarah. *Langland's Early Modern Identities*. New York, 2007.

Kennedy, Kathleen. *Maintenance, Meed, and Marriage in Medieval English Literature*. New York, 2009.

Kerby-Fulton, Kathryn. "Authority, Constraint and the Writing of the Medieval Self," in *The Oxford Handbook of Medieval Literature in English*, ed. Elaine Treharne and Greg Walker. Oxford, 2010, pp. 413–33.

"Langland 'in his Working Clothes'?: Scribe D, Authorial Loose Revision Material, and the Nature of Scribal Intervention," in *Middle English Poetry: Texts and Traditions: Essays in Honour of Derek Pearsall*, ed. A. J. Minnis and Derek Persall. Woodbridge, Suffolk, 2001. pp. 139–68.

"*Piers Plowman*," in *The Cambridge History of Medieval English Literature*, ed. David Wallace. Cambridge, 1999, pp. 513–38.

Reformist Apocalypticism and "Piers Plowman." Cambridge, 1990.

Kerby-Fulton, Kathryn and Justice, Steven. "Langlandian Reading Circles and the Civil Service in London and Dublin, 1380–1427," *NMR*, 1, 1997, pp. 59–83.

Kim, Margaret. "Hunger, Need, and the Politics of Poverty in *Piers Plowman*," *YLS*, 16, 2002, pp. 131–68.

King, John. "Robert Crowley's Edition of *Piers Plowman*: A Tudor Apocalypse," *Modern Philology*, 73, 1976, pp. 342–52.

Kirk, Elizabeth. "Langland's Narrative Christology," in *Art and Context in Late Medieval English Narrative*, ed. Robert R. Edwards. Cambridge, 1994, pp. 17–35.

"Langland's Plowman and the Recreation of Fourteenth-Century Religious Metaphor," *YLS*, 2, 1988, pp. 1–21.

Kiser, Lisa J. "Animal Economies: The Lives of St. Francis in Their Medieval Contexts," *Interdisciplinary Studies in Literature and Environment*, 11, 2004, pp. 121–38.

"Chaucer and the Politics of Nature," in *Beyond Nature Writing: Expanding the Boundaries of Ecocriticism*, ed. Karla Armburster and Kathleen R. Wallace Charlottesville, VA, 2001, pp. 41–56.

"The Garden of Saint Francis: Plants, Landscape, and Economy in Thirteenth-Century Italy," *Environmental History*, 8 no. 2, 2003, pp. 229–45.

Lampert, Lisa. *Gender and Jewish Difference from Paul to Shakespeare*. Philadelphia, 2004.

Lavezzo, Kathy. *Angels on the Edge of the World: Geography, Literature and English Community, 1000–1534*. Cornell, 2006.

Lawler, Traugott. "Conscience's Dinner," in *The Endless Knot: Essays on Old and Middle English in Honor of Marie Boroff*, ed. M. Teresa Tavormina and Robert Yeager. Cambridge, 1995, pp. 87–103.

"The Pardon Formula in *Piers Plowman:* its Ubiquity, its Binary Shape, its Silent Middle Term," *YLS*, 14, 2000, pp. 117–52.

"Piers Plowman," in *The Oxford History of Literary Translation in English*, ed. Roger Ellis. Oxford, 2008.

"The Secular Clergy in *Piers Plowman*," *YLS*, 16, 2002, pp. 85–117.

Lawton, David. "Alliterative Style," in *A Companion to "Piers Plowman*," ed. John A. Alford. Berkeley, CA, 1988, pp. 223–50.

"The Bible," in *The Oxford History of Literary Translation in English*, ed. Roger Ellis. Oxford, 2008.

"The Diversity of Middle English Alliterative Poetry," *Leeds Studies in English*, 20, 1989, pp. 143–72.

"Englishing the Bible: 1066–1549," in *The Cambridge History of Medieval English Literature*, ed. David Wallace. Cambridge, 1999.

"The Idea of Alliterative Poetry: Alliterative Meter and *Piers Plowman*," in *"Such Werkes to Werche": Essays on "Piers Plowman*," ed. David C. Fowler and Míceál F. Vaughan. East Lansing, MI, 1993, pp. 147–68.

Middle English Alliterative Poetry and its Literary Background. Cambridge, 1982.

"*Piers Plowman*: On Tearing – or Not Tearing – the Pardon," *PQ*, 60, 1981, pp. 414–22.

"The Subject of *Piers Plowman*," *YLS*, 1, 1987, pp. 1–39.

"The Unity of Middle English Alliterative Poetry," *Speculum*, 58, 1983, pp. 72–94.

Lees, Clare. "Gender and Exchange in *Piers Plowman*," in *Class and Gender in Early English Literature: Intersections*, ed. Britton J. Harwood, and Gillian R. Overing. Bloomington, IN, 1994, pp. 112–30.

Lerer, Seth. *Boethius and Dialogue: Literary Method in the Consolation of Philosophy*. Princeton, 1985.

Levinas, Emmanuel. "The Proximity of the Other," in *Alterity and Transcendence*, trans. Michael Smith. New York, 1999, pp. 97–110.

Lindenbaum, Sheila. "London Texts and Literate Practice," in *The Cambridge History of Medieval English Literature*, ed. David Wallace. Cambridge, 1999, pp. 284–309.

Little, Lester K. *Religious Poverty and the Profit Economy in Medieval Europe*. Ithaca, NY, 1978.

Machan, Tim. "Language Contact in *Piers Plowman*," *Speculum*, 69, 1994, pp. 359–85.

Mann, Jill. *Chaucer and Medieval Estates Satire*. Cambridge, 1973.

    From Aesop to Reynard: Beast Literature in Medieval Britain. Oxford, 2009.

    "'He Knew Nat Catoun': Medieval School-Texts and Middle English Literature," in *The Text in the Community: Essays on Medieval Works, Manuscripts, Authors, and Readers*, ed. Mann and Maura Nolan. Notre Dame, IN, 2006.

    "The Power of the Alphabet: A Reassessment of the Relation Between the A and B Versions of *Piers Plowman*," YLS, 8, 1994, pp. 21–49.

    "Troilus' Swoon," *ChR*, 14, 1980, pp. 319–35.

Marx, C. W. *The Devil's Rights and the Redemption in the Literature of Medieval England*, Rochester, NY, 1995.

McNamer, Sarah. *Affective Meditation and the Invention of Medieval Compassion*, Philadelphia, PA, 2009.

Middleton, Anne. "Acts of Vagrancy: The C-Version 'Autobiography' (C.5.1–108) and the Statute of 1388," in *Written Work: Langland, Labor, and Authorship*, ed. Steven Justice and Kathryn Kerby-Fulton. Philadelphia, 1997, pp. 208–317.

    "The Audience and Public of *Piers Plowman*," in *Middle English Alliterative Poetry and its Literary Background*, ed. David Lawton, Cambridge, 1982, pp. 101–23.

    "The Idea of Public Poetry in the Reign of Richard II," *Speculum*, 53, 1978, pp. 94–114.

    "Making a Good End: John But as a Reader of *Piers Plowman*," in *Midde English Studies Presented to George Kane*, ed. Edward D. Kennedy, R. Waldron, and J. S. Wittig, Woodbridge, Suffolk, 1988, pp. 243–66.

    "Narration and the Invention of Experience: Episodic Form in *Piers Plowman*," in *The Wisdom of Poetry: Essays in Early English Literature in Honor of Morton W. Bloomfield*, ed. Larry D. Benson and Siegfried Wenzel. Kalamazoo, MI, 1982, pp. 91–122.

    "Two Infinites: Grammatical Metaphor in *Piers Plowman*," *ELH*, 3, 1972, pp. 169–133.

    "William Langland's 'Kynde Name': Authorial Signature and Social Identity," in *Literary Practice and Social Change in Britain, 1380–1530*, ed. Lee Patterson. Berkeley, CA, 1990, pp. 15–82.

Minnis, A. J. *Chaucer's "Boece" and the Medieval Tradition of Boethius*. New York, 1993.

    "Langland's Imaginatif and Late-Medieval Theories of Imagination," *Comparative Criticism*, 3, 1981, pp. 71–103.

Minnis, A. J. and Johnson, Ian, eds. *The Cambridge History of Literary Criticism, vol. II: The Middle Ages*. Cambridge, 2005.

Minnis, A. J. and Scott, A. B. *Medieval Literary Theory and Criticism, c. 1100–c. 1375: The Commentary Tradition*. Oxford, 1995.

Mitchell, Bruce and Robinson, Fred C. *A Guide to Old English*. Malden, MA, 2007.

Mitchell, J. Allan. *Ethics and Eventfulness in Middle English Literature*. New York, 2009.

Morey, James. *Book and Verse: A Guide to Middle English Biblical Literature*. Champaign, IL, 2000.

Mula, Stefano. "Muhammad and the Saints: The History of the Prophet in the *Golden Legend*," *Romance Philology*, 101, no. 2, 2003, pp. 175–88.

Narin van Court, Elisa. "The Hermeneutics of Supercession: The Revision of the Jews from the B- to the C-Text in Langland's *Piers Plowman*," *YLS*, 10, 1996, pp. 43–87.

Nauta, Lodi. "The *Consolation*: the Latin Commentary Tradition, 800–1700," in *The Cambridge Companion to Boethius*, ed. John Marenbon. Cambridge, 2009.

Nolan, Maura. "The Fortunes of *Piers Plowman* and its Readers," *YLS*, 20, 2007, pp. 1–41.

Olson, Glending. "Geoffrey Chaucer," in *The Cambridge History of Medieval English Literature*, ed. David Wallace. Cambridge, 1999, pp. 566–88.

Orme, Nicholas. *English Schools in the Middle Ages*. London, 1973.

Ormrod, W. M. "Who Was Alice Perrers?," *ChR*, 40, 2006, pp. 219–29.

Patterson, Lee. *Negotiating the Past: The Historical Understanding of Medieval Literature*, Madison, WI, 1987, pp. 77–113.

Paxson, James. "Sick of Allegory: A Response to Lawrence Clopper's 'Langland and Allegory, A Proposition,'" *YLS*, 15, 2001, pp. 47–51.

Pearsall, Derek. "Poverty and Poor People in *Piers Plowman*," in *Medieval English Studies Presented to George Kane*, ed. E. Kennedy, R. Waldron, and J. Wittig. Woodbridge, Suffolk, 1988, pp. 167–85.

Pickering, O. S. "The Temporale Narratives of the *South English Legendary*," *Anglia*, 91, 1973, pp. 425–55.

Pollock, Frederick and Maitland, Frederic William. *The History of English Law Before the Time of Edward I*, vol. 1. Cambridge, 1968.

Rappaport, Roy. *Ecology, Meaning, and Religion*. Richmond, 1979.

Raskolnikov, Masha. "Promising the Female, Delivering the Male: Transformations of Gender in *Piers Plowman*," *YLS*, 19, 2006, pp. 81–105.

Rhodes, James. *Poetry Does Theology: Chaucer, Grosseteste, and the "Pearl"-Poet*. Notre Dame, IN, 2001.

Robertson, Elizabeth. "Measurement and the 'Feminine' in *Piers Plowman*: A Response to Recent Studies of Langland and Gender," in *William Langland's "Piers Plowman": A Book of Essays*, ed. Kathleen Hewett-Smith. New York, 2001, pp. 167–94.

Robertson, Kellie. *The Laborer's Two Bodies: Labor and the "Work" of the Text in Medieval Britain, 1350–1500*. New York, 2006.

Roger, William. "The C-Revisions and the Crusades in *Piers Plowman*," in *The Medieval Crusade*, ed. Susan J. Ridyard. Woodbridge, Suffolk, 2004.

Rouse, Richard H., and Rouse, Mary A. "Biblical Distinctions in the Thirteenth Century," *Archives d'histoire doctrinale et littéraire du moyen âge*, 41, 1974, pp. 27–37.

Rubin, Miri. *Charity and Community in Medieval Cambridge*. Cambridge, 2002.

Scanlon, Larry. "King, Commons, and Kind Wit: Langland's National Vision and the Rising of 1381," in *Imagining a Medieval English Nation*, ed. Kathryn Lavezzo. Minneapolis, MN, 2003, pp. 191–233.

Narrative, Authority, and Power: The Medieval Exemplum and the Chaucerian Tradition. Cambridge, 1994.

Scase, Wendy. *Literature and Complaint in England, 1272–1553*. Oxford, 2007.

"Piers Plowman" and the New Anticlericalism. Cambridge, 1989.

"Two *Piers Plowman* C-Text Interpolations: Evidence for a Second Textual Tradition," in *Notes and Queries*, 232, 1987, pp. 457–63.

"Writing and the Plowman: Language and Literacy," *YLS*, 9, 1995, pp. 121–39.

Schmidt, A. V. C. *The Clerkly Maker: Langland's Poetic Art*. Cambridge, 1987.

Scott, Anne M. *"Piers Plowman" and the Poor*. Dublin, 2004.

Simpson, James. "The Constraints of Satire in *Piers Plowman* and *Mum and the Sothsegger*," in *Langland, the Mystics and the Medieval English Religious Tradition: Essays in Honour of S. S. Hussey*, ed. Helen Phillips. Cambridge, 1990, pp. 11–30.

"Desire and the Scriptural Text: Will as Reader in *Piers Plowman*," in *Criticism and Dissent in the Middle Ages*, ed. Rita Copeland. Cambridge, 1996, pp. 215–43.

"Piers Plowman": An Introduction to the B-Text. London, 1990.

"The Power of Impropriety: Authorial Naming in *Piers Plowman*," in *William Langland's "Piers Plowman": A Book of Essays*, ed. Kathleen Hewett-Smith. New York, 2001, pp. 145–65.

Smith, D. Vance. *Arts of Possession: the Medieval Household Imaginary*. Minneapolis, MN, 2003.

The Book of the Incipit: Beginnings in the Fourteenth Century. Minneapolis, MN, 2001.

Smith, Jeremy J. "'The Metre Which Does Not Measure': The Function of Alliteration in Middle English Alliterative Poetry," in *Approaches to the Metres of Alliterative Verse*, ed. Jefferson and Putter. Leeds, 2009, pp. 11–23.

Smith, Macklin. "Langland's Alliterative Line(s)," *YLS*, 23, 2009, pp. 163–216.

"Langland's Unruly Caesura," *YLS*, 22, 2008, pp. 57–101.

Somerset, Fiona. "'Al þe comonys with o voys atonys': Multilingual Latin and Vernacular Voice in *Piers Plowman*," *YLS*, 19, 2005, pp. 106–36.

Clerical Discourse and Lay Audience in Late Medieval England. Cambridge, 1998.

Spearman, Alan. "Langland's 'Corlew': Another Look at *Piers Plowman* B xiv.43," *MÆ*, 62, 1993, pp. 242–58.

Spearing, A. C. *Medieval Dream Poetry*. Cambridge, 1976.

Staley, Lynn. "The Man in Foul Clothes and a Late Fourteenth-Century Conversation about Sin," *SAC*, 24, 2002, pp. 1–47.

Steiner, Emily. "Commonalty and Literary Form in the 1370s and 1380s," *NMR*, 6, 2003, pp. 199–221.

Documentary Culture and the Making of Medieval English Literature. Cambridge, 2003.

"Naming and Allegory in Late Medieval England," *JEGP*, 106 no. 2, 2007, pp. 248–75.

"*Piers Plowman*, Diversity, and the Medieval Political Aesthetic," *Representations*, 91, 2005, pp. 1–25.

"Radical Historiography: Langland, Trevisa, and the *Polychronicon*," *SAC*, 27, 2005, pp. 171–211.

Stokes, Myra. *Justice and Mercy in "Piers Plowman": A Reading of the B Text Visio*. London, 1984.

Swanson, Robert. *Indulgences in Late Medieval England: Passports to Paradise?* New York, 2007.

Szittya, P. R. *The Antifraternal Tradition in Medieval Literature*. Princeton, 1986.

Tavorima, M. Teresa. *Kindly Similitude: Marriage and Family in "Piers Plowman."* Rochester, NY, 1995.

Trigg, Stephanie. *Congenial Souls: Reading Chaucer from Medieval to Postmodern*. Minneapolis, MN, 2002.

"Learning to Live," in *Oxford Twenty-First Century Approaches to Literature: Middle English*, ed. Paul Strohm. Oxford, 2007, pp. 459–71.

"The Traffic in Medieval Women: Alice Perrers, Feminist Criticism, and *Piers Plowman*," *YLS*, 12, 1998, pp. 5–29.

Turville-Petre, Thorlac. *The Alliterative Revival*. Cambridge, 1977.

Wallace, David. *Chaucerian Policy: Absolutist Lineages and Associational Forms in England and Italy*. Stanford, CA, 1997.

Premodern Places: Calais to Surinam, Chaucer to Aphra Behn. Malden, MA, 2004.

Wallace, David, ed. *The Cambridge History of Medieval English Literature*. Cambridge, 1999.

Warner, Lawrence. "Becket and the Hopping Bishops," *YLS*, 17, 2003, 107–34.

"The Ending, and End, of *Piers Plowman* B: the C-Version Origins of the Final Two Passus," *MÆ*, 76, 2007, pp. 225–50.

"Langland and the Problem of *William of Palerne*," *Viator*, 37, 2006, pp. 397–415.

The Lost History of "Piers Plowman." Philadelphia, 2010.

"The Ur-B *Piers Plowman* and the Earliest Production of C and B," *YLS*, 16, 2002, pp. 3–39.

Watson, Nicholas. "Censorship and Cultural Change in Late-Medieval England: Vernacular Theology, the Oxford Translation Debates, and Arundel's *Constitutions* of 1409," *Speculum*, 70, 1995, pp. 822–64.

"*Piers Plowman*, Pastoral Theology, and Spiritual Perfectionism: Hawkyn's Cloak and Patience's Pater Noster," *YLS*, 21, 2007, pp. 83–118.

Richard Rolle and the Invention of Authority. Cambridge, 1991.

"Visions of Inclusion: Universal Salvation and Vernacular Theology in Pre-Reformation England," *Journal of Medieval and Early Modern Studies*, 27, 1997, pp. 145–87.

Wenzel, Siegfried. *The Sin of Sloth: Acedia in Medieval Thought and Literature*. Chapel Hill, NC, 1967.

Wetherbee, Winthrop. "The 'Consolation' and medieval literature," in *The Cambridge Companion to Boethius*, ed. John Marenbon. Cambridge, 2009.

Whatley, Gordon. "Heathens and Saints: *St. Erkenwald* in Its Legendary Context," *Speculum*, 61, 1986, pp. 330–63.

Williams, Deanne. "Boethius Goes to Court: The *Consolation* as Advice to Princes in the Poetry of Chaucer and Elizabeth I," in *The Erotics of Consolation: Desire and Distance in the Late Middle Ages*, ed. Catherine Léglu and Stephen J. Milner. New York, 2008, pp. 205–26.

Woolf, Rosemary. "The Tearing of the Pardon," in *Art and Doctrine: Essays on Medieval Literature*. London, 1986, pp. 131–56.

Woolgar, C. M. *The Great Household in Late Medieval England*. New Haven, CT, 1999.

Zeeman, Nicolette. *"Piers Plowman" and the Medieval Discourse of Desire*. Cambridge, 2006.

Zieman, Katherine. *Singing the New Song: Literacy and Liturgy in Late Medieval England*. Philadelphia, 2008.

Index